16.75

D0918598

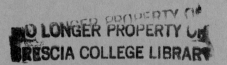

Historical Perspectives:
Studies in English Thought
and Society

Historical Perspectives
Studies in English Thought and Society

in honour of J. H. Plumb

Edited by
Neil McKendrick

London
Europa Publications

Europa Publications Limited
18 Bedford Square, London, WC1B 3JN

© the authors 1974

ISBN: 0 900 36277 4
Library of Congress Catalogue Card No: 74 80445

Printed and bound in England by
Staples Printers Limited
at The Stanhope Press, Rochester, Kent

Contents

CONTENTS

Notes on Contributors

G. V. BENNETT, Fellow and Tutor in Modern History, New College, Oxford; formerly Lecturer in History, King's College, London (1954–59); ordained in 1956 and is an Honorary Canon of Chichester; author of *White Kennett, Bishop of Peterborough* (1957) and editor of *Essays in Modern English Church History in Memory of Norman Sykes* (1966); is soon to publish a new life of Francis Atterbury.

J. W. BURROW is Reader in History at the University of Sussex; and was formerly Fellow of Christ's College and Downing College, Cambridge. He is the author of *Evolution and Society, a Study in Victorian Social Theory* (1966). His chief current research interest is nineteenth-century historiography.

A. RUPERT HALL, like Professor Plumb, is a product of Alderman Newton's School, Leicester, and of Christ's College, Cambridge, where he was also a Fellow. He is Professor of the History of Science and Technology at Imperial College, London. His main interest has been in seventeenth-century science and its relations with technology. He is the author of *The Scientific Revolution* (1954), a *Brief History of Science* (1964), and co-editor of *A History of Technology* (1953–58).

J. P. KENYON was a research student at Christ's College, Cambridge (1951–54), when he took his Ph.D. under J. H. Plumb's supervision, and was a Fellow of the College (1954–62). He is now Professor of Modern History at the University of Hull. His books include *The Stuart Constitution* (1960) and *The Popish Plot* (1972), and he is now engaged in a study of early eighteenth-century political thought in England.

NEIL McKENDRICK, a former Fellow of Christ's College, Cambridge, is now Fellow, College Lecturer and Director of Studies at Gonville and Caius College, Cambridge, and University Lecturer in

English Economic History at Cambridge University. He is currently engaged on a study of Josiah Wedgwood and the Industrial Revolution on which he has published numerous articles.

J. J. SCARISBRICK (Christ's College, 1948–54) is at present Professor of History at the University of Warwick. His major research interest is sixteenth-century ecclesiastical history and his principal publication is *Henry VIII* (1968).

QUENTIN SKINNER is a Lecturer in History at the University of Cambridge and a Fellow of Christ's College. He has been a visiting research fellow at the Australian National University (1970) and at the Institute for Advanced Study, Princeton (1974–75). He has published a series of articles on Hobbes in the *Historical Journal*, has contributed essays to several collections, acted as a co-editor as well as a contributor to the series *Philosophy*, *Politics and Society*, and has also published articles in *Comparative Studies*, *History and Theory*, *New Literary History*, *Past and Present*, *The Philosophical Quarterly*, *Philosophy*, *Political Studies*, *Political Theory*, etc.

ERIC STOKES is Smuts Professor of the History of the British Commonwealth at Cambridge University and Fellow of St. Catharine's College. He is the author of *The English Utilitarians and India* (1959) and is currently engaged in writing *The Peasant Armed: The Agrarian Background of the Indian Mutiny*.

BARRY SUPPLE was educated at the London School of Economics and Christ's College, Cambridge. He has taught at Harvard and McGill Universities and is now Professor of Economic and Social History at the University of Sussex. His principal publications are *Commercial Crisis and Change, 1600–1642* (1959); *The Experience of Economic Growth*, editor (1963); *The Royal Exchange Assurance: A History of British Insurance, 1720–1970* (1970); and *The State and the Industrial Revolution* (1971). He is co-editor of the *Economic History Review*.

Introduction

These essays were written to mark the retirement of Professor J. H. Plumb from his Chair in Modern English History at Cambridge University. The contributors are all ex-pupils of Professor Plumb, all are primarily English historians, and all are past members of Christ's College – where they have been either undergraduates or fellows, and, in some cases, both.

This book is a personal tribute and a Cambridge-inspired one. And, as such, it cannot do full justice to all of Professor Plumb's research interests or to all the fields in which he has published, nor can it include all the historians who would have wished to honour him. Indeed, to have attempted to do so would have created an impossible task for the editor and publisher alike. It would have required a series, not a single volume. So the lacunae will be obvious to all. There are no contributions from the American universities with which Professor Plumb has such close ties. There is nothing here on the Italian Renaissance, nothing on African exploration, nothing on the nature and purpose of history, nothing to call attention to Plumb's introductions to the *History of Human Society* which range so freely from pre-history to the present day, from the world of Rome to that of the United States, from the Chinese Empire to the sea-borne empires of Spain and Portugal.

But by limiting the range to modern English history, this *Festschrift* will, I hope, pay tribute to the area of Professor Plumb's major contributions to scholarship, and yet not be so restricted in its vision as to be uncharacteristic of the man. To have presented the most vivid writer and most readable historian of our day with an unwieldy portmanteau would have been grotesque. To have presented him with no more than narrowly based scholarship which gave no sense of the wide-ranging perspective of his own vision would have been little better. For these reasons I have taken the title for this volume from the regular column which, for several years, Professor Plumb wrote in the *Saturday Review*. There he examined a series of problems, personalities and events with a remarkable combination of precise scholarship and an unfailing ability to set them within their political and historical perspective. I hope I have encouraged the contributors to attempt to match that rare combination. The measure of our success may be judged by the difficulty of the task. With that apologia I seek the indulgence of the many distinguished historians, and the many more young historians of promise, who told me that they would have wished to contribute to this volume.

NEIL MCKENDRICK

I

J. H. Plumb:
A Valedictory Tribute*

NEIL McKENDRICK

There must be tens of thousands whose interest in history and
literature he has awakened and informed by his pen, and who
would gladly know what manner of man it was that has done
them so great a service.

[George Otto Trevelyan on Macaulay]

Let me confess at once how daunting I find the task of paying an
adequate and fitting tribute to someone who is not only a colleague,
but who is also my oldest and closest friend, and who is, unarguably,
one of the outstanding historians of his day – arguably, in the world's
eyes, the most famous living English historian. To do justice to my
own sense of personal debt, to his distinction as an historian, and to his
contribution to Cambridge is not easy.

But fortunately Cambridge's tribute has, in some ways, already been
paid, and in a very appropriate way. It was paid at his last formal
lecture as a university teaching officer last week. This was, in itself, a
very instructive and revealing and characteristic performance.

It was characteristic of Jack Plumb's energy that he had written a
completely new set of lectures for his last term's stint – a feat not
performed, I am told, since Clapham did so in his last year back in the
1930s. It was revealing, too, of Jack's creativity and versatility. For the
lecture was a descriptive *tour de force* on the eighteenth century as a
consumer society. This is not itself a novel idea (though it is a fairly

* This is a revised version of a speech made at the dinner given by the Faculty of History
in honour of J. H. Plumb's retirement, on 5 December 1973, in Selwyn College,
Cambridge.

recent one) but the way in which it was demonstrated, in terms of the commercialization of leisure, was wholly original and based on wholly original research – the detailed scholarship was as impressive as the literary and lecturing skills. In the deluge of words (enough, I would guess, for three normal lectures) we were regaled with the commercial significance of the Mendoza-Humphries fight, the financial implications of the stud fees of Eclipse, and the social significance of auricula societies; to demonstrate the new potentialities of the market, we were shown how Newbery made a fortune out of children's books, Spilsbury out of jigsaw puzzles, and Henry Wise out of gardening – all part of the demonstration of the growth of a mass audience for sport, literature and all the other manifestations of leisure. The willingness to tackle and to master a whole new field of social history is telling in itself, but even more instructive was the reception the lecture received.

Firstly the audience was huge. Room 3 was packed to capacity, packed with both undergraduates and senior members. One awed voice was heard to murmur, 'Half the faculty must be here'. It was that rare lecture performance for which the audience had queued in advance. Indeed, those (like myself) who loftily turned up late had great difficulty getting in. An excited member of the staff, clearly unused to such packed lecture rooms, was busily turning people away, having already run out of extra seats. When one did get in one had literally to sit at the feet of the master: Jack was able to pause in mid-paragraph to note with some satisfaction that he had never seen so many distinguished backsides together on the floor at the same time.

The audience was not only huge, it was ecstatic. When the lecture finished, and the thunderous applause died down, the audience was not prepared to let the lecturer slip away – there was a sudden popping of champagne corks and Jack was seen to be waving a magnum of Louis Roederer. The impromptu party which followed had more the appearance of a theatrical happening than a Cambridge lecture – but it was not an inappropriate finale for the most popular lecturer in the History Faculty over the last twenty years or so.

Obviously Jack was delighted with the reception; it suited both his nature and his expectations to go out with a bang, not a whimper. And it may momentarily have warmed his heart to Cambridge and his colleagues – not a place or a group he has always looked on with unambiguous approval.

Perhaps the explanation for this recurring coolness is that, while most people here were welcomed to Cambridge, Jack Plumb was initially rejected. Most retirement speeches start, even if they don't all finish, on a note of triumph – in the entrance examination or the Tripos lists. Jack's does not. He took the St John's Scholarship Examination in December 1929, and failed. At least he failed to get what he wanted and needed, an award.

Those brief statements of fact conceal a more interesting sequence of events, as a glance at the St John's group scholarship book reveals. On the first round of marks, the name of J. H. Plumb is well up among the leading scholars, but after the second round (when the men who had interviewed him had done their remarking),[1] it was dropped to the top of the Exhibitioner list – still a signal triumph for a boy from an obscure grammar school, but not a sufficient one. For in those days colleges *had* to take scholars, but they could reject Exhibitioners. So the young Plumb was informed that he had been placed in the Exhibition class but not awarded one. He could have a place if he wished it and could afford it. He could do neither. So he went to Leicester University and got the first First in History ever achieved from that university. (Perhaps when colleges, in penance, recognize their mistakes rather than, in self-congratulation, honour their successes, an honorary fellowship from St John's might not come amiss.)

The rest of the story is in *Who's Who*, and I see little point in rehearsing the details of the research studentship at Christ's while he worked as Trevelyan's only pupil; of the research fellowship at King's; of his official fellowship back at Christ's; of the lectureship, readership, personal chair and Litt.D., F.B.A., honorary degrees in both England and America; of the numerous visiting professorships, the Ford Lectures: all of this – and his time at the Foreign Office during the War – is easily available in the obvious works of reference. But it is, perhaps, worth saying that while he was collecting all the academic honours, he was also taking on all the academic chores. Unlike so many of the stars of the history world, Plumb has not prospered on effortless promotion and unlimited research time. On the contrary, he has been college lecturer, director of studies, tutor, steward and vice-master of

---

[1] In his memorable and brilliant reply to this speech Professor Plumb gave an hilarious account of why *he* thought he did not get a scholarship. The reasons ranged from the fact that he arrived at St John's in a bowler hat to his current preoccupation with the psycho-pathology of everyday life, and one can only hope that one day he will allow his explanation to appear in print.

Christ's. He was, I am told, once within a single vote of being bursar too, and even now after retirement he is still the Wine Steward – a much-coveted, and suitably Walpolian, title which is thought to require a twenty-year apprenticeship in Plumb's college.

But if I am not to rehearse the well-known details of his career, what should I rehearse? Here my problem is – to be both frank and immodest – that I know too much of my subject to have space to tell it. I have known him well for the last twenty-five years, and I know most of his friends. I went to the same school and to the same Cambridge college. I was taught by the same schoolmasters and, having lived in the same street in Leicester in the 1930s, I know his background at first hand. In Christ's I shared with him the same First Court staircase for five years – three as an undergraduate, one as a research student, and one as a research fellow. As he supervised me, directed my studies, was even briefly my tutor, and as I went to his lectures and did research in his century, I inevitably acquired some knowledge of him both as a pupil and as a colleague. Having shared a country cottage with him for the last fifteen years I have learnt even more as a friend. Inevitably as a result, the anecdotes I could tell are legion. Equally inevitably not all are appropriate. But some might surprise, and others might be instructive.

I could tell, for instance, of his youth in Leicester, but the picture of the young long-haired Plumb in canary-yellow sweaters and purple trousers might be too difficult to accept for those familiar only with his present-day image. But from all accounts they would recognize at once the radical, sceptical, optimistic, agnostic Plumb of the early '30s. His attitudes to politics and religion have not changed. Then as now they showed little trace of his Tory, nonconformist upbringing. In the same way his enthusiasm and eagerness for life were already fully apparent – perhaps even more so before the bruises and disappointment of later defeats.

I could tell you of his debt to that extraordinary schoolmaster H. E. Howard (a debt I share), who inspired so many young historians, but the account could scarcely be held to be exemplary – for the schoolboy Plumb was something of a rebel; his frequent contributions to the school newspaper and magazine were not infrequently censored; he was never allowed much power in the school; and his relations with Howard, although sometimes achieving a certain epic quality, were scarcely a model for such relationships. Discussions were not conducted in a spirit of polished courtesy or amiable give and take. The cut and thrust was of the claymore variety, and the blows, one feels, were sometimes intended to be lethal. One famous argument between the two raged all over Leicester and finally finished, at three in the morning outside the gates of the town gaol, with a splendid, but I imagine rare, dismissal from master to his star pupil: 'Sir, you've misunderstood your facts, you've misread your psychology, you've got a third-rate mind, and you're probably impotent. Good night.' Howard, as I came to know, believed in treating his pupils as equals. This had enormous advantages over the more conventional attitude of schoolmasters but it required a robustly built personality to survive some of the demands of such egalitarian treatment. No one would doubt that Professor Plumb's temperament was equal to the task, and few of his own supervision pupils would doubt that Howard's methods had left some mark. Plumb as a supervisor was not a paragon of all the old-fashioned virtues of charm, restraint and tolerance. He was not unfailingly reasonable like all those dons in the obituary columns. In compensation he was never dull, and often brilliant. In his supervisions you were informed, enthused and apprised of the importance of your subject. You were required to work, and you were expected to succeed. Some of us felt that we were also subjected to psychological warfare, a seemingly random pattern of praise and blame which, we finally worked out to our total satisfaction, was designed to ensure that no one, however dim, got no encouragement, and no one, however bright, got complacent. To judge by results it seemed to work, and Jack's genuine dedication to teaching can be judged from the fact that he is that very rare Cambridge don who continued to teach after he got his chair. The fact that professors cannot receive supervision fees is usually interpreted by professors to mean that they cannot supervise. Of course they can, and Plumb did. He continued to entertain Christ's undergraduates to a regular weekly seminar-cum-dessert at which they read papers, and he delivered his judgement and encouragement. And this despite the fact that he also ran the liveliest and one of the largest teams of research students in the faculty.

I could tell you, too, of the literary aspirations of his youth – of the industrial history of his father's firm which he wrote and published while still a student and of the novel he wrote in his twenties which came very close to publication; its rejection probably saved him for history.

I could tell you of his passion for punctuality. He says he almost glows with anxiety at the prospect of being late himself, and many can testify that his reaction to *their* being late is equally apparent – a sustained smoulder rather than a glow might be a suitable description. As a result he likes to do everything at speed. He eats fast, he talks fast, he works fast, he travels fast. He enjoys decisions and he takes them quickly. It was once said of him that while others are still admiring the landscape, Jack has bought it. If he is going anywhere he likes to arrive first. If he's in a race he wants to win it. He is the fastest driver I have driven with, and as my wife and I have driven all over Europe and America with him we have a fund of stories of the joint terror his driving has inspired in us. I fear we sometimes dine out on the stories, but since I suspect his appetite for them is less well developed than ours I will suppress them here. He is also, although this is less well known, one of the fastest sailors I know. At least in the sailing club we both belonged to he always finished first. There were those in the club – the real *cognoscenti* – who held that there were other better helmsmen, and that Jack won only because he started earlier, or because he had bought the fastest boat, or because he had picked the best crew (or even that his superb cooking and even better wine attracted the best crew) – all of which he would, I am sure, happily concede, mildly pointing out that those without a touch of natural cunning must get used to not winning. Being a pure helmsman no more makes a successful sailor, in his book, than being a pure research worker makes a successful historian.

His passion for speed and efficiency is very evident in his work. It explains why he is able to do so many jobs at the same time with such success. Where others agonize for days over a testimonial, Plumb writes a single paragraph with an unambiguous verdict, and is promptly back to his own research. Where many faculty boards regularly meet for five hours at a time, the History Faculty Board under Plumb's chairmanship rarely lasted an hour. Those who arrived three minutes late were likely also to be three items on the agenda late; and I recall Professor Ullmann once leaving the Board Room almost reluctantly at 2.45 having entered only half an hour before, and recalling the days under more expansive and more deliberate chairmen when he could not expect to leave before the sun had set behind King's Chapel.[2]

Speed, however, does not mean lack of care or accuracy. Happily

---

[2] These were days before the Faculty moved into the Stirling building on the Sidgwick Avenue site.

endowed with an omnivorous appetite for work and a prodigious and
certain memory, Plumb is able to work more surely as well as faster
than most. And he is a craftsman as well as an artist with words. He
prides himself not only on meeting his deadlines but also on meeting
his brief. If an editor asks Plumb for eight thousand words, then he gets
eight thousand, give or take a dozen; if he asks for twelve hundred or
five hundred, then he may well get precisely that, neither more nor
less. His pleasure in providing what is asked for, when it is asked for,
is so unusual as to be regarded as almost perverse. The virtues are, by
subtle alchemy, transmuted by some into vices. His speed and his
versatility will always make him suspect to some, but not, understandably, to his publishers, editors and readers. Hopefully, posterity,
too, will be on the side of the angels.

I could tell, too, of my experience as an undergraduate accompanying
Jack on research expeditions. The first time I went with him was to
Houghton, the magnificent house which Sir Robert Walpole built.
To work there and enjoy the superb hospitality of the Marquess and
Marchioness of Cholmondeley must be to research in the ideal environment. So Utopian indeed that some have cynically wondered at the
motives for Jack's choice of research topic. They, perhaps understandably, find the somewhat romantic explanation he gives in the first
volume of his biography of Walpole not wholly convincing. There he
wrote: 'My interest in Sir Robert Walpole was first roused by sitting
beneath his picture, which hangs over the High Table at King's, during
many silent dinners as a junior fellow.' The thought of Jack sitting
silent for long is, for many, intrinsically unacceptable, and with it they
reject the whole explanation. In support of their theory they point out
that it could not be sheer luck which led Jack's war-time 'lodgings' to
be with the Rothschilds, and the current tipple at his 'billet' to be
Latour 1920!

But I can assure such sceptics that research was not always conducted
in such blissful comfort. The contrast of working at Blenheim on the
Marlborough papers was marked indeed. Instead of the charm of Lady
Cholmondeley's welcome, one entered Blenheim very much at the
tradesman's entrance and then only after paying an entrance fee.
Instead of the warmth and splendour of Sir Robert's library at
Houghton, one got the chill of a white-tiled cellar which passed as an
archive room. So incensed was Jack at this environment – or merely
so cold – that he spent several freezing January days there wrapped in

the royal standard for warmth, discontentedly but efficiently working his way through the evidence of the behaviour of the Cabinet under Queen Anne; when I, encouraged by his boldness, reached for some lesser ducal pennant to wrap myself in I was sharply told to desist – to keep copying the documents, not him. 'Youth will keep you warm, McKendrick' was the cold comfort I received.

It is held by some that Jack developed his taste for fine wine and food, for fine porcelain, silver and painting on these sorties through the aristocratic archives of the eighteenth-century magnates he studied. The truth is that the gastronomic tastes, if not the aesthetic, had started earlier, but it can scarcely have been discouraged by the main area of his research. And whatever the inspiration, it is now well known that he has one of the finest cellars for old claret in Cambridge (some would say in England); he has a superb collection of Vincennes and Sèvres – markedly superior to the Fitzwilliam's collection – and an interesting and growing collection of silver and paintings. It is against the elegant setting of such possessions that he entertains so generously in Christ's. He is one of the few survivors of the Cambridge tradition of bachelor hosts who serve superb food and sybaritic wine in splendid college rooms. There can be few tables at which one can still experience pre-phylloxera claret, or enjoy a whole evening of nineteenth-century Bordeaux, or taste each of the great 1920s wines, one against the other. Such evenings are always lively and often combative, for if Plumb is one of the most generous hosts he is not one of the most relaxed or long suffering. His anxiety on his guest's behalf – and, perhaps, sometimes even more on his wine's behalf – is notorious. It does not always make for serenity.

All this may, in G. O. Trevelyan's words, tell you something of 'what manner of man [he] was', but it is obviously too personal and too subjective a view to be really convincing. When addressing an audience of historians, one does well not to rely on a single source of evidence, however well informed it thinks it is. So I thought that before delivering this tribute I should avail myself of other authorities. There are after all ample primary and secondary sources to consult.

First I sampled the memory of my colleagues but this, alas, yielded a meagre harvest. I have always envied those historians who can rely on oral evidence – but no longer. If trained and practising historians remember so little and so inaccurately, what hope can there be for others? To add frustration to disappointment, what little they did remember they frequently forbad me to repeat. But one important and instructive judgement did emerge – and that was the markedly different response which Jack Plumb inspires from the young and the old. One colleague spelt this out quite clearly when he said, 'The difficulty with Jack is that he gets on indifferently with his seniors, adequately with his contemporaries, and superbly with those junior to him.' Indeed when I approached senior members for information and help in preparing this tribute, and explained my problem and my needs, all too often the reply was, 'Mm, difficult, very difficult', and it was by no means clear whether they meant my task or my subject. In splendid contrast the response of the young was a chorus of praise and appreciation. 'The marvellous thing about Jack', 'The wonderful thing about Jack', was the way their replies began. They spoke with one voice of his generosity, his enthusiasm, the prodigality of his ideas for research, his unabashed pleasure in their success, his remarkable lack of envy. Their gratitude is both justified and readily evidenced, as the prefaces of so many monographs on seventeenth- and eighteenth-century English history indicate. But if the acclaim of the young is easy to understand, how does one account for the coolness of others?

Partly no doubt it stems from the fact that Jack, as well as relishing the success of others, also relished his own. And there has been plenty to relish. Partly, too, it stems from his frank enjoyment of the pleasures of life. Not for Plumb the life of what he describes as 'the quiet rich'. He spends his royalties with gusto which few could match, and he would not be above pointing out that few could match the royalties. No one would call him self-effacing, and I cannot imagine that he was an especially dutiful, or invariably modest, junior colleague.

Moreover, although occasionally prepared to suffer fools briefly, he rarely suffers mediocrity gladly, and he sometimes finds the academic world rather over-supplied with men of middling gifts. There was a time when he was much given to pondering aloud on the reasons for the apparently effortless success of the dull and the humdrum. 'Why', he would ask himself, and others too if they were available, 'is it that some men of such limited ability do so well?' Powerful connections, and the subtle workings of nepotism, he recognized, but found too banal to be wholly satisfying. Being an imaginative man he formulated several new theories to explain the phenomenon and to satisfy his curiosity. They had the added advantage that they took note of his impatience with the slow speaking, the pompous and the ponderous.

The first was Plumb's *Theory of Face Acreage* which runs: 'Given any two men of equal ability, the one with the larger face will go further.' The second was the *Voice Velocity Theory* which runs: 'Given any two men of equal ability, the one who speaks the more slowly will go further.' In a faculty which, I am told, once included a fair proportion of large-faced, slow-speaking men it is little wonder that he did not achieve universal popularity. The failure of my first attempt at oral history was, perhaps, pre-conditioned by my subject.

In secondary sources I was much luckier. My subject has not only produced an astonishing array of evidence in his own words, but has also attracted others to write about him, for it is well known to his friends (but little known to others) that Jack has been the subject of at least three works of fiction by distinguished contemporary novelists. Admittedly he is not always easily recognized by the uninitiated. In one he is the sparkling young director of a museum ruthlessly weeding out the dead wood among the staff (a task one can easily imagine him enjoying); in another he is a young provincial lawyer pursuing hilarious amorous adventures, carefully disguised as a red-haired, Jewish solicitor; in a third he is a brilliant research scientist, humbly born, richly gifted, highly ambitious – in this incarnation he is uxorious, creative and, although often on the brink of disaster, ultimately satisfyingly successful. In many Cambridge colleges it is a set book for research students in their first term, and deservedly so, for it teaches one a great deal about the academic life. It is, I think, the best portrait of Jack Plumb. In it he is described much as he is:

By the time he was twenty-one our subject had reached his full stature physically, that is to say five feet six inches. He was a sturdy young man inclined to be plump. He had a fair amount of muscle sleeked over by a thin layer of fat that gave his body a faintly pneumatic look. He had a hefty chest and buttocks and high waist. His body was strongly-made, tough and resilient, but there was nothing of the cart-horse about it. He had a certain fineness of grace. The flick of his eyelids was rapid, the movement of his hands was delicate.

His head was round like a ball and he had long dark silky hair. His face was small and broader than it was long. His big grey eyes protruded so far that he swore his eyeballs got sunburnt in summertime – he was short-sighted and wore spectacles. His nose was short and rather stubby, his mouth wide with red slightly pouting lips. It was a good, clever, homely, sensitive, pleasing, English lower middle-class face – not specially beautiful.

Many would find it difficult not to recognize Jack from that description, but my wife will not accept that it is a fair or adequate description
– reasonably pointing out that it could apply almost equally well to
nearly all of the recent professors of history in Cambridge. (It is true
that if one superimposed Professors Elton, Coleman, Postan, Ullmann,
Wilson, Joslin, Cheney, Stokes, Gallie, even Gallagher, one would
emerge with a human prototype not very dissimilar to the description
of J. H. Plumb.) Indeed this has led the more irreverent of the young
to match Plumb in formulating theories: *The Stunted Stature Theory*
runs, 'Given any two men of equal ability, the one most closely
approximating to the height of five foot six will go further' – at least
in the Cambridge History Faculty.

I should add that none of these fictional portraits is by his old friend,
C. P. Snow. Despite frequent assumptions to the contrary and feverish
searches through *The Masters* and *The Light and the Dark*, Plumb does
not appear in the *Strangers and Brothers* sequence. Indeed at Jack's
fiftieth birthday Snow explained why he had never written extensively
about him. He was often asked why he had not exploited one of the
most 'novelogenic' of his friends, and the answer, he said, was very
simple. Jack was too difficult, too complex, too contradictory. No one
would believe him if he were faithfully written down. I think this is
perhaps true and explains why the existing portraits are somewhat
one-dimensional. They have explored only bits of the man, and
therefore, though they are often revealing, even brilliant, they are not
wholly satisfying – not, that is, to historians seeking an accurate version
of J. H. Plumb; to the ordinary reader they are marvellously
satisfying.

Having exhausted the fictional, I turned to the factual – this time to
the remarkable bulk and variety of Plumb's own publications. When
I feel more than usually depressed at my own inadequacies, I remind
myself that at my age Professor Plumb had published only a single
scholarly article, but the comfort is short-lived because it serves only
to emphasize the phenomenal amount of publications that he has
packed into the last twenty-five years. He now has four pages to himself
in the University Library catalogue. Including the supplementary
catalogues there are now some forty-five entries under his name – and
some of those are single entries for a multi-volume work. I say nothing
for the moment of the high quality of his work, but it is clear that he is
prolific even among the productive. To give you, as it were, the current

Cambridge rate of exchange, only Professor Ullmann rivals him for space in the catalogues; Professor Chadwick and E. H. Carr fill only half the space; and Professors Grierson, Elton and Wilson less than a third. The rest simply do not compete.

Not that the University Library has a comprehensive collection of his works: little that has been published abroad is included and so there is no mention of his sparkling introductions to Goldsmith, Fielding and Defoe, nor of his memorable introduction to the *Memoirs of Fanny Hill*. It does not include, for instance, a recent joint venture published in the United States last year, the four volumes of documents, *Great Britain: Foreign Policy and Span of Empire, 1689 to 1971* by Plumb and Wiener. But, even incomplete, it indicates the prodigious range and variety of his interests.

As most of us have good reason to know, history is a humiliating subject to try to know, and most professional historians try to minimize the humiliation by restricting their range. Even those who lecture and teach outside their own patch, very rarely publish outside it. We tend our tiny Japanese gardens with ever greater care and erudition. Intruders are fought off with frightening vigour by those defending their chosen territory. But Jack has little use for *bonsai* and the more comic exercises in the territorial imperative. He prefers the grand sweep of the landscape to the confines of the pot. From time to time he demonstrates his mastery of the more pot-bound skills, as the pages of the scholarly journals show – even the pages of the *Economic History Review*. And he has, of course, his own area of greatest expertise. As a recent reviewer said, there is Tawney's century and there are Namier's decades, and in between lies Plumb territory – that hybrid century that runs from roughly 1660 to roughly 1745 – into which no one strays without due acknowledgement to the master. This is the area of his first research, this is the area of his scholarly articles, of his first serious publication in the *Cambridge Historical Journal*, of the magnificent two volumes on Walpole, of his masterly Ford lectures *The Growth of Political Stability*. This is the area of his work which I most admire. This is the area which provides the solid, central core of his professional reputation, and rightly so. But there is so much more besides – the countless essays and articles in which he has revealed his native optimism in the material progress of mankind, in which he has introduced a wide public for the first time to the exciting new work of young and little-known scholars, in which he has pleaded for governments and politicians to recognize the historical dimension – to read their statistics and interpret the evidence on a scale large enough to allow for the historical perspective.

And there are, of course, all the other books – from the vivid, brief biography of Chatham to the controversial polemic of *Crisis in the Humanities*; from the Hogarthian vigour of *The First Four Georges* to the deeply felt and densely evidenced arguments of *The Death of the Past*. What does one say of a specialist English historian who has written a history of the Renaissance which has outsold all but Burckhardt and is available in thirteen languages? What does one say of a specialist English historian who has written a book (or at least edited, and written a considerable slice, of a book) on the West African explorers, which drew a full-page rave review from Graham Greene welcoming an historian who could really write – a master of English prose? What does one say of a specialist political historian who has written the best general history of eighteenth-century England – a Pelican which is still unsurpassed, still on every university booklist, and which has sold nearly a million copies in English alone?

Few historians have ever reached such a remarkably wide audience on such a range of historical subjects. The depth of the audience is such that his recent 'Love letter to New York' drew an enormous fan mail including a letter from the staff of the Algonquin – that a Cambridge professor should extend the friendly hand of an admirer to that beleaguered city moved even the chefs to reply. The width of the audience is well attested by the Plumb volumes on my shelves in translation. They are there in French, Italian, Spanish, German, Czech and Russian. I even have one of his books published in English in Tokyo with Japanese footnotes: a restricted form of scholarship, I thought at first, but the catalogue at the back, in which Plumb lies between Plato and Edgar Allan Poe, makes it clear that here Plumb has been published as a model piece of prose, as an advanced exercise in English composition, and that the Japanese footnotes are there to guide the unwary through his more daring flights of literary fancy.

But perhaps the best example I have of the size and exotic nature of his audience is a book on my shelves, written by Plumb and published in a language and in a script which defeated the collective scholarship of my college. From internal evidence I knew it was Plumb's Pelican *England in the Eighteenth Century*, and I was confident that one of the experts in Caius would identify the language and beautiful script.

They could not. Or rather with characteristic confidence they did identify it, but each identified it differently. Within minutes I was assured that it was Armenian or Turkish, that it was Tamil or Thai or Urdu, that it was Bengali, Burmese or Sinhalese. No, that it was Malayalam. The majority vote was narrowly for Burmese, but whatever it is,[3] it is surely evidence of the unusual range of his readers, and, since Jack would always rather measure his success by the common reader he gets through to rather than by the scholarly controversies he inspires and the research he sparks off, the existence of such works must be sweet confirmation of his achievements.

He has always written to be read. He is always as concerned with the quality of his prose as he is with the quality of his argument or the precision of his evidence. In intention alone, such literary concern marks him out from the mass of practising academic historians, and the results of his endeavours mark him out even more clearly. His writing is, for pace, vigour and flow, unrivalled among contemporary historians and sometimes it is held to be too vivid. His figures of speech are not always appreciated by the profession: when he wrote, for instance, of Walpole's attempt to muzzle the youthful Chatham, 'As well might he attempt to stop a hurricane with a hairnet', there were not a few reviewers who tut-tutted at the extravagance of the idea and its expression, but fortunately most have welcomed a writer who can present the product of massive scholarship elegantly and compactly and vividly. For his work can convey an unusual sense of intellectual excitement, and its polish and panache make him one of the most readable historians. He is also one of the most quotable, and yet one whom, I think, it can be most unfair to quote. For he is not characteristically an epigrammatic writer, not a man who delights in intellectual paradox, or the elegant encapsulation of the recondite theory or obscure idea in an arresting or quirkish phrase. He is a man to read for the larger scale and the developing vision. He is an historian to read for the changing relationship between political allies and rivals, for the battle between moral scruple and tactical skill in political factions, for the narrative curve of a politician's career, for the unfolding of a man's character in the face of opportunity, triumph, setback or defeat. I once wrote that I knew no one else who could at the same time master the technical problems of conveying the

[3] The author later assured me that it was Sinhalese or, more properly, Sinhala.

sweep of history – the *tour d'horizon* of international relations, balance
of power, economic development, social structure, cultural achievement and national ambition – and at the same time stud these landscapes
of the past with perceptive and original interpretations of the major
figures bestriding the stage he had set. Plumb switches from the
telescope to the microscope with unusual ease. He delights as much in
the vagaries of the individual psyche as in the human behaviour of the
crowd, or of society as a whole. He enquires into the motives and
aspirations of the great men of the past with the pleasure of a gourmet
peeling off layer after layer in search of the *coeur d'artichaut*, and few
can rival his sense of the past in which such men moved. In this he is
one of the few who can marry the gifts of the traditional historian with
those of the modern professional academic: the literary intentions of
the one with the demanding techniques of the other. Indeed to do so
is one of the major motives behind his historical method. His intention
is, I think, to use his literary gifts to try to rescue professional history
from its flight from any sense of social purpose into the arcana of ever
more specialized scholarship; to use them to convey some sense of the
poetry of the past together with the stark reality of the way our
forebears lived; to capture at once a sense of the continuity of the past –
the unchanging response to the daily rhythms of men's lives and to the
human compulsions which drive us all – and yet to explain why the
social arrangements man has chosen have changed so dramatically over
the centuries.

It is interesting to note that some twenty years ago (when his major
reputation was as a political historian) he wrote: 'social history, in
the fullest and deepest sense of the term, is now a field of study of
incomparable richness and the one in which the greatest discoveries
will be made in this generation. Its purpose has long ceased to be merely
evocative.' His prediction has been fully borne out, and he has followed
the dictates of his own prophecy – first in an editorial capacity in the
History of Human Society, and more recently in his own research for his
Stenton lecture on the commercialization of leisure in the eighteenth
century, and his forthcoming book *The Growth of Leisure, 1660–1800*.

But there are, I think, even more compelling reasons for his need to
write, and more satisfying explanations of his desire to write in the
way he does, and about the subjects he chooses. Some twenty years ago
Jack Plumb wrote the following words on the motives which drive
the historian to write: 'Men write history for many reasons; to try and

understand the forces which impel mankind along its strange course; to justify a religion, a nation or a class; to make money; to fulfil ambition; to assuage obsession; and a few, the true creators, to ease the ache within.' When he wrote those words he was doing honour to George Macaulay Trevelyan, but the personal, the autobiographical note was clear to those who knew him. Many of the motives listed would apply to himself – his intellectual fascination with historical causation, and the yeast which stirs different societies to pursue their manifest destinies, and the remarkable justifications with which they seek to uphold them; his need to assuage, and to indulge, his own obsession with the past (plus, of course, a realistic worldly concern for both his career and his pocket); but the dominant drive has always been the creative one. His need to write is such that every day which passes – whether holiday or Christmas Day – without several hundred words safely down on paper in publishable form leaves him restless, fretful and miserable. He alone, among contemporary professionals that I know, is one of those 'few, the true creators, who write to ease the ache within'.

Fortunately he was blessed with the phenomenal energy to give his creative drive its fullest expression. That so many of his colleagues should describe him as Balzacian is a proper acknowledgement of both the nature and the character of his gifts. It is no more an accident that a prodigiously gifted and productive novelist should be chosen as his exemplar than that so many novelists should have intruded into this tribute. It is characteristic of both his friends and his qualities as a writer. For all the respect he receives as a scholar and for all the research and admiration he inspires among his students, it is the creative artist who most readily responds to his aims and to his achievements. When the artists are scholars themselves, the affinity is complete.

Therefore, although it would be banal (and doubtless embarrassing to the recipient) to quote from the countless professional tributes to his gifts as a scholar, I might, perhaps, be forgiven for quoting from two perceptive comments on Plumb's work by two famous contemporary novelists. For they touch on important aspects of his work which the professional academic historian tends to overlook.

The first is Angus Wilson, speaking as Orator and professor of the University of East Anglia at a recent honorary degree ceremony. In identifying Plumb's gifts and motives as an historian, Professor Wilson rightly draws attention to his belief in the material progress of mankind, to his belief in history's social purpose, and to his distrust of the academic's flight into specialization to which his own career runs counter:

Professor Plumb is outstanding among contemporary historians in fighting this diminished scope of his chosen discipline. It is shown, of course, in the breadth of his historical interests where his editorial work and his essays demonstrate his remarkable historical range. But it emerges more powerfully in the depth of his probing, and the constantly held wide perspective in which he has studied and made his own a portion of English history – the interrelation of political and social order in the late seventeenth and early eighteenth centuries – which in more timid hands, through blinkered eyes, could have been *par excellence* that sort of academic, specialist refuge he so stongly condemns.

Reading the fluent narrative of fascinating detail that informs the two volumes of his biography of Robert Walpole and his Ford Lectures upon the growth of political stability in England from 1675 to 1725, one is constantly and increasingly aware of the presence in the background of two interrelated conflicts, perhaps the most vital of our time. Again and again J. H. Plumb brings to our consciousness by inference the triumphant victory of humanity in the last centuries, despite all setbacks, over material squalor, disease and brutality of manners; equally insistent is his sense of the tragic shortness of men's lives set beside their aspirations, of their persistent proneness to cruelty, to lethargy or to corruption.

To confront this principal dilemma of our day, from which so many of his contemporaries, humanist and scientist alike, seek refuge in assumed boredom, despair or myopic specialization, J. H. Plumb seems peculiarly fitted by a combination of temperament and circumstances which have made him at once a very sensitive and a very tough-minded man. To this constantly implied confrontation between the forces of optimism and the forces of despair, he has added at the very core of his specialized historical work a more overt statement of another important related dilemma which presses upon our time. In Robert Walpole's life he has found the exemplar of that need for political stability without which social stability is impossible; yet, as the concluding remarks upon political stability of his Ford Lectures show, he is intensely aware that this very banishment of the chaos which haunts us all, holds in itself the nemesis of an inertia upon which social instability feeds. To have maintained such profound and pressing human problems as the constant background of works of exceptional detailed scholarship has surely been Professor Plumb's own splendid answer to the urgent demand he posed in his penetrating lecture "The Death of the Past" of 1969, when he called for a renewal of a meaningful study of history in an age when the past no longer gives the old simple linear answers that helped to hold civilization together from the age of Eusebius to the century of Karl Marx.

The second quotation is from an appraisal of Plumb's work by an old friend, C. P. Snow. It provides the right note on which to end this tribute for it echoes much of what I have tried, and would wish, to convey about Jack Plumb as an historian:

Creative energy is one of Professor Plumb's most obvious gifts – another is his sense of reality. No other historian can convey so vividly the feeling for how men breathe, eat, breed, enjoy themselves, go about their business, hope, worry and die. He is not too fastidious, he has a brotherly sympathy for the lusts of the flesh and the pride of the eye. All his books are written in what the French used to call the odour of man.

Lord Snow concluded, 'Vigorous, empathetic, sane, Professor Plumb is one of the tonic spirits of our day'. These, I think, are some of the qualities for which he will be best remembered – that tonic spirit, that vigour and realism, that life-enhancing quality, that lack of envy, that generous spirit which, as so many of his pupils have said, changed the quality of their lives – and which certainly changed the quality of mine. Where the world is divided into those who detract from life and those who enhance it, Jack Plumb invariably comes out high among the life-enhancers – and that is a rare and valuable attribute among contemporary historians.

I shall say no more in explaining why we are honouring a remarkable man and a great historian. I shall merely affirm it. And with that affirmation I shall ask you to drink to Professor J. H. Plumb.

II

Robert Persons's Plans for the 'true' Reformation of England*

J. J. SCARISBRICK

By any standards the English Jesuit, Robert Persons, was a remarkable man; and one of the more remarkable things about him was his *Memorial for the Reformation of England*, a comprehensive master-plan for building a new Jerusalem in England when that country should return to the household of the Faith.[1]

He wrote it in Seville[2] in 1596, shortly before he left Spain to attend to the affairs of the English College in Rome; but he had been gathering his ideas for seventeen or eighteen years beforehand, that is, since before he set out in 1580 with Edmund Campion to launch the first Jesuit mission to England. It was not published in his lifetime – it was, after all, intended for the guidance of the leaders of his own communion and not something to be broadcast in advance among the adversary. But its existence was well known. The author showed it to a 'few confident friends'; one or two manuscript copies circulated, apparently. It occasioned a good deal of consternation, especially among those who had not read it.

* I must thank Dr J. A. Bossy of Queen's University, Belfast, for doing much to stimulate my interest in this topic and generously providing detailed suggestions about it.

[1] Ireland is also included in these proposals, Persons says in the introduction to his work. Apart from T. H. Clancy's 'Notes on Persons's "Memorial for the Reformation of England" ', *Recusant History*, v (1959), 17–34, remarkably little attention has been given to this book by modern historians. Dr Clancy's article is primarily concerned with the ecclesiastical contents, rather than the social and economic proposals, and admirably sets them in their context. I am much indebted to him. I have used the text published by Edward Gee in 1690; but I have modernized spelling and punctuation throughout.

[2] So he tells us in *A manifestation of the great folly and bad spirit of certayne in England calling themselves secular priestes* (Antwerp, 1602), p. 56.

The question it posed was not how England was to be brought back to the Faith or, rather, how the Protestant regime was to be ended. This was presumably to be accomplished by force of Spanish arms or by the accession to the throne at Elizabeth's death of one of the Catholic claimants whose cause Persons had advanced in the previous year in his celebrated book *A conference about the next succession to the crowne of Ingland*. One way or another, England would one day return to Holy Mother Church; one day soon, he fervently believed. That being the case, it was necessary to give careful thought now to what was to be done after that blessed day had dawned to bring about a true reformation, a true renewal under the Spirit. Unlike some of his fellow-Catholics, Persons felt no pride in Mary Tudor's reign. There had been no plans, no preparation. A merely external reconciliation had been effected, without any true repentance and without any positive renewal. The Marian restoration had never deserved to succeed.

How would true reformation begin? How would it set about sifting friend from foe? How would it present itself to a people who had known three generations of schism and heresy, been subjected to decades of anti-Catholic and anti-papal propaganda and already been convulsed by a series of religious upheavals?

Mary had compromised and tried to use many of the tainted servants inherited from her brother and father. This time, says Persons, only 'known Catholics, which have been constant ... are to be used and employed by the Commonwealth in all principal charges, rooms and offices'.[3] Schismatics could be admitted, after careful preparation and due repentance, but not heretics. They must be cast out, and all gifts and favours bestowed upon them by the Crown rescinded, or at least suspended. Indeed, even truly repentant heretics should be allowed to receive the sacraments in public 'but by little and little, and with moderation, humiliation and after reverent ceremonies appointed for that purpose'; and it was 'to be considered whether Catholic service may be said again in our old churches before they be consecrated of new or hallowed publicly from profanation of heretics'. But there was to be no persecution – not at the start. A period of clemency would be allowed, to enable those in heresy to perceive the errors of their ways, a tactic which Persons claimed had worked admirably in the Low Countries. Temporary connivance of heretics (who would not be

[3] *Memorial*, pp. 29–30.

allowed to 'teach, preach or seek to infect others') was not to be taken as a first step to religious liberty. 'Nothing is so dangerous, dishonourable or more offensive to Almighty God in this world.'[4] He probably believed that the number of convinced English Protestants was small. He certainly believed, thanks to an exaggerated confidence in human reasonableness and the rightness of his cause, that only a brief respite was required before the errant of their own free will would have returned to the straight and narrow. Let there be 'full, free, equal and liberal disputation as could possibly be devised' between Catholic and Protestant divines in London, Oxford, Cambridge and elsewhere, with adequate warning for both sides to prepare themselves, each to have three or four experts in attendance and as many books as they required. The public debates were to be conducted with scrupulous fairness (Persons gives elaborate detail) and subsequently published. This, he rightly remarked, was the very thing that had always been refused to Catholic missionaries. 'I am of opinion', he concluded, 'it would break wholly the credit of all heresies in England and that afterwards few books would be needful on our part.' He believed, too, that it was only necessary to set alongside one another the controversial writings of Jewel and Harding, Whitaker and Stapleton, for the truth to emerge and that if, say, Jewel's sources were examined in public he would be 'discovered to make so many shifts and to slide out at so many narrow holes and creeks to save himself and to deny, falsify and pervert so many authors, doctors and Fathers as his side within a few days would be ashamed of him and give him over'.[5] And what if they did not? What if they remained obstinately loyal to the persecutors of the true Church, the heresiarchs and false bishops? 'It belongeth not to a man of my vocation to suggest.'[6] There would be recourse to the stake.

Persons underestimated the extent and constancy of English Protestantism in part because he maintained that much of its strength derived simply from the distribution among lay folk of former Church lands. Of course he was right to see this as a key issue. And he was sure that the solution agreed in Mary's reign could not be satisfactory. It was scandalous that ex-monastic lands should be in the hands of notorious heretics and active enemies of the Church. They must be dispossessed at once. But those who returned to the fold were to be allowed to

---

[4] Ibid., pp. 33, 108, 141–3, 207.
[5] Ibid., pp. 36–40.
[6] Ibid., p. 44.

compound for their lands by paying an annual rent (a 'rent of assize')
to a central, national fund out of which colleges, universities,
seminaries, schools, hospitals and religious houses (of new orders and
old) would be financed, and to which the income from the confiscated
lands would also be paid.[7] Persons's proposals, of course, provided a
powerful incentive for any non-Catholic to change sides; but their
primary purpose was to provide a large and steady income for re-
furbishing the Church and providing England with all those institutions
which had, as he believed, either languished or perished at Protestant
hands. He also knew enough of the English scene to appreciate that the
spoliation had not been confined to the religious houses: the reigns of
Henry, Edward and Elizabeth had seen relentless nibbling at the
possessions of bishops, cathedral chapters and colleges. All thus taken
away was to be handed back directly. Finally, there was the enormous
problem of the impropriated livings, with the tithes and patronage that
went with them, that had passed into lay hands at the Dissolution.
These, too, he boldly asserted, would be liable for return to the
Church.[8]

Responsibility for directing the restoration of Catholicism was to be
vested for the first few years in what Persons calls the 'Council of
Reformation' (in preference to 'Inquisition', which is 'somewhat odious
and offensive'),[9] consisting of the Archbishop of Canterbury, at least
three other bishops and lesser clerics. They were to administer the fund
just mentioned and have complete charge of the economic affairs of the
Church. They would appoint to all vacant parishes, license foreign
clergy, invite religious orders to send to England exemplary members
to refound their houses. They were to see to the foundation in every
diocese of what would later be called a 'junior' seminary providing an
education in grammar, rhetoric and humanities, and 'major' seminaries
in the universities, in which senior students would complete their
training – the costs of these to be met also by 'searching' every benefice.
The Council would send commissioners into every shire 'from time
to time' to discover what was needed by way of preachers, confessors,
seminary buildings, schools, monasteries, hospitals and parish churches

---

[7] Ibid., pp. 53–64. The term 'rent of assize' is somewhat obscure; but what Persons
meant, I think, was a fixed rent (*assisus reditus* of the Assizes of Clarendon) based on
the going rates at the time of the Dissolution. Cf. Clancy, art. cit., p. 33 and n. 44.

[8] *Memorial*, pp. 64–9.

[9] Ibid., p. 70.

(their repair, enlargement and furnishing), etc.[10] As long as Catholic clergy were in short supply it might be necessary to gather the laity of several parishes to hear Mass. Perhaps foreign clergy could be brought in to help. Worthy laymen might be employed to conduct Sunday services, even to read a homily.

The Council must produce a new ecclesiastical calendar for England. It must consider whether a third archbishopric was not required, say, at Bristol, with Wales as its province. It must direct visitations of the universities, Inns of Court and Chancery to reform learning and teaching there, and 'consider whether a third university were not necessary in the North parts of England, as at Durham, Richmond or Newcastle or the like'. To it would belong oversight of syllabuses and books used in schools, as also of 'all bookbinders, stationers and booksellers' shops', which were to be searched for dangerous wares.[11]

England would need a military order, like the Santa Hermandad in Castile, to mobilize 'our young gentlemen and nobility' for the campaign against heresy and, when there were heretics no more, against pirates, thieves and highwaymen. Every parish should have its pious brotherhoods and sodalities to take charge of religious education of the young, to accompany the Blessed Sacrament when it was carried abroad, etc. These were to be instituted by the Council, which was also to encourage every kind of pious society for performing such good works as visiting the sick and prisons, and helping the poor. Societies of these kinds abounded in Rome, Naples, Milan, Madrid, Seville, and ought to become a familiar part of the English scene.[12] Finally, the Council was to appoint men of 'ability, zeal and judgement' to write the history of the persecution of the English Catholics, petition the Holy See to honour their martyrs, build churches where they suffered and perhaps make Tyburn a centre of pilgrimage.[13]

Such was the programme of the Council of Reformation during the few years of life envisaged for it. When its work was done 'it would be very much necessary' that it should be succeeded by 'some good and sound manner of Inquisition' – something less harsh than the Spanish

[10] Ibid., pp. 70–82.
[11] Ibid., pp. 83–5, 90–1, 94–5, 184. Persons also proposed that new dioceses should be carved out of Lincoln and York, which were still too large.
[12] Ibid., pp. 78–80, 96.
[13] Ibid., pp. 97–8.

model, but a tribunal that would doubtless have outstripped the Court of High Commission in severity.[14]

Persons has plenty to say about the clergy of recatholicized England – their formation and manner of life. Bishops must live without pomp or riches, be devoted to the poor, the sick and the orphans, widows and the rest, and be ever-vigilant pastors of their flocks. They must keep close watch on their clergy and keep a list of their 'ages, talents, manners, merits and conversations'. Archbishops should do the same with the bishops of their provinces. All candidates for the priesthood must be closely examined and all preferment kept in the hands of bishops and chapters. All clergy, including bishops, should be removable or liable to demotion (translation to a lesser see in the case of bishops). There were to be frequent provincial synods, and so on.[15] In short, England was to feel the full force of Trent's decrees; and even as commissioners visited all the parishes to assess their spiritual and material needs, the clergy were to submit to continuous supervision by bishops and archdeacons and to a regime of meetings of 'priests of each circuit' every two or three months to examine priestly conduct and to enjoy 'sermons, conferences and exhortations' in the presence of certain learned men appointed to resolve doubts.[16] In the meantime the Council of Reformation would have overseen the return of the religious, showing preference for those orders which 'in our days [are] more reformed than others' and giving special preference to orders of nuns. It would be for the Council, too, to distribute to all these sufficient lands, 'which shall be restored according to present necessity, without respect of former possessors'.[17]

The success of the Council of Reformation inevitably depended on the co-operation of Parliament (which would be required to repeal all anti-Catholic legislation immediately) and this in turn would depend on its membership. Until such time as there were heads of religious houses to sit in the Lords once more, their places could be taken by provincials and the like of new orders. Perhaps there should also be

[14] Ibid., pp. 98–9; there should also be held quickly a National Synod to continue the work of enforcing the Council of Trent's decrees in England (ibid., p. 101).

[15] Ibid., pp. 121–38.

[16] Ibid., pp. 145–6. For comment on this proposal, see below, p. 40.

[17] Ibid., pp. 75–7, 188. But it is a fair comment that Persons had earmarked so much of this capital and income to hospitals, schools, colleges, seminaries, etc. (as well as to succouring the secular clergy) that there would not have been a great deal left for the religious.

clergy in the lower house: deans, archdeacons, heads of colleges? Every prospective lay member ought to make public profession of his faith and only tested Catholics be allowed to stand. For a while the local bishop could be given a hand in the matter, at least as far as having 'a negative voice'. At the opening of Parliament let 'every man be sworn to defend the Catholic Roman faith; and moreover that it be made treason for ever for any man to propose anything for change thereof, or for the introduction of heresy.' Parliament should adopt the custom of Venice, 'where suffrages are given by little balls of different colours signifying yes or no to the matters that are proposed'. Every bill should have three days' discussion. The law of mortmain, as well as anti-Catholic legislation, should be repealed, to encourage pious endowments.[18]

The English educational system was badly in need of overhaul. First, there must be a commission from Prince and Parliament, confirmed by the Pope, 'to certain men of experience, learning and wisdom' to attend to the universities. Certain reforms could be proposed immediately. College teaching was wasteful and 'doth greatly hurt and hinder the public profit of students in their learning'. There should be public lectures only 'in public schools that are fair and largely builded for the purpose', given by university lecturers for adequate remuneration, and thus leaving the colleges with a merely ancillary teaching role. Indeed, there could be lectures on the same subject at the same time by different teachers, 'so that scholars be left free to go to which they shall like best, for by that means the two concurrents will try who shall read best and have the most hearing' – a good example of Jesuit *emulatio*.[19] Persons has pages of detail on revising syllabuses (including, of course, the restoration of canon law), on the different apparel to be worn by teachers and students, on the organization of fellowships and scholarships, on a common purse to meet heavy expenditure of individual colleges and to provide for the new lecture rooms, hospitals, infirmaries, libraries, etc.[20] He proposes that all existing heads of colleges, fellows and the rest should be removed in one clean sweep and appointments made afresh. Thereafter heads should hold office for two or three years only; and a visitation should take place at the end of each term of office.[21]

There should be 'greater and more principal colleges as are in other

---

[18] Ibid., pp. 102–7.   [19] Ibid., pp. 152–5.
[20] Ibid., pp. 166–9, 176–7.   [21] Ibid., pp. 170–1.

universities', which, like All Souls', would provide no teaching but act
as storehouses of learning for 'prince and commonwealth to lay hands
on' and supply religious leaders. Perhaps there would be virtue in
specialization within colleges – some in divinity, some in law, some in
natural science, and so on – and even grouping of students among
halls and colleges by subject. Such an arrangement could greatly aid
the students themselves. It would allow a college specializing in natural
science, for example, to collect specimens from all over the world and
a college specializing in medicine to build up an anatomical museum,
as at Padua.[22]

Grammar schooling in England needed much improvement. The
fundamental defect was that schools had only one master, which meant
that the different age-groups could not be organized into classes; this
led to problems of discipline, which in turn caused 'overmuch beating
of children'. England must follow the continental pattern (which
Jesuits themselves did much to spread): four or five classes per school,
each with a master in charge and an examination system controlling
promotion of students to higher classes; a grammar school in every
town and village.[23]

Commissioners would be appointed to enquire into not only the
teaching methods, syllabus, discipline and daily life of the Inns of Court,
but also every aspect of the administration of the English law. Persons
was a severe critic of the legal profession and the courts. 'The rigour
of our temporal laws in putting men to death for theft of so small
quantity or value as is accustomed in England' should be moderated
'and some lesser bodily punishments invented for the purpose'. Indeed,
the death penalty was being meted out with horrifying readiness, often
by hastily summoned juries. The defendant, Persons complained, had
no time to prepare his defence, seek legal advice and gather witnesses.
Our laws touching life and limb 'do savour much of tyranny' and
offended against natural justice, not least by resting so much on 'twelve
silly men' and putting the defendant at heavy disadvantage.[24] Persons
was urgent and eloquent here, and doubtless recalled as he wrote the
trial of Campion and the others of the Society who had trodden the
same path to martyrdom.

<hr />

[22] Ibid., pp. 180–3.   [23] Ibid., pp. 159–60.

[24] Ibid., pp. 241–53. Persons was to develop his criticisms of the English legal system in
his exchanges with Sir Edward Coke. See Clancy, *Papist Pamphleteers* (Chicago,
1964), pp. 111–16, 118–20.

The costs of litigation were inordinate. The poor should receive free legal aid for all cases – as (he claims) they did in Catholic countries. A religious order should provide the necessary services. The courts were clogged with 'infinite suits', partly thanks to the lawyers themselves. There should be more outlying tribunals than merely those of the North and Wales. The number of suits brought to London should be limited; and perhaps the flow of appeals could be stemmed by adopting the Spanish practice of requiring a large cash deposit from the appellant, to be shared between the court and the defendant if the appeal was lost.[25]

Commissioners would attend to the urgent task of giving the overgrown and tangled Common Law 'some more clear order and method'. But some major reforms Persons proposed at once. Primogeniture should be abolished and replaced by the sharing among children provided by Roman Law. The law concerning dowries (for which Parliament should lay down a scale) and jointures should be amended to protect the wife, particularly by preventing her dowry from being wholly absorbed into her husband's estate; and the whole matter of wardship required immediate amendment.[26] Finally, every corner of the legal profession was to be subject to regular visitation by royal visitors, a provision which in Spain, for example, had done much to reduce corruption.

And what kind of society, lay society, was to emerge from all this? In some respects, Persons is entirely conventional. Since order, hierarchy and deference were divinely ordained, the nobility and gentry were to be restored 'to their ancient honours, dignities and privileges', including special preferment in the Church, and the commonalty to return to that 'old simplicity, both in apparel, diet, innocency of life and plainness of dealing and conversation' from which heresy had lured them. Let the rich uphold true religion, edify by virtuously avoiding excesses in food and apparel, bring up their children in 'order and discipline' and show to their servants 'ancient love and tender care'; and let the commons become once more the most contented in the world.[27] And so on.

But it would be unjust to accuse Persons of doing no more than

---

[25] *Memorial*, pp. 212–13, 245.
[26] Ibid., pp. 226–9, 280–2, 246. Both Cardinal Allen and Persons felt particular hostility towards the Court of Wards, on the grounds (primarily) that it debilitated the nobility, especially by preventing adequate education for wards. Cf. Clancy, op. cit., pp. 40–1.
[27] *Memorial*, pp. 220–4, 256–7.

dressing up traditional social conservatism in Arcadian pieties or of complacently assuming that it was enough to uproot heresy for the 'Commonwealth' to flourish once more. His belief in hierarchy and degree was accompanied by a passionate concern for the 'bare and needy common husbandman' and indignation at 'known public oppression of the common people'; nor was social injustice simply the creature of heresy. Let there be, he says, another set of commissioners to enquire into 'what oppressions, injuries, vexations, losses or other injuries have been laid upon the commonalty, or any part thereof, by the heretical estate of these last years, or by bad landlords, nobles, or gentlemen of puissance, to the end it may be remedied; also what landlords principally have most raised or racked their rents, to the end they may be dealt withall for some moderation'. All rights of common, wood, grazing, etc., which have been taken away or violated must be restored. Parliament must impose the old rents of assize and control all rents thereafter. Rack-rents and short leases must go; and the landlord who tried to offset the disadvantage of leasing for life by imposing high entry fines must also be baulked. We must return to the ancient manner 'of letting and setting lands for term of life after the rates of the old rents'. No commoner ought to be vexed with law suits: no tenant required to stand as surety for his lord. The 'often markets and fairs' in England are admirable and should be multiplied. Coin must be minted in sufficiently small denominations to be of use to the poor. Finally, in every city or great shire town there should be set up a poor man's bank or treasure, modelled on the Monte della Pietà, 'where poor men either freely or with very little interest have money upon sureties and [be not] forced to take it up at intolerable usury'. Responsibility for providing the necessary money would rest initially with the Council of Reformation, who would assign rents and other income (from ex-religious sources) to this fund; thereafter it could be maintained by private benefaction.[28] Thus the poor would be delivered from the tyranny of the usurious moneylender and that vicious circle which could easily bring a debtor tenant into ever more abject dependence upon his lord.

The *Memorial* shows well the power and energy of Persons's versatile, dedicated mind. It is full of shrewdness and imagination. It is executed with enormous assurance, passing without apparent effort from, say,

[28] Ibid., pp. 256–60.

plans for redirecting no small share of the total wealth of England or remodelling Parliament to details of the collars which dons should wear and the terms of their fellowships. Time and again it produces striking, and often modern-sounding, ideas, such as the proposal that confessors should impose the penance of visiting hospitals and prisons rather than reciting of prayers, and that, to encourage this, hospitals should be 'kept fine, cleanly and handsome and public prisons . . . be enlarged with courts and open halls for people to visit them'.[29] The book is the fruit of wide travel and keen observation – as frequent reference to the laws and usages of other countries or the structure of their nobilities or universities, and so on, shows. Though Persons had been out of England for fifteen years before he wrote, he clearly retained (as his remark about entry fines on leases, for instance, indicates) an informed interest in his homeland. Indeed, his book is redolent of patriotism. The 'true' reformation will leave England a 'light and lantern' to other nations; her universities will be the best in Europe; London will be another Rome and provide 'seminaries for the help of our neighbours oppressed or infected with heresy, as namely, Denmark, divers parts near to us of Germany, Poland, Gothland, Sweden, Scotland, Muscovy and the Isles of Zealand'. English priests could go thither, too, 'among which the writer of this Memorial would offer himself for one' – and thus revive the glories of the Saxon missionaries.[30] We should remember this when we listen to the enemies of the Jesuits rehearsing their charge that Persons and his party were disloyal, un-English, 'Hispanomaniacs', etc.

On the other hand we may be tempted to agree with the charge that Persons was seriously out of touch with the realities of the English scene. As has been suggested, he probably seriously underestimated the strength of the Elizabethan Settlement and the English Protestant cause; he surely underestimated English anti-papal and anticlerical sentiment. In the light of what Mary Tudor and then James II experienced, his proposals for swift repeal of anti-Catholic legislation and the thorough purging of all office-holders, Parliament and the universities will seem optimistic. In view of the difficulties which Whitgift, Bancroft and, above all, Laud encountered in their efforts to halt and reverse lay spoliation of the English Church's resources, and to recover land, tithes and patronage, Persons's plans for the economic restoration of the old Church seem to be no less ignorant of the fierce resistance

[29] Ibid., p. 96.
[30] Ibid., pp. 100, 150–1.

that awaited neo-clericalism everywhere. Property, Parliament and Protestantism would have closed ranks against the Roman Catholic version no less instinctively and no less formidably than they did later against Archbishop Laud. But Persons's solution of the problem of the abbey lands, namely, that all who conformed would be allowed to keep them in return for an annual rent to the Church, is perhaps more convincing. In the first place, it was an arrangement already fairly widespread in Ireland[31] (to which the provisions of the *Memorial* also applied). In the second, it somewhat paradoxically gave greater security to the lay owners than they could ever have derived from Mary Tudor's settlement – because it was less generous. Cardinal Pole, in the Pope's name, had formally released the new possessioners from any obligation to restore ecclesiastical property to the Church. But how could anyone be sure that this was not merely a tactical retreat? There was scarcely any oath, any vow, any undertaking which had not been or could not subsequently be found wanting and declared null and void by some willing papal canonist. Rome had only itself to blame for others' lack of trust and for the fact that no protestations of good faith could match the security of a Protestant Settlement. The virtue of Persons's design was that it would help to stifle any later papal demand that all ex-monastic lands be returned, since they would already be yielding a steady income for pious and ecclesiastical purposes. On the other hand that income would have been becoming decreasingly valuable on account of inflation – as, too, the income from those long leases to favoured lay folk of ecclesiastical lands, which concerned Laud greatly (and which Persons does not seem to know much about).

Persons rather skated over the problem of what exactly was to be done in those critical days immediately after the 'Conquest' or the queen's death to secure England for Catholicism; how, in other words, the religious *coup* was to be mounted. Some years after he wrote, and perhaps only a few months before Elizabeth actually died, another Jesuit hand (possibly Garnet's) produced a further 'Memorial' which tried to make good this omission and to spell out a detailed plan of campaign.[32] It also made some refinements to Persons's programme.

[31] As Dr Bossy has pointed out to me.
[32] P.R.O., SP 12/275, fos. 104–13. It is headed 'Discourse of the providence necessary to be had for the setting upp the Catholick faith when God shall call the queen out of this life'; and is endorsed 'A project of Jesuits'. It is possibly a copy in the hand of Sir Thomas Wilson. A second copy follows immediately. The manuscript seems to have been written *c.* 1602.

First, if possible, the Pope should announce on the eve of Elizabeth's death the name of that one who, out of 'the multiplicity of competitors to the crown', was to succeed to the throne. Next, because the 'interior party' of active English Catholics was small and Spanish help slow and unreliable, the Pope was to rally support for the Catholic cause in England by solemnly promising the following: that all former abbey lands would remain in the hands of those who adhered to the Catholic cause (saving only the annual rent to the Church); that a heretic's ex-monastic lands would pass to a Catholic brother and, if there was none, revert to the Church and thence be given in reward to 'gentle-men, captains and soldiers' aiding the Catholic cause; that all 'debts of usury' of adherents to that cause were to be wiped out; that the Court of Wards would be abolished; that supporters would be exempt for life from parliamentary taxation and military service outside the realm; that all enclosed lands would be restored; that Catholics would have free legal aid; that 'franklins and serving men' who conformed would be advanced to the degree of gentlemen and receive a share of the lands of their masters if the latter were heretics; that all obstinate heretics and persecutors of the Church would lose their possessions.[33]

All this – and the author frankly conceded that it was unblushing bribery (which rivals might try to outdo with counter-offers) – was to be contained in proclamations published by the Jesuit provincial or the Archpriest on the queen's death. To protect his candidate, the pope must threaten to excommunicate anyone who supported James VI of Scotland or the son of the King of France. Meanwhile the Fathers of the Society would have chosen a captain to seize the dead queen's ships in the Medway and thence to gain control of the Thames, and another to surprise the Tower, with the guns from which 'the better to threaten the City of London to accept of this intended Reformation'. It would be necessary to take and fortify a line of towns from Cornwall to Lancashire from which to succour the Irish (who should also have risen under papal direction to expel the heretics) and places in the Thames estuary to receive aid from the Low Countries. Since the Puritans, the really dangerous opponents, were 'commonly artisans and burgesses' and not warlike, they would withdraw to fortified towns themselves and (presumably) be reduced piecemeal; and once the Catholics had gained the key positions, Spanish troops and ships would shortly

[33] Ibid., fos. 104–8.

provide overwhelming superiority. 'The danger is little, the charges nothing, the hope to be great, the profit infinite of souls to God, service to the Apostolic See, glory to the name of his Holiness and good of the whole Christian monarchy.'[34] And the recovery of England would be the first step to winning back Scotland, to bringing the Dutch to heel, to opening up the Baltic lands to the Faith, and so on.

Before this second 'Memorial' was written, Persons's work had become known to English Catholics, especially those bitterly opposed to him and his policies. They had not read it. They assumed the worst about it – because they wanted to. Hence the *Memorial* came to play a not inconsiderable part in the lamentable conflict between seculars and Jesuits which broke out in the last decade of the sixteenth century and inflicted a grave wound on English Catholicism.

The conflict reached from England to English exiles in the Low Countries and to Rome (indeed, it had had a first kindling in the English College there). It sprang from jealousy, personal animosities, insensitivity (on both sides), frustration and the anguish of persecution. Eventually two sets of protagonists emerged, one consisting of a group of seculars confined in Wisbech Castle and their supporters, the other of Robert Persons and his circle. The conflict had by then become a fierce clash of policy and ideology – between those who, like Persons, saw victory at hand, looked to Spain to produce it, preached the crusade and the *coup d'état* to unseat Elizabeth, and lived a militant Counter-Reformation Catholicism which neither gave any quarter to the heretical, usurpatious enemy nor expected any in return; and on the other hand, those who, fortified by the obvious loyalty to the queen of so many recusants at the time of the Armada, rejected Spain and her aggressive imperialism (masquerading as zeal for Holy Church), denounced the plots and violence of 'total war', proclaimed their loyal Englishness over and against 'Hotspur Jesuits and the Spaniard',[35] and believed that the survival of the Faith in England could be secured only by winning concessions from a monarch who was, after all, a good deal less intolerant than most of her contemporaries, and would respond favourably if her Catholic subjects could give firm proof of their loyalty and moderation. They had tired of violence; outgrown the *simpliste* policies of Persons which, they believed, had provoked and

[34] Ibid., fo. 112v.
[35] The phrase comes from A. Copley, *An answere to a letter of a Jesuited gentleman* (1601), p. 74.

always would provoke the English government into counter-attacking with fines, the rack and 'Bloody Questions', etc., and hence were the main reasons for the sufferings of the Catholic community; they had glimpsed the futility of living in a past heroic age of brutal martyrdoms, *Regnans in Excelsis*, and plots centred on such as Mary Queen of Scots. And they resented two further things: the way in which a handful of exiles, led by Persons and out of touch with the realities of the English scene, sought to manage the English mission and was able to exercise considerable influence over papal policy; and the papal decision in 1598 to appoint George Blackwell as Archpriest (an extraordinary office which carried some jurisdiction over the whole English mission) instead of giving England a much-needed episcopate – a decision which was quickly assumed to have been procured by Persons in order to leave the Society untrammelled, and indeed, since Blackwell was known to be an admirer of Jesuits, to enable it by typical subterfuge to exercise complete, but unseen, control over the whole of English Catholic affairs.

'No bishop, no regiment, no order.' 'No bishop, no property.' Jesuits, as well as being arrogant, violent, Machiavellian, 'Spanish' and heirs to odious Huguenots and the Ligue, threatened the whole structure of society, 'so lawless is all their carriage'.[36] They were more dangerous than the Puritans, they were 'Anabaptisticall' and atheists, for they preached popular sovereignty and tyrannicide, they would claw down nobility and were the enemies of episcopacy. As Anthony Copley, a lay supporter of the Appellants (that is, those who appealed to Rome against the appointment and then the activities of the Arch-priest), concluded, 'Cathay or cannibal country were their abode rather than so civil a land as England'.[37]

When news of Persons's *Memorial* reached his opponents the conflict was already mature and being conducted with scandalous spleen and bitterness. A garbled report of the book came to them and they were not slow to construe it in the most hostile light. The book was yet another example of Persons's overweening arrogance: he demanded that everything in England should be changed – laws, customs, property, habits, the hospitality of prelates, the authority of nobles.[38]

---

[36] Ibid., p. 27; cf. Clancy, *Papist Pamphleteers*, esp. pp. 79ff.
[37] Copley, op. cit., p. 95.
[38] So the author of the *Brevis Relatio*, an Appellant statement of the case against the Jesuits, in T. G. Law, *The Archpriest Controversy* (1898), ii, 108.

And this could not come about without establishing a tyranny. 'See the doting man', exclaimed Copley, 'he hath framed an ecclesiastical Utopia to himself, whereunto he hath given the same to be exhibited at the next Parliament to be holden after the Conquest, *viz. anno* I of Philip the third'.[39] Of course, Persons kept his book like a precious jewel 'in his bosom' and for the moment showed it 'only once on a time to a very dear friend of his'; but it would have been blazoned forth in print by the time the Spanish assault came and England was reduced to a province of Spain under a viceroy – like the Low Countries. Copley rehearses the familiar anti-Jesuit sentiments in the name of 'we that are England's upon English and let all foreign rule go by',[40] but he fastens in particular on scurrilous charges of feathering of nests and gulling the pious, especially women (and he is full of innuendo here), into showering lands and money upon the Society. 'A Jesuit is a *piscator*, but not like St. Peter, *animarum*, so much as *pecuniarum*', and seeks a life of ease in elegant company.[41] The *Memorial*, however, shows that the Society aspires to much larger financial successes. After the 'Conquest' all the secular clergy, from bishops to parsons, will simply 'be pensionary to the Pope's Holiness', that is, they will receive stipends from a central 'Exchequer', the income for which will consist of a levy on the laity in respect of all 'abbey lands and other the old Church lands of England' and spiritualities ('all devotionary supplements'), and be gathered in by four Jesuit collectors, assisted by 'only two seculars of their own choosing', who shall also be responsible for disbursing the annual stipends. Moreover, any surplus left in that fund shall be 'pursed up' by these papal collectors and dispatched to Rome.[42] Copley is right about the national fund into which the rent on ex-monastic lands would be paid; and Persons had foreseen that, at least initially, income from parishes might also be paid into that fund to provide stipends for clergy, until such time as parochial and diocesan structures has been reorganized and incumbents could be appointed once more to benefices. He had also suggested that the Council might enquire into bishops' incomes, particularly with a view to augmenting them. But the rest of the story – about Jesuit collectors turning seculars into pensioners (and, readers were doubtless expected to suppose, in the process skimming off a good deal of wealth for themselves as well as for Rome) – was mischievous. Whether knowingly or not, Copley had

---

[39] Copley, op. cit., p. 99.
[41] Ibid., p. 82 and *passim*.
[40] Ibid., p. 65.
[42] Ibid., pp. 99–100.

somehow acquired enough of the truth to be plausible and added enough of the false to convince the Jesuits' many ill-wishers that they were now beginning to discover the full extent of the sinister ambitions of their antagonists.

Indeed, what more easy for them than to believe that the *Memorial* was a secret master-plan full of the most objectionable designs for reducing England to servitude under Spaniard and Jesuit? And the very fact that it had not been published (and scarcely could ever be), as well as enabling imaginations to run riot, heightened the sense of conspiracy. To those among the secular who detected Jesuit '*libido dominandi*' and Machiavellism at every turn, Persons's 'ecclesiastical Utopia' could easily assume nightmarish qualities. His *Memorial* was also the most arrogant example yet of the way in which, despite the fact that they had long since left England (fled from the fray, even), he and his like never hesitated to dispose of the fortunes, if not lives, of those who had remained on the mission. It went hand in hand with his *Conference about the next succession* (published in 1597 and immediately a further cause of consternation); it was all of a piece with the appointment of the wretched Blackwell.

In 1602 William Watson, a secular priest who had served the English mission long and at one time undergone torture at the hands of Topcliffe, but who was now taken up with an implacable, almost pathological, hatred of Jesuits and Jesuitry, attained new heights of abuse in a book entitled *A Decacordon of Ten Quodlibeticall Questions*. It was devoted largely to exposing the 'impiety, irreligiosity, treachery, treason and Machiavellian atheism' of the 'bastardly runagate Persons'[43] and it paid considerable attention to the *Memorial*. Watson, of course, had not read it. He had received, or his own frenetic mind had generated, a blood-curdling travesty of its contents. Persons and the General of the Jesuits in Rome had produced, he declared, a set of 'statutes' (contained in a volume entitled *The high court of reformation for England*) laying down the policies to be followed when the 'Catholic conqueror of Spain or Austria should be invested with the sceptre royal of our noble Eliza and sit enthronised in her princely seat as sole monarch of all the Albion's or great Britain's isles'.[44]

It provides for a 'Jesuitical commonwealth' which would finally make England what she already was fast becoming under the arch-

[43] Watson, *Ten Quodlibeticall Questions* (1602), pp. 112, 128.
[44] Ibid., p. 92.

priest, namely, 'a Japponian monarchy' or 'a Japponian island of Jesuits', with 'our petty king father, Fr. Persons', hand in glove with the Spanish viceroy.[45] No religious orders were to be allowed into the country, save Jesuits and Capuchins, the Holy Spirit having forsaken all others (or, to be more exact, the Capuchins being the only sort whom Jesuits could live with). Next, the income of all the bishops of England, Ireland and Scotland, plus the 20,000 parish clergy and all the colleges and religious houses, was to be handed over to four Jesuits (as Copley has told), abetted by two seculars who must be 'demi-Jesuits'; these would assign to all the clergy 'competent stipends and pensions to live upon', as competent, that is, as a Turk's ration to janizaries. What was left over would not go to the Pope in Rome, as Copley had predicted, but be 'employed *in pios usus* as Father General of Rome shall think good'. And if anyone should demand a public account of what had become of their revenues, lands and lordships, 'this shall be their answer: "*mirantur superiores, etc.*", or in plain terms: "how dare you seem to inquire how a Jesuit disposeth of any thing, being peculiarly guided by the spirit".'[46] And there was worse to come.

'They have made a Puritanian division of the ecclesiastical estate in their High Council of Reformation for England, wherein, amongst other things, a statute is made for the abrogation of all episcopal dignity; and that, just like to the Puritanian or the Cartwrightian or the Brownistian or the Genevan . . . a new order or government [shall] be brought into the Church, whose governors shall consist of six seniors or elders . . . whereof the seculars shall be as it were the chaplains to the Jesuits, as pater rector and pater minister, that is, Father Persons and his minister.' As for secular clergy, they would bring in foreigners – the better to control them (like the janizaries, again) – and reserve the highest offices to themselves.[47]

'All the whole state must be changed', all 'altered, abridged and

---

[45] Ibid., pp. 170, 209, 303. I take the allusion to 'Japponian' monarchy to refer to the monopoly of the Japanese mission which Rome had granted to the Jesuits (thus excluding, in theory, friars from such places as the Philippines), rather than to suggest some extreme form of despotism, as has been proposed.

[46] Ibid., pp. 92–4.

[47] Ibid., p. 142. Persons had certainly suggested that foreign clergy might be imported, at least initially, and given key offices even. Watson was quick to seize upon this useful point. His remark (quoted above) about the Capuchins being the only other religious who would be allowed in is interesting – for they were the only new order whom Persons mentioned by name. Watson seems, therefore, to have had some detailed information about the book with which to fabricate his hostile account.

quite taken away' including the lands and lordships of nobleman and gentleman. What retinue gentlemen might keep, how much they might spend yearly, 'what diet they should keep at their tables', would be controlled; all land held in fee simple and by other tenures was to be 'brought into villeiny, scoggery and popularity';[48] any fine house required by the Society would be liable to confiscation (and 'this ignoble bastard Persons, in his vain, childish but arrogant hope hath already in conceit confiscated Cecil house to be a *Casa Professa* and another thereby to be *Novitiatum*').[49] They would overthrow the Common Law and have 'Caesar's civil imperial brought in among us . . . all whatsoever England yields being but base, barbarous and void of all sense, knowledge or discretion . . . and on the other hand, all whatsoever is or shall be brought in by those outcasts of Moses, stain of Solon and refuse of Lycurgus, must be reputed for metaphysical, semi-divine and of more excellence than any other were'. And to prove the point they planned that 'all the great charter of England [i.e. Magna Carta] must be burnt'.[50]

They had ready another 'statute' forbidding anyone from speaking against any Jesuit, including 'Fr. Persons, that blessed live saint', or criticizing the High Council of Reformation – though the fathers them-selves shall be licensed to calumniate anyone, 'noble, peer, or prince or bishop, cardinal or pope himself', as we have already seen them doing all too readily in recent years. But anyone whom they had traduced in his lifetime, they would be free to praise to the skies when dead or 'if his back be broken with slaunders or other mishap so as he is never able to rise to any honour afterwards'.[51] This was how they were. They would pick up and drop protégés and patrons. They exploited the gullible and unwary. There was doubtless much else 'in that statute book or huge volume of the High Council of Reformation for England', Watson remarks, 'notable stuff' too, which would come to light if ever it were made public. And doubtless there was one statute that Persons would want his Council to attend to promptly: provision for a less strict law for legitimization of bastards. It was a constant cry of the more bitter among the Appellants that Persons was the son of a Henrician priest called Cowback and a 'very base quean', and Watson took obvious pleasure in suggesting that, 'once this whole monarchical Isle is made a province depending on Spain and Jesuitism', some statute

[48] Ibid., p. 95.
[50] Ibid., pp. 94–5.
[49] Ibid., p. 144.
[51] Ibid., pp. 95–6, 103.

would be 'closely made and covertly foisted in for enabling some bastards . . . to be capable of any honour or dignity, either in the Church or Commonwealth'.[52]

Persons was quick to reply – in a book which took in the whole gamut of Appellants' charges, not just those concerned with his *Memorial* – and to expose the 'absurdities and notorious lies' which Watson had written. There were no *statutes*; nothing had been drawn up or decreed. He did not propose the abolition of fee simple or the overthrow of the customs and Common Law of the land; his book shows forth his patriotism and his high esteem for both the prince and for nobility.[53] He turns angrily on the now-familiar charge that he (and all Jesuits) was opposed to episcopacy and had engineered the erection of Blackwell's 'archpresbytery' in England because he was a crypto-Puritan. He recalls, as he well might, how vigorously he had pressed Rome to appoint bishops, two of them, for England and how he had written to the pope, touted cardinals, in vain.[54] He could justly point to the *Memorial* itself in which, writing without *arrière-pensée*, he had assumed that the full (and enlarged) hierarchy would be restored as soon as England returned to the household of the Faith, had devoted pages to the responsibilities and manner of living of those who were to be promoted to the English sees and had nominated bishops to direct the supremely important body, the Council of Reformation. No, it was egregious mischief-making to put it about among the English Catholics that his *Memorial*, which, of course, none of them had read, would dispossess England of its ecclesiastical superstructure. What had been written about the place which he accorded the Jesuits in England after the conversion was no less wanton. As he rightly remarked, he did not mention the Jesuits once in the whole book. He envisaged that all religious orders would return to England, without exception. What Copley and Watson had supposed about the financial proposals for the restored Church were entirely wrong. Furthermore, it was his intention that the Common Law should be overhauled, not abolished; there was nothing ever thought, let alone written, resembling Watson's statute 'concerning calumniation'; and as for the passage referring to

---

[52] Ibid., p. 109. It is fair to add that this hysterical book shocked the Appellants themselves and earned Watson sharp rebuke from no less personages than Christopher Bagshaw and William Bishop. See Law, op. cit., ii, 183, 194–5.

[53] Persons, *A manifestation of the great folly, etc.*, 56v, 112v.

[54] Ibid., p. 61. He develops the story about his efforts with pope and cardinals in his *A brief apology or defence of the Catholic ecclesiastical hierarchie, etc.* (n.d.), pp. 101–2.

his plans to relieve illegitimacy, it deserved nothing but 'contempt and compassion'.[55] Persons quoted a few lines of the *Memorial* verbatim: but short of publishing the whole work there was little that he could do to give weight to his denials, and very little to persuade those who would have assumed that whatever he said was shot through with equivocation.

Persons's work was one of the most influential unread books ever written. Despite its author's disclaimers, it continued to haunt the anti-Jesuit party and to provide Bancroft with yet further, and ever more welcome, opportunity to pursue his policy towards Catholics of 'divide and debilitate'. It was exactly the sort of thing which William Gifford, a staunch Appellant, had in mind when he warned his sister against being associated with Jesuits, for they preached and practised treason, incited the prince to impose penal laws upon Catholics and did 'vainly promise reformation or rather subversion of the state'.[56]

For us the *Memorial* will have further significance. It was the only plan produced by the Counter-Reformation for creating afresh a restored, model Catholicism. Apart from the author of that other 'Memorial' already mentioned, and that maverick Thomas Blacklo, who fifty years later brooded over designs to refashion English Catholicism,[57] Persons seems to have been the only one ever to try to sketch the future building, the only one who dared draw up a master-plan.

What he produced was a grand design for a theocracy – blatantly clerical, triumphalist and ultramontane, but something new, and something beyond any previous order.

Like Laud, Persons grasped that there was a fundamental economic problem confronting him. Like the Puritans (and not only they), he grasped that 'true reformation' was above all a matter of producing an adequate clergy. Though he never uses the term 'lordly prelate', his discourse on the model bishop would have been scarcely less acceptable to Grindal than to Borromeo; he may not speak of 'dumb dogs', but preaching matters to him, too. He provided for as stringent 'proving' or testing of candidates for the ministry as the first *Admonition to*

---

[55] *A manifestation of the great folly, etc.*, 111v, 112v.
[56] Law, op. cit., ii, 178.
[57] Cf. R. I. Bradley, 'Blacklo and the Counter-Reformation: An Inquiry into the Strange Death of Catholic England', in *From the Renaissance to the Counter-Reformation* (1966), ed. C. H. Carter, esp. pp. 360–5.

Parliament ever sought. There is a striking similarity between his plans for meetings of clergy of every 'circuit' and the prophesyings and exercises which the hot-gospeller Protestant regarded as so important an instrument in raising the standard of the English clergy, and which (so Elizabeth believed) could easily mature into a subversive Puritan infrastructure. Persons could go one better than the Puritan: he had at hand the institution that, more than any other, could eradicate the ignorance and worthlessness of so many benefice-holders in the Elizabethan Church, namely, the seminary. He had founded more seminaries than had anybody else; he had spent much of his life on them.

Calling Jesuits 'puritans' was, of course, easy slogan-mongering. But Persons made the task very easy. When he called for a new ecclesiastical calendar for England he had in mind, among other things, that this would prune away many holy days. He denounced sloth and seemed almost as obsessed with the sin of idleness as any Protestant zealot. Let some feast days be half-holidays, he proposed: Mass in the morning and back to work in the afternoon. On a full day's rest exercises must be devised (to keep the faithful out of mischief) which combined spiritual activity with entertainment. He is more human than the stage Puritan. But he urged that every master should keep his servants from idleness with 'some honest exercise', and that bishops and justices should make sure that no child grew up without a skill or profession.[58] Indeed, England needed an officer like the Roman censor, 'to look that no man lived idly nor brought up his children without some exercise and means to live . . . to call to account such men as lived scandalously, as by carding or dicing, or spent riotously any way his own goods or his wife's'.[59]

He preached a 'total', Hildebrandine Christianity. Heaven has begun. True reformation consisted in 'putting our Commonwealth in joint again' from head to toe. He looked for much more than a merely theological or ecclesiastical restoration, therefore; there must be a renewal of the whole of society and one that embraced 'the poor commons'. There was truth in the charge that Jesuits like Persons, for all that they said about order and degree, and for all their praise of godly bishop and God-fearing gentleman, were at heart populists. The spirituality of the Catholic Reformation was essentially that of

[58] *Memorial*, pp. 86–7, 260–1.   [59] Ibid., pp. 89–90.

'sanctification by good works' and everywhere that it spread it brought a new kind of clergy, the new male and female orders, and lay sodalities, dedicated to an apostolate of charity among the poor and the suffering. Persons's *Memorial* showed forth the same concern. It speaks repeatedly of the lay confraternities and the new religious who will undertake visiting the sick, caring for the old and orphaned, etc.; it returns many times to the need for hospitals and infirmaries and schools; bishops must set aside a portion for the poor; the Council of Reformation will undo enclosures and set up interest-free banks for the poor, and so on.

Concern with excessive holidays, idleness, unworthy clergy and the like was not, of course, a Puritan monopoly. It had been the stock-in-trade of the Commonwealth men and Protestants decades before we can usefully speak of Puritans. Likewise, many others had pleaded passionately, as passionately as did Persons, for the poor, for more schools, for 'good works'. Persons stands in direct line of succession to More, Starkey, even such as Crowley and Latimer. He also pointed to later days. His *Memorial* spoke harshly about the brutality of the English law and promised thorough reform. The English legal system, Persons noted, was the work of Norman invaders and imposed on his ancestors by them.[60] A 'Norman yoke' theory is here in embryo that decades later would be fully grown. Persons stands half way, and is a most unexpected link, between the Tudor Commonwealth men and the radicals of the Commonwealth.

That was why, in the last analysis, the *Memorial* shocked the anti-Jesuit party. Its activism and 'holy worldliness' were alien to them. But in fairness to them it should be quickly added that it was surely a lamentable and unnecessary misfortune that the cause should have been gratuitously associated with plots and treason, and with those millstones around the necks of righteousness, the Habsburgs. Philip II cooked Rome's goose. Persons's magnificent vision never really had a chance. The quieter, even quietist, and conservative world of the Appellants won through not because it was less Christian but because it was more realistic. 'Seigneurial' Catholicism became less 'total' and turned away

---

[60] Ibid., p. 248. Cf. Clancy, op. cit., pp. 111–13, for Persons's further contribution to 'Norman yoke' theory. Persons also suggested that parliamentary seats be redistributed, or at least that smaller boroughs lose their representation (*Memorial*, p. 103), a suggestion which could be taken as further evidence of the way in which he anticipated later radicals, especially Levellers.

from Spain to Gallican France because Spain was such a liability and Rome so insensitive to the English scene. Inevitably the *Memorial* was misunderstood and rejected.

It was to have another day – when, in 1685 and in circumstances that Persons himself could never have envisaged, a Catholic prince ascended the English throne at last. The book had been kept at hand in the meanwhile, and a Jesuit father presented a copy to James II:[61] perhaps Fr Petre himself, that supreme proponent of a 'forward' policy?

James did not have the time to follow its directives, even if he had wanted to do so. After his fall, a copy came into the hands of his opponents, who had been trying hard to procure it during his reign. No less a person than the redoubtable William Lloyd, Bishop of St Asaph and one of the Seven Bishops, acquired it and alluded to it in a sermon preached before William and Mary on 5 November (Guy Fawkes' Day) 1689. Edward Gee was one of his audience. He was quick to see the use to which the bishop's find could be put. By publishing this *Memorial*, 'naked Jesuitism' could at last be exposed and a greater service rendered to 'the Protestant interest than ever I was able to do by anything I wrote against popery during the controversies of the last reign'. In the *Memorial*, then, Protestant England had one of the most complete reasons for thanking the Almighty for 'deliverance by their present majesties';[62] even as the Appellants had had for believing that they were standing firm against power-mania and subversion, and defending the best interests of Holy Church.

---

[61] So Edward Gee tells us in his Dedication to William Lloyd, Bishop of St Asaph, of his edition of the *Memorial* in 1690. Gee was, of course, a vigorous anti-Roman protagonist in James II's reign.

[62] *Memorial*, A3v – Gee's Dedication.

III

The Revolution of 1688:
Resistance and Contract

J. P. KENYON

In the midst of the elections of 1710 a Whig journalist irritably remarked:

We live in a nation where at present there is scarce a single head that does not teem with politics. The whole island is peopled with statesmen, and not unlike Trinculo's kingdom of viceroys. Every man has contrived a scheme of government for the benefit of his fellow subjects, which they may follow and be safe.[1]

To many it was a matter of concern that politics and the constitution should still be in a state of flux, twenty years after the so-called 'Settlement', and that this instability should implicate the Revolution of 1688 itself, which the Whigs at least, and some of their political opponents, regarded as basic to the religious safety and the political well-being of the English people. Benjamin Hoadly voiced his deep and passionate disquiet in 1709:

The case of the Revolution is a public, national case of conscience . . . [and] it hath, I think, become absolutely necessary that, one way or other, it should be put as much out of doubt as possible. For the matter is now reduced to this; whether we lie under a national guilt, or not.[2]

This national guilt was by then focused on the question of resistance. Had the Revolution of 1688 been an act of resistance to constituted authority, and if so, was such resistance in special cases justified, notwithstanding the non-resistance oath of 1661, and its subsequent

[1] *The Whig Examiner*, 12 October 1710.
[2] *Works* (1773), ii, 177–8.

endorsement by the leaders of Church and State right up to 1688? The Church of England, once it emerged from the trauma of the Revolution itself, was alive with contestation on this point. Whig writers gloried in the fact that resistance had been used to James II in 1688, but their opponents declared that this invalidated the whole Revolution Settlement (though where this left Queen Anne, or the Pretender, was not clear). To the Whigs' contention that James had been ejected by a national act of will, they replied that William had been invited over by an interested clique of men acting in a private capacity – a damaging admission made by Hoadly himself.[3]

But it was left to Henry Sacheverell to demonstrate the contempt of the high Tories for Whig theory, and stand the whole problem on its head, in a sermon first preached at St Mary's, Oxford, on 23 December 1705 and repeated, on a much more famous occasion, at St Paul's on 5 November 1709. There he announced:

Our adversaries think they effectually stop our mouths, . . . when they urge the Revolution of this day in their defence. But certainly they are the greatest enemies of that, and his late Majesty, and the most ungrateful for the deliverance, who endeavour to cast such black and odious colours upon both. How often must they be told that the [late] king himself solemnly disclaimed the least imputation of resistance in his Declaration; and that the Parliament declared, that they set the Crown on his head upon no other title but that of the vacancy of the throne. . . . So tender were they of the regal rights, and so averse to infringe the least tittle of our constitution.[4]

The Whigs' immediate reaction was one of scorn. At Sacheverell's trial the following winter Robert Walpole sarcastically remarked: 'My lords, it cannot now be necessary to prove resistance in the Revolution; I should as well expect that your lordships would desire me to prove, for form's sake, the sun shines at noon day.'[5] Daniel Defoe was even more scathing:

How merry a tale it is to hear [Sacheverell] prove the doctrine of non-resistance from the Prince of Orange's declaration, and reconcile the Revolution to the principle of unconditional subjection, because it was founded on the vacancy of the throne. As if the Prince of Orange had not brought an army with him to resist, but came with 14,000 men at his heels, to stand

---

[3] *The Revolution No Rebellion* . . (1709), p. 11.

[4] 'Perils of False Brethren both in Church and State', *State Trials* [ed. W. Cobbett and T. B. Howell (1809–28)], xv, 80–1.

[5] Ibid., 91.

and look on while the English gentry and clergy, with prayers and tears, brought King James to run away and leave the throne vacant! What a banter on King James is this new-started whimsy, to tell the Revolution was no breach of non-resistance; as if inviting and bringing over the Prince was not the effectual and original cause of the throne being vacant.[6]

True enough, but not to the sophists on both sides whose task it was to fashion a political theory which would reconcile the Revolution of 1688 with the deepest prejudices of the nation. The general disfavour into which left-wing political thought had fallen as a result of the 'murder' of Charles I and the 'tyranny' of Oliver Cromwell left little room for manoeuvre, and if the enormously strong conventions of an age of deference – deference of wives to husbands, children to parents, servants to masters, tenants to gentry, gentry to nobility – were an embarrassment to Tory theorists who had to pretend that the Revolution had not infringed them, they were more than an embarrassment to the Whigs. Because the history of the late seventeenth and eighteenth centuries has been written largely by Whigs and because the two-party interpretation of English history (one which is remarkably tenacious) implies a fifty-fifty split between Whigs and Tories, it is too often assumed that the Whigs triumphed in a fair fight because of the originality of their ideas and the general acceptance they gained. Nothing could be farther from the truth. The difficulty the Whigs experienced in gaining a working majority in Parliament is reflected in the weakness of their political theory within the context of the times; indeed, it must be doubted if their theories appealed to more than a small minority of the articulate governing class. They were a minority party whose success was due to their ability to provide war-time leadership – a fact demonstrated in reverse by their defeat at all the peace-time elections of the period, 1698, 1700, 1710 and 1713[7] – and if they triumphed in the end it was because of the maladroitness of their opponents, which led some of them to flirt with the Pretender and bring down on the whole Tory party the wrath of George I. Even then, the conduct of the Whig leaders from 1710 to 1716 and beyond is not the conduct of party leaders conscious of a sound ethical and political base.

By 1710 it was clear that their principal totem or *ju-ju*, the Revolu-

---

[6] *The Review*, vi, 426–7.

[7] For this purpose I count 1710 as a peace-time, 1701 as a war-time election.

tion of 1688, was an idol with feet of clay. Their response to Sacheverell's criticisms was vigorous but unconvincing. It was not in fact easy to find hard evidence of resistance in the Revolution. It was true that in his Declaration of 30 September 1688, William had denied any intention of offering force to James II, and announced that his army was merely intended to protect his own person from the violence of the King's 'evil counsellors'; in his Additional Declaration, published on 14 October, he had protested that his forces were 'utterly disproportioned to that wicked design of conquering the nation'.[8] In the processional campaign that followed, the two armies had never come within a hundred miles of one another, and the local magnates who rose against James announced that they did so to secure the assembly of a free parliament under the terms of the Prince's declaration, sheltering behind such vague and unexceptional abstractions as 'the Protestant Religion, our Laws and Liberties, and the Ancient Constitution of England'.[9] Lord Delamere, typically enough, broke through this curtain of constitutionality to announce: 'I am of opinion, that when the Nation is delivered, it must be by Force or by Miracle. It would be too great a presumption to expect the latter, and therefore our deliverance must be by force.'[10] But apart from this, the only attempt to justify the use of force against King James was made by 'the nobility, gentry and commonalty at the rendezvous at Nottingham' on 22 November, whose published declaration roundly stated:

We hope all good Protestant subjects will with their Lives and Fortunes be assistant to us, and not be bug-beared with the opprobrious Terms of *Rebels*, by which they [James II and his advisers] would fright us to become perfect *Slaves* to their Tyrannical Insolences and Usurpations; for we assure ourselves that no rational and unbiased Person will judge it Rebellion to defend our Laws and Religion, which all our Princes have sworn at their Coronations. . . . *We own it Rebellion to resist a King that governs by Law, but he was*

---

[8] *State Tracts* (1693), pp. 424, 426.

[9] This was at Plymouth; see *Correspondentie van Willem III*, ed. N. Japikse, 2nd ser. (The Hague, 1932–7), iii, 69. For Norwich and King's Lynn, see *State Tracts*, p. 437; and for Derby, ibid., p. 438. It does not seem that a declaration was issued at York, though one was in preparation when Danby struck; Andrew Browning, *Thomas Osborne Earl of Danby* (Glasgow, 1944–51), i, 400. 'The Thoughts of a Private Person, about the Justice of the Gentlemen's Undertaking at York', *State Tracts*, p. 461, adopts some advanced positions, but it was written weeks, if not months, later, and it is to be doubted if it was endorsed by Danby.

[10] 15 November 1688, *State Tracts*, p. 435. Though described as a 'speech', it was in fact a letter to his tenants.

always accounted a Tyrant that made his Will his Law; and to resist such an one we justly esteem no Rebellion, but a necessary Defence.[11]

This was valuable material, which gained in piquancy from the fact that Henry Compton, Bishop of London, now a rock-ribbed Tory, and the Princess Anne, now Queen, arrived in Nottingham four days later and took shelter under the Declaration. It was given great prominence by the author of *Vox Populi Vox Dei*, the most influential Whig tract of this generation, and this is in itself suggestive.[12] For it was an isolated instance, and it was never necessary to carry it into effect, for the total collapse of James's position left his opponents in bloodless possession of the country. A case for the use of resistance had been made, but had resistance been used?

The Whigs' answer was that the decision to grant the crown to William in 1689 was an implied act of resistance; in fact, it implied James's deposition. There was superficial justification for this. During the Convention debates in 1689, or soon after, several pamphlets were published asserting in crude terms that the deposition of an unjust sovereign was justifiable by scripture, the law of nature, or plain common sense.[13] Commons and Lords debated the Original Contract, and it featured prominently in the resolution on the state of the nation finally agreed by both Houses. Moreover, late in the year John Locke published his two treatises *Of Civil Government*, the second of which was a detailed exposition of contract theory, and he avowed in his preface that his intention was to justify the Revolution just accomplished. This gave many contemporaries the illusion that James II had been deposed for breaking the Original Contract, and this is a misconception shared by some historians down to the present.[14]

For it is a misconception. True, in the famous Commons debate of 28 January 1689, several M.P.s wholeheartedly embraced contract theory. Sir Robert Howard, a long-time servant of Charles II and

[11] Ibid., p. 436. [Italics as in original.]
[12] *Vox Populi*, p. 32. (For this tract, see p. 62 below.)
[13] E.g., 'An Argument for Self-Defence', *Somers Tracts* (ed. Walter Scott, 1809–15), x, 277ff.; *An Essay upon the Original and Design of Magistracie* (1689), pp. 4, 6, 9 [from internal evidence it seems that this was published even before the Convention met]; and 'Proposals humbly offered to the Lords and Commons in the present Convention', *State Tracts*, p. 455. See also 'The Thoughts of a Private Person', note 9 above, and *Sydney Redidivus*, note 47 below.
[14] A notable example is George F. Sensabaugh, 'Milton and the Revolution Settlement', *Huntington Library Quarterly*, ix (1945–6), 178–9. As is often the case, Macaulay had it exactly right; *History of England* (Everyman ed.), ii, 184–5.

James, boldly said, 'The constitution of our government is actually grounded upon pact and covenant with the people', and John Maynard agreed: 'Tis no new project [he said]; our government is mixed, not monarchical and tyrannous, but has had its beginning from the people. There may be such a transgression in the Prince that the people will be no more governed by him.'[15] He cited a few legal precedents, and John Somers followed in the same vein, with painful and learned examples from Polish and Swedish history. But clearly this was not the sense of the House, and another Whig lawyer, George Treby, put forward instead the 'alibi' theory that James had in some way abdicated. He quoted with approval the remark of his Tory opposite number, Dolben, that the king had 'fallen from the crown', and declared that the question some members had posed, whether or not they could depose a King, was fortunately irrelevant: 'We have found the throne vacant', he assured them, 'and are to supply that defect; we found it so, we have not made it so.'[16] Sir William Williams, a former Exclusionist who had served King James with some distinction, testily agreed: 'Should you go into the beginning of government', he said, 'we should be much in the dark; every man in town and country can agree in fact on the state of things.'[17]

In the event, the devotees of contract were strong enough to insert it into the final resolution of the House, but they could not give it teeth. The resolution ran:

That King James the Second, having endeavoured to subvert the Constitution of the Kingdom, by breaking the Original Contract between King and People, and by the advice of Jesuits, and other wicked persons, having violated the fundamental laws, and having withdrawn himself out of this kingdom, has abdicated the Government, and that the throne is thereby become vacant.

But the key word was 'abdicated'. If James had abdicated, then his previous conduct, though historically suggestive, was not directly relevant, and the reference to the original contract was merely descriptive.[18] The resolution did not say that he had *forfeited* the Crown.

[15] A. Grey, *Debates of the House of Commons* (London, 1769), ix, 12, 20.
[16] Ibid., 12–15. Repeated in much the same terms 26 February, ibid., 116.
[17] Ibid., 15.
[18] And rather muddled. It would surely have been more accurate to say that James had broken the Contract by trying to subvert the Constitution. But this cloudiness may have been intentional.

Nevertheless, when the resolution came before the Lords 'it was desired that the learned counsel of the law might give an account of what the original contract is, and whether there be any such or not'. These legal assessors to the House were all Whigs or Whiggish, appointed to replace James's notorious judges. Their reply was affirmative, but not especially convincing; according to them it was implicit in Common Law, though not often mentioned, and they affected to find proof of it in the preamble to 25 Henry VIII c. 21 and James I's speech to Parliament on 21 March 1610, neither of which uses the term, though the latter does have some glimmerings of the idea.[19] The Lords concurred, for the matter was irrelevant; in the long discussions which followed between the two Houses it was clear that the word 'abdicated', or the Lords' preferred choice, 'deserted', both implied a voluntary act, if not a rational choice, on James's part. The Commons went along with this, as it was in their interest to do, and when the Tory peers, led by Clarendon, tried to attack contract, they insisted that the question was closed. Contract re-appeared only when the Lords argued that abdication implies a formal act of renunciation, and in reply Sir John Holt argued from the analogy of a trust in law:

The government and magistracy is under a trust, and any acting contrary to that trust is a renouncing of the trust, though it is not a renouncing by formal deed; for it is a plain dereliction, by act and deed though not in writing, that he who hath the trust, acting contrary, is a disclaimer of the trust.[20]

However, soon after that the Lords bowed to the Commons' wishes, and Holt's idea was not pursued. Indeed, contract was dropped altogether. The Declaration of Rights submitted to William and Mary on 14 February 1689, and enacted in statutory form as the Bill of Rights later in the year, contained no mention at all of the Original Contract; it merely listed the more spectacular of James's crimes, and concluded that they were all 'utterly and directly contrary to the known laws and statutes and freedoms of this realm'. But this was not the reason for his removal; indeed, he had not been removed at all, for the next paragraph goes on to say that he had abdicated the government.[21] Nor was William's acceptance of the crown conditional on this document; having heard it read out, he replied:

[19] *House of Lords Papers 1688–90*, p. 15.
[20] J. Torbuck, *A Collection of the Parliamentary Debates* (London, 1741), ii, 196.
[21] W. C. Costin and J. Steven Watson, *The Law and Working of the Constitution* (London, 1952), i, 68–9.

This is certainly the greatest proof of the trust you have in us that can be given, which is the thing that makes us value it the more; and we thankfully accept what you have offered. [That is, the Crown] ... And as I had no intention in coming hither, than to preserve your religion, laws and liberties, so you may be sure that I shall endeavour to support them, and shall be willing to concur in anything that shall be for the good of the kingdom, and to do all that is in my power to advance the welfare and glory of the nation.[22]

Yet the haste and confusion of the occasion, the ambiguity of hastily drafted documents, made it possible for most Whigs (many of them no doubt sincerely) to believe that James II had been deposed because he had broken the Original Contract, and that the Crown had been granted to William conditionally. On this, with the abstract assistance of Locke and Algernon Sydney, they had no difficulty in building an edifice of principles lovingly known as 'Revolution Principles', which enshrined the people's right to depose unjust sovereigns and alter the magistracy at will. At first there was some resentment at the Whigs' effrontery in appropriating as their own an event as bipartisan as any in English history. In 1695 Lord Halifax mordantly criticized those he called 'Pretenders to exorbitant merit in the late Revolution': 'The men who only carried mortar to the building [he wrote], when it is finished think they are ill dealt with if they are not made master workmen. They presently cry out, "The Original Contract is broken", if their merit is not rewarded at their own rate.'[23] But with the conservative reaction which gathered force during the 1690s and broke out in full flood under Queen Anne, competition to be associated with the Revolution lessened, and the Whigs' insistence on it laid them open to a derision. A cynical pamphleteer of 1712 remarked:

If your mouth be ever, on all occasions, in all places and company, full of encomiums of this Revolution, if your tongue be well turn'd to speak but those two words REVOLUTION PRINCIPLES, with a grace. If you derive the very bread you eat, and the bed you lie upon, from thence, and do really profess yourself to believe that if that had not happened you would have been starved of course, or lain in a barn, or upon a hurdle, then you are truly sound and perfect. ... But if at the mention of Revolution, though it be one to come, you frown, shake your head, shrug your shoulders, or look down, nay, if you allow one to have been attended with very good conse-

---

[22] *Lords Journals*, xiv, 127–8. This point was first brought to my attention by Lucille Pinkham, *William III and the Respectable Revolution* (Harvard, 1954), p. 234.

[23] *Complete Works*, ed. J. P. Kenyon (London, 1969), p. 184.

quences, and to have been justifiable because it was necessary, yet if you spoil all with an IF or a BUT, there is no further need of witness, you are condemned from your own mouth.[24]

By 1712 'Revolution Principles' had undoubtedly been blurred and magnified. The issues had been clearly stated in 1698 and 1699. In the former year a memorial was published which was supposed to have been drawn up for submission to the plenipotentiaries at the peace congress of Ryswick, but never presented. It may even have been genuine. This memorial flatly stated:

The late King [James] chose to desert his government. . . . By his so doing he set his subjects free from any farther tie to himself, and made it necessary for them to seek their own safety, which they did by continuing the ancient government, with no other interruption than what their present circumstances made unavoidable. . . . Nothing was done in the progress of the whole revolution, but that which he made inevitable by some act or other of his own.[25]

A Tory pamphlet of 1699 sharply drove this lesson home, reminding the Whigs that:

[So] that the honourable Convention might not seem to make dangerous precedents to posterity, give the people a scandalous authority, or render the monarchy of England precarious, and not worth acceptance, they cautiously and honestly avoided such pretences [of deposition], and settled the nation upon the express renunciation of James the Second, his voluntary withdrawing himself out of the kingdom, and the necessity of providing for the nation when the throne was vacant; and therefore would never depart from the words 'Abdication' and 'Vacancy of the Throne'. So that what the Convention did upon that extraordinary occasion was, when the late king went hence, but shutting the door after him.[26]

Of course, to the party of Locke, Sydney, Russell and Shaftesbury, shutting the door after King James was an inglorious anti-climax, nor was it easy to found upon it a scheme of political theory appropriate to an on-going, forward-looking party. To accept any such position would be to line up with the Tories, without the support of the Church

[24] *An Old Story that Everyone Knows: or the Religion of the Whigs enquired into* (1712), pp. 9–10.
[25] 'A Memorial drawn up by King William's special direction, intended to be given in at the Treaty of Ryswick', *Somers Tracts*, xi, 110.
[26] 'Cursory Remarks upon some late Disloyal Proceedings', ibid., xi, 172–3.

which the Tories enjoyed, and to try and do the Tories' business with the aid of the dissenters, who as the period progressed became an ever-greater liability. (It took from 1694 to 1709 to put through a simple measure for the naturalization of foreign Protestants, and even then its repeal two years later was blocked only by the Lords.) The need for a more positive interpretation of the events of 1688–9 became the more pressing with the death of Anne's son, the Duke of Gloucester, in 1700. In 1701 the Act of Settlement vested the reversion to the crown in the Hanoverians, but they were far from popular, and Queen Anne herself had doubts as to the morality of excluding the Pretender, doubts shared by the majority of the Tories if their ardently expressed views on non-resistance, divine right and hereditary succession were pressed to their logical conclusion. The fact that such views were not so pressed, that doubts were not aired when it mattered, in 1714, did not make the situation any less menacing from the standpoint of 1702 or 1710. The death of Anne might easily bring a crisis of the magnitude of 1688, and to meet it the Revolution must be rescued from the status of an historical event, a morality tale, and made into a tool which could be applied to future events.

The trouble was, how? The attitude of the governing classes was deeply confused but deeply conservative. Roughly since 1660 the tendency of European development had been towards autocracy, consolidated by the King in alliance with the nobility.[27] The England of Charles II had been no exception to this rule, and the rise of a new office-holding nobility, active and trusted in government, was offset by a marked decline in the middle-class parliamentary gentry. It is no accident that the strict settlement, enabling the great landowners to transfer their estates intact from one generation to the next, was fashioned under Charles II.[28] In the gradual development of this process 1688 was an aberration, produced solely by religious differences between James II and the nobility. (The loss of office and freehold was a side-issue; very few noblemen, as distinct from gentlemen, lost office, and they were usually replaced by Catholics or compliant Protestants of the same rank. Nothing is more significant than the way in which men like Godolphin, Feversham and Clarendon stuck by James to the

---

[27] See Henry Kamen, *The Iron Century* (London, 1971), ch. 12, and F. L. Carsten, *New Cambridge Modern History*, v, 12.

[28] H. J. Habakkuk, 'Marriage Settlements in the Eighteenth Century', *Transactions of the Royal Historical Society*, 4th ser., xxxii (1950), 15.

bitter end.) But once the break had occurred, the nobility was adrift; they were makers of autocracy without an autocrat. William III would not do, and not only because of his dubious title, but because he was a professional soldier and a foreigner without children to succeed.

The attitude of the conservatives is well known. Nottingham remarked in February 1689: 'I must confess any government is better than none, but I earnestly desire we may enjoy our ancient constitution'.[29] At least twenty peers refused the new oath imposed by the Act of Association in 1696, 'that his present Majesty King William is rightful and lawful king of these realms', and in 1701 Nottingham again led a famous protest against the Act requiring him to abjure the Pretender.[30] Nor was he alone in his attitude. At the height of the Revolution the Earl of Danby was plagued by doubts: 'Were there any visible hopes under heaven [he wrote] of saving the Protestant religion in England but by this opportunity that God has given us, I think you know me well enough to believe that I am the last man in the kingdom that would attempt to have it rescued by force.' And in February 1689 he grudgingly admitted that William and Mary had been crowned King and Queen, 'yet no man could affirm they were rightfully so by the constitution'.[31] Halifax 'confessed that there was no great hopes of a lasting peace from this settlement'.[32]

Naturally, the Church was subject to graver doubts, and especially on the moral propriety of accepting the Settlement. Though the great majority of the clergy took the oaths in 1689, the Church was almost immediately rent by a furious controversy as to whether they ought to have done so or not, a controversy focused in the years 1690–2 on William Sherlock, the new Dean of St Paul's, who preached the Hobbesian doctrine that obedience was owing to any government which could offer security and protection to the individual.[33] Clearly the Revolution had fractured the theory of Divine Right, and the stance of non-jurors like Sancroft, who had opposed James II yet declined to

[29] Torbuck, *Debates*, ii, 255.

[30] *House of Lords Papers 1695–7*, p. 208; J. T. Rogers, *Complete Protests of the House of Lords* (Oxford, 1875), i, 68–9.

[31] Browning, *Danby*, i, 432; ibid., ii, 142 (letter to Sir John Hanmer, 30 November 1688). See also his remarks to Reresby, *Memoirs of Sir John Reresby*, ed. A. Browning (Glasgow, 1936), p. 521.

[32] Reresby, *Memoirs*, p. 553.

[33] Charles F. Mullett, 'A Case of Allegiance: William Sherlock and the Revolution of 1688', *Huntington Library Quarterly*, x (1946–7), 83ff.

acknowledge his abdication, was felt by many to be logically and morally correct. After toying weakly for a few years with the theory of the 'Divine Right of Providence' – that the Revolution was a divinely ordained miracle, therefore it would be impious to question its results[34] – the leaders of the Church settled for the re-imposition of the strict theory of passive obedience, though this now applied to the new government, and could apply to Parliament as well as the King (in this, as in nothing else, they agreed with Locke and Sydney). The new doctrine was put to the House of Lords by Archbishop Sharp in a sermon preached on 30 January 1700. He told them: 'Let the form of government in any country be what it will, in whomsoever the Sovereign Authority is lodged, whether in one or in many, they are the principalities and powers to whom we are subject.' The implication was that those who could not stomach King William could transfer their allegiance to a sovereign Parliament, but those who still had doubts after that must obey: 'Even where we doubt of the lawfulness of their commands we are bound to obey; so long as we only *doubt* of their lawfulness, but are not *persuaded* that they are unlawful.' But, with this qualification, Sharp had no doubt that passive obedience was unreserved, and his peroration was reminiscent of Sibthorpe or Manwaring at their most extreme:

That there is such a submission due [he said], from all subjects to the Supreme Authority of the place wherein they live, as shall tie up their hands from opposing or resisting it by force, is evident from the very nature and ends of political society. And I dare say there is not that country on earth, let the form of their government be what it will (Absolute Monarchy, Legal Monarchy, Aristocracy or Commonwealth) where this is not a part of the constitution. Subjects must obey passively where they cannot obey actively, otherwise the government would be precarious, and the public peace at the mercy of every malcontent, and a door would be set open to all the insurrections, rebellions and treasons in the world.[35]

It is easy to see that High Church doctrine on this point, re-affirmed by Simon Harcourt at Sacheverell's trial, strengthened the doctrine of

---

[34] See Gerald M. Straka, *Anglican Reaction to the Revolution of 1688* (Madison, Wisconsin, 1962), ch. 6, and 'The Final Phase of Divine Right Theory in England 1688–1702', *English Historical Review*, lxxvii (1962), 638ff. I am not sure that Straka is not trying to elevate into a formed political theory what was in fact the small change of intercessory vocabulary, freely used by laymen as well as the clergy.

[35] Sharp, *Sermons preached on several occasions* (London, 1729), ii, 51–2, 56, 59–60.

parliamentary supremacy. Some went further. Preaching on 8 March 1705 (the anniversary of the Queen's accession), Offspring Blackall admitted that though supreme political power was originally in God's gift, its precise distribution was a matter of human concern only; therefore once a ruler condescended to share his power with his subjects this grant could not be withdrawn except by general consent. He applied this text to the Revolution, and warned his audience of the dangers of such proceedings, 'it being very rarely that any considerable change can be made in the forms of a government that has been long established without more danger of hurt than hope of good'. His text was Proverbs 24:21, 'Fear thou the Lord and the King: and meddle not with them that are given to change'.

In the mouths of men like Sacheverell High Church doctrine was pressed even further, the doctrine of passive obedience raised to such a pitch that it was clearly impossible to accommodate the Revolution to it. But there were deeper issues. It was suspected, and rightly, that the Whigs and King William wanted to secularize politics completely, and deny the relevance, ultimately, of Christian doctrine to constitutional law. The High Church reaction was a passionate affirmation that Church and State were one, that religion was politics and politics religion, and that every Christian priest had the right and the duty to discharge his conscience on the matter. In his sermon of 1700 just cited, Sharp defended the right of the clergy to air their views, as trained experts in theology, and therefore in politics:

We meddle not with Politics; we meddle not with the Prerogative or Property; we meddle not with the disputes and controversies of law that may arise about these matters. But we preach a company of plain lessons of Peaceableness and Fidelity, and Submission to our Rulers, such as the Law of Nature teaches, such as both Christ and his Apostles did preach in all places wherever they came.[36]

There is every sign that this clerical assault on the Revolution caught the Whig leaders unprepared. Indeed, their political views are hard to come by; few accounts of parliamentary debates for this period survive, and when they do they reveal men like Wharton and Montague at odds with one another on important points of principle;[37] and though

[36] Ibid., 49.
[37] For instance, Montague opposed the triennial bill of 1693, while Wharton called for annual elections; see Grey, *Debates*, x, 329–31, 370.

the Junto must have sponsored some political pamphleteers we do not know which. We can only suspect that Daniel Defoe, who from 1697 to 1701 produced a stream of pamphlets and poems re-affirming the strong Whig view that James II had been deposed by the will of the people for breaking the Original Contract, was in their employ.[38] It was seriously questioned by contemporaries whether men of the stature of the Junto peers were much troubled with political principles or theories at all, and there is some truth in the remark thrown off by one anonymous pamphleteer in 1710:

These distinctions of Whig and Tory do properly belong to the second class, or inferior rank of men; for persons of the first rank, who either by their birth or abilities are entitled to govern others, do not really list themselves in those parties, but only put themselves at the head of either of them.[39]

Be this as it may, by 1700 the Whig leaders needed a viable political doctrine they could at least appear to espouse. Here they were much less well-equipped than they appeared. As we have seen, the architects of the Revolution had taken good care to dissociate it from contract theory, but even if this association were made it was of doubtful value. The English approach to political thought was strictly legalistic and historical; roughly speaking, oldest was best, and the antecedents of any doctrine were almost as important as its intellectual validity. Clarendon remarked in 1689: 'This breaking the original contract is a language that hath not been long used in this place, nor known in any of our law books or public records. It is sprung up, but as taken from some late authors, and those none of the best received.'[40] Indeed, it was well known that the parents of contract theory were the Jesuits, and in his *Discourses concerning Government* Sydney found himself treading a very narrow plank between Filmer on the one hand and Suarez and Bellarmine on the other. Worse still, it was indissolubly linked with the name of Hobbes, the great bogeyman of the seventeenth century,

---

[38] A. E. Levett, 'Daniel Defoe', in *The Social and Political Ideas of Some English Thinkers of the Augustan Age*, ed. F. J. C. Hearnshaw (London 1928), p. 157ff. An exception to be noted are the many pamphlets putting the Government's case on the standing army, Irish land grants and secret diplomacy, published between 1698 and 1701, particularly *Jura Populi Anglicani*, often attributed to Somers. But these were mainly concerned with very specific questions of law and fact.

[39] 'A Letter from a Foreign Minister in England to Monsieur Pettecum', *Somers Tracts*, xiii, 67.

[40] Torbuck, *Debates*, ii, 204 (5 February 1689).

whose name was associated with the total despiritualization of political behaviour and the reduction of political motivation to the merely animal. Finally, and most serious, contract theory, as interpreted by Hobbes, was the prime justification for the Great Rebellion and the execution of Charles I, which were still live political issues, perhaps more alive than any. The straits to which advanced thinkers could be reduced is shown by the title of the tract William Sherlock issued in 1692 in reply to his adversaries: *Their Majesties Government proved to be thoroughly Settled, and that we may Submit to it without asserting the Principles of Mr Hobbes: Shewing also that Allegiance was not due to the Usurpers after the late Civil War*. Similarly in 1702, eight years after he had laid down his pen, James Tyrrell was moved to publish the fourteenth dialogue of his *Bibliotheca Politica*, 'shewing', ran the sub-title, 'that the arraigning and murder of King Charles I can by no means be justified by the proceedings of the Convention Parliament against King James II, upon his abdication, the grounds and manner thereof being wholly different'.

In these circumstances, though they were reprinted in 1694 and 1698, it is easy to see why Locke's *Two Treatises* failed of their intended effect. The high posthumous reputation of this book was not reflected in contemporary popularity; as John Dunn remarks, 'The book at no time secured the sort of unquestioned acceptance and esteem which it is customary to assert for it today'.[41] His friend James Tyrrell made use of his ideas in the *Bibliotheca Politica*, a series of ponderous dialogues between 'Mr Meanwell, a Civilian' and 'Mr Freeman, a Gentleman', published between 1692 and 1694. The influence of this work is problematical; certainly it is time Tyrrell was properly investigated and assessed;[42] it was republished in a collected edition in 1694, but great as the appetite then was for constitutional argument, a distinctly unlively book of nearly a thousand closely-printed pages must have been somewhat daunting, and it was not reprinted until 1718. Moreover, his debt to Locke can be exaggerated; he made only five references to the *Two Treatises* and three of these deal with patriarchalism.[43] Yet apart from Tyrrell, the only subsequent authors to cite him were William

---

[41] *The Political Thought of John Locke* (Cambridge, 1969), p. 8. See also his remarks in *John Locke: Perspectives and Problems*, ed. John Yolton (Cambridge, 1969), pp. 56–7.

[42] I have been able to find only one brief assessment, by Caroline Robbins, in *The Eighteenth Century Commonwealthman* (Harvard, 1959), pp. 73–6.

[43] *Bibliotheca Politica* (1694), pp. 72–4, 81–3, 88–9, 100, 155–6.

Molyneux, in a distinctly unlucky attempt to prove the independence of the Dublin Parliament, in 1698, and the Jacobite polemicist Charles Leslie, who launched a full-scale attack on him in his periodical *The Rehearsal* in 1705.[44]

Of course, Locke's ideas probably had a diffused influence; they can be traced in such unlikely sources as Defoe's doggerel *The True-born Englishman*,[45] and it can be argued that Leslie's attack was an indirect proof of his influence. Perhaps so, but Leslie may equally well have chosen to attack him because he was at once the most famous supporter of the Whigs and a source of weakness to them; he was a notorious advocate of toleration, plausibly accused of deism, and though his work was purged of virtually all political and historical references, it was profoundly radical. For instance, what Locke had to say on the actual circumstances of the Revolution, by abdication, was particularly radical. According to him, unless the Monarch in abdicating makes provision for his successor, 'the Government visibly ceases, and the People become a confused Multitude, without Order or Connexion'; yet in such circumstances 'the People are at liberty to provide for themselves, by erecting a new Legislative, differing from the other, by the change of Persons, or Form'.[46] This was precisely the possibility which most alarmed a majority of responsible people, especially in the House of Lords, in 1689, and which the myth of James's 'abdication' had been designed to prevent. Yet it was with this kind of republicanism that Whiggism was too often associated, and to its cost. It is easy to forget that in 1689 Monmouth's extraordinary Taunton Declaration, with its principles (borrowed from the Levellers) of annual parliaments, election of magistrates by freeholders, complete religious toleration and much else, was only four years away.

The perfect embodiment of the Whigs' embarrassing past was Algernon Sydney. The House of Lords had reversed his attainder in 1689, on the legal grounds that the jury which tried him had not been composed of freeholders and there had been only one proper witness against him, but this did not imply any endorsement of his principles, which were well enough known; his views were summarized in a

---

[44] *The Rehearsal*, nos. 55–66 (August–September 1705); summarized in book form in *The New Association: Part II* (1705). For Molyneux see Charles Bastide, *John Locke* (Paris, 1907), pp. 286–7.

[45] *Poems on Affairs of State* (Yale ed.), vi, 292. See also *A Free Discourse, wherein the Doctrines which make for Tyranny are Display'd...* (1697), pp. 32–3.

[46] *Locke's Two Treatises*, ed. Peter Laslett (Cambridge, 1960), p. 429 (II: 219–20).

pamphlet issued for the edification of the Convention in 1689, and in 1693 the paper he had handed to the sheriffs on the scaffold was reprinted in *State Tracts*. This contained a bald summary of his theories:

That God had left nations unto the liberty of setting up such governments as best pleased themselves.
That magistrates were set up for the good of nations, not nations for the honour and glory of magistrates.
That the right and power of magistrates in every country was that which the laws of that country made it to be.
That those laws were to be observed, and the oaths taken by them having the force of a contract between magistrate and people, could not be violated without danger of dissolving the whole fabric.[47]

These propositions were discussed at great length, and extended, in his *Discourses concerning Government*, first published in 1698 and reprinted in 1704.

In Sydney, as in Locke, there was considerable doubt as to who 'the People' were in whom the power to erect and throw down governments was vested. The tenor of Locke's argument supposed a representative assembly, once the Commonwealth was too populous to admit of a mass meeting, and Sydney, more specific in his approach, spoke often and approvingly of the function of parliament.[48] However, though in one instance Sydney remarked that by 'the People' he meant 'Freemen', he did not enlarge on this, and the precise meaning he attached to the term remained in doubt. Did he mean 'freemen' in the English sense of 'freeholders', or did he mean 'free men' as against slaves? His preoccupation with ancient history makes the latter interpretation at least plausible.[49] But in any case he spoilt himself almost at once by bringing in the idea of the people as 'the multitude', and denying that it could ever be sedition for this multitude to set up a new Commonwealth. 'Till the commonwealth be established', he wrote, 'no multitude can be seditious, because they are not subject to any human law', and the context makes it clear that he was thinking not merely of the original foundation of the state but of revolutions in established states. Elsewhere he baldly announced: 'The general revolt of a

---

[47] *State Tracts* (1693), p. 268. Cf. *Sydney Redidivus: or the opinion of the late Honourable Colonel Sydney as to Civil Government . . . by which the late proceedings of the nation against James II are justified* (1689).
[48] *Discourses*, 3rd ed. (1751), p. 457ff. (III: 46).
[49] Ibid., p. 75 (I: 5).

nation cannot be called a rebellion.'[50] Moreover, from a close study
of Roman history, Sydney derived the conclusion that such periodic
revolutions were positively advantageous, and a sign of political
health. 'All human constitutions', according to him, 'are subject to
corruptions, and must perish, unless they are timely renewed, and
reduced to their first principles', and the heading of the section in which
this statement appears is: 'There is no disorder or prejudice in changing
the name or number of magistrates whilst the root and principle of
their power continues entire.'[51] Elsewhere he remarked that 'Good
governments admit of changes in the superstructure, whilst the foundations remain unchangeable.'[52]

Sydney's *Discourses*, like Locke's *Treatises*, was a book of great power
and intellectual distinction. Its influence on subsequent generations was
profound, nor was it negligible in the period up to 1714.[53] But his ideas
were still running against the general tide of accepted political thought;
that tide was perhaps just on the turn, but it is doubtful if it had begun
to ebb. It was difficult for most men to accept that man was born to
govern, not to be governed, that all men were equal in a political sense,
and that government was a convenient superstructure not basic to
society and not necessarily ordained and constantly monitored by
Almighty God. Under Queen Anne, as under Charles II, there is no
doubt that the most influential political theorist was still Sir Robert
Filmer, who was, as Laslett remarks, 'that extremely rare phenomenon,
the codifier of conscious and unconscious prejudice'.[54] His influence
can be measured by the fact that Sydney's *Discourses* and Locke's
Treatises were not so much independent and positive contributions to
political thought as elaborate refutations of Filmer's *Patriarcha*; indeed,
but for Filmer it is to be doubted if either book would have been
written. And Filmer's ideas were kept alive by Tory journalists like
Charles Leslie, who in 1705 published *A Full Answer to Mr Locke . . .
and all others who assert the power of the People: with a short account of the
Original of Political Government in the first division of Nations after the
Flood.*[55] As late as 1709, when Hoadly published his considered defence

[50] Ibid., pp. 81, 413 (I: 5, III: 36).   [51] II: 13 (ibid., p. 117).
[52] Ibid., p. 134 (II: 17).   [53] Caroline Robbins, op. cit., p. 41 ff.
[54] Filmer, *Patriarcha*, ed. Peter Laslett (Oxford, 1949), p. 41. Cf. Gordon J. Schochet,
'Patriarchalism, Politics and Mass Attitudes in Stuart England', *Historical Journal*, xii
(1969), 413ff.
[55] Already cited under the title *The New Association*, note 44 above.

of the social contract in *The Original and Institution of Civil Government Discussed*, he felt it necessary to devote fully half the treatise to a painstaking refutation of patriarchalism step by step, from Adam down to the British Heptarchy.[56]

Meanwhile, the dismissal of Anne's Tory Ministers in 1703 and 1704, though it postponed the Tory millennium, also raised the temperature of the party conflict, and again the fury of the High Churchmen seems to have caught the Whigs by surprise. They found that their appropriation of the credit for the Revolution was now an embarrassment; their view of the events of 1688 and 1689 was generally contested, and for advocating it they found themselves branded as republicans and Levellers. At the same time the publication in 1699 of Toland's *Life of Milton*, and in 1702, 1703 and 1704 of Clarendon's *History of the Rebellion*, intensified the continuing dispute over the rights and wrongs of the Civil Wars.[57] Clarendon's son Rochester used the prefaces to his father's great work as an unashamed vehicle for party propaganda, and in the third preface, in 1704, he argued that the Revolution had been a serious blow to political stability – 'Such deliverances have their pangs in the birth, that much weaken the constitution in endeavouring to preserve and amend it' – and that the Whigs were the sworn allies of republicans and dissenters.

But [he went on] let any impartial person judge to whom all the libertines of the republican party are like to unite themselves; and whether it is imaginable that the established government, either in Church or State, can be strengthened by them. They must go to the enemies of both, and pretend there is no such thing as a republican party in England, that they may be the less observed, and go on the more secure in their destructive projects.[58]

Later that year, in November 1704, the Whig journalist John Tutchin was found guilty of treason for publishing in *The Observator* what was only a slightly exaggerated restatement of Algernon Sydney's central doctrine:

---

[56] *Works* (1773), ii, 182ff.
[57] Symptomatic was the controversy throughout the 1690s on the authorship of the *Eikon Basiliké*, for which see Francis Madan, *A New Bibliography of the Eikon Basiliké* Oxford, 1950), *passim*, and *Eikon Basiliké*, ed. Philip A. Knachel (Cornell, 1966), Intro. See also Helen W. Randall, 'The Rise and Fall of a Martyrology', *Huntington Library Quarterly*, x (1946–7), 153.
[58] Clarendon, *History*, ed. W. D. Macray (Oxford, 1888), vol. I, pp. xlvii, liii.

This is a prerogative of singular advantage to the people of England, in that their representatives are the judges of the maladministration of their governors; that they can call them in question for the same, and can appoint such to wear the Crown who are fittest for the government, which they have often done, and indeed which is the privilege of all free people, who are authorized by the laws of God and Nature to choose their own governors.[59]

In the prolonged and bitter disputes of the next six years, culminating in Sacheverell's trial, the lead was taken by the clergy; principally by Francis Atterbury and Offspring Blackall (rather unwillingly) for the Tories, and Benjamin Hoadly for the Whigs. Hoadly's singular eminence was acknowledged in December 1709, when, immediately after moving Sacheverell's impeachment, the Commons decided to recommend Hoadly to the Queen for preferment, 'for having often strenuously justified the principles on which his [late] majesty and the nation proceeded in the late happy Revolution'.[60] It is worth remarking that Hoadly was not seconded by the lay Whigs, except gutter journalists like Tutchin and Defoe, and anonymous pamphleteers of no great ability; and that he himself throughout his extensive polemical writings eschewed all mention of Locke and Sydney, preferring to base his case on Hooker and St Paul, whose chequered career under the government of Imperial Rome he put to remarkably good use, though it may be that his central proposition that government was created to ensure the comfort and happiness of the people was an echo of Sydney. It is unhappily clear that in 1709 and 1710 the Whigs were not anxious to be associated in the public mind with what we now regard as the fathers of Whig political thought; the managers of Sacheverell's trial did not mention them, either; nor did the anonymous author of *Vox Populi Vox Dei*, published in the summer of 1709.

Vox Populi Vox Dei: or True Maxims of Government is remarkable as the only serious and practical piece of Whig political philosophy (considering Locke, Tyrrell and Sydney as academics) written in this period by a layman.[61] It was a remarkably competent and concise piece of work, now undeservedly forgotten.

[59] *State Trials*, xiv, 1126. Cf. Sydney, *Discourses*, I: 19. Tutchin's conviction was quashed, but only on a technicality.

[60] *Commons Journals*, xvi, 242 (14 December 1709). See Norman Sykes, 'Benjamin Hoadly', in Hearnshaw, op. cit. [note 38 above], p. 112ff.

[61] From internal evidence we may assume the author was not a clergyman, but beyond that it is difficult to go. It has been attributed to Defoe or Somers. Defoe can be dis-

It opened with the admission that God was the originator of all political power, but it asserted that he had set limits to the ruler's use of power in what was rather mysteriously called 'the Charter of Nature and Revelation'.[62] Thus God himself was the guarantor of the social contract; yet, it went on, 'The principles of natural religion give those who are in authority no power at all, but only secure them in the possession of that which is theirs by the law of the country.'[63] For the history of parliament showed that this was the designated body through which the rights of the people were to be enforced, and this avoided any implication of outright democracy. It explains:

The Prince has his Authority from the People, or the Law which chooses or appoints him to be supreme, of which he is only executor while separated from the Legislative Authority. The Law is the rule and power of the Government (and the measure of the People's submission and obedience), beyond which he has no power, except he acts by fraud or force.

Moreover:

The Supreme Authority of a Nation belongs to those who have the legislative authority reserved to them, but not to those who have only the executive, which is plainly a trust when it is separated from the legislative power; and all trusts by their nature import that those to whom they are given are accountable, though no such condition is specified.[64]

To buttress his position the author also invoked the Law of Nature, though he was wise enough not to attempt a definition: 'No power can exempt princes from the obligation to the eternal laws of God and Nature. In all disputes between Power and Liberty, Power must always be proved, but Liberty proves itself, the one being founded upon positive law, the other upon the Law of Nature.'[65]

He next linked these generalities with the Revolution of 1688 by affirming, with the support of examples drawn from the history of France, Spain, Portugal, Denmark and England itself, as well as Old

---

missed; it is not in his style at all, and it is to be doubted if he had the necessary legal or historical knowledge. Somers had, but so had several other Whig lawyers, such as Lechmere or Jekyll; the trouble is, we do not have a sufficient body of well-authenticated work by Somers to make a stylistic comparison. There are echoes of Vox Populi in The History of Resistance, published in 1710 by John Withers (Somers Tracts, xii, 249ff.), but this is no doubt plagiarism.

[62] Vox Populi (1st ed., 1709), pp. 3-4.   [63] Ibid., p. 13.
[64] Ibid., pp. 11-12.   [65] Ibid., p. 13.

Testament Israel, that nations had an entire freedom to depose their rulers and appoint others, 'And when it is done upon just and urgent causes, and by public authority of the whole body, the justice thereof is plain; as when the Prince shall endeavour to establish idolatry, or any religion which is repugnant to Scripture, [or] contrary to the laws of the land.'[66]

Moreover, his readers were firmly reminded that the leaders of such revolutions in the past were not remembered as moral outcasts or lepers, or reviled as republicans. On the contrary:

The chief instruments of the great revolutions and changes that have happened in the world from slavery to liberty have always been accounted as heroes, sent by Almighty God from time to time for the redemption of Man from misery in this world. They were accordingly honoured and respected while they lived, and their memories have been and will be held in veneration by all posterity.[67]

The weakest part of the whole tract, predictably, was that which dealt specifically with the Revolution of 1688. The author made great play with the Nottingham Declaration of 22 November 1688,[68] but he had no supporting evidence of overt resistance, and to prove that the Revolution involved the application of contract theory he could only appeal, rather disingenuously, to the Commons Resolution of 28 January 1689.[69] But he finished strongly, with a firm denial that his theories implied continual revolutions; the enforcement of the original contract was not the concern of any individual, or even a group; it was a national act of will, executed by 'the body of the People' as represented in Parliament.

Vox Populi Vox Dei sold well – it went through eight editions in 1709 alone – but the Tories were not abashed. In *A Letter to a Noble Lord* (probably Evelyn Pierrepoint, Marquess of Dorchester) Charles Leslie expressed surprise at finding the aristocracy allied with the common people. 'Was your Lordship's noble family first raised to that honour by the People?' he enquired. 'Did the Mob first summon your ancestor[s] to Parliament? And is that the tenure by which you hold your baronage?'[70] Atterbury hysterically accused the author of being:

[66] Ibid., p. 20.
[67] Ibid., p. 26.
[68] P. 46 above.
[69] *Vox Populi*, p. 32.
[70] *A Letter to a Noble Lord about his dispersing around Mr Hoadly's Remarks* . . . (1709), p. 7.

A Leveller, and consequently an implacable enemy to anything above himself, which is the most dangerous of enthusiastical delusions, or rather, a desperate contrivance of the needy to bring all things into common, or under that colour to thrust themselves into the estates they have not title to.[71]

Hoadly was now preparing his laborious *Original and Institution of Government*, to be published in December, but this battle of books seemed unlikely to reach any definite decision. Sacheverell offered the Whig leaders the chance of putting their theories to the collective wisdom of the House of Lords. They made Sacheverell's remarks on the Revolution (by any assessment not the most inflammatory or dangerous part of his sermon) the subject of the first article of the impeachment, and drafted in the rising young Whig politicians, Stanhope and Walpole, to second the efforts of their lawyers on this point.

It is difficult to tell whether this action was offensive or defensive. Edmund Burke had no doubt that it was the action of self-confident men, who felt that they had their opponents on the run, and his interpretation has gained general acceptance.[72] Sacheverell's impeachment is usually regarded now as a wilful and gratuitous mistake, arising from an optimistic misinterpretation of public opinion. It seems just as likely that it was a gamble, intended to re-establish Whig political ideology when all else had failed.

However, whatever their initial motives, the Whig managers soon found themselves on the defensive when the trial opened in February 1710. From the first they had the greatest difficulty in proving that resistance had been used to James II, or that it mattered; indeed, whether any of the issues involved merited this kind of treatment was in question throughout. Moreover, their insistence on the point that if the Revolution was not acknowledged to be an example of the enforcement of the Original Contract then every Act of State since 1689 was invalid, was distinctly unwise. According to Lechmere, for instance:

The denying the Original Contract is not only to disavow the whole proceeding at the time of the Revolution, but to renounce the Constitution itself, to disclaim those many and undeniable proofs and testimonies of ı which almost every part of our history, our records and memorials of antiquity will furnish. To deny the original contract of government is to contradict and condemn the voice and tenor of all our laws, of every act of

---

[71] *The Voice of the People No Voice of God* (1709), p. 24.
[72] 'Appeal from the New to the Old Whigs', *Works* (World's Classics), v, 52.

the supreme legislative power, the force and efficacy of which exists upon the consent of Crown, Lords and Commons.[73]

Since it was the Whigs, not the Tories, who were applying contract theory to the Revolution, they thus laid themselves open to the accusation that they, not their opponents, were imperilling the Constitution. But in any case they could not prove that the Convention had proceeded according to contract theory; they all skirted the question except Sir Joseph Jekyll, who argued that the Commons had chosen the word 'abdicated' because it carried the implication of maladministration, boldly (but unspecifically) referring his audience to 'the Journal'. But even he dared not argue that James had been deposed.[74] The Duke of Leeds, whose share in the Revolution made him an authority, put the point succinctly when he said: 'They ought to distinguish between Resistance and Revolution; for Vacancy and Abdication was the thing they went upon, and therefore Resistance was to be forgot, for had it not succeeded it had certainly been Rebellion, since he knew of no other but hereditary right.'[75] His old companion-in-arms, Shrewsbury, supported this common-sense view, and so, more predictably, did Nottingham and the young Earl of Anglesey. 'As to the Revolution . . .', said Anglesey, 'the Vacancy of the Throne was properly the thing, and therefore the mentioning the necessary means was mere nonsense.'[76] Lord Haversham, a former Whig who had sat in the Convention, agreed. 'If any man denies [this]', he said, 'I appeal to the papers that were then writ, and are now in print on this subject.'[77]

Indeed, if Wharton had not prevented the Lords voting on each article of the impeachment separately, they would almost certainly have voted Sacheverell 'not guilty' on Article I.[78] As it was, when they voted on all the articles together, they found him guilty by a majority so small (69:52) as to constitute a defeat for the Government and the Whig leaders.

Nor was this simply a defeat which left the *status quo ante*. In at least one respect the Whigs had damaged their reputation by their unashamed Erastianism. Jekyll, for instance, had remarked that:

[73] *State Trials*, xv, 412–13. [74] Ibid., 101.
[75] *Parliamentary History*, vi, 847.
[76] Ibid., 846–7. For Nottingham, see H. Horwitz, *Revolution Politicks* (Cambridge, 1968), p. 219.
[77] *Parl. Hist.*, vi, 846.
[78] *Memoirs of the Life of . . . Thomas . . . Wharton* (London, 1715), pp. 70–2.

Of later times, patriarchal and other fantastical schemes have been framed, to rest the authority of the law upon; and so questions of divinity have been blended with questions of law, when it is plain that religion hath nothing to do to extend the authority of the prince, or the submission of the subject, but only to secure the legal authority of the one, and enforce the due submission of the other, from the consideration of higher rewards and heavier punishments.[79]

Lord Haversham probably spoke for many when he expressed distaste for this, and noted with alarm that the Whig managers had said nothing of 'the divine appointment or institution of government', which obliged men to submit to it 'for conscience' sake'. He went on:

And I the rather mention this, because of notions that some people have of late advanced of their own (and have found their advantage, too, in so doing) of a discretionary obedience only; that is [to say], in my opinion, whilst the government is for them they will be for it, and [otherwise] think themselves bound to obey no longer.[80]

Worse still, the trial confirmed in the public mind the association of the Whigs with popular rights, the legalization of indiscriminate rebellion, and democracy. And yet the Whig managers had taken every precaution to represent themselves as conservatives on this point, even to the extent of confirming the application of contract strictly to the Revolution of 1688, and forswearing its future use. Lechmere explained the anxious care with which they had chosen the term 'the necessary means' to describe resistance to James II, and stressed that it had been legalized only out of overwhelming necessity.[81] Jekyll eagerly denied any wish 'to state the limits and bounds of the subject's submission to the sovereign', or to 'put any case of a justifiable resistance, but that of the Revolution only'.[82] Walpole was 'very sensible of the difficulty and nicety that attends the speaking to this point', and feared that he might be 'misconstrued and misrepresented, as maintaining anti-monarchical principles'.[83] Sir John Holland would not have it thought that he was pleading for a licentious resistance, as if subjects were left to their good will and pleasure when they are to obey and when they are to resist'.[84]

But it was all quite useless. In the wake of the Sacheverell trial came

[79] *State Trials*, xv, 97.
[81] Ibid., 60.
[83] Ibid., 113.
[80] Ibid., 476.
[82] Ibid., 97.
[84] Ibid., 111.

a flood of pamphlets denouncing the Whigs for the very faults they had so strenuously denied. A mock political glossary explained the term 'revolution principles' thus:

Revolution comes from the Latin word *revolvere*, which signifies 'to turn about', so that by revolution principles are meant such principles as, under the specious pretence of justifying the last happy Revolution, prepare mankind for any, and allow of the same proceedings, without the same necessity.[85]

It is significant that when *Vox Populi Vox Dei* was reprinted in 1710, going through six further editions, it was under the heftier but less provocative title *The Judgment of Whole Kingdoms and Nations Concerning the Rights, Power and Prerogative of Kings, and the Rights, Privileges and Properties of the People*, but two years later their opponents were still elaborating on the same theme. Said one:

Our forefathers, it seems, for many generations were so dull, illiterate and undiscerning as to derive all government and authority from God alone, to imagine that the supreme power bore his immediate commission . . . and was accountable to none but him. . . . But these quick-sighted and ingenious gentlemen have made us happy in discovering another account of the original right of government, quite different from all this. They make government and authority to ascend from the people, tell us of an original contract made, no one knows where, or at what time, or by whom; but from them it comes, to them is the *dernier ressort*, and the last appeal to be made. Thus in their scheme the very splendour of the Crown is like a shining vapour drawn up from a dunghill, which may blaze for a time, whilst the exhalation continues to feed it, but if the jakes be covered, or refuse to send up a steam, the meteor drops to the ground from whence it was taken.[86]

And Charles Hornsby, a bitter enemy of the Whigs, advised them for their own good, as well as the nation's, to moderate their ideas:

I wish that the Whigs would strip themselves of their political opinions, and lay aside those dangerous principles of rebellion which they still seem so fond of, which tend not so much to support the late Revolution as to draw us from the basis of our government into an eternal whirl of fresh revolutions.[87]

The Whigs did not give up. In 1714 their pamphleteers were still arguing that James II had not abdicated, and insisting that if the Revo-

---

[85] 'An Explanation of Some Hard Terms now in Use', *Somers Tracts*, xii, 661.
[86] *An Old Story that Everyone Knows* (1712), pp. 25–6.
[87] *Caveat against the Whiggs*, pt. I (1710), p. 105.

lution had not involved resistance then it was nothing but 'a successful rebellion' or 'a fortunate usurpation'.[88] Yet in terms of immediate political utility their ideology had failed. They had failed to prove that their interpretation of the Revolution was the correct one (because it was not) and, despite the august assistance of Locke and Sydney, they had failed to gain acceptance for the view that royal authority depended on an implied contract. As late as 1717 they were still having to defend themselves against the charge that their opinions made them the true heirs of the murderers of Charles I.[89] The misfortunes of the Harley Ministry saved them, and in the event Jacobitism proved weaker than most people had supposed; but had a Tory parliament repealed the Act of Settlement between 1710 and 1714, they would have found it difficult to apply the supposed principles of 1688 to the new situation, and justify resistance to the Pretender.

Note: Unfortunately, *The Trial of Doctor Sacheverell*, by Geoffrey Holmes (London, 1973), was published too late for me to incorporate in this essay the important new evidence he has discovered and his con-clusions upon it. However, these do not affect my basic argument.

J.P.K.

---

[88] *Revolution Principles Fairly Represented and Defended* (1714), p. 33ff.; *Whiggism Vindi-cated: in a Letter to a Tory*, pp. 12–13. [The latter work is dated 1715, but internal evi-dence suggests that it was written before Queen Anne's death.]
[89] *A Rebuke to the High–Church Priests* (1717), preface [unpaginated].

IV

Jacobitism and the Rise of Walpole

G. V. BENNETT

In a magisterial biography J. H. Plumb has told the vivid story of the rise of Robert Walpole to the position of undisputed First Minister of George I. Within the space of three years, good fortune and a rare political acumen took a relatively junior member of the Sunderland-Stanhope administration to the point where he had obtained not only the confidence of the King but a clear mastery over the House of Commons. The extraordinary nature of this transformation needs little emphasis. After the great Whig split of 1717 Walpole and his brother-in-law, Viscount Townshend, had been glad to return to office at all. Their reconciliation with the ministers in June 1720 was more apparent than real and their portfolios represented no advance on their former status. Sunderland himself retained the warm regard of King George and a firm grasp on the strings of Treasury patronage. And yet, by the spring of 1723 Walpole had attained supreme power. Professor Plumb has illuminated much that was previously obscure. He has modified the traditional notion that it was Walpole's financial skill in dealing with the crisis of the South Sea Bubble which won the applause of King and Parliament, and he has shown that Sunderland's influence, especially in the royal closet, remained a significant political factor down to his sudden death in April 1722. Walpole's premiership can be said to date only from the critical moment when the senior minister was removed from his path, and much still remained to be done before his new position was consolidated. Professor Plumb has called attention to the skilful use which he made of the Jacobite issue in the House of Commons which met in the autumn of 1722. Much of the story, however, remains untold; and a careful study of the Stuart papers at

Windsor provides new evidence from the Jacobite side. It reveals not only the strange dealings of Sunderland himself with the English Jacobites but Walpole's exploitation of the most successful political scare in the eighteenth century.[1]

1

At the time of Walpole's return to office in 1720 English Jacobitism was almost wholly ineffectual. In 1717 the Pretender, James Edward Stuart, had been forced to retire beyond the Alps into Italy and it became impossible for him to retain any close supervision of his affairs. Letters to and from England took at least a month on the road and were always at risk from the diligent efforts of the French and British intelligence services. It was inevitable that James should become increasingly dependent on his agents in Paris and notably on the doubtful advice of General Arthur Dillon, an Irish professional soldier in the French army. Dillon was loyal and assiduous, but he was not a trained diplomat and he was quite incapable of making a realistic estimate of the situation in England. But the Chevalier's greatest difficulty lay in his inability to recruit men of sufficient ability and social status to direct his affairs in England. After the flight into exile of Bolingbroke and Ormonde there was virtually nobody. Repeated applications to the Earl of Arran, Ormonde's brother, produced only lame excuses and procrastination. For a while James had great hopes of Robert Harley, Earl of Oxford, who was always ready to dictate letters replete with elaborate assurances and complex advice. Certainly Oxford's friends were experienced Tory politicians such as Lords Poulett, Foley, Dartmouth, Mansel and Bingley, but they were not particularly active in Parliament and they were, in fact, to play no significant part in any Jacobite conspiracy.

It is clear that the English politician from whom James had most to hope was Francis Atterbury, Bishop of Rochester. Though mercurial and quick-tempered, he was possessed of passionate Tory principles

[1] I am grateful to Her Majesty Queen Elizabeth II for her gracious permission to consult and quote from the Stuart papers in the Royal Archives at Windsor. These will be referred to as R.A. Stuart. They have been used by G. H. Jones in his general survey *The Main Stream of Jacobitism* (Cambridge, Mass., 1954). P. S. Fritz has used some of the material in his Cambridge Ph.D. thesis, 'Jacobitism and the English Government, 1717–1731' (1967), but his work differs in substance and argument from the present essay.

and he was an effective and witty debater in the House of Lords. Gradually he had come to be recognized as the leader of a determined group of opposition peers, men who looked upon the hesitations of the Harleian circle with contempt and who were even willing to take upon themselves the considerable risk of writing directly to James. Lords Arran, Orrery, Strafford, North and Bathurst, with William Shippen and Sir William Wyndham in the Commons, could have been the real nucleus of a Jacobite movement in England, but their willingness to serve was diminished by their extreme distrust of those who managed James's affairs in Italy and Paris. Their fears rested upon bitter experience, for in the early months of 1717 Dillon and the Earl of Mar, the Chevalier's secretary-of-state, had brought them within an ace of disaster. The previous summer Dillon had entered into a secret negotiation with Swedish agents and, though the Swedes promised nothing definite, Mar and Dillon persuaded themselves that it would be possible to launch an invasion of the British Isles with substantial assistance from the army of Charles XII. It was on the strength of their assurances that Atterbury accepted a commission as James's official 'resident' in England, and he and his friends raised no less than £10,000 in gold and dispatched it abroad. All their hopes, however, were suddenly dashed to the ground when it was publicly announced that the British Government had intercepted and deciphered the entire correspondence of Baron Görtz, the Swedish ambassador-at-large, and Count Gyllenborg, the envoy in London. It was only by the narrowest chance that Atterbury and his associates escaped detection.

The deep suspicion caused by the discovery of the 'Swedish Plot' virtually ruined the possibility of an effective Jacobite organization in England for the next three years. Indeed, when in 1718 James was presented with his greatest opportunity since 1715 there was no one at home prepared to lift a hand to help him. Cardinal Alberoni's offer of a Spanish fleet, a trained force of 5,000 men and weapons sufficient for an irregular army of 30,000 English supporters, was the very stuff of Jacobite dreams. Yet the fact was that the British Government knew far more of the coming invasion than did the Chevalier's English friends.[2] When in March 1719 George I announced to the House of Lords that an armada was actually on its way, none could have known better than the Jacobite group of peers that no preparations at all had

---

[2] See B.M. Stowe MSS. 231, fo. 225, Stair to Robethon, 29 Oct./9 Nov. 1718.

been made to meet and support the invasion force. By the summer of 1719 English Jacobitism was utterly dejected. James's friends had ceased to meet and their overriding concern was that nothing should be attempted which might bring down upon them the full weight of their political enemies' spite.[3]

The revival of Jacobite activity which took place in the early months of 1721 was due then not to a spontaneous recovery of spirits but to a remarkable political initiative taken by the Earl of Sunderland. It was a moment of great difficulty for him. All during the autumn and winter of 1720 the financial world had been in wild motion following a spectacular crash in the value of the shares of the South Sea Company. Sunderland and some of his closest associates had been involved in highly dubious transactions connected with the floating of the 'bubble', and by the new year they were in deadly danger of impeachment. Robert Walpole's hastily devised schemes to raise the price of stock had been coolly received, and it was apparent that the two Houses, urged on by the anger of the thousands who had suffered terrible losses, were intent on a searching inquiry. Soon John Aislabie, Chancellor of the Exchequer, and Charles Stanhope, Secretary of the Treasury, were on the rack before parliamentary committees. As one perceptive Tory put it, 'Will the chief minister stand firm when underlings are torn off?'[4] Sunderland was well aware that this was his moment of peril; he knew that in Walpole and Townshend he had colleagues who would seize any opportunity to strip him of power and influence. His position in the Commons had been undoubtedly shaken and soon he was forced to retire from the Treasury to a Court sinecure. But he still possessed one considerable advantage: the personal confidence of the King. Relying on the royal trust, he therefore determined upon a subtle and ingenious political manoeuvre. He would diminish his dependence on his colleagues and blunt the edge of the parliamentary attack by opening negotiations with the Jacobite leaders. That he should do so occasioned no great surprise among informed political commentators. For some time they had been speculating that he might form a new mixed administration as a way of countering the influence of Walpole and the Prince of Wales. Indeed, in the spring of 1720 the Prince himself had expected as much and had felt himself compelled to submit to his father

[3] R.A. Stuart 46/93, Orrery to James, 1 May 1720; ibid. 46/147, Sir William Wyndham to James, 14 May 1720.
[4] H.M.C. *Portland MSS.*, vii, 287, Canon Stratford to Lord Harley, 24 June 1721.

because of just such a persistent report 'that the ministers were sure of
the Tories [and] that Atterbury said he would come up to anything
personal against the Prince'.[5]

Certainly the Jacobites themselves were not averse to an intrigue
with Sunderland, for they were genuinely uncertain what to do. It
would have been possible to carry on with an all-out parliamentary
attack but the Bishop himself doubted whether any Tory action in the
two Houses would have an effect other than to aid one Whig faction
in its struggle against another. In fact he had always secretly believed
that the surest way by which James could be 'restored' was by a secret
agreement with the Minister in power. Otherwise the Jacobites had no
real plans, for the financial crisis had taken them as much by surprise as
anyone else. Strafford, Orrery and the rest had dispatched urgent letters
to Dillon in Paris and James in Urbino, telling them of the critical
moment and the glorious opportunity, but they had no advice except
that the courts of France and Spain should be asked for military aid.
The Chevalier was equally nonplussed. He drew up a dramatically
phrased declaration; Ormonde in Madrid was told to press King Philip
for another naval expedition; and Dillon dutifully took himself to
Versailles, though he knew that his chances of success were minimal.[6]
The managers in Paris busied themselves with drawing up plans for a
small-scale landing by the Duke of Ormonde without the assistance of
a foreign army, and in mid-October this scheme was sent over to the
Bishop of Rochester with an urgent request that he should at once
begin to organize friends at home so that they could rise to meet
Ormonde and give him sufficient support before the British army
could capture him.[7] In such a hare-brained project Atterbury would
have absolutely no part. He advised holding everything and waiting
until the time of the General Election due to be held in the spring of
1722. This would give time for really adequate preparations to be made
on both sides of the Channel; but even then, he warned, James was to
expect nothing from his English supporters 'unless the forces to be sent
were in much greater quantities than is proposed'.[8] By the end of 1720
it was clear that his condition could not be met. The British diplomatic

[5] *The Diary of Mary, Countess Cowper, 1714–1720*, ed. Spencer Cowper, 1865, p. 133.
[6] R.A. Stuart 49/45, for the declaration, dated 29 Sept./10 Oct. 1720; ibid., 49/79,
James to Ormonde, 12/23 Oct. 1720.
[7] Ibid., 49/99, Dillon to Atterbury, 14/25 Oct. 1720; ibid., 49/98, Dillon to James,
17/28 Oct. 1720.
[8] Ibid., 49/78, Atterbury to Dillon, 22 Oct./2 Nov. 1720.

service had done its work exceptionally well and, though Jacobite agents continued to submit memorials at most of the courts of Europe, there was now no possibility of foreign military aid.[9]

It was a deeply frustrating situation, and in January 1721 Atterbury and his associates seemed almost to go out of their way to invite some approach from the Ministry. When a significant body of Tory peers and M.P.s was seen to be abstaining from the parliamentary attack, rumour was soon going around that a reconstruction of the Ministry was in the offing. Not all Tories were entirely happy with such a tactic and Lord Orrery was sufficiently unsure of this 'waiting for the Ministry' to complain bitterly to James himself of 'the ill consequences of some false steps which several of them have lately taken. Their business is certainly to give George and the Ministry all the disturbance, all the uneasiness and all the opposition possible in Parliament . . . so that I hope there will be better managements among them than has been of late'.[10] In fact there was not long to wait. In late February Sunderland arranged a meeting with Lord Orrery, using as an intermediary the Scottish M.P., Alexander Urquhart, and when this proved abortive, because of mutual antipathy, he set out his offer directly to Atterbury himself. James Hamilton, a Jacobite agent in London, reported the terms to the Chevalier on 10 March. Sunderland promised that if the Tories would preserve him from impeachment he 'would order all things as they desired'. Parliament would be suddenly dissolved and 'if the Tories do not take the opportunity then it will not be his fault'.[11] On 15 March in the Commons Sunderland was acquitted by a handsome majority, and it was noted that a good number of Tories had voted for him. During the Easter recess the conversations which senior Ministers were having with Atterbury and Lord Trevor were an open secret.[12]

Of course, the Jacobites were well aware that they were playing a dangerous and uncertain game. In their discussions with Sunderland they were elaborately careful not to reveal any Jacobite secrets, and the meetings took the form of an elaborate and wary sparring match. As the Bishop recalled it later, 'he could assure the world that whatever

[9] Ibid., 50/91, James to Dillon, Rome, 2/13 Dec. 1720.

[10] Ibid., 51/53, Orrery to James, 16 Jan. 1721.

[11] Ibid., 52/165, James Hamilton to James, 10/21 Mar. 1721. See also H.M.C. *Portland MSS.*, vii, 293, 7 Mar. 1721.

[12] H.M.C. *Portland MSS.*, vii, 295, 9 Apr. 1721. See also Blenheim MSS. F. 1–31, Atterbury to Sunderland [30 Mar. 1721].

he made of Lord Sunderland was a secret, but that Lord Sunderland made nothing of him'.[13] Yet the offers made were unnervingly tempting and presented with every appearance of sincerity. At the end of April Sunderland went so far as to assure Atterbury that he regarded the Prince of Wales as his deadly enemy; rather than that such a creature should come to the throne he was prepared to embrace the cause of the Chevalier. He promised to procure a dissolution of the present Parliament and to form a new 'mixed administration' in which Trevor, Orrery, Strafford and North should find places along with moderate Whigs.[14]

Thus beguiled, the Jacobite leaders threw caution to the winds. Until this time every one of them of any standing had insisted in letters to James that there was no chance of a widespread rising in England without the encouragement of a strong force of professional soldiers which could meet the British army on level terms. Now in the heady excitement of the moment they dispatched a message to James, urging that he should set out immediately, even though this meant that he came with only a small personal entourage. 'The time is now come', wrote the Bishop, 'when, with a very little assistance from your friends abroad, your way to your friends at home is become safe and easy. The present juncture is so favourable, and will probably continue for so many months to be so, that I cannot think it will pass over without a proper use being made of it.' Even Lord Orrery, usually the very soul of self-concern, was won over to hope for success 'without foreign assistance'.[15] In a fateful moment of euphoria they set in motion in France and Italy the machinery of preparation for an expedition to England.

As the summer days of 1721 passed, the meetings and negotiations with Sunderland went their way. In June he seemed almost to parade his discussions with Atterbury and Trevor, and the town buzzed with speculation when the coaches of Cabinet Ministers stood outside the Bishop's door in Dean's Yard, Westminster. Sunderland himself arrived with Lord Trevor; and Lord Carteret, the Minister's able young follower, was 'often in close conference' inside. Atterbury later

[13] Cholmondeley (Houghton) MSS. [hereafter referred to as C(H) MSS.] 1292, J. Sample to Horace Walpole, 19/30 Mar. 1726, reporting Atterbury's conversation.
[14] R.A. Stuart 53/79, C. Caesar to James, 4 May 1721.
[15] Ibid., 53/48, Atterbury to James, 22 Apr. 1721. See also ibid., 53/137, H. Goring to James, Paris, 15/26 May 1721; ibid., 53/87, Orrery to James, 6 May 1721.

described the manner in which Sunderland 'pressed him several times to act with him', and they even discussed the disposition of portfolios in the new administration.[16] Yet it was agonizingly difficult to probe what was really meant by all these offers. It was clear that King George knew about the talks and had given them his consent, and this very fact made the Bishop suspect that there was a trick 'to render him suspected by the Tory party'. In later years he insisted 'that neither he nor Lord Trevor would engage till we saw the Church and the Army new modelled'.[17] The trouble was that Sunderland never quite got to the point. When the bishopric of Winchester fell vacant on 19 July he at once came to Atterbury and offered him translation to this wealthy see 'if he and his friends would only now come into the new scheme'.[18] But still 'he could never be prevailed upon to come into necessary measures for securing a good Parliament, though he professed his zeal for one'. Clearly, Sunderland did not intend real concessions to the Jacobites but he still wanted to manipulate them. In August he and Carteret made a renewed bid to mobilize support, and their overtures now extended not only to Hanoverian Tories such as William Bromley but even to sturdily independent Jacobites such as William Shippen who had hitherto held aloof from all negotiations. In June Walpole had thought it worthwhile himself to call on Atterbury and discuss the situation with him. Now at the end of August it seemed that the intrigue with the Tories, carried on with the King's full consent, had become dangerous enough for him to return in haste from Norfolk to face what seemed like an urgent threat to his political position.[19] It was a situation which he would not readily forgive or forget.

2

The new session of Parliament in October made it clear to the Jacobites, however, that there was nothing more to be gained from Sunderland. If his negotiation with the Tories had been intended to counter the slow rise to effective power of Walpole and Townshend, then it had failed in its objective, for it was they who now drew up the King's

[16] H.M.C. *Portland MSS.*, vii, 299, 23 June 1721; B.M. Add. MSS. 9129, fo. 61, Sample to H. Walpole, 31 Oct. 1726.
[17] B.M. Add. MSS. 32686, fo. 330, J. Macky to R. Walpole, 21 Sept. 1723, reporting a conversation with Atterbury.
[18] R.A. Stuart 55/67, Orrery to James, 28 Oct. 1721.
[19] J. H. Plumb, *Sir Robert Walpole*, i, 363 *et seq.*

Speech and arranged the business. But if he had merely intended to confuse the Tories, then he had succeeded amply. In September the Scottish Jacobite, George Lockhart, had come south to seek the advice of English friends on the astonishing offers which he had received from Sunderland with regard to the coming elections in the Scottish burghs. To his alarm he found Shippen and others whom he approached seething with resentment at the part which the Bishop of Rochester and his collaborators had played.[20] Even the amiable Lord Bathurst had intimated that he wished henceforth to dissociate himself from the intrigue.[21] Lord Orrery reported to James in pungent terms the lame excuses which Sunderland made to them. It had been, the Minister explained, not his fault that Parliament had not been dissolved but the unfortunate influence of Walpole in the closet; he assured them that he was himself 'still a well-wisher to the Tories'.[22] But this was nonsense, and the business proposed to both houses on 26 October showed plainly that there was to be another regular session. So far from there being cause for further trust in Sunderland's promises, it was clear that the Government wanted time to make elaborate preparations for the General Election in the spring, and that the full weight of ministerial influence was to be exerted against the Tories.[23] The shock of this realization brought about an immediate closing of the opposition ranks. Atterbury, Orrery, Strafford, Bathurst and North, for the Jacobites, held an emergency meeting with Archbishop Dawes of York and Lords Guilford and Foley for the Hanoverian Tories; and the Opposition Whig, Earl Cowper, attended the discussion. It was resolved to sink their differences so far as to agree to work under the leadership of Cowper in the Lords, and to launch an all-out attack on the Government, using the kind of issues which could provide useful ammunition in the coming election campaign.[24]

During November, however, the Jacobites were facing a harsh dilemma. What of the pressing invitation which they had dispatched to the Chevalier and upon the strength of which he was even now collecting money and organizing an expedition? Were they to fulfil

[20] *The Lockhart Papers* [ed. A. Aufrere], 2 vols. (1817), II, 68–71, G. Lockhart to James, 5 Dec. 1721.
[21] SP 35/28, Bathurst to Atterbury, 19 Aug. 1721; *The Correspondence of Alexander Pope*, ed. George Sherburn, 5 vols. (Oxford, 1956), ii, 87, Atterbury to Pope, 15 Oct. 1721.
[22] R.A. Stuart 55/67, Orrery to James, 28 Oct. 1721.
[23] Ibid., 55/57, Hamilton to James, 23 Oct. 1721.
[24] SP 35/40/423, for a paper in Atterbury's hand.

their promises and make ready for a landing of Ormonde during the election, even though he came virtually alone and with no foreign army? Already James was asking for news, and at the beginning of October Dillon and Lord Lansdowne in Paris had sent over an outline plan to be put into effect the moment polling began in March 1722.[25] Ormonde was to land secretly at some strategic spot by sailing up the Thames to a point near London; and a diversionary force was to land in Scotland or the West Country to draw off the Hanoverian troops. But it was stressed that everything depended on the support which could be provided by the English Jacobites: money had to be collected at once and dispatched abroad in large quantities, and there had to be set up a clandestine military organization which could rise and give instant support to the Duke. He must not be overwhelmed before the revolution was properly under way.

On receiving this set of papers the Jacobite group was plunged into vehement dispute. Orrery made his position clear: the scheme was wholly impracticable; as a professional soldier he knew that it was not possible to organize an effective army in secret; in his opinion every penny which could be raised was to be devoted to the Tory election campaign, not sent abroad. 'There are', he wrote off to James, 'so many little venal boroughs that 'tis to be apprehended a majority will hardly be carried by the inclinations of the people only.'[26] Lords Gower and Bathurst agreed with him, but a party consisting of Strafford, Arran and North took the opposite view. For them the sudden appearance of the great Protestant hero, Ormonde, in the midst of the elections would do more to accomplish 'the king's restoration' than any amount of tedious electioneering. Obviously much depended on Bishop Atterbury and after a terrible hesitation he agreed to fall in with the project.[27] At once the plan sent over from Paris was amended by the conspirators and returned. The Earl of Arran was to be in command in England until his brother actually arrived; Strafford was to rouse the gentry of the north as Danby had done in 1688; Lansdowne was to land in Cornwall to prepare for a rising in the west; and weapons would be required for at least 20,000 irregulars. They promised that money would

[25] R.A. Stuart 55/137, James to Strafford, 11/22 Nov. 1721; ibid., 55/82, James to Lansdowne, 22 Oct./2 Nov. 1721. See also ibid., 65/18, for the memorial, dated 4/15 Oct.

[26] Ibid., 55/67, Orrery to James, 28 Oct. 1721.

[27] Ibid., 65/33, Hay to Mar, 3/14 Apr. 1722; ibid., 63/33, Hamilton to James, 9/20 Nov. 1722.

be collected in England and sent to Paris and Madrid to finance the foreign preparations. On 20 November, in the name of five conspirators, himself, Strafford, Arran, North and Sir Harry Goring, the Bishop dictated the detailed proposals to the Reverend George Kelly, an Irish non-juring clergyman, and dispatched him to France.[28] Lord Sunderland's initiative with the Jacobites had produced a strange effect which perhaps he had not foreseen. It had propelled them into a rash and dangerous venture.

During the whole of December the Chevalier's agents were involved in intense activity. An appeal was sent to the Czar, Sweden was asked to repay the money lent in 1718, and arms and ammunition were purchased in large quantities in Hamburg. In January and February Ormonde was engaged in fitting out a small force of three ships in the port of Cadiz.[29] Commissions were sent from Rome, authorizing the English conspirators to act in James's name, and in London the rudiments of a financial organization were set up when Captain Dennis Kelly came over from France prepared to transfer money to continental bankers by means of bills of exchange. Everything, however, depended on one thing: whether the leading Jacobites could really put their promises into effect and transform a mere conspiracy into a movement which represented a real threat to the British Government. By the beginning of February it was clear that this had not been done and could not be done. At a meeting with his associates the Bishop was horrified to learn of the true state of their preparations. No plans had been made to divide the country into military districts, no commissions had been distributed and, worst of all, virtually no money had been collected. The grandiose scheme for a general uprising was still only a figment of the conspirators' imagination, and the elections were only two months away. Atterbury realized that his friend Ormonde was being led into a trap, prepared by the empty promises of a few highly placed but totally unrealistic English Jacobites. After a bitter quarrel with them he dissociated himself completely from the whole foolish project and wrote off to warn the managers in Paris of the lamentable

[28] The letters to James and Dillon have not survived in the Stuart papers, but their contents are evident from R.A. Stuart 57/1-7, James's replies of 24 Dec. 1721/4 Jan. 1722.

[29] H.M.C. *Moray MSS.*, p. 171, Dillon to Gordon, 26 Dec. 1721; see *Reports from Committees of the House of Commons*, vol. I, 1715-1735: 'Report from the committee appointed to examine Christopher Layer and others', 1 Mar. 1723 [hereafter referred to as *C.R.*], document A.A.5, Ormonde to Lansdowne, *c.* 4/15 Apr. 1722.

state of affairs.[30] On every ground of reason and calculation the conspiracy should have been abandoned then and there.

Instead of being broken off, however, it entered a new stage: that in which the managers in Paris proceeded to place in the hands of the British Ministry a most potent political weapon. Dillon and Lord Lansdowne, James's official agents, were prepared to recognize that nothing could be done during the elections which would not risk an utter disaster. But they and James in Italy were desperately reluctant to abandon Ormonde's preparations in Spain and they all now listened to advice from a quarter which should have been utterly suspect. It came from the Earl of Mar, who had been out of favour with the Chevalier since 1719 but who had, with some persistence forced himself into the company of Dillon and Lansdowne in Paris. James was aware that in 1720 Mar had made his submission to the British Government and was actually in receipt of a pension from George I.[31] And yet, unaccountably, they all accepted from him a suggestion that the Jacobite expedition should now be mounted in the summer of 1722 when King George would be on his annual visit to Hanover. Mar was even allowed to take over part of the correspondence with England and to attempt to recruit Bishop Atterbury and the Earl of Oxford as leaders of a new conspiracy and a new collection of money.[32]

It was a wholly unreal scheme, as the Bishop at once saw when, on 12 April, George Kelly brought Mar's proposals across. Oxford was an ailing man and Atterbury himself was grievously incapacitated by gout.[33] Within a few days Atterbury's determination to do nothing at all was confirmed by the news that on 19 April Lord Sunderland had dropped dead of an apoplexy. While that Minister remained in office the Bishop felt reasonably secure, for both Sunderland and Carteret had maintained constant contact with the Jacobites.[34] Indeed, Sir Luke Schaub, the envoy in Paris and closely connected with both, had gone out of his way to assure Dillon and Lansdowne that his patrons were secretly in the Chevalier's service. Clearly if these professions and offers

---

[30] R.A. Stuart 58/74, Mar to James, 5/16 Mar. 1722; ibid., 65/33, Hay to Mar, 3/14 Apr. 1722; ibid., 59/118, Strafford to James, 18 May 1722. See also *The Political State of Great Britain*, xxv, 429.

[31] R.A. Stuart 52/54, James to Mar, 11/22 Feb. 1721.

[32] Ibid., 58/91, Mar to James, 12/23 Mar. 1722; ibid., 58/113, 19/30 Mar. 1722.

[33] For Kelly's report to Mar, 16/27 Apr. 1722, see ibid., 59/14.

[34] B.M. Add. MSS. 9129, fo. 61, Sample to H. Walpole, 31 Oct. 1726, reporting Atterbury's conversation. See also *Pope Corr.*, ii, 110, Pope to Atterbury, 19 Mar. 1722.

had become public property it would have been impossibly embarrassing for Sunderland, and it was thus highly unlikely that he would ever have initiated prosecutions for treasonable activities against the more eminent English Jacobites. But after 19 April the situation was quite altered, and for Robert Walpole the discovery and following through of a Jacobite plot offered every political and personal advantage.

3

Sunderland's unexpected death is rightly accounted the moment of Walpole's opportunity, and it removed from his path the one politician who could still challenge his bid for pre-eminent power. But there was still much to be done to establish his position. The existing Ministry contained many of the dead man's immediate followers, notably the brilliant young Secretary of State, Carteret, who was clearly *persona grata* at court. Walpole and Townshend still laboured under a weight of suspicion from the King which stemmed from the circumstances of their dismissal in 1717. It was certain that Sunderland had done little to reconcile his rivals to their royal master. But in one respect at least, the dead man had caused King George considerable unease and that was in the matter of his negotiation with the Jacobites. The King had consented to it with the greatest reluctance and had viewed its progress with dire suspicion. Indeed, Walpole himself, sensing this, had always made a show of taking 'the other point, of standing and falling with the Whigs, which was not only the King's own entire opinion, but had been much confirmed in the past by my Lord Sunderland himself'.[35] The discovery of a Jacobite plot, with all the possibility that it could be worked up into a national emergency, was thus of special importance for Walpole. It was, as Speaker Onslow later wrote, the 'most fortunate and the greatest circumstance of Mr Walpole's life. It fixed him with the King, and united for a time the whole body of Whigs to him, and gave him the universal credit of an able and vigilant Minister.'[36] Not only did it allow him to throw suspicion on those of Sunderland's friends who had been involved with the Jacobite negotiation, but it meant that he could meet the newly elected House of Commons in the autumn of 1722 in the full excitement of a plot, in the prosecution of which he would sustain the chief and directing role.

[35] H.M.C. *Carlisle MSS.*, p. 38, Sir John Vanbrugh to Carlisle, 5 May 1722.
[36] H.M.C. *Onslow MSS.*, p. 513.

For some months the Secretaries of State had been receiving vague reports of increased Jacobite activity abroad but on 21 April, only two days after Sunderland's death, definite information was obtained. On that evening there came an express from Sir Luke Schaub, conveying an urgent warning from the French Premier, the Cardinal Dubois.[37] His intelligence service had been picking up hints of Dillon's preparations, and now reported that money was coming across from England and that Irish officers were moving towards ports in Brittany as if to embark on some expedition. The ministers acted at once with all the appearance of a national emergency. At a specially summoned Cabinet Council on 23 April orders were issued to open all letters between England and France, to search cross-Channel shipping, and for the regiments of foot-guards to set up a camp in Hyde Park.[38] That very evening the Post Office intercepted three letters which the Bishop of Rochester had dictated to Kelly for Dillon, Lansdowne and Mar. For some reason which remains obscure Kelly had actually sent these through the ordinary letter-post and, though they were disguised in code, the gist of their contents presented little difficulty to the Government's cipher experts.[39] In subsequent days a rich harvest of letters between other lesser Jacobites was gathered in, copied, resealed and allowed to pass on through the post. Although the false names employed were puzzling, the ministers knew quite well who the leading Jacobites were. That the Bishop of Rochester was involved and had dictated the three most important letters they did not doubt at all. The problem was to find legal proof.

On 25 April Walpole and Townshend moved into action. They had a private meeting with Carteret, and the luckless secretary realized that his political career depended on joining in an energetic pursuit of the plot with as much enthusiasm as he could muster. Obviously his own and Sir Luke Schaub's extensive Jacobite intrigue could be very dangerous to both of them, if misrepresented by political enemies. It was agreed that a formal letter should be sent to Schaub, to be shown to the French Ministry, announcing the absolute unanimity of the

---

[37] B.M. Stowe MSS. 250, fo. 73, Schaub to Carteret, 19/30 Apr. 1722.

[38] SP 35/31/72: 'At the duke of Newcastle's house, 23 Apr. 1722'.

[39] The ciphered letters are to be found in C(H) MSS. 69/4. The Government experts' decoded versions are *C.R.* D.10–12, and the versions corrected from the codes in R.A. Stuart are in *The Stuart Papers*, ed. J. H. Glover, 1847, i, appendix, pp. 11–15.

three Ministers at home in the face of a grave crisis.[40] And it was decided to entrust Colonel Charles Churchill, Marlborough's bastard nephew, with a special mission in Paris. He was instructed to press the French Government for further information but also to see whether any of the Jacobites could be bribed or persuaded to reveal the plans or correspondence of their English associates. On 28 April Walpole and Townshend made a further bid to secure evidence by a forcible search of Sunderland's private papers. Despite the Duchess of Marlborough's excited protests, the dead man's desk was opened and his files scrutinized. Virtually nothing incriminating was found but the wide publicity given to the event left no doubt that Sunderland's friends were under suspicion.[41]

Churchill was amazingly successful in Paris. His first action was to call on the Earl of Mar, bearing a 'peremptory message' from the three Ministers in London requiring him to reveal the whole plot on pain of forfeiting his pension and any hope of future rehabilitation to his title and Scottish estates.[42] There is evidence that he was induced to talk freely and even to write a letter to Atterbury, using the false names of the previous correspondence, so that this could be 'intercepted' in the post. Taking advantage of Schaub's established connections with the Jacobites, Churchill went on to discuss with them the possibility that Walpole and Townshend might embrace their cause as Lord Sunderland had done.[43] When Cardinal Dubois expressed utter amazement at this contact with known enemies of the Hanoverian regime, Carteret explained that it was 'parcequ'il y a longtemps que Mar a eu des obligations au Roy'.[44] Little of the evidence which Churchill obtained could be used in a court of law, but it is clear that after his mission the Ministry had a much clearer view of the personnel and actual extent of the conspiracy. And from Walpole's point of view there was one invaluable by-product. Churchill's visits to the French

---

[40] B.M. Add. MSS. 22517, fo. 48, Carteret to Schaub, 25 Apr./6 May 1722, quoted *British Diplomatic Instructions, 1689–1789*, vol. iv (ed. L. G. Wickham Legg, 1927), pp. 30–1.

[41] Plumb, *Walpole*, ii, 40; *C.R.* E.35, Kelly to Glascock, 30 Apr./11 May 1722; H.M.C. *Sutherland MSS.*, p. 190, unidentified correspondent to Gower, 1 May 1722.

[42] R.A. Stuart 60/88, James to Lansdowne, 17/28 June 1722; ibid., 75/136, Atterbury to James, 31 July 1725, quoting from letters found among Mar's papers.

[43] *C.R.* F.23, Dillon to Kelly, 16/27 May 1722; *C.R.* D.24, Mar to Atterbury, 11/22 May 1722.

[44] B.M. Add. MSS. 22517, fo. 116, Carteret to Schaub, 7/18 June 1722.

court, where he was received by Dubois and the Regent himself, produced a series of accusations against Sunderland at the highest level, based on information which the French intelligence service had gleaned. Although Carteret wrote formally to Schaub that neither King George nor his Ministers believed that such turpitude could have existed, it is clear that Walpole was more than content that the King should peruse these reports from Paris in his usual review of the diplomatic correspondence.[45]

Meanwhile, the Ministry moved to the creation of an emergency. On 7 May troops were camped in Hyde Park, the price of Bank stock fell from 90 to 77, and the next day, in a letter to the Lord Mayor, Townshend announced the discovery of a detestable plot, the existence of which would soon be proved by His Majesty's vigilant Ministers. George I put off his visit to Hanover, and the world waited to see what the evidence could be for all these extraordinary precautions. In fact, there was precious little, certainly not enough to lay before Parliament when it met in the autumn. The Post Office continued to intercept Jacobite correspondence between England and France, but it was obvious that these were the letters of minor agents and did not indicate any widespread activity in England. Some dextrous undercover work by the British secret service found out that the Reverend George Kelly was the principal correspondent in London, and he was arrested and closely questioned by the Committee of Cabinet. This examination gave Walpole his first real break. Inadvertently, Kelly implicated the Bishop of Rochester by naming him as the recipient of a French spotted dog named Harlequin which had been mentioned in certain of the intercepted letters. This dispelled any possible doubt in Walpole's mind about Atterbury's involvement and it impressed the Cabinet Council. But there was still insufficient evidence publicly to justify the emergency which had been created.[46] Indeed, from all its agents abroad the Government continued to receive reports which indicated that what remained of the Jacobite expedition had folded. Certainly the ministers were no longer in any real alarm, for their precautions had been massive. In mid-May all strain went out of the situation when news

---

[45] B.M. Add. MSS. 9129, fo. 49, Schaub to Carteret, 1 June 1722; ibid., fo. 50, Carteret to Schaub, 21 June 1722. The letters are in French for the King's benefit.
[46] C.R. E.4: 'At a committee of council, May 23rd 1722'; C.R. E.47, Kelly to O'Brien, 11/22 June 1722; W. Coxe, *Memoirs of the Life and Administration of Sir Robert Walpole*, 3 vols. (1798), ii, 220–2, R. Walpole to H. Walpole, 29 May 1722.

came that the Regent had ordered all foreign officers in the French army to rejoin their regiments immediately and that the Spanish Government had arrested Ormonde's ships.[47] It was now apparent, even to Dillon and Lansdowne, that their project was ruined, and in early June they cancelled everything. The British Embassy in Paris could assure London that there was nothing further to fear.

During the summer months, even when his colleagues appeared to have lost interest in the game, Walpole continued with his relentless search for evidence. For a while it seemed a hopeless pursuit. Atterbury, Strafford, North, Arran and Orrery had retired to their country estates in justifiable fear, knowing that their every move was being watched. The Post Office was still intercepting five or six letters a week but their contents were disappointing. Though the cipher experts had now mastered the codes in which the minor Jacobites put their trust, it was clear that little treasonable activity was going on. George Kelly's letters were those of a man who knew that he was being spied on, and there was nothing in them. Dennis Kelly, whose work in London had been discovered by Schaub in May, was desperate to escape back to France. If Walpole had had to rely on this kind of evidence, he would certainly have had nothing in his hand with which to meet Parliament. Fortunately there were other figures in the Jacobite underworld who could provide him with what was wanted. There was a set of letters, intercepted in the post from London to Paris, from a correspondent calling himself 'Rogers', and these were full of the direst menace. 'Rogers' told of a vast plan to raise a rebellion in the autumn before Parliament assembled; he described in detail discussions with the French and Spanish envoys who were said to have pledged their support. On 4 July he even outlined a plan for the assassination of George I. The ministers were delighted rather than alarmed. Enquiries in Paris and Madrid produced horrified denials that their ambassadors were engaged in such Jacobite schemes, and Sir Luke Schaub professed himself amazed at projects which were wholly out of accord with everything else they knew about the state of Jacobite affairs.[48] In fact, Walpole had intercepted the correspondence of a broken-down Irish

[47] B.M. Add. MSS. 22517, fo. 56, Carteret to Schaub, 2/13 May 1722; H.M.C. *Clements MSS.*, p. 342; *C.R.* A.15, Stanhope to Carteret, 28 May/8 June 1722.

[48] SP 78/177/84, Schaub to Carteret, 7/18 July 1722; B.M. Add. MSS. 22517, fo. 145, Carteret to Schaub, 7/18 July; B.M. Sloane MSS. 4204, fo. 80, Schaub to Carteret, 18/29 July.

confidence trickster named James Plunket, written on behalf of his employer, Christopher Layer. It was a world of pure fantasy, quite unconnected with the real Jacobite conspiracy which had existed earlier in the year. Layer was a simple-minded and busy romantic who, under Plunket's influence, had actually visited the Chevalier in Rome in the summer of 1721. On his return to England he had tried pathetically to have himself accepted into the inner Jacobite circle and to be accounted a fellow-conspirator. He had been snubbed and rejected at every attempt, and avoided as the dangerous meddler he was. All his schemes were concerted to recommend himself by showing his boldness and ingenuity, though in fact he knew practically nothing. Now, as the senior English Jacobites tried to fade into obscurity, he went on inventing plots and submitting them for approval.

Even more fortunate for Walpole was the information volunteered by the Reverend Philip Neyno, an Irish non-juror who occasionally acted as secretary or amanuensis to George Kelly. On 1 August Neyno visited Walpole at Chelsea with evidence to sell, and was gratefully received.[49] Neyno was flattered, bribed, tricked and finally terrorized. On 4 August he broke down completely and soon he was blabbing out everything he knew. He repeated over and over again that the Bishop of Rochester was the real leader of the conspiracy in England, and he did not spare his lesser colleagues. His only reticence was a refusal to commit any of this evidence to writing or sign a statement.[50] Yet it was on the strength of Neyno's oral testimony that Walpole moved on 24 August to his most serious step: the arrest of Bishop Atterbury and his confinement in the Tower on a charge of high treason. He had now staked his political career on a successful prosecution of the Jacobite plot, and for the next nine months he was to devote himself day and night to proving to the satisfaction of King and Parliament that there had been indeed a grave threat to the national security. And he had to do this in spite of the fact that in the summer of 1722 there was ample evidence that the danger from abroad had never been anything more than slight and that the English conspirators had been divided and confused at all times. It became more and more obvious that Neyno was the key witness, and during September he was mercilessly interrogated in an effort to make him swear to his testimony.

---

[49] See B.M. Add. MSS. 34713, fos. 55–56, for Walpole's testimony, 13 May 1723; B.M. Add. MSS. 32686, fo. 232, Poyntz to Newcastle, 3 Aug. 1722.

[50] R.A. Stuart 100/45, Hamilton to James, n.d., but after 29 Sept. 1722.

But in this Walpole went too far. On the night of 25 September, in desperation, Neyno escaped from custody by throwing himself into the Thames. When in the first light of morning his drowned body was recovered from the river, the Ministry had lost its best chance of obtaining legal evidence. Now only Christopher Layer remained. On 18 September he was taken up and his confused information used as an excuse for arresting Orrery and North and ransacking the home of William Shippen. Still there was no concrete evidence until, on the 29th, to Walpole's relief and delight, two large bundles of material which was plainly treasonable were discovered in Layer's lodgings. The wretched young man had preserved every item of his imaginary conspiracy, including an elaborate scheme for seizing the City of London.[51] It was mostly nonsense, but sufficiently menacing in tone gravely to alarm the King and influential members of the Cabinet such as the Duke of Newcastle. It was poor stuff but it would have to serve.

4

Whatever his own doubts may have been, Walpole began the new parliament with all the appearance of a grave crisis. In the speech from the throne on 11 October the King devoted himself almost entirely to the plot and called for the loyal assistance of both Houses in bringing conspirators to justice. A Bill to suspend the provisions of *habeas corpus* was proposed and rushed through all its stages to receive the royal assent on the 17th. Although Shippen and his band of Tories fought until the small hours of the morning, they were powerless in the face of an overwhelming government majority. In debate Walpole made his own position clear: he was determined to secure a conviction, at least against the Bishop of Rochester, whom he did not hesitate to name as the real master-mind of the Jacobite cause. The method by which this was to be done, however, still remained unclear, and a cruel game was to be played out before a decision could be made. On 27 November Christopher Layer was sentenced to death in the Court of King's Bench. With all the evidence against him his case was hopeless from the start, but now the poor wretch was subjected to a torture by hope. There was a series of last-minute reprieves before execution, and after each he was pressed for new information. If he could have done

---

[51] The originals are in C(H) MSS. 69/9.

anything to procure his life he would have done it. The fact was, quite simply, that he knew nothing.[52]

During December Walpole and his two assistants spent hours going through the intercepted letters, and the Cabinet Committee met almost daily to examine a host of small fry who might provide a few extra crumbs of information. When the Chancellor of the Exchequer went home to Norfolk for Christmas he carried with him a trunkload of documents, so that he could work up his case even over the season of goodwill.[53] But on his return to Westminster he had reached a painful decision. All the evidence was collected into neat folders and he knew that it was not sufficient to proceed at all against Orrery, North or Dennis Kelly. There was not even enough to prosecute Atterbury, George Kelly or James Plunket by any method which required ordinary proof at law. Impeachment was out of the question, and if the plot were not to fall to the ground he had to set aside legal restraints and resort to wholly political action. The Bishop, Kelly and Plunket must have pains and penalties imposed upon them by an Act of Parliament, and then all that had to be done was to persuade a majority in each House that it was right and expedient to punish men who were dangerous to the State. It was a dangerously arbitrary procedure and would require most careful management. Accordingly on 15 January a Commons Committee of reliable ministerial supporters was set to work to compile a report on the evidence. In the succeeding days and weeks they went through the motions of examining Layer, Plunket and others, but it was clear that there was nothing new to be added to the files which Walpole had so carefully marshalled. Nevertheless the report, when it was read on 1 March, created an immense sensation.[54] Walpole had created a massive and intricate piece of detective-work which managed to construct an intelligible narrative of the plot from a bewildering variety of evidence. The careful deciphering of the letters was particularly impressive. But it was not easy for the casual reader to detect that the report invented as much as it disclosed. It confused and conflated quite separate Jacobite correspondences and thereby created the impression of a single widespread conspiracy when in fact

[52] C(H) MSS. 989, Layer to Walpole, 27 Nov. 1722; SP 35/34/167, Layer to Townshend, 4 Dec. 1722.

[53] H.M.C. Portland MSS., vii, 345, 8 Jan. 1723.

[54] The Parliamentary Diary of Sir Edward Knatchbull, 1722–1730, ed. A. N. Newman, 1963, p. 14.

there had been only a series of distinct movements. It was never made clear that Layer's plot had been almost wholly imaginary. Yet it was at this point that the majority of ordinary M.P.s made up their minds and accepted the Committee's unanimous verdict that an extensive and dangerous conspiracy had been only narrowly averted. That the report was founded on circumstantial evidence alone and there was not a single living witness to swear to the essential facts seems to have mattered little to the ordinary members of either House.

The 'trials' of Plunket, Kelly and Atterbury provide one of the more discreditable episodes in the history of the administration of British justice. The 'pains and penalties' voted against them in the Commons were inserted at the third reading of their respective Bills, and in the Bishop's case it was proposed that he should be deprived of all his preferments and sent into perpetual exile. When his case came before the Lords his status was not so much that of a defendant in a court of law as of a witness called by counsel against a Bill. The procedures and the rules of evidence adopted were not those of the common law but what a majority of peers decided they should be. Atterbury accepted that nothing could prevent his banishment, and he devoted such of a case as he was allowed to present to making one point: that the whole prosecution stemmed from the political ambition of one man, Robert Walpole.[55] Monday, 13 May, was later remembered as the dramatic high point of the trial, when the two principal antagonists faced each other: a confrontation between an able politician, now on the very threshold of power, and a priest who represented all those political and religious opinions which Walpole so heartily detested.[56] Arthur Onslow, standing at the bar when the Bishop cross-examined Walpole, was awed by the encounter. 'A greater trial of skill this way', he wrote, 'scarce ever happened between two such combatants, the one fighting for his reputation, the other for his acquittal.'[57] Vigorously Walpole denied that there had ever been a plot to destroy his political opponents, and by his assured performance, in a crowded House of Lords with the Commons pressing at the bar, did much to allay the accusations against him.

[55] Pope Corr. ii, 165, Atterbury to Pope, 10 Apr. 1723; H.M.C. Bromley-Davenport MSS., p. 78, Atterbury to Bromley, 9 Apr. 1723.
[56] The notes of Lord Chancellor Macclesfield, B.M. Add. MSS. 34713, fos. 34–78, give the fullest record of the Bishop's examination of witnesses.
[57] H.M.C. Onslow MSS., p. 463.

The banishment of Bishop Atterbury was a turning-point in British politics, and a decisive blow to the Tory cause. Though Lords Orrery and North were set at liberty, a deep fear was implanted in the Jacobite ranks that some other of their number might receive the kind of treatment meted out to the Bishop. In the summer of 1723 they sought refuge in silence and categorically refused to correspond with James or with any of his known agents. Immediately after Atterbury's departure Sir William Wyndham, Lord Bathurst and Lord Gower contacted Walpole and 'declared themselves weary of the situation they were in, and ready to enter into measures'. By the summer of 1724 Orrery had to admit that the Chevalier's friends in England 'quite despond and almost abandon all hopes of relief'.[58] One by one the possible leaders were coming to terms with the Government, and Abingdon, Anglesey and Hanmer had ceased their opposition. Eventually a paid Jacobite agent had to be sent to England to investigate the situation and his account of the prevarication and shuffling he met with was so dismal that James was forced to agree that there was not a vestige of real support to be expected from England.[59]

Jacobitism had served Walpole well. While, like most English politicians, he was uncertain of the extent of Jacobite sympathy in the country, he was perceptive enough to realize that fear of conspiracy and invasion was a powerful weapon in political life. Not least important, Jacobitism caused deep unease to King George I. At a time when his own position was by no means established, Walpole had the dexterity to turn Sunderland's over-clever intrigue with the Tories to his own advantage. The real Jacobite plot of 1721–22 was a poor thing, ill-managed and abortive, but it provided an able minister with a unique opportunity. Seizing the fortunate chance of Sunderland's death, he could go on to discredit Carteret in the King's eyes, gain the support of influential colleagues like the Duke of Newcastle, and begin the new House of Commons with an issue in which Walpole was undoubtedly the leading spirit. In the process he destroyed the effectiveness of that Tory–Jacobite opposition in the Lords which had proved such a thorn in the side of previous Whig administrations. By the end

---

[58] B.M. Stowe MSS. 251, fo. 14, R. Walpole to Townshend, 23 July 1723; R.A. Stuart 74/59, Orrery to James, 10 May 1724.

[59] R.A. Stuart 81/71, James to Atterbury, 11 Apr. 1725; ibid., 81/133, Atterbury to Hay, 30 Apr. 1725.

of the parliamentary session of 1722–23 Robert Walpole was firmly established as the King's Minister. He had made so effective a use of the Jacobite issue that in succeeding years he searched about diligently to see whether he could collect enough evidence to employ it again.

V

The Principles and Practice of Opposition: The Case of Bolingbroke versus Walpole

QUENTIN SKINNER

1

In the discussion of his political career, as in his career itself, Bolingbroke has been much less fortunate than his lifelong rival, Sir Robert Walpole. Both Walpole's rise to power and the conduct of his administration have been splendidly analysed by Professor Plumb in the two volumes of his biography.[1] But the conduct of Bolingbroke's opposition has been far less satisfactorily discussed. This can no longer be explained simply by citing Burke's famous dismissal: 'Who now reads Bolingbroke?' A growing number of scholars do, and a lengthening list of studies have in consequence been devoted in recent years to establishing the facts about Bolingbroke's political career and to analysing his political works.[2]

---

[1] J. H. Plumb, *Sir Robert Walpole*, vol. I, *The Making of a Statesman* (London, 1956), vol. II, *The King's Minister* (London, 1960). See also J. H. Plumb, *The Growth of Political Stability in England, 1675–1725* (London, 1967), esp. Ch. VI.

[2] Jeffrey Hart, *Viscount Bolingbroke, Tory Humanist* (London, 1965); S. W. Jackman, *Man of Mercury* (London, 1965); Harvey C. Mansfield, Jr., *Statesmanship and Party Government: A Study of Burke and Bolingbroke* (Chicago, 1965); Isaac Kramnick, *Bolingbroke and his Circle: The Politics of Nostalgia in the Age of Walpole* (Cambridge, Mass., 1968); H. T. Dickinson, *Bolingbroke* (London, 1970). See also Caroline Robbins, *The Eighteenth Century Commonwealthman* (Cambridge, Mass., 1959); Archibald S. Foord, *His Majesty's Opposition, 1714–1830* (Oxford, 1964), and articles by Isaac Kramnick, 'Augustan Politics and English Historiography: The Debate on the English Past, 1730–35', *History and Theory*, 6 (1967), pp. 33–56; J. H. Grainger, 'The Deviations of Lord Bolingbroke', *The Australian Journal of Politics and History*, 15, no. 2 (1969), pp. 41–59; and Pat Rogers, 'Swift and Bolingbroke on Faction', *The Journal of British Studies*, 9, no. 2 (1970), pp. 71–101. There is an exceptional article, however, by J. G. A. Pocock, to which I am much indebted, originally published in *The William and Mary Quarterly*, 22, no. 4 (1965) and reprinted as Ch. 4 of J. G. A. Pocock, *Politics, Language and Time* (New York, 1971), pp. 104–47.

What is unsatisfactory about these studies is not that they have failed
to agree about the facts or in general to present them fairly and well.
It is rather that the facts seem to have been fitted into inappropriate
schemes of explanation. My aim in what follows will thus not
primarily be to provide new information about Bolingbroke and
his party of opposition to Walpole's Ministry. It will rather be to
argue that the existing facts – which have by now been much repeated,
and do not seem to be in dispute – fit a theory about the behaviour of
Bolingbroke and his party which does not seem to have been enter-
tained by any of Bolingbroke's interpreters, but which nevertheless
seems to offer the best explanation of his political beliefs and actions.

The thesis I wish to advance can be stated in a general as well as a
specific form. My specific claim is that both the main types of explanation for Bolingbroke's opposition to Walpole which have hitherto
been suggested mis-state the nature of the connections between
Bolingbroke's professed political principles and his actual political
behaviour. My more general claim is that these misinterpretations
derive from a more general incapacity – which is shared by most
recent writing in political history – to give any coherent account of the
nature of the relations between political thought and action. Correspondingly, my specific aim in what follows will be to provide a new
account of the role which needs to be assigned to Bolingbroke's
professed political principles if we wish to explain the actual conduct
of his opposition to Walpole's Ministry. My general aim will be to
provide a framework of explanation which may be more widely
applicable in discussions – in this and other historical periods – of the
interplay between principles and practice in political life.[3]

2

The relevant facts about the opposition to Walpole's Ministry can for
the most part be found in any of the recent studies of Bolingbroke's
career, and will be set out here as briefly as possible. The attack took

---

[3] Two other examples of current debates in which the conceptual scheme I attempt to
set out here could, I believe, be directly applied would be the debates about the role
of ideology in the American Revolution, and about the role of Benthamism in
nineteenth-century English government reform. For a survey of the literature
relevant to the first of these debates, see Gordon S. Wood, 'Rhetoric and Reality
in the American Revolution', *The William and Mary Quarterly*, 23 (1966), pp. 3–32,
and for a survey of the second, see Jenifer Hart, 'Nineteenth-Century Social Reform:
A Tory Interpretation of History', *Past and Present*, 31 (1965), pp. 33–61.

two main forms. The first was journalistic, and began in earnest in December 1726 with the first publication of *The Craftsman*, set up by Bolingbroke and Pulteney to expose the crafts by which Walpole governed.[4] The other line of attack was mounted in Parliament itself. Pulteney had already spent the sessions of 1726 and 1727 in opposition, but it was after the opening in 1728 of the first session of the new Parliament that the organized attack on Walpole's Ministry really began to become effective.[5] Bolingbroke himself was obliged to pour most of his energies into the journalistic attack, for despite the pardon (for his Jacobite adventures in 1715) which he had received in 1723, he was still debarred from taking his seat in the House of Lords.[6] He was able, however, to gather around him a brilliant opposition coterie which met at his retreat at Dawley,[7] as well as a considerable amount of support within the Commons, led by William Pulteney, William Bromley, Samuel Sandys and Lord Morpeth, and joined for a number of crucial debates and divisions by such prominent high Tory leaders as William Shippen and Sir William Wyndham.[8] Both these lines of

[4] Jackman, *Man of Mercury*, p. 41, gives a different date. For the correct details, see either Hart, *Bolingbroke*, p. 61, or (more fully) Kramnick, *Bolingbroke*, pp. 17–24; and Dickinson, *Bolingbroke*, 185, 188–9. For the Government side of the journalistic war, see L. Hanson, *Government and the Press* (London, 1936), esp. pp. 106–18.

[5] The unexpected death of George I in the previous year had necessitated a general election, otherwise not due until 1729. It seemed that Walpole might not survive the change of monarch, and the opposition obviously hoped that his capacity to manage the new Parliament might be impaired. On Walpole and the change of monarch, see Plumb, *Walpole*, II, pp. 157–72; and on the general election, ibid., pp. 176–85. Archdeacon Coxe, in his biography of Walpole, dated the rise of effective opposition from this point. C. B. Realey, however, in *The Early Opposition to Sir Robert Walpole* (Kansas, 1931), points out (pp. 224, 231) that the opposition did not in fact succeed in gaining much advantage at this time, and remained relatively muted until the 1730 session.

[6] This part of Bolingbroke's career can be followed in Hart, *Bolingbroke*, pp. 45–59, or in Jackman, *Man of Mercury*, pp. 34–42, or (most fully) in Dickinson, *Bolingbroke*, pp. 154–83. For Walpole's attitude towards Bolingbroke's pardon, see Plumb, *Walpole*, II, pp. 124–7.

[7] For the 'literary aspects' of Bolingbroke's opposition, see Hart, *Bolingbroke*, pp. 61–3, and Dickinson, *Bolingbroke*, pp. 212–19.

[8] Dickinson, *Bolingbroke*, p. 220, warns against assuming that these leaders merely acted out Bolingbroke's schemes. There can be no doubt, however, that the opposition platform adopted in the Commons was the product of discussion between Bolingbroke and such leaders. See, for example, the views of the French ambassador cited in Dickinson, *Bolingbroke*, p. 231, and the account in Plumb, *Walpole*, II, pp. 139–41 and 145–6. It is even possible that Bolingbroke wrote some of the speeches used by the opposition in the Commons. See Hart, *Bolingbroke*, p. 68. I shall continue, therefore, to use (though obviously as a shorthand) the phrase 'Bolingbroke's campaign' to include the opposition campaign in Parliament.

attack were then kept up unremittingly until the life of the Parliament
ran out in 1734. The end of Bolingbroke's leadership of this most
concerted attempt to unseat the ruling Whig oligarchy came only after
the General Election of that year, which duly returned Walpole to
power with a still comfortable majority.[9] The opposition ground on
in the new Parliament,[10] but Bolingbroke himself suddenly lost heart
and retired to France within the year to enjoy the consolations of
philosophy in his second exile.[11]

Bolingbroke and his party, both in the press and in Parliament,
naturally tried to make use of every possible issue and expedient to
embarrass the Ministry. As Professor Plumb puts it, writing of the
particularly troublesome session of 1730, Walpole found himself confronted and denounced on a bewildering variety of issues: 'gaols, the
renewal of the East India Company charter, the Africa Company, the
complaints of London shopkeepers, the peculiarly difficult by-election
petition from Liverpool.'[12] It is a very important fact about the conduct
of the opposition, however, which the recent studies of Bolingbroke
do not seem to bring out, but which Professor Plumb has again
stressed, that underlying these flurrying attacks there were several
'perennial' issues to which the opposition consistently returned. These
were the issues especially 'dear to independents', the issues which could
absolutely be guaranteed to animate their most 'cherished attitudes'.
In fact, the demand for these issues to be debated in each session
became, as Professor Plumb puts it, 'almost a part of the formal ritual
of the Parliamentary session'.[13]

There were two particular issues which constantly recurred in this
pattern of opposition. The first was the repeated denunciation of the
fact that, even after the conclusion of Britain's involvement in any
major European wars, the Ministry was prepared to go on keeping up
a sizeable land force, and even on one occasion to pay for the hire of
Hessian mercenaries.[14] This policy was attacked in virtually every

---

[9] For the (particularly elaborate) election preparations, and the (relative) success of the
Whigs, see Plumb, *Walpole*, II pp. 314–24.

[10] So did *The Craftsman*, but with diminished success. It eventually changed sides. For
this later history, see Plumb, *Walpole*, II, p. 141 and note.

[11] He took up residence at Chanteloup, where he died in 1751. For this part of his
biography, see Dickinson, *Bolingbroke*, pp. 247–96.

[12] Plumb, *Walpole*, II, p. 216.

[13] Ibid., pp. 216, 303, 305.

[14] For this issue see ibid., pp. 207–8.

session of this Parliament. In the opening session there was an attempt to prevent the addition of 8,000 men to the existing land forces.[15] In the second session both Pulteney and Shippen 'strongly opposed' the vote to keep the land forces at their existing strength.[16] In the third session Shippen mounted exactly the same attack.[17] In the fifth session Morpeth successfully demanded a further debate on Sir William Strickland's motion to continue the forces at their existing strength.[18] In the sixth session Morpeth led yet another debate on the same issue, prompting Walpole himself to reply, and both Shippen and Wyndham to counter-attack.[19] And finally, in the seventh and last session, Wyndham returned to the same attack, supported by Pulteney and the whole group of Bolingbroke's sympathizers.[20]

The other set of issues which the opposition attacked with equal consistency concerned the Ministry's control of the House itself. Two particular policies were recurrently denounced: the award of government places by the Ministry to its supporters in Parliament; and the award of government pensions to those who supported the Ministry. The climax of this attack on Walpole's devices for managing Parliament came in the final session, with the motion proposed by Bromley (evidently prompted by Bolingbroke himself) for the repeal of the Septennial Act, which the Whigs had first passed in 1717, and which the opposition saw (correctly) as the linchpin of Walpole's managerial success.[21] The award of places and pensions had meanwhile been denounced in virtually every session. In the third session Sandys brought in a bill 'for making more effectual the laws in being, for disabling persons from being chosen Members of, or sitting and voting in, the House of Commons, who have any pension . . . or any office held in trust for them, from the Crown'.[22] This actually passed the Commons,

---

[15] *The Parliamentary History of England*, 36 vols. (London, 1806–1820), VIII, pp. 642–3. For the debate on the Hessian troops, see VIII, pp. 643–4.

[16] Ibid., VIII, p. 677.

[17] Ibid., VIII, p. 771.

[18] Ibid., VIII, p. 882. Hervey replied to Morpeth's attack on 26 January. The debate took place next day; see pp. 913–4.

[19] Ibid., VIII, pp. 1184–5.

[20] Ibid., IX, p. 262.

[21] On Pulteney's opposition to the introduction of the bill, and the role played by Bolingbroke, see Kramnick, *Bolingbroke*, pp. 29–30, and Dickinson, *Bolingbroke*, p. 243, quoting the personal attack on Bolingbroke as 'anti-minister' which Walpole launched in the course of the debate. For the debate see *Parliamentary History*, IX, pp. 394–479.

[22] *Parliamentary History*, VIII, p. 789.

and Walpole had to rely on the Bishops to throw it out of the Lords. In the fourth session Sandys mounted the same attack. He failed to get a list of Members of Parliament who held pensions published, but he again succeeded in getting a pension bill past the Commons, and again Walpole had to use the Lords to throw it out.[23] In the fifth session Sandys again led exactly the same attack, and in the sixth session he attempted to carry over the same bill, prompting the Tories to join the attack, and Walpole himself to reply.[24] Finally, in the last session, Sandys changed his tactics, and instead sought leave 'to bring in a bill for securing the freedom of Parliament, by limiting the number of officers in that House'. This too was supported by Wyndham and the Tories, and although it failed, it proved to be the first of a new series of Place Bills which the indefatigable Sandys continued to introduce.[25]

The crucial point is thus that it is not quite accurate to say, as Bolingbroke's most recent biographer has done, that Bolingbroke and his group of supporters in the Commons simply looked around 'for any and every expedient and issue, real or imagined' with which to denounce the Ministry.[26] They also followed a basic pattern in their opposition, which was not only consistent, but so much so that within a few years it had become completely predictable. Thus one of Lord Chesterfield's pieces of advice to his son, at the time when he was about to enter Parliament, was to rehearse a speech either about the size of the land forces or about the award of places and pensions. These were the best subjects for prepared eloquence, simply because these were the issues which could absolutely be relied upon for a debate.[27]

It is equally crucial that, as well as concentrating on this particular pattern of opposition, Bolingbroke and his supporters consistently

---

[23] Ibid., VIII, on the Bill, p. 841; on the attempt to get the list published, p. 857. For Walpole's use of the Lords in connection with this and the earlier bill, see Foord, *Opposition*, pp. 183–4.

[24] *Parliamentary History*, VIII, pp. 882, 992, 1177–9.

[25] Ibid., IX, p. 336. See also Foord, *Opposition*, p. 184, noting that this was followed by other Place Bills, all brought in by Sandys, in the 1735, 1736, 1740 and 1741 sessions.

[26] Dickinson, *Bolingbroke*, p. 113. See also Hart's account, *Bolingbroke*, pp. 60–1 and 66–7. Neither Mansfield nor Kramnick discusses the parliamentary campaign at all, so that neither is able to give an account of Bolingbroke's political ideas in relation to the practice of opposition. Dickinson, however, gives a good general account at pp. 193–4, and does speak at one point (although this happens to be a mistake) of the 'almost annual' Place Bills, p. 242.

[27] Charles Strachey and Annette Calthrop, eds., *The Letters of the Earl of Chesterfield to his Son*, 2 vols. (London, 1901), Letter of 26 March 1754, II, p. 341.

professed the same political principle for the sake of which, they claimed, they were pursuing these lines of action. They all claimed, simply and invariably, to be activated by the spirit of patriotism. This term did not of course suffer at this time from any of the equivocal and potentially ironic overtones with which it has since become invested. It was both a strongly favourable evaluation to apply to anyone's behaviour, and one with a clear meaning. By the concept of patriotism both Bolingbroke and his opponents understood the ideal of acting in such a way as to defend and preserve the political liberties which their fellow-countrymen enjoyed under, and owed, to the constitution. Thus when Bolingbroke wanted to allude in his own epitaph to his professions of patriotism, what he spoke of was his 'zeal to maintain the liberty and to restore the ancient prosperity of Great Britain'.[28] His Whig opponents did not, of course, for a moment accept Bolingbroke's professions of patriotism, but they all agreed about the meaning of the term. They agreed, that is, that if it could sincerely be said of any political group that they had 'a mighty concern for the public good',[29] and specifically that they were 'the guardians of our liberties', animated by 'the spirit of liberty',[30] and 'continually at work in the support and defence of our liberties',[31] then it could certainly be said of such a group that they were entitled to 'the language of a patriot' and that their behaviour deserved 'the honourable name of patriotism'.[32]

The facts I am concerned to explain can thus be summarized as follows. The principle for the sake of which Bolingbroke and his

[28] This is cited in Jackman, *Man of Mercury*, p. 3 and in Hart, *Bolingbroke*, p. 82. For a famous near-contemporary definition of patriotism in similar terms, see George Berkeley, 'Maxims Concerning Patriotism' in *The Works*, ed. Alexander Fraser, 4 vols. (Oxford, 1901), IV, pp. 559–63. This prevailing definition of patriotism in terms of the defence of constitutional liberty is well brought out by Betty Kemp, 'Patriotism, Pledges and the People', in *A Century of Conflict*, ed. Martin Gilbert (London, 1966), pp. 37–46, esp. p. 39. See also Bonamy Dobrée, 'The Theme of Patriotism in the Poetry of the Early Eighteenth Century', *Proceedings of the British Academy*, 35 (1949), pp. 49–65. The definition seems to be somewhat mis-stated by several of Bolingbroke's recent interpreters. See, for example, Mansfield, *Statesmanship and Party Government*, pp. 68–9.

[29] [Edmund Gibson], *The Lord Bishop of London's Caveat against Aspersing Princes and their Administration* (London, 1731), p. 4.

[30] [Sir William Yonge], *Sedition and Defamation Displayed* (London, 1731), pp. vii and 38.

[31] [Lord Hervey], *The Conduct of the Opposition and the Tendency of Modern Patriotism* (London, 1734), p. 7.

[32] [William Arnall], *Opposition No Proof of Patriotism* (London, 1735), pp. 9 and 16.

supporters consistently claimed to be acting was that of patriotism, by which they meant (in Bolingbroke's own words) the 'cause of liberty and their country' and of 'the honour and interest of the nation'.[33] And the actual courses of action in which they then consistently engaged, in their opposition to Walpole's Ministry, were those of attacking the size of the land forces and the control of the House of Commons.

3

If those are the relevant facts, the question I wish to consider can now be directly raised. It is a question which has of course been raised by every interpreter of Bolingbroke's opposition to Walpole. It concerns the nature of the connections between the principle for the sake of which Bolingbroke and his party claimed to act, and the actual courses of action which they then pursued. What role was played by the opposition's professed principle of patriotism in governing their actions? Or, to put the same question the other way round, what weight should be placed on the opposition's professions of principle in attempting to explain their actual political actions?

One answer to these questions has until recently enjoyed the status of an orthodoxy. It can quite aptly be labelled the Namierite answer. The premise is that the tactics of Bolingbroke and his party were solely motivated 'by an insatiable ambition for power'.[34] It is then claimed to follow that their professions of principle, since they merely played the role of providing *ex post facto* rationalizations for this pursuit of 'ambition born of hate',[35] ought not to be given any weight at all in the attempt to explain their actual political behaviour. To assign Bolingbroke's ideas any independent role in directing the conduct of his opposition is simply to be 'off the track'.[36]

---

[33] Lord Bolingbroke, *The Works*, 4 vols. (London, 1844, reprinted London, 1967), I, p. 327 and II, p. 169. See also II, pp. 48, 171. The scepticism which greeted the attempt by Bolingbroke and his party to arrogate to themselves the title of 'patriots' was soon reflected in the generating of a new lexical entry for the term. The best-known example is in Samuel Johnson, *A Dictionary of the English Language*, 4 vols. (London, 1805 edition), *sub* 'Patriot': '1. One whose ruling passion is the love of his country. 2. It is sometimes used for a factious disturber of the government'.

[34] G. C. Robertson, *Bolingbroke* (The Historical Association, General Series pamphlet G6) (London, 1947), p. 3.

[35] H. J. Laski, *Political Thought in England: Locke to Bentham* (London, 1920), p. 90.

[36] Robert Walcott, ' "Sir Lewis Namier Considered" Considered', *The Journal of British Studies*, 3, no. 2 (1964), pp. 85–108, at p. 90.

Namier himself treated it as virtually an axiom about all political behaviour that the actors engage in it solely out of a desire to acquire and exercise political power. It follows that their professed principles, or rather their 'party names and cant', as Namier characteristically preferred to put it in *The Structure of Politics*, form no guide at all to the 'underlying realities' of politics.[37] They are invoked merely to ensure that the 'unconscious promptings' and 'inscrutable components' of personal ambition and the quest for domination which actually drive men into politics[38] are 'invested *ex post facto* with the appearance of logic and rationality'.[39] It follows that all such 'abstract ideals' must be mere epiphenomena, which play no independent role in determining any courses of political action, and which not only can but ought to be bypassed if we are to give realistic explanations of political behaviour. As Namier himself put it in his essay on 'Human Nature in Politics', 'what matters most is the underlying emotions, the music, to which ideas are a mere libretto, often of very inferior quality'.[40] And, as several recent commentators on his work have stressed, it was his express hope in studying eighteenth-century politics (and a large part of the attraction which the subject held for him)[41] to be able to show that 'considerations of principle or even of policy had only limited relevance' in this period,[42] that 'what mattered in politics' at this time 'was not attachment to principle but the struggle for office',[43] and in general that 'political ideas' are 'rarely in themselves the determinants of human action'.[44]

Namier 'empties Hanoverian Whiggery of principle',[45] and this approach has in turn had a profound impact on the more recent study of the period. The same assumptions are clearly embodied, for example,

[37] L. B. Namier, *The Structure of Politics at the Accession of George III*, 2nd ed. (London, 1957), Preface, p. vii. Walcott also speaks of 'cant' and attacks those who take Bolingbroke's writings 'at their face value', loc. cit., p. 90.

[38] L. B. Namier, *Personalities and Powers* (London, 1955), p. 3.

[39] L. B. Namier, *England in the Age of the American Revolution* (London, 1930), p. 147.

[40] Namier, *Personalities and Powers*, p. 4.

[41] This fact is brought out by Henry C. Winkler, 'Sir Lewis Namier', *The Journal of Modern History*, 35, no. 1 (1963), pp. 1–19, at p. 19.

[42] Geoffrey Holmes, *British Politics in the Age of Anne* (London, 1967), p. 6.

[43] Jack P. Greene, 'The Flight from Determinism: A Review of Recent Literature on the Coming of the American Revolution', *The South Atlantic Quarterly*, vol. 61 (1962), pp. 235–59, at p. 253.

[44] John Brooke, 'Namier and Namierism', *History and Theory*, 3 (1963–4), pp. 331–47, at p. 341.

[45] A. J. P. Taylor, *Rumours of War* (London, 1952), p. 17.

in Brooke's discussion of political parties in eighteenth-century England. The sole aim of the politicians, it is said, 'was simply to get into office'. They 'dignified' this 'struggle for power' as 'a conflict between opposing political ideas'. But these professed principles merely served to provide 'a respectable façade' for their otherwise naked desire for power. The historian will merely be allowing himself to be deceived by appearances if he comes to believe either 'that ideas, rather than instinctive aggressive forces, impel men towards conflict' or that men in politics are ever 'activated by public principle' rather than 'solely by the desire for office'.[46] A further important example of these same assumptions is provided by Foord's discussion of Bolingbroke's attack on Walpole in his recent book *His Majesty's Opposition, 1714–1830*. Although Bolingbroke may have claimed, it is said, that his opposition was governed by his political principles, such 'verbiage' cannot disguise 'his underlying belief that the situation which then existed forced this course of action upon a man of spirit and action'. Bolingbroke's professed principles are again taken to be mere rationalizations which were 'manufactured as debating points'. And, since they merely 'sprang from calculations of advantage', so they are taken to be 'in the final analysis irrelevant' to the explanation of Bolingbroke's political behaviour.[47]

It is clear, however, as some recent historians of eighteenth-century politics have begun to point out, that there is something unsatisfactory about this Namierite type of account. It seems, even if not actually mistaken, at least to be incomplete. For there seem to be certain features of Bolingbroke's campaign which this type of explanation remains unable to account for at all. The Namierite succeeds in giving an explanation of why Bolingbroke and his party chose to conduct *some* form of opposition to Walpole's Ministry: it is said that they wanted power for themselves, and evidently believed that their denunciations of Walpole in the Press and Parliament constituted a rational means of attaining this desired end. But none of these historians is able to offer a satisfactory explanation of why Bolingbroke and his party chose to conduct their opposition to Walpole according to a particular pattern, focusing their attack specifically on the issues of the land forces and the

---

[46] John Brooke, 'Party in the Eighteenth Century', in A. Natan, ed. *Silver Renaissance* (London, 1961), pp. 21–2, 24–5. See also John Brooke, *The Chatham Administration, 1766–1768* (London, 1956), p. 218.

[47] Foord, *Opposition*, pp. 78–9, 114 note, 136, 150.

control of the House of Commons. They have not, of course, failed
to notice that the policies pursued by Bolingbroke and his party in the
name of patriotism had a specific content, so that their professed
principles at least give the impression of having propelled their
behaviour in certain specific directions. It is rather that they have failed
to take seriously the possibility that there might be anything to be said
about the content of these ideas. Thus Namier himself, in referring to
the discussion of the same pattern of ideas by the young George III,
could only manage to dismiss their content as 'flapdoodle'.[48] Similarly,
Brooke's discussion of the contents of Bolingbroke's party programme
merely invokes the question-begging idea that there are 'fashions' in
opposition;[49] Foord's explanation falls back on the equally question-
begging claim that 'all political programmes need an altruistic key-
note';[50] and even Sutherland only manages to speak in a puzzled but
dismissive tone of the peculiar and unexplained fact that Bolingbroke's
party programme expressed 'an archaic, academic Whiggism'.[51]

Suppose it is conceded, however, that all the professions of patriotic
principle made by Bolingbroke and his party amounted to nothing
more than fashionable (or perhaps archaic) flapdoodle. There is still a
decision on the part of Bolingbroke and his party to be explained, the
decision to propagate one brand of flapdoodle rather than another,
and to propagate one particular brand with such remarkable consistency. We still need, that is, to be able to provide an explanation,
which the Namierites do not seem to be in a position to provide, of a
further belief which Bolingbroke and his party evidently held, as well
as their belief that their attack on Walpole's Ministry constituted a
rational means of trying to get power for themselves: the belief that it
was rational, granted their desire to attain power for themselves, to
choose to carry out their campaign in this particular way.

Once this lacuna in the Namierite type of explanation has been
detected we are left with two theoretically possible ways of trying to
account for it, and thus of trying to replace it with a better explanatory
scheme. Either the Namierites' argument must be *untrue*, or else the
form of their argument must be *invalid*. It is a striking fact that all the

[48] Namier, *American Revolution*, p. 95.
[49] Brooke in Natan, ed., *Silver Renaissance*, p. 25.
[50] Foord, *Opposition*, p. 150.
[51] Lucy Sutherland, 'The City of London in Eighteenth Century Politics' in *Essays Presented to Sir Lewis Namier*, ed. Richard Pares and A. J. P. Taylor (London, 1956), p. 58.

recent critics of the Namierite scheme of explanation have converged on the first possibility, while no one seems to have considered the second.[52] The thesis I now wish to argue, however, is that it is in fact the second possibility which needs to be investigated if the Namierite scheme of explanation is to be effectively criticized.

4

I turn first to consider the numerous attempts which have recently been made to deny the *truth* of the Namierite argument. These have all taken the same form. They have focused on the premise from which it has been said to follow that we do not need to assign any weight to the professed principles of Bolingbroke and his party in order to explain their actual political behaviour – the premise that Bolingbroke and his party were motivated solely by the desire to gain power for themselves. They have then argued that this premise is empirically mistaken, since Bolingbroke and his party were in fact sincere in their professed fears about the security of English political liberties. Their principle of patriotism is thus taken to have provided not just a rationalization of their desire for power, but a genuine motive for their attacks on Walpole's Ministry. It follows, according to this increasingly accepted scheme of explanation, that since the principle professed by Bolingbroke and his party was among their motives for action, it is not irrelevant but essential to cite it in order to explain their actual political behaviour.

This approach obviously reverts to an older, moralizing tradition of historical explanation which was first revived specifically as an anti-Namierite way of discussing eighteenth-century politics by Butterfield in his polemic *George III and the Historians*. What the Namierites had failed to allow for, according to Butterfield, was 'the operative force of ideas', deriving from the fact that at least some political agents are in fact 'sincerely attached to the ideals' for the sake of which they claim to act.[53] This possibility seems by now to have touched the conscience even of some of Namier's professed followers,[54] and it has recently

---

[52] The possibility is hinted at, however, at the start of the valuable essay by J. H. Burns, 'Bolingbroke and the Concept of Constitutional Government', *Political Studies*, 10 (1962), pp. 264–76.

[53] H. Butterfield, *George III and the Historians* (London, 1957), p. 209.

[54] See, for example, Ian R. Christie, *Myth and Reality in Late Eighteenth-Century British Politics* (London, 1970), esp. at p. 27.

been used by Holmes to provide the theoretical framework of his massive and avowedly anti-Namierite analysis in *British Politics in the Age of Anne*. Holmes's entire account is written in terms of the belief that the political conflicts of Anne's reign were concerned not merely with 'power and the quest for office', but were also 'concerned with real issues, involving the conflict of sincerely held principles'.[55]

When these assumptions are applied specifically to explain Bolingbroke's opposition to Walpole, it is of course true that a marked gain in explanatory power over the Namierite view is achieved. They can be deployed, first of all, to give a rival account of why Bolingbroke and his party engaged in *any* opposition to Walpole's Ministry. The explanation, it is said, is that they were genuinely motivated by a fear that liberty was being subverted, and thus by a genuine spirit of patriotism.[56] This is the assumption governing Hart's book on Bolingbroke's humanism, in which Bolingbroke's political behaviour is seen as 'essentially informed by principle'.[57] This is also the assumption governing Mansfield's book on Burke and Bolingbroke. It is a mistake, according to Mansfield, to think that Bolingbroke merely collected 'commonplace slogans in order to make his way into office'. His professed antipartisan principles were 'seriously meant and competently argued'. 'Patriotism' is in fact '*the* political theme of Bolingbroke'.[58] The same assumption again governs Kramnick's study of the whole Bolingbroke group. Their opposition, it is claimed, was genuinely 'based upon political ideals and principles and not merely the common interest of the outsider'.[59] Finally, the same assumption underlies both Grainger's recent account of Bolingbroke's political 'deviations' and Dickinson's recent biography. As Grainger puts it, Bolingbroke was in fact 'the leading exponent of a disinterested patriotic political theory'.[60] And, as Dickinson insists, 'though often regarded as an ambitious,

---

[55] Holmes, *Politics in the Age of Anne*, p. 114. See also pp. 93, 111, 113, etc.

[56] According to Hart, *Bolingbroke*, p. 57, and Dickinson, *Bolingbroke*, p. 183, the opposition were genuinely motivated by this fear *and* by the desire to gain office. The issue is similarly evaded in Bernard Bailyn, *The Origins of American Politics* (New York, 1968), in an account which appears to hover between regarding Bolingbroke as a 'cynical' and a 'sincere' political agent. Both these terms are actually used, p. 53.

[57] Hart, *Bolingbroke*, p. 26.

[58] Mansfield, *Statesmanship and Party Government*, pp. 59, 66. See also pp. 47–8, 112, 118–19.

[59] Kramnick, *Bolingbroke*, p. 5.

[60] Grainger in *Australian Journal*, 1969, p. 61.

self-seeking adventurer, Bolingbroke showed in his opposition to Walpole a clear vein of political principle'.[61]

The greater explanatory power of these assumptions lies in the fact that they can also be deployed to explain, in a way not open to the Namierites, why Bolingbroke and his party engaged in the *specific* course of action in which they in fact engaged in their opposition to Walpole's Ministry. The recent historiography divides at this point. One explanation, first suggested by Hart and much developed by Kramnick,[62] is that Bolingbroke and his party concentrated on the issues of the land forces and the control of the Commons out of a nostalgic regard for an older scheme of aristocratic political values which these policies, among others, were particularly felt to undermine. According to Hart, the whole of Bolingbroke's conduct 'should be understood as an attempt to preserve a variety of traditional values during a period of drastic social and intellectual change'.[63] Kramnick takes up the same point. Bolingbroke's 'reactive conservatism', as he calls it, should be seen as the 'product of his social existence', and specifically of his 'nostalgic flight from the political and economic innovations of his day'. His attack on the maintenance of the land forces must therefore 'be understood partly as a rejection of an impersonal professional and rootless organization'. His attack on the control of the Commons in particular, and on the corrupt world of the money economy in general, must be understood to follow from his perception that this was 'the major force contributing to the depersonalization of society and the destruction of the traditional bonds which naturally held men together'.[64] Correspondingly, the whole opposition platform of 'annual Parliaments, a militia, exclusion of placemen' must all be seen as 'steps to a freer past'.[65]

The other and simpler explanation, however, is that Bolingbroke and his party concentrated their attacks on the issue of the land forces and the control of the Commons simply because they genuinely feared that these were the policies most likely to undermine political liberties.[66]

[61] Dickinson, *Bolingbroke*, p. 184.

[62] It is also mentioned by Dickinson, *Bolingbroke*, at pp. 207–8 and p. 301.

[63] Hart, *Bolingbroke*, p. 164. See also pp. viii–ix and p. 142.

[64] Kramnick, *Bolingbroke*, pp. 8, 72–3, 150, 166.

[65] Kramnick in *History and Theory*, 1967, p. 40.

[66] This explanation is hinted at in H. N. Fieldhouse, 'Bolingbroke and the Idea of Non-Party Government', *History*, 23 (1938–9), pp. 41–56, at p. 50ff. It is sometimes adopted by Hart. See his *Bolingbroke*, pp. 20, 58, 64, 119. Jackman, *Man of Mercury*,

According to Mansfield, the reason for Bolingbroke's decision to concentrate his attack on the political privileges usurped by the ruling Whigs was 'not because he wanted similar privileges, but because he really believed that such privileges were unnecessary to the working of the constitution'. His 'attack on partisanship' is similarly said to have arisen from his genuine 'fear of religious parties and of divisive doctrines in general'.[67] Dickinson makes the same point. The focus of Bolingbroke's opposition, he claims, reflects his 'considerable sympathy' with the views of the independent gentry, and his 'genuine concern' about 'the increasing numbers of placemen in Parliament and the infrequency of elections. And his fears about the corruption of the constitution are similarly said to have provided 'a constant motivating force in his political career'.[68]

This new line of interpretation of Bolingbroke's political principles and practice follows exactly the account of his behaviour which Bolingbroke always insisted upon himself. This is perhaps quite enough in itself to make one suspicious. And it is I think true that the gain in explanatory power which this set of assumptions generates is more than outweighed by the *naïveté* and sheer loss of plausibility which is involved in having to rest the entire interpretation of Bolingbroke's political conduct on the presumption of his unwavering sincerity. I do not intend to try, however, actually to disprove these claims being made on behalf of Bolingbroke and his party as genuine men of principle. They would be very difficult actually to falsify, just as they would be very hard to substantiate, and have not of course been substantiated, but have merely been asserted, by the scholars I have cited. What I wish to suggest is rather that there is a shared and mistaken assumption underlying both this and the Namierite view of the connections between professed political principles and actual political behaviour.

The key assumption shared by the Namierite and the revisionist view of eighteenth-century British politics is that it is only if we can show that a given political principle genuinely acted as a motive for engaging in a given course of political action that we can hope to establish the need to refer to the principle in order to explain the action. The

---

moves inconsistently between this and the Namierite type of explanation, e.g. at
p. 141. Kemp in Gilbert, ed. *A Century of Conflict*, takes up a similar position, p. 38.

[67] Mansfield, *Statesmanship and Party Government*, p. 11. See also pp. 46, 66.

[68] Dickinson, *Bolingbroke*, pp. 184, 188.

Namierites take the view that such principles seldom if ever serve as motives, and thus seldom need to be cited. The revisionist view is that such principles serve as motives more often than not, and thus usually need to be cited. I now wish, however, to consider instead the possibility of denying this assumption itself, and thus of denying not the truth but the *validity* of the Namierite type of argument.

The focus of this line of argument would again be on the premise from which it has been said (by the Namierites) to follow that we do not need to assign any weight to the professed principles of Bolingbroke and his party in order to explain their political behaviour – the premise (to repeat) that Bolingbroke and his party were exclusively motivated by the desire to gain power for themselves. The argument would then be not that this premise is empirically false (as the revisionists have all sought to show) but rather that the argument involves a *non sequitur*.

It is this suggestion that I now wish to develop – the suggestion that the Namierite orthodoxy rests not on an historical but on a logical mistake. I shall not attempt in what follows to dispute the truth of the premise of the Namierite type of argument. I shall assume, indeed, that the Namierites are right in claiming – and the revisionists naïvely mistaken in denying – that the motives of Bolingbroke and his party were entirely unprincipled and self-interested. What I shall argue is that it is in the claim that *it follows from this* that no weight should be placed on their professions of principle when we come to explain their behaviour that the fallacy in the Namierite form of argument lies.

5

The point of departure in this attempt to connect the professed principles of Bolingbroke and his party with their actual political behaviour must be with the fact, which all students of this period of British political history have emphasized, that to engage in the sort of 'formed opposition' to the King's ministers which Bolingbroke and his party conducted between 1728 and 1734 was to engage, according to the constitutional conventions of the time, in an activity which (as Namier himself put it) was regarded as 'immoral' and 'tainted with disloyalty'.[69]

[69] Namier, *American Revolution*, p. 58. The idea of opposition as 'immoral' is taken up by Walcott in *Journal of British Studies*, 1964, p. 87. This issue is not properly raised in either Hart or Dickinson. But there is a good discussion in Mansfield, *Statesmanship and Party Government*, pp. 11–12 and pp. 112–16. Kramnick, *Bolingbroke*, pp. 155–62,

Bolingbroke's Whig opponents left him in no doubt, of course, about the unconstitutional character of his campaign against Walpole. Their accusations – conveniently summarized in the title of William Arnall's pamphlet *Opposition No Proof of Patriotism* – took two main forms. First and most dramatically, Bolingbroke was accused in a more or less explicit way of fomenting sedition and treason. The opposition, as an anonymous Whig pamphleteer put it, was engaged in 'such notorious acts as call their loyalty in question'. They were engaged in 'treasonable insolencies towards the throne'.[70] The most unguarded of these accusations were made by Walpole's friend Sir William Yonge in his pamphlet *Sedition and Defamation Displayed*. The opposition, he claimed, were 'attempting to raise sedition or rebellion'. They were 'infamous retailers' of 'sedition and treason', who 'publish seditious and traitorous libels against the Government and his Majesty himself'. They may appear to be acting under a veil of loyalty, but once this is torn off then 'sedition and treason stalk abroad'.[71] The other and more telling line of attack, however, simply consisted of pointing out that Bolingbroke and his party *were* engaged in an opposition[72] to the Ministry, and that this was in itself an enterprise of very doubtful legality. Arnall put the point by way of a rhetorical question. 'Can there be a more unjust thing than opposing measures necessary to the support and being of a State?' And later in the same pamphlet he answered himself. 'Where the laws rule, where liberty flourishes', as he claimed was the case in England, then *'General Opposition* ought to be out of countenance and cease.'[73] It followed, according to this prevailing view of the constitutional proprieties, that Bolingbroke's 'general opposition' was in itself a course of action 'repugnant to patriotism' which 'all calm and disinterested men will condemn'.[74]

The crucial importance for my present argument of the fact that

---

also takes up the point about Bolingbroke's rejection of party, and the consequent need to justify his opposition. See also Caroline Robbins, ' "Discordant Parties": a Study of the Acceptance of Party by Englishmen', *The Political Science Quarterly*, 73 (1958), pp. 505–29.

[70] Anon., *A Coalition of Patriots Delineated* (London, 1735), p. 4.

[71] [Yonge], *Sedition and Defamation*, pp. 1–2, 20, 33.

[72] The concept of opposition as an *activity* first dates from this period, according to the O.E.D.

[73] [Arnall], *Opposition*, p. 11.

[74] Ibid., pp. 7, 11. See also Anon., *A Persuasive to Impartiality and Candour in Judging of the Present Administration* (London, 1731), esp. p. 26ff.

'general opposition' was normally regarded as immoral at the time of Bolingbroke's campaign is that this meant that Bolingbroke and his party were engaged in a *prima facie* unjustifiable course of political action, and needed to be able to supply an explicit and plausible justification to their Whig opponents for this apparently unconstitutional behaviour. The need to provide such a justification, however, presented them with an intractable, as well as inescapable, ideological task. The task was inescapable since they would otherwise be unable to continue with the attack on Walpole – and thus with their undoubted ambition to oust him and offer themselves as an alternative government – except at the paradoxical cost of hearing their own conduct attacked in even more unfavourable terms. But the task was also, for two reasons, extremely difficult to perform. On the one hand, they could not (and did not)[75] seriously attempt to deny the fact that they were engaged in a 'general opposition' to the King's chosen Ministry. But on the other hand, they also could not deny the fact (since it was a fact about common usage) that this description was standardly used at this time as a means of attacking and condemning any course of action which could properly be described in this way. They were thus bound by the strongest motives of self-interest to continue with their 'general opposition', while they were also bound to accept (and did accept)[76] that the applicability of this description to their conduct implied a strongly unfavourable evaluation of it.[77]

It was thus essential for Bolingbroke and his party, as one of the conditions of being able to continue with an effective campaign of opposition, to try to offer a rival evaluative description of their own behaviour, in terms of which their Whig opponents might in effect be given a reason for believing, and might thus be forced to accept, that despite its *prima facie* appearance of unconstitutionality, their campaign

---

[75] This admission is made by Bolingbroke both at the start of his 'Remarks on the History of England' in *Works*, I, p. 301 (see also I, p. 428) and at the end of his 'Letter on the Spirit of Patriotism' in *Works*, II, pp. 358, 364, 369–70.

[76] This admission is also made at the start of the 'Remarks' in *Works*, I, pp. 304–5 and p. 329.

[77] I am making use here of the idea of an 'evaluative-descriptive' term in the way in which this concept has been used by recent ethical naturalists. For a discussion of the class of terms (of which the term 'opposition' in its eighteenth-century meaning is an instance) which are applicable in virtue of the facts of the case, but which are also standardly used, wherever applicable, to perform the speech-act either of commending or condemning, see John R. Searle, 'Meaning and Speech-Acts', *The Philosophical Review*, 71 (1962), pp. 423–32.

was justifiable in the circumstances. Now there are several theoretically possible tactics for trying to bring off the ideological task which, I am arguing, it was essential for Bolingbroke and his party to be able to perform – that of attempting to legitimate their *prima facie* unjustifiable course of action by means of redescribing it in an alternative (favourably instead of unfavourably) evaluative way.[78] One of the most powerful of these tactics, which Bolingbroke and his party in the event attempted to adopt, consists of trying to establish that one's opponents are simply failing to perceive certain facts about the situation in which one is acting, in failing to perceive that the ordinary indicators[79] for applying a favourable description to one's action are in fact present in the given situation. To be able to make this empirical claim look plausible is to be able to argue either that the applicability of this new and favourable description to one's action entails the *defeat* of the original and unfavourable description, or at least to argue that the new description, even if it does not defeat the original one, can at least be seen to *override* its unfavourable evaluation by providing a more powerfully favourable evaluation.

It will by now be clear why it was rational and indeed essential for Bolingbroke and his party to try to exhibit a plausible relationship between some political principle and their actual course of political action, even if they were not really motivated by, and did not really believe in, any political principles at all. Since it was a condition of being able to continue with an effective campaign of opposition that they should be able to supply some recognizable justification for their *prima facie* unconstitutional behaviour, it follows that it was essential to be able to refer to some already accepted political principle as a means both of characterizing their opposition and their alleged motive for engaging in it, and thus as a means of seeking to legitimate as well as to redescribe their own behaviour. It will also be clear why it was rational for Bolingbroke and his party to redescribe and legitimate their behaviour specifically by choosing to profess the principle of patriotism. If they could somehow make it plausible to claim that their

---

[78] For an account of the relations between social principles and actions, setting out ways in which one can try to legitimate an action by redescribing it, see my article 'Some Problems in the Analysis of Political Thought and Action', *Political Theory*, 2, August 1974.

[79] I follow Hilary Putnam's use of this term, in preference to speaking of 'criteria', for reasons which he has stated in 'Dreaming and "Depth Grammar"' in R. J. Butler, ed., *Analytical Philosophy*, Series I (Oxford, 1962), pp. 211–35.

apparently unconstitutional attack on the King's Ministry was genuinely motivated by the spirit of patriotism, and could properly be characterized as a patriotic act, then they could hope to fulfil two vital ideological tasks on their own behalf. They could hope, first of all, plausibly to claim that it must be an empirical mistake for their Whig opponents not to perceive that the action of opposing the Ministry over the issue of the land forces and the control of the Commons was a case of defending the political liberties of their fellow-countrymen, and was thus a case of patriotism, since their action could be seen to yield these accepted indicators for the application of this favourable descriptive term. They could then hope to use this new description of their motivation and corresponding action to defeat, or at least override, the existing and unfavourable descriptions which had been given of their behaviour. First, the claim that their behaviour could properly be described as patriotic would entail the defeat of most of the wilder accusations which had been made against them. A course of action, for example, which can properly be described as patriotic cannot also be described as seditious or treasonable. Secondly, and even more importantly, the same claim could also be used to override the one major criticism of their campaign which they could not hope to defeat – the criticism implied by the description of it as a case of 'general opposition'. No Whig would dare to argue that the preservation of a constitutional convention should be ranked higher as a political value than the preservation of the political liberties of Englishmen. It followed that Bolingbroke and his party would be able, if only they could succeed in presenting themselves plausibly as patriots, to concede that their campaign might properly be described in unfavourable terms as a case of general opposition, for they would be able to insist that, since it was also an act of patriotism to engage in general opposition in the circumstances, this doubt about the justifiability of their conduct could safely be overridden.

This brings me to what I take to be Bolingbroke's great *coup* as a politician. He not only recognized his inescapable need to be able to claim (however disingenuously) to be motivated by some accepted political principle in order to be able to confront his Whig enemies with a plausible justification for his attack on Walpole's Ministry. He also recognized that a special plausibility, as well as an obvious value, would in fact attach to claiming that the specific principle motivating his behaviour was that of patriotism. What he perceived was that if his party professed this particular principle, this would give them the best chance of being able to justify their opposition in the circumstances. And this strategy was in turn owed to Bolingbroke's fundamental perception that if his party concentrated their attack on two particular policies being pursued by the Whig Ministry – the issue of the land forces and the control of the Commons – this would in turn give them the best chance of being able to make the Whig Ministry's conduct appear unpatriotic in the light of the Whigs' own most cherished beliefs about political liberty.

The essence of Bolingbroke's *coup* was thus to perceive that, according to the most impeccably Whig canons of beliefs about the nature of the agencies by which political liberties are usually and most readily jeopardized, the Whig Ministry could in fact be claimed to be pursuing certain policies which could quite plausibly be made to look like a threat to such liberties. Bolingbroke's corresponding strategy then consisted of concentrating on just those policies, magnifying their importance with a good deal of cynical emphasis, and insisting that since the Whigs themselves professed to believe that such policies normally had the effect of undermining political liberties, to oppose them must, in the circumstances, be an act of a true patriot, since it was to be concerned with the preservation of the political liberties of one's fellow-countrymen.

6

The precise mechanics of this *coup* can readily be illustrated if we now turn to the great tradition of seventeenth-century Whig political theory, and to the nature of the beliefs which Bolingbroke's Whig opponents had inherited from this tradition on the subject of political liberty and the means by which such liberties are most readily sustained or lost.

The main source in the Commonwealth period itself for the ideas of the so-called 'Whig canon'[80] of 'Commonwealthmen' lay in James Harrington's *Oceana*, first published in 1656. Harrington's views on political liberty, which in turn derived to a great extent from

---

[80] For a general survey of the writers in the 'Whig canon', see the book by Caroline Robbins and the article by Pocock (which makes use of Robbins's research) cited in note 1, above. For the seventeenth-century background, see Z. S. Fink, *The Classical Republicans*, 2nd ed. (Northwestern, 1962).

Machiavelli's *Discourses*, were first generally propagated, in a somewhat modified form, by a group of Whig 'neo-Harringtonians' associated with Shaftesbury's campaign at the time of the Exclusion Crisis,[81] a group which included Nevile[82] and Petyt[83] among political writers, and Somers among the Whig grandees.[84] The most crucial period, however, for the propagation of this pattern of ideas came at the turn of the century. The beginning of this renewed publicity can perhaps be dated from the re-issue in 1694 of the translation of Machiavelli's complete political works which Nevile had published some twenty years before.[85] The same year saw the publication of *Bibliotheca Politica* by Locke's Whig friend James Tyrrell,[86] as well as an *Account of Denmark* by the 'independent Whig' Molesworth, which contained a Machiavellian analysis of the causes of Denmark's loss of political liberty in the *coup* of 1660.[87] But the most important years for the establishment of the Whig canon of ideas about political liberty were between 1697 and 1700. The year 1697 saw the publication of the first version of Andrew Fletcher's *Discourse on Government*,[88] as well as the collaboration of John Trenchard with Walter Moyle, at that time sitting as an 'independent Whig' in the House of Commons.[89] The

[81] For this group, and its modifications of Harrington's doctrine, see Pocock, *Politics, Language and Time*, pp. 115–33. For a discussion of Machiavelli's apparent influence on Harrington, see Felix Raab, *The English Face of Machiavelli* (London, 1964), pp. 185–217.

[82] Henry Nevile's main tract was *Plato Redivivus*, first published 1681, reprinted in Caroline Robbins, ed., *Two Republican Tracts* (London, 1969), with details of Nevile's life and works, pp. 5–20, 61–200.

[83] Petyt's main tract was *The Ancient Right of the Commons of England Asserted* (London, 1680). Petyt is discussed in J. G. A. Pocock, *The Ancient Constitution and the Feudal Law* (London, 1957), pp. 186–93.

[84] Somers's main literary contribution to the debate at this stage was his anonymously published tract *The Security of Englishmen's Lives* (London, 1681).

[85] Nevile had (anonymously) published *The Works of the Famous Nicholas Machiavel* (London, 1675), 'newly and faithfully translated into English.'

[86] [James Tyrrell], *Bibliotheca Politica* (London, 1684). Tyrrell's work, like Petyt's, mainly took the form of a 'Whig' account of the Ancient Constitution. For the connections between the two writers, see Pocock, *Ancient Constitution*, pp. 187–8.

[87] [Robert Molesworth], *An Account of Denmark, As it was in the Year 1692* (London, 1694). Ch. VII is devoted to analysing 'the manner how the kingdom of Denmark became hereditary and absolute'.

[88] [Andrew Fletcher], *A Discourse Concerning Militias and Standing Armies* (London, 1697) is identical with the same writer's *A Discourse of Government* cited in note 90 below.

[89] [John Trenchard and Walter Moyle], *An Argument, Shewing, that a Standing Army is inconsistent with a Free Government* (London, 1697). According to the British Museum

following year saw the publication of further tracts by both Fletcher and Trenchard,[90] as well as the publication for the first time of both the *Discourses concerning Government* by the Whigs' own martyr, Algernon Sydney,[91] and the Republican Edmund Ludlow's *Memoirs* of the Civil War and Commonwealth periods.[92] Finally, the year 1700 saw the publication of the first collected edition of Harrington's political works. This was edited by John Toland,[93] who also contributed in his own right to the establishment of the Whig canon of ideas with the publication in 1695 of his *Danger of Mercenary Parliaments* and in 1701 of his *Art of Governing by Parties*.[94]

The attitudes voiced by these writers were to be repeated again in a number of works published in the years surrounding the crisis of the South Sea Bubble. Thus the year 1720 saw the reissue of Nevile's translation of Machiavelli and of Ludlow's *Memoirs*; the following year saw the publication of Molesworth's essay on the principles of an independent Whig;[95] and the same period saw the collaboration between Trenchard and Thomas Gordon, which eventually resulted in the publication of *Cato's Letters* in 1724.[96] Two years later there

---

catalogue, Walter Moyle was the exclusive author of *The Second Part of an Argument, Shewing, that a Standing Army is inconsistent with a Free Government* (London, 1697). For this collaboration, see Kramnick, *Bolingbroke*, pp. 244 and 254–6. But Kramnick appears to confuse the above works with the separate *History of Standing Armies* which Trenchard published in the following year. See note 90, below.

[90] [Andrew Fletcher], *A Discourse of Government with Relation to Militias* (Edinburgh, 1698). [John Trenchard], *A Short History of Standing Armies in England* (London, 1698).

[91] Algernon Sydney, *Discourses Concerning Government* (London, 1698).

[92] Edmund Ludlow, *Memoirs*, ed. C. H. Firth, 2 vols. (Oxford, 1894). See esp. I, pp. 114–5, 151–67, 203–5 and 245–6.

[93] James Harrington, *The Oceana . . . and his Other Works*, ed. John Toland (London, 1700).

[94] [John Toland], *The Danger of Mercenary Parliaments* (n.p., n.d.). The British Museum catalogue ascribes this work to Toland (though it is not mentioned in his *D.N.B.* entry) and dates it to 1695. [John Toland], *The Art of Governing by Parties* (London, 1701).

[95] This was published as a preface (pp. i–xxxvi) to the 1721 ed. (not the 1711 ed., as Kramnick claims, *Bolingbroke*, pp. 252–3) of *Franco Gallia . . . translated . . . by the Author of the Account of Denmark, The second edition, with additions and a New Preface by the Translator* (London, 1721).

[96] Between January 1720 and June 1721 they published a weekly, *The Independent Whig*, which appeared later in 1721 in book form. Between November 1720 and July 1723 they published a series of letters signed by 'Cato', first in the *London Journal*, later in the *British Journal*. These appeared, with a number of additions by Gordon, as *Cato's Letters*, 4 vols. (London, 1724).

appeared a collected edition of Moyle's works,[97] and two years after that an edition of Tacitus by Gordon, with a long introduction pointing up the Whig morals of Tacitus's *History*.[98] It remains true, however, that the most important years for the formation of the Whig canon of ideas about political liberty were the years around 1698, and it is on the doctrines set out in the writings published at that time that I shall concentrate.

In discussing the topic of political liberty, all these writers advance the same three major claims. The first is the claim, derived from a Polybian and ultimately an Aristotelian vision of the special virtues of mixed constitutions, that political liberty is assured whenever the constitution of a nation is 'balanced' between its executive and legislative parts, and is threatened whenever that balance is encroached upon or lost. There is a clear source for this belief in Machiavelli's *Discourses* with their constant stress on the need (as Nevile translated it) to preserve popular liberty 'with vigilance' and to 'secure it against the encroachments of others'.[99] This ideal of a balanced constitution is then taken up by Harrington, who devotes the whole of the start of his 'Preliminaries' to analysing the relations between various forms of constitutional balance and various degrees of political liberty.[100] And from *Oceana* this assumption passed into the whole Whig canon. Thus Sydney's discussion of regulated monarchy ends with a plea for the 'medium between tyranny and popularity' as the only constitutional guarantee against 'vice and corruption', while his discussion of political liberty includes the insistence that a 'mixed' constitution represents the best means of maintaining it.[101] Similarly, Molesworth's chapter on the Danish form of government is based on the claim that it was only while a balance between the elective kingship and the frequent meetings of the estates was maintained that Denmark was able to maintain her political liberties.[102] Again, the whole aim of Toland's attack on

[97] Thomas Sargent, ed., *The Works of Walter Moyle Esq.*, 2 vols. (London, 1726), a collection of Moyle's unpublished works. His previously published works were issued in the following year by Anthony Hammond as *The Whole Works of W. Moyle Esq.* (London, 1727).

[98] Thomas Gordon, *The Works of Tacitus*, vol. I (1728). The translation is prefaced by a series of ten 'Discourses', the last of which is 'Of Armies and Conquest'. This preface was commended by Bolingbroke, *Works*, I, p. 315.

[99] [Nevile], *Machiavel*, p. 274.

[100] *Works*, ed. Toland, esp. at pp. 54–57.

[101] Sydney, *Discourses*, pp. 145, 241.

[102] [Molesworth], *Account*, esp. pp. 44–5.

mercenary parliaments is to suggest that his fellow-countrymen will 'fruitlessly bewail the loss of our liberties' unless they now act to maintain 'a poise and balance' in the constitution, and to prevent 'encroaching power'.[103] And in dedicating his edition of Harrington's works to the Lord Mayor and Aldermen of London, Toland begins with a passionate declaration that 'liberty is the true spring' of their 'prodigious trade', and that their liberty is in turn owed to the balanced workings of the constitution.[104]

The second major claim about political liberty advanced by all these writers is that to study the cause of liberty and its loss is inevitably to study the history of the various European countries which have passed from a state of popular freedom into the slavery of absolutism. This stress on the need to learn from the lessons of history again has a clear source in Machiavelli's *Discourses*, which begin with an attack on ignorance of the past and an expression of the hope that (as Nevile translated it) 'the records of ancient history will serve our turn'.[105] The importance of seeking such lessons in the past is again taken up by Harrington, whose 'Preliminaries' to *Oceana* include his famous fictional history of England and his discussion of the morals which he believed to follow from it.[106] And again this stress on the exemplary significance of historical study then passed into the whole Whig canon. Thus Sydney's *Discourses* are organized in a completely historical way, his points being variously illustrated from the histories of ancient Athens, Rome and Sparta as well as modern Denmark, France and Italy.[107] Similarly Molesworth not only writes an historical account of Denmark's loss of political liberty, but specifically commends a combination of travel and historical study on the grounds that this will 'teach a gentleman who makes right use of it by what steps slavery has within these last two hundred years crept upon Europe'.[108] Again, Tyrrell's *Bibliotheca Politica* mainly consists of a conventional Whig history of the English ancient constitution, while Toland's *Art of Governing by Parties* consists of a history of the way in which this art

---

[103] [Toland], *Mercenary Parliaments*, pp. 1–2. Compare the *Art*, with the fulsome tribute in its opening chapter to the liberties of the subject guaranteed by the proper working of the mixed constitution.
[104] *Works*, ed. Toland, Dedication, pp. ii–iii.
[105] [Nevile], *Machiavel*, p. 288.
[106] *Works*, ed. Toland, pp. 66–70.
[107] Sydney, *Discourses*, e.g. at pp. 153, 155, 226, 249, 284, etc.
[108] [Molesworth], *Account*, Preface, Sig. B, 3a.

'was set on foot among us' by the Stuarts, and of the morals to be drawn from the disastrous results.[109]

The third major claim advanced by all these writers about political liberty concerns the nature of the agencies which history shows have been employed with the greatest frequency and success by aspiring absolutist courts to alter the balance of free constitutions and thus to extinguish the political liberties of the citizens living under them. All these writers in fact focus on two main agencies which, they all claim, have always been particularly liable to undermine free constitutions. The first is the employment by the king and the court of a standing mercenary army. Again, a clear source for this fear can be found in Machiavelli's *Discourses*, with their constant denunciations of all auxiliary and mercenary armies, and their corresponding insistence that a free nation ought to be defended only by its own armed and independent citizens.[110] This essentially Aristotelian theme is again taken up by Harrington, two of whose 'Political Aphorisms' summarize the significance of this theme in relation to political liberty. One is the claim that 'where the spirit of the people is impatient of a Government by arms, and desirous of a Government by laws, there the spirit of the people is not unfit to be trusted with their liberty'. The contrasting aphorism claims that 'where there is a standing army, and not a formed Government, there the army will have dictatorial power'.[111] And again, this stress on the danger of standing armies, and the corresponding need for any state which prizes its freedom to allow its citizens to bear arms for themselves, passed into the whole Whig tradition – eventually becoming enshrined, with ironic consequences, in that most Harringtonian of official documents, the American Constitution.[112] Thus Sydney, as well as giving a Machiavellian analysis of the use of a standing army to corrupt the republican constitution of ancient Rome, also discusses modern France and Denmark in the same terms. He claims that it was 'the strength of a mercenary soldiery' which allowed the King of Denmark to 'overthrow all the laws of his country', and that it is the power of his standing armies which prevents the subjects

---

[109] [Toland], *Art*, p. 8. See also p. 119, for a list of historical examples.
[110] See especially Discourse I, Chs. 21, 43; Discourse II, Chs. 10, 16, 30. See [Nevile], *Machiavel*, pp. 293–4, 312, 344–6, 351–3, 372–3.
[111] *Works*, ed. Toland, pp. 515, 521.
[112] For this pedigree of ideas, see Robbins, *Commonwealthman*, and Bernard Bailyn, *The Ideological Origins of the American Revolution* (Cambridge, Mass., 1967).

of the King of France from being able even 'to defend their own rights against him'.[113] Molesworth makes the same point about Denmark, claiming that the reason the Danes lost their political liberties, and cannot be expected to regain them, is that their King maintains against them 'a standing army composed for the most part of foreigners'.[114] Similarly, both Ludlow and Tyrrell in effect draw the same moral from even nearer home. Ludlow's *Memoirs* contain an account of the behaviour of the army during the interregnum which scared every good Whig for generations,[115] while Tyrrell's savagely hostile account of the reign of James II includes the charge that the King had begun 'to maintain a standing army' which he hoped might be put to the characteristic purpose of fighting 'against the religion and liberties of the country'.[116]

There is a special group[117] of these Whig writers, moreover, including Fletcher, Moyle and Trenchard, who concentrate virtually the whole of their attention on discussing the threat to political liberty which a standing army invariably represents. Fletcher's *Discourse* discusses 'the alteration of Government which happened in most countries of Europe about the year fifteen-hundred' and 'was fatal to their liberty'. There was originally 'a balance that kept those Governments steady' and 'an effectual provision against the encroachments of the crown'. Liberty gave way to tyranny when this balance was disrupted. And the major agency of this disruption was that princes 'were allowed to raise armies of volunteers and mercenaries', so that 'the power of the sword was transferred from the subject to the King', who was thus able to use the sword against his own subjects' liberties.[118] Trenchard and Moyle take up exactly the same theme, studying Europe's relapse into absolutist rule, and claiming that 'if we enquire how these unhappy nations have lost that precious jewel, liberty', the simple answer is that they all 'permitted a standing army to be kept

---

[113] Sydney, *Discourses*, pp. 148, 156.

[114] [Molesworth], *Account*, p. 268.

[115] They are cited, for example, in Trenchard's *History of Standing Armies*, with the exhortation to read them 'if any man doubt whether a standing army is slavery', p. 1.

[116] [Tyrrell], *Bibliotheca*, pp. 666, 687.

[117] For a paraphrase of their arguments, and those of their opponents, and for the background to the discussion, see E. Arnold Miller, 'Some Arguments Used by the English Pamphleteers, 1697–1700, Concerning a Standing Army', *The Journal of Modern History*, 18 (1946), pp. 306–13, and J. R. Western, *The English Militia in the Eighteenth Century* (London, 1965).

[118] [Fletcher], *Discourse*, pp. 5–6, 9, 114–15.

among them', with the result that the free 'Gothic balance' of rulers and people was disrupted, and liberty was in consequence lost.[119] Moyle later repeats the same point, claiming that 'in all ages and parts of the world, a standing army has been the never-failing instrument of enslaving a nation'.[120] And Trenchard later draws the same moral from the history of England, claiming that it has always been standing armies which 'have brought us from one tyranny to another'.[121] Throughout this literature on standing armies the unvarying claim, as Trenchard and Moyle put it, is that 'to know whether a people are free or slaves, it is necessary only to ask whether there is an army kept amongst them'.[122]

The second and more insidious way in which the political liberties of a free nation are most readily lost, according to all these writers, is when the citizens are prevented from involving themselves, in a free and independent spirit, in the business of government. Machiavelli had laid it down that to be vigorously involved in political life, even at the cost of encouraging 'tumults', was to be a citizen of *virtù* (which Nevile often translated as 'public spirit');[123] to lose or be prevented from enjoying such a sense of involvement was to be politically corrupt. Harrington took over both these technical terms, as well as Machiavelli's corresponding belief that political liberty can be assured only where such corruption[124] is checked and balanced by the maintenance of political virtue. Harrington's 'model' of a Commonwealth in *Oceana* is in fact filled with detailed suggestions about the sorts of devices which may serve to ensure that the citizens at large do not lose a sense of active involvement in political life – the devices of annual elections, rotation of offices, and the whole paraphernalia of

---

[119] [Trenchard and Moyle], *An Argument*, p. 4.
[120] [Moyle], *The Second Part of an Argument*, p. 10.
[121] [Trenchard], *History of Standing Armies*, pp. iv–v.
[122] [Trenchard and Moyle], *An Argument*, p. 11.
[123] See especially Discourse III, Chs. 19–22, 29–31. See [Nevile], *Machiavel*, pp. 404–8, 413–17. On the meaning of *virtù*, and its place in the development of Machiavelli's thought, see Hans Baron, 'Machiavelli: The Republican Citizen and the Author of *The Prince*', *The English Historical Review*, 76 (1961), pp. 217–53. On the value of 'tumults', see Discourse I, Ch. 4, in [Nevile], *Machiavel*, p. 273.
[124] For the special meaning of the term 'corruption' as inherited from the Machiavellian tradition, see especially Pocock, *Politics, Language and Time*, pp. 125–6, 129–32. See also Hart, *Bolingbroke*, p. 93, and Mansfield (a defective statement of the point), *Statesmanship and Party Government*, p. 67. It sometimes seems that the Namierites, in discussing the claim of the eighteenth-century opponents of the Whigs that the constitution was being corrupted, use the term 'corruption' in an anachronistically narrow sense.

constitutional checks and balances which American 'empirical' theorists of democracy continue to celebrate. And again, this Machiavellian stress on the need for independence and *virtù* then passed into the whole Whig tradition. Thus Sydney gives an intensely repetitious account of the general need for 'strength, valour and spirit' as 'essentially necessary to the establishment and preservation of liberty', and the specific need for each citizen to involve himself in 'the public good' with 'industry and affection'.[125] Similarly, Molesworth's whole discussion of how Denmark became an absolute monarchy can be read as an attack on 'the enslaving of the spirits of the people', which made it so easy for the King to trick the nobles and Commons into signing away their political rights.[126] And Toland's chief fear about 'mercenary Parliaments' is their encouragement of 'supineness and base neglect', so that the citizens at large, having lost any sense of either independence or political concern, may then 'give away with their own breath and free consent all their rights to their estates and lives'.[127] The twin poles of political liberty and slavery are thus represented in all these writers by the corresponding Machiavellian terms 'virtue' and 'corruption'. A virtuous people will be active, will 'check and curb' any 'ambitious and overgrown statesmen', and will thus be able to maintain their political liberties. A corrupt people will be supine, will avoid or be prevented from acting as anything more than 'unconcerned spectators' of the nation's political life, and will in consequence allow the 'debauching of their honest principles' to be brought about by those whose ambition it is to subvert their political liberties.[128]

7

It is precisely this pattern of ideas which we find once more if we now turn to Bolingbroke's two most important political works, written during the most active period of his opposition to Walpole's Ministry, the *Remarks on the History of England*, and the *Dissertation on Parties*. First of all, we find in the *Remarks* a complete endorsement of the Whig belief in the fundamental importance of maintaining a balanced

[125] Sydney, *Discourses*, pp. 215, 218, 221.
[126] [Molesworth], *Account*, Preface, Sig. B, 3a. See also the Conclusion, in which Molesworth stresses that the King of Denmark has 'taken care' to make 'all the people poor in Spirit, as well as in purse', p. 267.
[127] [Toland], *Mercenary Parliaments*, p. 8.
[128] Ibid., pp. 4–5.

constitution. Bolingbroke summarizes the doctrine in a much-repeated epigram to the effect that 'in a constitution like ours, the safety of the whole depends upon the balance of the parts, and the balance of the parts on their mutual independency on each other'.[129] To preserve this 'balance of power', it is said, is to assure that we 'secure to ourselves, and to our latest posterity, the possession of that liberty which we have long enjoyed'.[130] But to disrupt this balance is to assure the collapse of those liberties. This is the main lesson which Bolingbroke continually seeks to derive from his outline of English history. The unique grandeur of Elizabeth's reign is said to have been based on her exact understanding of this essential link between political liberty and the balance of the constitution. The collapse of political liberty, both in the Wars of the Roses and under the Stuarts, is correspondingly said to have been brought about by the attempts which were made during both those periods to alter the balance of the constitution.[131]

Bolingbroke also endorses the characteristic Whig belief that any study of the ways in which political liberties are usually gained or lost must necessarily be an historical study. Both his own main political works are organized as histories. The *Dissertation on Parties* contains a sequence of chapters in which the loss of political liberty is explained in turn in the case of ancient Rome, modern Spain and modern France.[132] And it was of course Bolingbroke, typically, who coined the famous epigram which summarizes the key assumption governing this approach to the use of historical evidence. 'History', he said, 'is philosophy teaching by examples.'[133]

[129] This classic statement of the idea of the balanced constitution comes in Letter VII of the 'Remarks on the History of England' in Bolingbroke's *Works*, I, pp. 328–35, at p. 331. See also the account in 'A Dissertation on Parties' of the need for a mixed and balanced constitution in *Works*, II, pp. 114, 119, 148.

[130] Bolingbroke, *Works*, II, 112.

[131] The reign of Elizabeth is discussed in Letter XIII of the 'Remarks' in *Works*, I, pp. 363–9. See also I, pp. 392–3, 406. For the Wars of the Roses, see I, pp. 335–41, where (at p. 339) Trenchard's *History of Standing Armies* is approvingly cited. For the comparison with the Stuarts, see I, pp. 413–21 and p. 428. The connection between political liberty and the balance of the constitution is also traced in the 'Dissertation on Parties', in *Works*, II, esp. at pp. 80–1, 86, 95, 99, 112, 115, 126, and the summary at pp. 141–2.

[132] See Letters XIII to XV of the 'Dissertation', in *Works*, II, pp. 115–39.

[133] See Letter II of the 'Letters on the Study and Use of History', in *Works*, II, p. 177. Bolingbroke's use of history is discussed in Hart, *Bolingbroke*, pp. 99ff., in Jackman, *Man of Mercury*, pp. 44–69, by Mansfield, *Statesmanship and Party Government*, pp. 59ff., and by Kramnick in *History and Theory*, 1967, pp. 33–56.

The most important beliefs from the Whig canon which Bolingbroke endorses, however, concern the nature of the agencies by which
political liberties are most usually and readily subverted. First of all, he
finds that the same weapon was used to deliver the *coup de grâce* in the
destruction of political liberty both in ancient Rome and in modern
Spain: the use of 'the force of an army' against the people.[134] In Rome
'the principal men' finally brought about the collapse of the Republic
when they 'employed the commands they had of armies' as well as
their positions in the state to further their own ambitions.[135] And in
Spain the standing army played an even more direct role in the subversion of political liberty. Despite an ordinance of the Cortes 'against
increasing the standing forces of the kingdom', the kings continually
found 'pretences for keeping armies on foot'. The characteristic and
fatal outcome of this policy was finally revealed when Ferdinand, who
had raised 'a regular, disciplined army' ostensibly to defend Navarre
against the French, then turned it upon his own people, 'marched into
Castile, defeated the commons, and extinguished liberty'.[136] The
general moral is that 'standing armies have been generally the instruments of overturning free governments'.[137]

Finally, Bolingbroke also endorses the Whig belief that the other
characteristic way of subverting liberty and bringing about absolutism
consists of corrupting and encroaching upon the independence of the
citizen body, thus preventing them from involving themselves, in a
properly independent and public-spirited manner, in the nation's
political affairs. He follows Machiavelli in attributing the collapse of
the Roman Republican constitution to its 'want of a third estate', and
thus to the incapacity of the people to check and balance the power of
the executive. He makes exactly the same point in discussing the drift
of the French constitution into absolutism. 'The great original defect
of having but two estates to share the supreme power' with 'the constant desire of encroaching' and the lack of popular surveillance is said
to be a critical objection 'common to the Roman and to the French
constitutions'. It is in discussing the case of modern Spain, however,
that Bolingbroke gives the most unequivocally Machiavellian analysis
of the constitutional devices said to have been used by the rulers of
Castile to 'enslave' their subjects. The Castilians originally possessed,
in the Cortes, a representative assembly which might 'truly be com-

---

[134] Bolingbroke, *Works*, II, p. 132.   [135] Ibid., I, p. 304.   [136] Ibid., II, p. 129.
[137] Ibid., I, p. 427. See also I, pp. 341, 371, and I, pp. 92, 132.

pared to a British Parliament', and which guaranteed the citizens their liberties so long as they remained active and independent in running it. Their freedom was struck down, however, with 'an incurable, fatal wound' when 'prostitute wretches were found' who were prepared to maintain 'that the necessary independency of the prince could not be supported, without allowing a corrupt dependency of the Cortes on him'. The people were then rendered unable to check the encroaching power of the Court and its dependent ministers with their 'titles, places, pensions and grants'. The result was that the King gained 'such an influence over the Cortes as overturned at last the whole constitution' and enslaved the formerly free Castilian people'.[138] The general moral is that 'though it be proper in all limited Monarchies to watch and guard against all concessions or usurpations that may destroy the balance of power, on which the preservation of liberty depends, yet it is certain that concessions to the crown from the other constituent parts of the legislature are almost alone to be feared'.[139]

8

With this survey of the beliefs about political liberty held by the writers in the Whig canon, we are now in a position, I believe, to trace out the nature of the connections between the principle for the sake of which Bolingbroke and his party consistently claimed to be acting – that of patriotism – and the actual course of action which they then consistently followed – that of denouncing the size of the land forces and the Ministry's devices for controlling the House of Commons.[140]

---

[138] For this discussion of Rome, France and Spain – the source of all these quotations – see ibid., II, pp. 123, 125, 128, 132.

[139] Ibid., II, p. 126. See also II, pp. 26, 138.

[140] The connections between this Whig canon of beliefs about political liberty on the one hand, and the actual conduct of Bolingbroke's campaign of opposition on the other, has not been traced in the existing secondary literature. Neither Hart, *Bolingbroke*, nor Mansfield, *Statesmanship and Party Government*, discusses the views of the 'Whig canon' of writers at all. Pocock's analysis of the 'neo-Harringtonians' has been taken up both by Kramnick, *Bolingbroke*, Ch. IX, and by Dickinson, *Bolingbroke*, Ch. XI, but neither Pocock nor Kramnick discusses these ideas in relation to Bolingbroke's campaign of opposition, and Dickinson's account seems only to imply the connections. Both Kramnick and Dickinson, moreover, espouse general theories about Bolingbroke's motivation which seem to me to prevent them from establishing the nature of the connections between Bolingbroke's professed principles and the actual conduct of his opposition, while Pocock's account (see *Politics, Language and Time*, p. 105) remains deliberately uncommitted about the nature of this connection.

We can now explain, first of all, why Bolingbroke and his party adopted and consistently carried out this particular political programme. According to the writers in the Whig canon, the two policies most liable to undermine political liberties were the keeping up by the Crown of a standing mercenary army, and the interference by the executive with the capacity of the citizens and their representatives to maintain a sense of free and independent involvement in the nation's political life. First, we can now explain why Bolingbroke and his party concentrated on the issue of the land forces. Correspondingly, we can explain why they concentrated on their own demand for the establishment instead of an effective citizen militia. They chose to focus on this issue because they perceived that this would make it possible (and particularly plausible) to imply that what the Whig Ministry was doing in maintaining a large professional land force in time of peace could be described as a case of seeking to establish a standing mercenary army dependent only on the Crown. And secondly, we can explain why the rest of their attack was concentrated on the operation of the Septennial Act and on the award of places and pensions to government supporters in the House of Commons. Correspondingly, we can explain why they concentrated on their own demand for annual parliaments purged of placemen and pensioners. Again, they chose to focus on these issues because they perceived that this would make it possible (and particularly plausible) to imply that what the Whig Ministry was doing in managing Parliament could be described as a case of interfering with the balance of the constitution in such a way as to corrupt and limit the capacity of the citizens and their representatives to maintain a sense of free and independent involvement in the nation's political life. Bolingbroke was always too cautious, of course, to claim that these were the Ministry's actual intentions. But he was able to leave the very strong impression that this must be so, by means of his explicit claim that the Ministry was pursuing a set of policies known to be particularly liable to bring about these consequences.[141]

---

[141] For the claim that to alter the balance of the constitution *is* to endanger political liberty, see Bolingbroke, *Works*, I, p. 334, and II, pp. 62, 144. See also the constant stress on the idea of being a 'friend to the government', but an 'enemy to the constitution', e.g. at II, pp. 87, 89, 91, etc. For the implication that what the Walpole Ministry is doing *is* altering the balance of the constitution, see the disguised claims at I, pp. 306, 333–4, 417, and at II, pp. 91, 161–72, the latter section being a covert but clear attack on Walpole. The major discussions of 'corruption' are in the 'Dissertation', *Works*, II, pp. 61, 63, 95, 145, 147, 151, 153–4, 160, 163–4.

We can also explain why Bolingbroke appears so enthusiastically to endorse the Whigs' beliefs in his own political works. A number of Bolingbroke's recent interpreters have commented on the apparent paradox that it was Bolingbroke, the arch-enemy of the Whigs, who provided in his own political writings the clearest and most stylish survey of a number of key Whig political beliefs. The explanation which has usually been given, in somewhat question-begging style, is that Bolingbroke must in some way have been a 'pseudo-Whig' himself,[142] who was either powerfully under the influence of Machiavelli,[143] or was genuinely a 'neo-Harringtonian' who genuinely shared these characteristically Whig beliefs.[144] The correct answer, I am suggesting, is rather that Bolingbroke simply wanted to remind his Whig enemies, in the clearest possible style, of the views held by the accredited theorists of their own party about the concept of political liberty, in order to be able to make use of the immensely strong resonances of this tradition of thought to further his own wholly cynical and self-interested political ends.

Finally, we can also explain why it was the principle of patriotism for the sake of which Bolingbroke and his party consistently claimed to act. As I have suggested, the essence of Bolingbroke's *coup* lay in matching this principle to his party's practice in just such a way as to be able to imply to the Whigs, with maximum plausibility, that their own Ministry was pursuing at least two policies known to every good Whig to be peculiarly liable to endanger English political liberties. This made it possible to leave the correspondingly strong impression that to oppose these precise policies was, in the circumstances, to be concerned above all with the idea of preserving English political liberties. But to be concerned with the preservation of English political liberties was what was meant at the time by being a true patriot. This in turn enabled Bolingbroke and his party to claim with maximum plausibility

---

[142] This is the view of Robbins, *Commonwealthman*, p. 284.

[143] This is suggested in H. Butterfield, *The Statecraft of Machiavelli* (London, 1940), pp. 135–65. Hart, *Bolingbroke*, pp. 117–43, stresses the humanist origins of Bolingbroke's thought, but uses a caricatured version of Machiavelli's political theory which he is then at pains to claim is largely rejected by Bolingbroke.

[144] This is Pocock's view in *Politics, Language and Time*. See p. 134 on Bolingbroke as 'the most spectacular of the neo-Harringtonians'. This view is adopted by Kramnick, *Bolingbroke*, pp. 177, 180 and Ch. IX, and by Dickinson, *Bolingbroke*, pp. 184–5. This seems to me the wrong way to resolve the paradox, though better than merely stating (as for example Jackman, *Man of Mercury*, does, p. 142) that 'Bolingbroke, the Tory, shows Whiggish traits'.

that they were genuinely motivated by the spirit of patriotism. And this provided them with the element of justification which, as I have sought to show, was essential if they were to be able to continue with the successful pursuit of their otherwise unconstitutional policy of conducting a 'formed opposition' to the King's chosen Ministry.[145]

What I have tried to argue is that until we put ourselves in a position to explain why Bolingbroke and his party evidently *believed it was rational* to concentrate on certain specific courses of political action, we cannot hope to explain why they chose to concentrate on just those courses of action. And what I have tried to show is that the reason they believed it was rational to act in just the way they did was that it *was rational* in the circumstances to act in just that way. I have not tried, however, to vindicate the honesty or sincerity of their actions. This is simply because I see no convincing evidence for saying (and I do not in fact believe) either that Bolingbroke and his party ever felt that English political liberties were genuinely in jeopardy, or that they felt any particular nostalgia for the passing of any of the alleged values of English political life. In one way, in fact, my argument goes even further in this direction than the Namierite view, for I have implied that the whole of Bolingbroke's political writings were designed simply to serve the polemical purpose of reminding the Whigs of their own beliefs and principles, rather than to set out any principles in which Bolingbroke himself necessarily believed. In another way, however, my account is completely opposed to the Namierite view, for I have insisted that it does not follow from the fact that Bolingbroke's professions of principle were merely *ex post facto* rationalizations that these principles ought to be by-passed when we come to explain his political behaviour. My aim has been to argue, on the contrary, that for at least two reasons it must be essential to refer to Bolingbroke's professed principle of patriotism, and to explain why he chose to profess it, in order to explain his actual courses of political action. First, I have sought to show that the range of actions which it was open to Bolingbroke and his party to perform in opposing Walpole's Ministry was limited to the range of actions for which they could hope to supply recognizable justifications, and was thus limited by the range of recognized political principles which they could plausibly hope to

---

[145] For Bolingbroke's reiterated insistence that a formed opposition, in the political situations he describes, would be the act of a true patriot, see *Works*, I, pp. 357, 428–9, 447, 450–3, and II, p. 166.

suggest as favourable descriptions (and thus as justifications) for their actions. Secondly, I have sought to show that the principle which Bolingbroke and his party actually chose to profess in this attempt to justify their behaviour then made it rational for them to act, and thus directed them to act, only in certain highly specific ways.

The general belief I have thus been concerned to isolate and criticize is the belief that it is only if an agent's professed principles can be shown to have served as a motive for his actions that it is necessary to refer to those principles in order to explain the agent's actions. The agent's principles will also make a difference to his actions whenever he needs to be able to provide an explicit justification for them. This will make it necessary for the agent to limit and direct his behaviour in such a way as to make his actions *compatible* with the claim that they were motivated by an accepted principle and that they can thus be justified. This in turn means that such an agent's professed principles invariably need to be treated as causal conditions of his actions, even if the agent professes those principles in a wholly disingenuous way. What I have thus been concerned to establish, by reference to the specific historical case of Bolingbroke versus Walpole, is the sense in which the explanation of political action essentially depends upon the study of political ideology – and thus with the way in which it is essential, and not optional, for any political historian to be an historian of political ideas.

Acknowledgements: This essay was written while I was visiting research fellow (1970) in the History of Ideas Unit, The Research School of Social Sciences, at the Australian National University. I am most grateful to Professor Eugene Kamenka for inviting me to deliver the seminar papers on which the essay is based. I am particularly indebted to John Dunn, as always, for helping me to shape my thoughts; to Geoffrey Mortimore for some very valuable discussions of my original draft; and to Karin Barber, John Burrow and John Thompson for reading subsequent versions. I have also learnt a great deal from discussions with Martin Hollis, who has included a critical account of the thesis of this essay in his paper 'My Role and its Duties', in *Human Nature and Conduct:* The Royal Institute of Philosophy Lectures, 1973-74.

Note: In citations from seventeenth- and eighteenth-century sources, spelling and punctuation have been modernized.

VI

What did the Industrial Revolution
in Britain owe to Science?

A. RUPERT HALL

Discussion of the intellectual origins of the Industrial Revolution has, like medieval philosophy, provoked a division between nominalists and realists. One school of historians seeks to apply, in one formulation or another, the word *scientific* either to the process of technical change in the eighteenth century or at least to the mental habits of those who effected these changes; others, the realists, search without success for precise examples of a technical innovation's being derived consciously from pre-existent theoretical knowledge of a non-trivial character, or at least write of the relations between science and technology in the eighteenth century as being so subtle and complex that such terms as *application* and *derivation* become wildly inappropriate.

It may be difficult, initially, to convince oneself that the two positions are separated by more than words. The facts about technological development in the eighteenth century are not in dispute, nor are the biographies of the inventors, and in any case the main burden of analysing and accounting for the occurrence of the early Industrial Revolution in Britain falls upon economic historians.[1] No one today

---

[1] Although T. S. Ashton followed Mantoux in the supposition that an English tradition of empirical inductive science contributed in a notable way to the technological changes of the Industrial Revolution, recent economic historians have adopted a more sceptical position. Thus David Landes (*Cambridge Economic History of Europe*, VI, C.U.P., 1965, p. 293) writes: 'in spite of some efforts to tie the Industrial Revolution to the Scientific Revolution of the sixteenth and seventeenth centuries, the link would seem to have been an extremely diffuse one. . . . Indeed, if anything, the growth of scientific knowledge [i.e., in thermodynamics] owed much to the concerns and achievements of technology; there was far less flow of ideas or methods the other way.' And

would argue (in this case, at least) that brilliant technical improvisation compelled industry to reorganize itself; rather, everyone agrees that economic opportunity offered unprecedented incentives to hasten in Britain a secular process of technological development common to all Europe. M. Maurice Daumas has presented forceful arguments to support his contention that even if the historian may be permitted to speak of an Industrial Revolution in the eighteenth century, he should certainly not postulate a concomitant *technical* revolution. Indeed, the well-known tradition of early, but futile, attempts to smelt iron with coal, to make textiles with machines (William Lee's stocking-frame being the earliest successful example) or to raise water by fire – all going back to Elizabeth's reign – illustrate M. Daumas's view that invention by a Darby or a Newcomen is not a unique, simple historical event, but rather 'une opération complexe qui bénéficie d'une expérience parfois longue de plusieurs siècles, accumulée de génération en génération'.[2] In a different, but strictly analogous manner, Professor Nef has in a lifetime's work traced the technological antecedents of the industrial revolution to the fuel famine of the sixteenth century, showing thereby how the line that led to Etruria and Paisley became differentiated from that leading to Sèvres and Gobelins. If one were to push this historical view to its logical limits it would seem that there is nothing out of the ordinary for the historian of technology to account for in the Industrial Revolution, nothing but a smoothly continuing course of evolution. Few historians have been able, however, to contemplate the introduction of steam-power or the beginnings of a synthetic chemical industry quite so calmly, even though they may feel that mechanical

---

he rightly draws attention to the crucial importance of the *engineering* development of the steam-engine (p. 333). Similarly, S. G. Checkland (*The Rise of Industrial Society in England, 1815–1885*, Longman, 1964, pp. 73–4) maintains that: 'It was impossible to bring together at this stage the brilliant generalized mechanics of d'Alembert and Lagrange and the experience of the artisan. . . . This is not to deny that the mechanical inventors were scientific in the sense of deliberately construing and solving their problems, nor to deny that they drew on the observations and experiences of others. But it is to say that the engineering progress of the day was made by men with little philosophical knowledge, working with what contemporaries called "mechanical instinct".' Phyllis Deane (*The First Industrial Revolution*, C.U.P., 1965) makes no mention at all of science as a predisposing factor to invention.

[2] M. Daumas in *Revue d'Histoire des Sciences*, XVI, 1963, 291–302; cf. a second article by the same author, ibid., XXII, 1969. To what remote ancestry the steam-engine may be traced is evident from Joseph Needham in *Trans. Newcomen Soc.*, XXXV, 1962–3, 3–56 (=*Clerks and Craftsmen in China and the West*, C.U.P., 1970, pp. 136–202).

ingenuity in the textile industry or innovations in the manufacture of iron do exhibit this 'normal' character. Moreover, there is strong evidence of a contemporary awareness both in France and England that technical change had assumed a new character in which scientific self-consciousness formed an important element (though one can, equally, find contemporary assertions of the not necessarily antithetical point of view that this change was not effected by cabinet philosophers). Whether one prefers to speak of a 'revolution' in productive technology or, instead, of an accelerating rate of change – and if it is appreciated that all revolutions have their historical antecedents the difference between these manners of expression is not very great – many historians write with the conviction that there is a phenomenon here deserving particular explanation.

The temptation, and it is a perilous one as Charles Gillispie has pointed out already,[3] is to assume that the explanation can be couched in simple terms. If a historian postulates as an explanation of innovation, either in science or technology, a direct, self-evident translation of one into the other, he is liable to slide over the essential logical distinction between *episteme* and *techne*, evident already in the Greek writings on machines. In societies prior to our own it was the concern of the natural philosopher (and is still that of the theoretical scientist today) to analyse and rationalize phenomena; to show that, far from being capricious, they may be set within a universal and acknowledged system of ideas. The scientist publishes the results of his investigations openly for the information and criticism of his peers, unlike the technologist who is normally most anxious to keep novel processes as secret as possible, and to prevent their dissemination by patent protection; if James Watt, for example, thought like a scientist, he behaved as secretively as any traditional craftsman. Scientific theories have been demonstrated as successful by their breadth and capacity for fruitful extension, by their internal consistency, and by their applicability to a multitude of confirmatory instances. Success is largely a question of esteem by fellow-scientists; it does not spring from popular acclaim – often voiced in favour of moribund theories – nor from practical usefulness, nor even from the absence of contrary instances. The technologist, on the other hand, is not esteemed according to the votes of his peers, or according to the consistency of his reasoning, or according to the skill with which

---

[3] In 'The Natural History of Industry', *Isis*, 48, 1957, 398–407.

he derives his methods from general principles. He is required only to succeed in what he undertakes to do; his opportunity to attempt a project and the measure of his achievement in it may be very much a matter of popular acclaim. Hence, in considering the history of technical development, it is no more necessary to enquire after abstract rationality than, in similarly considering the history of science, to enquire after utility. It is temptingly easy to over-intellectualize technical invention: even in the twentieth century careful analysis indicates that science is only one source of such innovation, sometimes a necessary source, never a sufficient one.[4]

No one can need much convincing that the origin and progress of technology were the work of unlettered craftsmen. Despite the myths of ancient civilizations, the names of the obscure individuals who were the first inventors remain unknown to us. So are the authors of the carpenter's plane, the rotary grindstone, the water-wheel and the water-raising machines of classical antiquity (unless we attribute the screw to Archimedes); in medieval times the mechanical clock, the wind-mill and the many water-powered devices are similarly anonymous. In all the process of transmission of technology from East to West only Gutenberg's name survives, and he may therefore be reckoned the first of the known inventors of modern times. Even in the early Industrial Revolution period the biographies of some early inventors are almost lost. We know their successors better because the importance of their work was recognized. But it would be rash, after this long history of development, to underestimate the capacity for innovation in the craft tradition, to imagine that to call a man an 'unlettered mechanic' was a term of abuse before a changing society made it so, or to believe that the inventions of the Industrial Revolution were of so high an order of sophistication that they could never have been made without assistance from a superior, scientific plane. Even where new working principles may have been drawn from science, experience and mechanical skill were needed for their realization in practical form; and the number of instances of this occurrence seems to be small. Even historians who have particularly striven to elicit the scientific contribution to the Industrial Revolution can write: 'We do not wish to push this thesis too far – to under-estimate the contributions of unscientific though intelligent practical craftsmen – but the evidence

[4] John Jewkes, David Sawers, Richard Stillerman, *The Sources of Invention* (rev. ed., London, Macmillan, 1962).

appears to necessitate some modification of the traditional view of the Industrial Revolution.'[5]

It is, I believe, particularly misleading to translate the logical and objective distinctions between science and craftsmanship into a social distinction between craftsmen and scholars, as though the former were of no significance in the historical interrelations between science and technology, and all failure of the one to merge with the other was to be ascribed to an artificial social barrier. So far as the study of the history of technology from literary sources is concerned, the postulation of this barrier is, for early times at least, self-defeating: these sources were, by definition, compiled by scholars and gentlemen. But there is much good reason for doubting the importance of class-division in this context. We have Needham's evidence from China of the ascription of important inventions to high officials and scholars who were, nevertheless, technically informed also.[6] In the classical Greek and Roman tradition educated men familiar with philosophy and mathematics engaged practically in both building and mechanical engineering; Vitruvius, one of this group, seems to find it noteworthy that Ctesibios was the son of a barber. A few of the high officials charged with superintendence of Rome's water-supply (Frontinus among them) were technical experts. Again, the common illusion that medieval architecture was entirely the creation of illiterate masons is a fallacy; medieval architects understood and applied clear design principles, though these were not based on scientific knowledge. So did shipwrights.[7] The role of monastic houses in the exploitation of waterpower and the development of time-keepers is well known. All such examples illustrate not only the unreality of a social barrier supposedly separating literacy and numeracy from manual skill, but the direction of skill by concepts or procedures that are not merely manual, and to which the trained eye and hand were irrelevant.

One may further argue on general grounds that it was not social distinction, causing ignorance of and contempt for the crafts among

---

[5] A. E. Musson and Eric Robinson, *Science and Technology in the Industrial Revolution* (Manchester U.P., 1969), p. 189.
[6] Joseph Needham, *Science and Civilization in China*, IV, Part 2 (Cambridge U.P., 1962), pp. 30–5.
[7] See F. C. Lane, *Venetian Ships and Shipbuilders of the Renaissance* (Baltimore, 1934, rev. ed. in French, 1965); R. L. Mainstone in *Architectural Review*, 1968, 303–10; and my survey article in *Society of Engineers Journal*, LX, 1969, 17–31.

educated men, that was the basic reason for the non-appearance of a fruitful interaction between science and technology in early societies. While elementary concepts may prove of some immediate value in mechanical engineering, most crafts depend on the empirical exploitation of properties of materials or chemical reactions that are quite complex; if shipbuilding had had to wait for rational fluid mechanics and brewing for biochemistry, men would have had neither ships nor beer. Technical progress in early science could occur only by fortuitous and empirical steps; in so far as the scholar attempted to immerse himself in craftsmanship he plunged himself more deeply into the craftsman's confusion. Military affairs have always been in the hands of men drawn from the upper strata of society without its being conspicuously obvious that military techniques have advanced faster than civilian ones. However far-reaching the tactical conceptions of a great engineer like Vauban, in their execution he was imprisoned by the craft skill of his age, not enabled to transcend it by his superior social status. Only Leonardo da Vinci – himself a product of the crafts – appears as an exception to this rule. Again, the temporary concern of the Royal Society for its histories of trades and that of the Académie Royale des Sciences for the *description des arts et métiers* was productive of little but materials for future historians. And, as it seems to me, necessarily so: one may solve intricate problems involving many variables by a lucky guess or by trial and error through the fruit of long experience, but one does not at once solve them by taking thought in the absence of a greatly extended theoretical structure, which must be created first.

For science must start at quite the other end, not by delving into the hopeless morass of agricultural or mineralogical detail but by investigating the apparently simplest phenomena and formulating the most general – and therefore practically useless – propositions. In antiquity and in recent centuries those branches of science in which such phenomena could be singled out, namely astronomy and mechanics, made the fastest progress; not because physiology or properties of matter were neglected for social reasons (in fact, the problems of these sciences, too, were constantly in debate) but because rationalization of the more simple must logically precede rationalization of the more intricate. On the other hand, where 'proto-chemists' and 'proto-geologists' deliberately prided themselves on a wide familiarity with craft secrets, the lore of still and mine, and cut themselves off from the general trends of natural philosophy, advance in these sciences was the more retarded. Whatever may be the case today, there was nothing to be gained in the past by maintaining that science and technology pursue the same ends, or that a *single* outlook, that of the 'scholar-craftsman', is sufficient to attain the ends of both.[8]

If it is neither profitable nor realistic, then, to pursue through the seventeenth and eighteenth centuries the gradual emergence of a single species of dual parentage, *Homo scientificus*, pursuing sometimes the purity of science, sometimes its applications to mundane affairs, one is left with a quite traditional conception that science was concerned with one class of problems and technology with another, and it remains to establish the relations between them. The commonest way of expressing a relation is to say that science is 'applied'; in their recent study of this question as it bears on the origins and course of the Industrial Revolution, A. E. Musson and Eric Robinson repeatedly refer to applied science as denoting a significant (though not the only significant) difference between technical innovation in that period and earlier innovation. Now the most obvious way of applying science would be to seek to practise the useful hints provided by scientists themselves. The seventeenth century is not without such hints: Descartes suggested that lenses should preferably be ground to a hyperbolic curvature; Galileo proposed the optimal shape for a loaded beam; Newton defined the solid of least resistance; Petty, if he may be classified as a scientist, advocated the catamaran construction for ships; Rømer and

---

[8] The opposite view has had its powerful advocates, notably among Marxist historians. Benjamin Farrington, starting from a definition of science as having its 'origin in techniques' with experience as its source and 'its aims practical, its only test that it works', has argued that the Milesians were successful because they were 'observers of nature whose eyes had been quickened, whose attention directed, and whose selection of phenomena to be observed had been conditioned, by familiarity with a certain range of techniques'. The 'positive content' of their science was 'drawn from the techniques of the age' (*Greek Science*, London, Penguin Books, 1944, I, pp. 14, 36–37). Similarly Edgar Zilsel, as well as Farrington himself, has emphasized the usefulness of the scholar-craftsman concept in accounting for the appearance of the 'modern' type of scientific investigator (see my 'Merton Revisited' in *History of Science*, 2, 1963, 1–15). Musson and Robinson (op. cit. note 5, pp. 11, 12) also incline towards the 'scholar-craftsman' hypothesis, suggesting that 'these distinctions between "pure" and "applied" science in the sixteenth, seventeenth and eighteenth centuries are to a large extent artificial'. All distinctions drawn by men are artificial, but they may well be conceptually important; and nothing could be more fatuous or more destructive of analytical enquiry than the view that 'after all, craftsmen and philosophers are all students of nature in their different ways'.

La Hire gave what they took to be an optimal profile for gear-teeth; Huygens and Newton worked out approximate solutions for the curve traced by a projectile in air. None of these and other suggestions from scientists for doing things better were adopted during the Industrial Revolution, though improved versions of these ideas have, of course, been applied in the nineteenth century or later.[9] The reasons are not far to seek: the novel designs were unnecessary or impracticable in the prevailing technical context. Evidently the scientists' notions of how to improve craft practice were not usually realistic; all Huygens's attempts to design a serviceable marine chronometer similarly failed, though his object was attained by working clockmakers in the following century. (The apparent exception to this general experience will be discussed later.)

It is true that the advocacy by writers on mathematics of more sophisticated and accurate methods of survey and navigation was rewarded with greater success, even though rudimentary methods were common through the Industrial Revolution. Their contribution to technology was minimal, however, and the advocacy was centuries, if not millennia, old. As Robert E. Schofield has put it, 'To demonstrate a relationship between aspects of an industrial revolution and science, we must show that those aspects influenced or were influenced by the development of contemporary theories in science.'[10] Trigonometry was no innovation of the eighteenth century. Surveyors and navigators also borrowed, through the scientific-instrument makers, practical improvements first devised for scientific purposes, such as telescopic sights; by the end of the eighteenth century navigation could be – but perhaps was not often – an 'applied science'. But this hardly goes near the root of the matter.

Turning now to the eighteenth century itself, one can again discover many scientific 'hints to craftsmen' concerning gunnery, optics, gear wheels, structures and so forth that were neglected for the time being, while it is correspondingly evident that an enormous proportion of scientific research in mechanics, astronomy, electricity, natural history, physiology and geology had no ascertainable bearing on technology

[9] The English mill-architect, Charles Bage, employed Galileo's theory of scaling in designing cast-iron beams for a mill at Shrewsbury (1796–97), and confirmed his results by full-scale breaking tests (A. W. Skempton in *Actes du VIIIe Congrès Inst. d'Hist. des Sciences*, Florence, 1958, III, pp. 1029–39).

[10] *Chymia*, 5, 1959, 186.

at all.[11] In fact the only obvious (and much discussed) instances of possible 'hints' from science that were gladly and effectively taken up by inventors and entrepreneurs both occurred at a time well after the inception of the Industrial Revolution in Britain, and perhaps played no crucial part in it: these 'hints' led to the introduction of chlorine bleaches, the manufacture of soda from salt, and the improved steam engine.

Chlorine bleaching was introduced in Britain in 1787. It is perhaps just worth noting that the name *chlorine* was conferred by Davy in 1810 when he established the elementary nature of this gas; the basic chemistry had been up to this point erroneous in that chlorine had been considered to be a compound, oxymuriatic acid. This basic investigation (by Scheele, Berthollet and Chaptal) was wholly continental, not British. The many confused and confusing attempts to make the new chemical agent effective in the absence of adequate scientific knowledge and manufacturing experience, involving the usual squabbles over patent rights, need not concern us here, save to note that commercial production of bleaching powder on a large scale was begun by Charles Tennant at Glasgow in 1799. Whatever the ethics of Tennant's commercial enterprise, it was certainly effective. By contrast, although from early 1787 James Watt (in association with his father-in-law James McGrigor) enjoyed the advantages of direct personal contact with Berthollet and other scientists in Paris as well as Joseph Black in Edinburgh, and possessed potentially valuable ideas about possible ways of manufacturing the bleach which he strove to keep as secret as possible, it does not seem that his acute interest led to commercial success. As usual in business, a great deal more was necessary for success than a short-lived lead in scientific knowledge. As early as 1790 Berthollet himself could claim that in this instance a scientific experiment had given birth to large manufactures but, whatever the propaganda value of this statement, it would be naïve to accept it as a complete summary of historical events. (In fact, in their first year of manufacture, Tennant's St Rollux works produced no more than 52 tons of bleaching powder.) A very great deal of what today would

---

[11] The discovery of electrostatic conduction generated, from 1753 onwards, a series of impractical proposals for telegraphs; this seems to be another example of frustrated scientific fertility in technical ideas. For a few years the electro-magnetic telegraph conception moved equally slowly, and one might argue that it was redeemed only by the needs of the railway.

be called 'development', much of it fruitless, had to be expended upon Berthollet's experiment before manufacture could be said to flourish. To my mind, this development would be more exactly classified as technical than as scientific research, for the problems to be solved by Watt and his multitudinous competitors were problems of economical, consistent and controllable manufacture to which science, though it indeed stimulated and inspired this technical research, was incapable of furnishing ready-made answers. Moreover, the solution of these problems contributed little or nothing to scientific knowledge whereas their technical profit was, in the end, considerable.

At a rather earlier period another technical investigation in chemical manufacture was begun in England, Scotland and France. Even before 1750 it was fairly generally known to chemists that soda could be prepared from other substances, chiefly common salt and Glauber's salt (that was itself made in the laboratory from common salt).[12] While an empirical relationship between these various materials was known, chemists were until after 1800 wholly ignorant of the element sodium common to them, and the nature of the carbonate ion $(CO_3^=)$ in soda. Leblanc, author of the ultimately successful process for preparing soda synthetically, employed limestone because he knew that it was used as a flux in iron metallurgy. Thus he was guided to a useful reaction not by chemical science but by false analogy.[13] Similarly James Watt, working in collaboration with the Scottish chemist Joseph Black, attempted (like several continental chemists) to work an utterly impossible process for making soda from salt;[14] in fact the soda yielded by this process seems to have come, not from sodium chloride, but from the sodium sulphate (Glauber's salt) also present in common salt made by evaporating sea-water. Partial success, in other words, came from a happy accident, not from a chemical science inadequate for an understanding of the reactions involved. Black's part in the collaboration with Watt has been described as enigmatic. 'He does not seem to have grasped the chemistry of the process, though it was well within his abilities to do so. He probably decided at an early stage that the process was worthless, but was reluctant to say so to Watt, and

[12] The events have been reviewed recently by A. and N. Clow in *The Chemical Revolution* (Batchworth, 1952) and A. E. Musson and Eric Robinson (op. cit. note 5, pp. 251–337).

[13] See Charles Gillispie in *Isis*, 48, 1957, 152–70; 398–407.

[14] On this, see A. and N. Clow (op. cit. note 12) and Musson and Robinson (op. cit. note 5, pp. 352–71).

temporized.'[15] The obvious implication is that Watt was *not* able to perceive the futility of his experiments (in which he continued for many years), and the same might be said of several more distinguished chemists than he. In short, we may credit chemical science on this occasion with at most a partially correct observation, for the facts were never properly understood at the time, and no assistance at all towards the development of commercial manufacture.

Leblanc, whose process was at least feasible (though it yielded him no personal advantage), was probably the least chemically distinguished of the inventors of a dozen or so methods for preparing soda synthetically. Their history demonstrates, certainly, both collaboration between scientists and entrepreneurs and the activity of chemists like Guyton de Morveau as entrepreneurs. But their history shows too how empirical the first steps towards the synthetic alkali industry necessarily were; those engaged in this technical investigation were hardly better equipped intellectually than the early metal workers learning how to smelt copper from malachite. Their knowledge of the composition of the materials with which they worked was inadequate, and they had no means of predicting which reactions would be likely to succeed. As Charles Gillispie has remarked in his excellent study of the origins of the Leblanc process, by the time it was fully understood by chemists it was moribund.[16] And, as he has also remarked, both in France and in Britain this technical investigation was entirely unaffected by the 'chemical revolution' of Lavoisier which was the chief event in the history of chemical science when all this was going forward.

Finally, turning to Watt's invention of the separate condenser for the Newcomen steam engine, it is hardly necessary to do more than emphasize the fact that the myth of Watt's 'application' of an already formulated science of heat to the problem of the atmospheric engine's relative inefficiency has been exposed many times already.[17] The myth

---

[15] W. V. and K. R. Farrar in Musson and Robinson, p. 371. This passage is based on their interpretation of Watt's work.   [16] *Isis*, 48, 1957, 170.

[17] See Donald Fleming in *Isis*, 43, 1952, 3–5, and D. S. L. Cardwell, *Steam-power in the Eighteenth Century* (Sheed and Ward, London, 1963). It is perhaps unfortunate that, in his recent co-operative volume with Dr. Robinson (note 5), Mr. Musson (on pp. 79–81) in treating Watt as a scientific inventor does not firmly disavow this myth. While he writes that Watt 'appears to have rediscovered the principle of latent heat, independently of Black' he also writes of his consulting with Black in the course of his experiments on steam. Although this statement is formally correct, it might lead a reader to imagine that Black's superior scientific knowledge decisively stimulated Watt's invention.

was wholly created by Black himself and by John Robison who was in this affair a better friend to Black than to Watt.[18] It is abundantly evident that, before saying a word to Black, Watt was in possession of the salient facts: (a) a great deal of steam was wasted by the necessity for reheating the cylinder after condensation had produced a partial vacuum;[19] (b) a surprisingly small quantity of steam would suffice to raise water to its boiling-point; hence the need for a great quantity of injection-water to cool both the cylinder and the steam in it, and the consequent difficulty of obtaining a good vacuum so that the piston would descend.[20] Essentially, all that Black did was to assure Watt that his observation (b) was correct, and tell him of its agreement with his own unpublished theory of latent heat, of which until then Watt knew nothing. It would have been no logical impediment to Watt's invention of the separate condenser had he remained always unaware of the latent heat of steam, and a *general* conception of the latency of heat could be of no value at all in solving his problem.

It is easy to overlook the fact that while particular facts and *ad hoc* correlations may be no more than awkward or intriguing to a scientist, they may be quite sufficient to permit an engineer or technologist to take an important step; conversely generalization, essential to science, may be a feeble prop for the practitioner. The literate and sophisticated engineer, like Watt, may enjoy his use of scientific labels and his

[18] In his evidence on Watt's behalf against Hornblower and Maberley in 1796 Robison wrote (speaking of the work on the Glasgow model engine): 'Mr. Watt had learned from Dr. Black somewhat of his late discovery of the latent heat of Fluids and Steams . . . a subject of much conversation among the young Gentlemen at College. Mr. Watt was one of the most zealous partisans of this Theory. . . .' Watt's annotation on this passage reads: 'Dr. Robison is mistaken in this. I had not attended to Dr Black's experiment or theory on latent heat until I was led to it in the course of experiments upon the Engines when the fact proved a stumbling-block which the Dr. assisted me to get over. JW.' (A. E. Musson and Eric Robinson, *James Watt and the Steam Revolution*, Adams and Dart, 1969, pp. 26–7). See also Watt's letter of May 1814 in John Robison, *A System of Mechanical Philosophy* (Edinburgh, 1822), II, pp. iii–ix. This important autobiographical statement of some length is not reprinted by Musson and Robinson in their volume on Watt just cited, though Watt's contemporary experimental notes there printed (pp. 39–40) fully support Watt's much later recollections.

[19] Watt had already taken practical steps experimentally to reduce this heat-loss, which Cardwell has shown to be more significant in full-scale engines than the second factor, the latent heat of steam.

[20] Watt also knew that this effect was made the more serious by the lowering of the boiling point of water within the cylinder as the pressure within fell below the atmospheric.

mastery of scientific rationalization while always actually working with particular facts and ideas. *Any* scientific theory may envelop his actual immersion in particulars, right or wrong. R. E. Schofield has noted Wedgwood's distinction between two white clays (pipe-clay and kaolin) by their supposed difference in phlogiston content as an example of Wedgwood's use of chemical theory. But, in practice, Wedgwood did not – as quoted by Schofield – measure phlogiston in order to distinguish the clays; he distinguished them by firing specimens and observing that one was consistently darker than the other. His phlogiston-language was no more than a way of rationalizing what was physically observable; Wedgwood could just as well have said that the kaolin contained more *ying* than the pipe-clay. Being familiar with chemists' terminology, he used it, but it had no technological (or logical) significance.[21]

If, then, the application of science consisted in exploiting direct suggestions concerning utility coming from scientists themselves, its role in the Industrial Revolution would seem to be rather trivial. However interesting and prophetic the instances concerning chemical manufacture, they can hardly be said to have been decisive for the growth of the British textile industry by 1800, or even by 1825. Watt's separate condenser, despite the vast attention it has always attracted, was not essential to this or any other aspect of eighteenth-century industry. Supposing that at least 1,500 steam engines were at work in Britain by 1800, when Watt's patent expired, no more than a third had come from the Soho works; the majority were Newcomen engines or even Savery pumps supplying water to mill-wheels.[22] And the total power obtained from steam engines was but a fraction of that obtained from water-wheels and windmills over the whole country (the largest water-wheel erected in the British Isles – for mine drainage – at Laxey, in the Isle of Man, was built as late as 1854). Moreover, it is indisputable that Watt's later improvements of the steam engine – the sun-and-

---

[21] Obviously the falsity of Wedgwood's phlogistic hypothesis has nothing to do with my argument. See *Chymia*, 5, 1959, 189.

[22] J. R. Harris in *History*, LII, 1967, 133–48; A. E. Musson and E. Robinson in *Science and Technology in the Industrial Revolution* (Manchester U.P., 1969), pp. 393–426. The first use of steam for spinning in Lancashire (atmospheric engine with water-wheel) was in 1783; Boulton and Watt erected a rotative engine in Nottinghamshire in 1785/6 (R. L. Hills, *Power in the Industrial Revolution*, Manchester U.P., 1970, pp. 136, 152ff. This writer puts recognition of the advantages of the Watt engine by the textile industry as late as 1790).

planet gear, double-action, the parallel motion and so forth – owed everything to Watt's mechanical ingenuity and nothing to science. Even if the myth of the separate condenser were true its significance would be psychological rather than economic.

The purposefully useful enterprises of scientists in the eighteenth century seem, then, like those of their seventeenth-century predecessors, to have been largely misdirected, though exact as far as their own age was concerned; at any rate the work of Amontons and Coulomb on friction, of Euler and Coulomb on structures, was quietly ignored by their engineering contemporaries.[23] Even Sadi Carnot's study of the heat engine (1824) – the classical instance of technological progress presenting a new problem to science – was long in bearing practical fruit. In earlier cases where scientists had actually abandoned technical projects as futile (Huygens the marine chronometer, Huygens and Papin the atmospheric engine), their hopes were in the end realized by practical mechanics employing different principles from theirs.[24] There is a logical sense in which a formally correct scientific analysis must be true, but scientists could, and can, often be wrong in matters of practice, judgement and experience. The assumptions which had necessarily to be made in applying mechanics or chemistry to the technical issue commonly, in the eighteenth century, enforced an excessive simplification rendering the formally accurate answer of little mundane value. Since all real fluids are viscous, for example, theorems true of ideal fluids may prove deceptive in engineering practice. One must, then, conclude that the 'application' of science to technology bears some more general connotation than that examined so far, at least in the eighteenth century; it must denote, not the exploitation for particular purposes of general scientific truths or even particular discoveries, but some more diffuse activity: the adoption of scientific method, or familiarity with the general context of science, the practice of analysing problems in a rational or experimental manner, or even the development of an acquaintance among scientists, or some combination of these characteristics. The historical problem then (in face of such an indefinite conception of applied science) is to determine the functional significance

[23] Of course I do not mean to include here the practical and analytical work of such men as Macquer who were responsible for the direction of manufactories.

[24] It has never been proved, however, that the first steam engineers, Savery and Newcomen, were cognizant of the experiments of Huygens and Papin from 1675 onwards.

for technology of any one of these characteristics considered singly. For otherwise the whole discussion remains nebulous.

It is certain, to take one point, that there was a considerable popularization of science in Britain during the eighteenth century, in which entrepreneurs, manufacturers and inventors participated as well as clergymen and poets. The movement took two chief forms: the circulation of popular books by authors as various as Benjamin Martin and James Ferguson, Oliver Goldsmith and John Wesley, and the foundation of local societies, of which the best known are, of course, the 'Lunar Society' (or rather club – it was never a society in the ordinary sense) and the Manchester Literary and Philosophical Society.[25] In addition, itinerant lecturers continued the tradition of popular scientific demonstration begun in London by Hauksbee and Desaguliers, while instrument-makers found a lively market for microscopes, telescopes, globes and other apparatus. Probably more people possessed a discursive knowledge of science in 1760 than in 1660, though it is impossible to measure the extent of self-education or to assess its significance objectively. Only a very few of the popular writers and society members were at all eminent in science: such men as Joseph Priestley in the Lunar Society, William Henry and later John Dalton in Manchester. Inventors, engineers and manufacturers read the books and joined the societies; some impressed themselves on contemporaries' recollections by their interest in scientific discussion and their command of what they had read. But to find a causal relationship between the popularity of science and innovation in technology in eighteenth-century Britain requires a degree of faith. Most of these same people were dissenters and northerners also; perhaps these correlations may be equally significant. Moreover, it is difficult to determine whether a private devotion to science among British manufacturers compensated for the defects of formal scientific education in Britain.[26] It was dormant in the English universities during the early

---

[25] Among recent publications, much detail may be found in R. E. Schofield, *The Lunar Society of Birmingham* (Clarendon Press, 1963) and in the volume by A. E. Musson and Eric Robinson so often cited in this essay, *Science and Technology in the Industrial Revolution* (Manchester U.P., 1969).

[26] R. E. Schofield quotes a letter from Wedgwood to Bentley (7 March 1779) in which he writes: 'Finding my young men often at a loss to form clear ideas of chemical affinities, solutions, compositions, decomposition and recomposition of particles of matter which they could not see . . .' he devised a pictorial symbolism representing chemical reactions. This indicates, presumably, an early experiment in industrial

Industrial Revolution, though not in those of Scotland. The Royal Society was not remarkable for great vigour and enterprise. There were no trade schools. There was no scientific bureaucracy. The Royal Military Academy at Woolwich (1741) was insignificant, while the Navy had no comparable institution at all.[27] The very popularity of science ensured its treatment as an entertainment, as it was regarded by Samuel Johnson and Joseph Wright of Derby. Taking science seriously – in its academies and factories – seems to have been very much a characteristic of religious dissent.

In France it was far otherwise. Since the time of Colbert technical education had been encouraged; there were trade schools, schools of design, schools of commerce; above all there was the *École des ponts et chaussées* (officially organized in 1755). A French school of mines, in imitation of earlier German mining schools, was founded in 1778. There were *écoles royales militaires* and an *École d'Ingénieurs-Constructeurs de Vaisseaux* (1769). Even the theorists of the virtues of manual education were French.[28] France, too, produced the first great theorists of technology (Amontons, Perronet, Coulomb, the Carnots *père et fils*); and there Macquer and Lavoisier became high officials; Lazare Carnot, the organizer of victory; and Laplace, son of poor Normandy peasants, made his way to great eminence from a career begun as a teacher in military schools.[29] Chemical industry was systematically developed under the direction of the state, and scientists were employed to carry out mineralogical and metallurgical surveys.[30] Like Britain, eighteenth-century France provides ample evidence of the popularity of science, from the *Encyclopédie* and Algarotti's *Newtonianisme pour les Dames* to the formation of provincial societies.

If interest in science, sophisticated analysis of technical methods and problems, and the provision of technical education were essential concomitants of industrial innovation it does not seem that France was

---

education to supply the want of formal training in schools, as well as Wedgwood's belief that chemical knowledge was useful to the conduct of his business. (See *Chymia*, 5, 1959, 193.)

[27] The first Chief Master of the R.M.A. was indeed Martin Folkes, also President of the Royal Society; but he possessed no ascertainable distinction in natural science.

[28] F. B. Artz, *The Development of Technical Education in France, 1500–1850* (Cambridge, Mass., 1966).

[29] D. I. Duveen and R. Hahn, *Isis*, 48, 1957, 416–27.

[30] Henry Guerlac, *Chymia*, 5, 1959, 73–112.

notably at a disadvantage as compared with the midlands and the north of England.[31] (And, indeed, development of the more 'scientific' types of manufacture such as the synthetic chemical processes did proceed about equally quickly there.) Of course, it might be argued that other aspects of the English industrial milieu, its traditions of intellectual, religious and financial independence, for example, had to be allied with scientific propensities and knowledge to make the latter effective. But if that argument is pursued it seems to imply that these other differences between England and France were more effective in bringing about an industrial revolution than a diffusion of science that was common to both countries.

Another line of thought, and to my mind a more promising one, would be to examine the role of 'applied science' considered as the rational and experimental study of techniques, without presupposing the injection of important elements of abstract theory, or of pure scientific discoveries. For I must certainly concur with Charles Gillispie's conclusion that 'if the question [of the relations between science and technology in the eighteenth century] be approached in any detail ... it proves extraordinarily difficult to trace the course of any significant theoretical concept from abstract formulation to actual use in industrial operations'.[32] And we have seen already how difficult it was straightforwardly to 'apply' a seemingly useful experimental discovery in science. Sometimes, indeed, scientific clarification post-dated the technical improvements which it ought to have preceded: the elementary chemistry of the differences between cast iron, steel and wrought iron (that is, the decreasing proportion of carbon in each) was established by Torbern Bergman (Sweden) and Guyton de Morveau and C. L. Berthollet (France) in the 1780s; this was the problem that had defeated Réaumur in 1722.[33] Meanwhile, in complete ignorance of chemistry, the Darbys at Coalbrookdale, Henry Cort and Benjamin Huntsman had respectively revolutionized the production of cast iron, wrought iron and steel. Moreover, if one supposes that what expert

---

[31] The point could be extended to practical mechanical skill also, with such obvious exceptions as the English lead in steam-engine building and (after 1770 and for a shorter period) in making textile machinery. Apart from the evidence of the *Encyclopédie*, the names of Vaucanson, Senot, Jacquard and Bréguet are in themselves demonstrative of the fact that excellence in mechanical craftsmanship was not confined to England.

[32] *Isis*, 48, 1957, 399.

[33] C. S. Smith, *Sources for the History of the Science of Steel, 1532–1786* (M.I.T. Press, 1968).

and scientifically literate technical men applied to problems of engineering and manufacture was not the content of science but a new rational methodology, the essential logical distinction already noted can be preserved; for the technical men directed their methodology to gain practical objectives, and judged its utility by its success in gaining them, while scientists directed their methodologies to the acquisition of knowledge. I do not mean at all to imply by this argument that there was a unique method of discovery (Hooke's 'philosophical algebra'[34]) that was simply transferred from science to technology; such a conception would be naïve. In scientific activity the basic logical structure was of far greater significance, and abstract concepts played a more vital role; science, moreover, was innocent of the 'scaling-up' problems (from pilot plant to factory, from model to full-scale engineering) that bedevil technological innovation. Yet it seems that, in the attempts made during the eighteenth century to analyse technical procedures with the object of improving their efficiency, one may detect contemporary notions of what constituted scientific procedure in (a) attempts to classify technical processes logically, notably in the *Encyclopédie*; (b) the employment of systematic experimentation, usually involving models; and (c) the treatment of data quantitatively.

One may speak of this empirical technical research – I have in mind such examples as Desagulier's and Belidor's investigation of water-wheels, Smeaton's model experiments on water-mills and windmills, young James Watt's experiments with his model Newcomen engine, Wedgwood's investigations of glazes and clays, or the quantitative data accumulated by structural engineers like John Rennie and Telford – as *imitative* (in a loose sense) of empirical science; it was not dependent on science, it did not apply science and, though it might sometimes use the language of science, it lay outside its conceptual structure. (There was no abstract conception of a heat engine until Carnot formulated one in 1824, even then defectively.) As R. E. Schofield has remarked, 'experiments, however cleverly performed, are not science unless they are guided by some sort of theoretical structure. Many things have been discovered by a process of empirical testing, but empiricism is not science.'[35] Such a process has very often, however, been sufficient to promote technology. Though ancient assay-masters were not chemists, they had great technical mastery of methods for determining exactly

[34] See Mary B. Hesse in *Isis*, 57, 1966, 67–83.
[35] *Chymia*, 5, 1959, 181.

the proportions of precious metal in an alloy, and for separating the metals. Stephenson, Fairbairn and Hodgkinson, for example, found empirical tests on model structures sufficient for the building of the Britannia Bridge.

Experimentation was no new means to technological innovation. Despite the occurrence of happy accidents it is hard to see how millennial progress could have occurred without it. When Darby experimented with coke for smelting iron, or Paul with rollers for spinning cotton (an idea later taken up by Arkwright), they were continuing very ancient traditions of technical innovation. What seems to have happened before the end of the eighteenth century is that such amorphous experimentation had been occasionally given a more systematic form, and that very gradually the design of mills, bridges or chemical plants was put on a more rational base. When an historical account assumes or implies that technological practices must be *either* derived from scientific knowledge *or* merely guided by tradition, chance, experience or rule-of-thumb, it necessarily ignores the role of coherent design procedures, which in many crafts (the shipwright's is the obvious example) constituted the core of technical skill. However ill-founded these procedures on abstract and demonstrable principles, they succeeded (if with far less than maximum economy and efficiency), and scientific knowledge was unable to supplant most of them before the mid-nineteenth century. Neither the shipwright nor the wheel-wright nor the millwright nor the clockmaker of the pre-Industrial Revolution age was governed by an inexpressible mystique, nor were they mere slavish copyists. Though less subject to changes of taste than joiners and cabinet-makers they were consciously, though unscientifically, cognizant of what constituted good design in their respective crafts.

Their successors in the Industrial Revolution, of whom some began to be known as engineers or mechanics, were men of the same stamp, though masters of more sophisticated methods. It is a great misunderstanding to suppose that if some of them were certainly more than inspired tinkerers, they were therefore applied scientists as though no other category were conceivable.[36] Men like Smeaton, Wedgwood, Watt, Telford, Trevithick, Stephenson, Rennie were above all great

---

[36] Unless, of course, the term 'applied scientist' is taken to have some special definition in the eighteenth-century context, quite distinct from that which it has possessed for the last century or so.

technical designers. Certainly they used more exact and sophisticated experimentation than their predecessors; they also relied far more on the analysis of quantitative data. But these novel characteristics – and their significance was still limited enough – should be regarded rather as incipient modifications of an ancient tradition, partly enforced by the desire to use new materials like cast and wrought iron, than as the effect of a revolution wrought within technology by an infusion of scientific theories and discoveries.

I do not believe that my arguments in favour of the historian's distinguishing between technical research and the improvement of technical design on the one hand, and science itself or its application to industry on the other, are inconsistent with contemporary statements such as Richard Watson's:

The uses of chemistry, not only in the medicinal but in every economical art are too extensive to be enumerated, and too notorious to want illustration; it may just be observed, that a variety of manufactures, by a proper application of chemical principles, might, probably, be wrought at a less expense, and executed in a better manner than they are at present. But to this improvement there are impediments on every hand, which cannot easily be overcome. . . . It cannot be questioned, that the arts of dyeing, painting, brewing, distilling, tanning, of making glass, enamels, porcelain, artificial stone, common salt, sal ammoniac, salt-petre, potash, sugar and a great variety of others, have received improvement from chemical inquiry, and are capable of receiving much more.[37]

Or James Watt's inclusion of the laws of mechanics, the laws of hydraulics and hydrostatics, the 'doctrine of heat and cold' and the volumes of water converted into steam at various pressures, among the requirements to be known by a steam engineer.[38] Or George Stephenson's encomium of Smeaton: 'The principles of mechanics were never so clearly exhibited as in his writings, more especially with respect to resistance, gravity, and the power of water and wind to turn mills. His mind was as clear as crystal, and his demonstrations will be found

---

[37] *Chemical Essays*, I (second ed., London, 1782), pp. 39–40, 42. This seems to me more of a programmatic statement, and less a positive statement of past achievement, than appears to be claimed by Musson and Robinson (op. cit. note 5), p. 169. It need hardly be insisted that the elementary chemistry or biochemistry of the manufactures listed by Watson was unknown when he wrote, and that none had originated from chemical science.

[38] Eric Robinson in *Notes and Records of the Royal Society*, 24, 1970, 224.

mathematically conclusive.'[39] For we must set these statements in their industrial context, as well as allowing for an eighteenth-century writer's use of language which is somewhat different from our own. The chemical manufacturer did not work with purified reagents in a laboratory. He worked with sand, sea-salt, clays, limestones, metallic compounds, and coal whose compositions were complex and far from fully understood. He had to learn, partly in the light of technical experience and partly with the aid of scraps of laboratory chemistry, so to treat these materials that they yielded the desired products, using again a few analytical tools from science but also much familiarity with how a preparation should feel when handled, or how its appearance changed during treatment. So smiths had long judged the heat of iron. Wedgwood's pyrometric experiments were one attempt to quantify such subjective appraisals, but their one field of application hardly impinged on the accumulated mass of craft experience.

Similarly engineering mechanics in the late eighteenth century owed hardly more than an indefinite concept of 'force' (commonly rendered as synonymous with 'power') to the progress of theoretical mechanics since the time of Huygens and Newton, nor were its mathematics the mathematics of science. Rational and experimental students of machines did not start from the laws of motion, though they knew them. They employed no clear concepts of momentum and kinetic energy. They began with information about the performance of actual machines, so as to compare one design with another (for example, an undershot wheel and an overshot wheel) or, like Smeaton, they made model experiments to obtain more precise comparative data.[40] They examined the relation between the speed of the wheel and that of the water moving it. They investigated the effect of employing blades of different shapes, or boilers of different design. They developed a unit of their own for measuring the power of machines, which did not yet enter into the scientific vocabulary. By such search for perfected machines, by their eagerness to build only according to the most rationally efficient design, by their willingness to exploit useful devices (as Watt took the centrifugal governor from the windmill and applied it to the

---

[39] Musson and Robinson (op. cit. note 5), p. 74.
[40] At about the same time (i.e. in 1770) a structural engineer, E. M. Gauthey, made the first tests of the strength of building-stone in connection with an actual construction (S. B. Hamilton in C. Singer, E. J. Holmyard, A. R. Hall and T. I. Williams, *A History of Technology*, IV, Clarendon Press, 1958, p. 480).

steam engine) they greatly hastened the evolution of techniques. If to seek for quantitative measure is science, then these men were scientific in their approach to engineering; but I do not believe that to be an adequate definition of science. And just as the metallurgists created new craft skills by learning to manage smelting or puddling, or the chemical manufacturers mastered their retorts, so a new kind of engineering was created in which quantitative use of tabulated empirical data and simple equations linking the variables of concern to the engineer became important. In a sense this new form of design was as empirical as the old shipwright's rules for shaping a hull, since no fundamental physical reasons could be given in most cases to explain why its principles were valid; they had been established by testing, measurement and analysis of the behaviour of actual, or model, machines and structures. Accordingly, no reason of principle could be stated in 1820 why a high-pressure steam engine should be more efficient than one working at low pressure; and Thomas Young could write of the Telford-Douglas proposal in 1798 to throw a single cast-iron arch across the Thames: 'It would be difficult to find greater discordance in the most heterodox professions of faith, or in the most capricious variation of tastes, than is exhibited in the responses of our most celebrated professors on almost every point [concerning this proposed bridge] submitted for their consideration.'[41] Quite frankly, the greatest English engineers were wholly unable to determine the stresses in such an elastic structure, though much of the basic theory had been set out many years before by Coulomb. They had inherited a sound though limited engineering tradition, and developed it much further, without borrowing from or themselves creating a rational science of structures.

Modern engineering, with its use of formulae and calculation, was indeed nascent in the late eighteenth century. But there was then, and to a less extent is still now, much more to progress in engineering than the application of science. Before a structure or a machine can be built it must be designed; so must the plant required for a chemical manufacture. And as Hugh Clausen has insistently remarked, design is as much an art as a science:

One sees articles dealing with the scientific, analytical, or experimental aspects [of engineering] illustrated by formulae, graphs, and tables ... but the next thing one sees is a photograph of the finished article, which tells

---

[41] Quoted idem, ibid., p. 484.

you nothing – except what the thing looks like from the outside. Of the really difficult and important thing, the transformation of ideas into iron-mongery, there is usually not a hint. It is apparently inferred that these things just happen by themselves – that there is nothing of real importance in them.[42]

The technicians and entrepreneurs of the early Industrial Revolution in Britain excelled in 'transforming ideas into ironmongery', a problem made all the more acute for them by their desire to adopt new materials and new methods. In order to make this double form of innovation effective they had to modify traditional design procedures, though not departing from them entirely. Moreover, they had to solve quickly the problems so created. They could not wait for a slow accumulation of experience in building with cast iron, such as architects had accumulated in masonry construction, nor could the steam engine, like the water-mill, evolve over the centuries. The opportunity for engineers to create large, fireproof buildings, more powerful engines and swifter transport could not be postponed. Hence they turned to calculation and experiment to discover what could be done, drawing in a minor way on the ideas of the physical sciences, but employing also their own experience and technical intuition of what constituted sound design. But the point is that it was engineers and inventors who experienced the opportunity, and who created the new design methods to exploit it. They did not find these methods ready made to their hand in science. And it was they who chose, according to their necessities, fragments of scientific theorization to fit into their new ideas of engineering design – it was not the force of scientific truth that compelled them to do this, but the desire to derive quickly a sound and economical answer to a design problem. The history of the Industrial Revolution in Britain shows amply how ready the technical innovators were to work out new ideas empirically when, as was then so often the case, science had little guidance to offer.

---

[42] Hugh Clausen, *Engineering Design – the Background and Basis of Contemporary Life* (Institution of Engineering Designers Lecture, 1958).

VII

Home Demand and Economic Growth: A New View of the Role of Women and Children in the Industrial Revolution

NEIL McKENDRICK

Man's inhumanity to man has, over the centuries, been surpassed only by his inhumanity to women and children. And few periods are as richly credited with such exploitation and brutal ill-treatment as that of the Industrial Revolution in Britain. This is, for most, the period *par excellence* of child and female labour, of sweat shops and their attendant Gradgrinds, of intolerably long hours and pitifully low wages, of frightful working conditions, scarcely better living conditions, and hopelessly inadequate diet. Judged by our standards such a portrait of an age is not unreasonable; and judged by any standards it is a portrait which contains much that is undeniably true.

That it is far from the whole truth is equally undeniable. But first let us acknowledge the black side.

The traditional view of the role of women and children in industry is one which justifiably evokes compassion. Their place in society as a whole was not a comfortable or a just one. Both were exploited groups and both were underprivileged. Their position was unambiguously dependent on, and subordinate to, that of men, and they were encouraged to make what they could of their dependence, to exploit their inferiority. As Mrs John Sandford wrote in 1837 in *Women in their Social and Domestic Character*, 'Women are something like children: the more they show their need of support, the more engaging they are.'[1]

In this appealingly inferior role women were allowed few rights.

[1] Quoted by Joan Evans, *The Victorians* (1966), p. 109.

Inequality of the sexes was the rule, not the exception:[2] adultery by a wife, for instance, justified divorce; adultery by a husband did not.[3] Even after the reforms of 1857 a wife had to show, in order to achieve a divorce, that her husband was guilty not only of adultery but also of cruelty, desertion, bigamy, incest, rape or unnatural offences. 'It was a failing common to mankind in general', said the Lord Chancellor, 'that, although the sin in both cases was the same, the effect of adultery on the part of the husband was very different from that of adultery on the part of the wife. It was possible for a wife to pardon a husband who had committed adultery; but it was hardly possible for a husband ever really to pardon the adultery of a wife.'[4] And this was only a modest echo of an earlier view that 'Forgiveness on the part of a wife ... is meritorious, while a similar forgiveness on the part of a husband would be degrading and dishonourable.'[5] In practice the limitations on women's rights were far greater than such discussions indicate. Legal debates on women's rights were purely academic for most of society, and the chances of most women being able to take advantage of the 1857 reforms would, of course, be virtually non-existent.[6]

Women's property rights were little better than their sexual rights. Although married women could benefit under a trust, they could own no property, a situation which Dr Joan Evans exemplified rather tartly when she wrote: 'Charlotte Brontë found with a certain surprise, after her marriage to her father's curate in 1854, that the ownership and direction of her copyrights, and the enjoyment of her royalties, had passed to her husband.'[7]

So much was the ownership of most women in England vested in men that it was widely believed abroad that Englishmen could sell their wives on the open market. Indeed such cases are not unknown: Thomas Heath bought the wife of George Fuller for '2¼d. the pound

---

[2] Keith Thomas, 'The Double Standard', *Journal of the History of Ideas*, 20 (1959).
[3] O. R. McGregor, *Divorce in England* (1957).
[4] Parliamentary Debates, 3rd Ser., Vol. 145, col. 490, quoted by Thomas, op. cit. p. 202.
[5] Sir John Nicholls in 1825, quoted in J. Haggard, *Reports on Cases argued and determined in the Ecclesiastical Courts at Doctor's Commons, and in the High Court of Delegates* (London, 1829–32), I, p. 752. See Thomas, op. cit. p. 202.
[6] For their redress working-class women often relied not on the law of the land, but on local custom. Instead of divorce there were local corrective devices such as *y ceffyl pren* (or wooden horse) of South-West Wales: see Trefor M. Owen, *Welsh Folk Customs* (1959), p. 168, and D. Williams, *The Rebecca Riots: A Story of Agrarian Discontent* (1955), pp. 53–6.
[7] Joan Evans, *The Victorians* (1966), p. 104.

in 1696',[8] navvies transacted similar sales in the mid-nineteenth century,[9] and many other transactions of this kind are well evidenced and recorded.[10] As Keith Thomas mildly remarked, 'One does not have to prove the widespread existence of wife-selling in order to be able to assert that until the mid-nineteenth century the ownership of most women was vested in men, but it provides an interesting if somewhat exaggerated illustration.'[11]

Women's political rights were even less encouraging for they scarcely existed at all. Their political activity was very limited, too. In the 1830s there were some local, and usually short-lived, efforts to get equal pay; and they were swept along by the general enthusiasm of the attempt at General Union in 1834,[12] but independent political action by women was rare. When it did happen, the reaction was revealingly alarmist. A prison-magistrate expressed his shock at the 'Spirit of Combination to dictate to their Employers and to raise the price of their wages' by a group of Loughborough women in 1811;[13] and the Leeds Mercury of 4 May 1832 reacted even more strongly to a wage-protest meeting of women cord-setters, writing: 'Alarmists may view these indications of female independence as more menacing to established institutions than the education of the lower orders.'[14]

Without the vote, without adequate legal protection and without adequate wages, women were politically, legally and financially an unambiguously underprivileged group. They were not allowed the same sexual freedom as men, nor the same educational opportunities. Their career choice was cripplingly limited; and, not surprisingly, their accomplishments could easily be disparaged. 'I have long sought for some instances of invention or discovery by a woman. And the best I have been able to find is Thwaites' soda water. A Miss Thwaites of Dublin, an amateur chemist, hit on an improvement of soda water, which enabled her to drive all others out of the market. But besides this, some small musical compositions, and some pretty novels and poems, are all the female inventions I can find.'[14a]

---

[8] Keith Thomas, The Double Standard, p. 213.

[9] Terry Coleman, The Railway Navvies (1965).

[10] H. W. V. Temperley, 'The Sale of Wives in England in 1823' in History Teachers' Miscellany (May 1925), 111, p. 5.

[11] Keith Thomas, op. cit. p. 5.   [12] Barbara Drake, Women in Trade Unions, pp. 4-5.

[13] J. L. and Barbara Hammond, The Town Labourer, p. 262.

[14] John Wade, History of the Middle and Working Classes, pp. 570-71.

[14a] Richard Whately, Miscellaneous Remains (1864). See Evans, op. cit. p. 118.

Women were allowed to undertake drudgery. Indeed they were held to excel at it. Most manual work – even dragging coal trucks in the mines – was open to them. And, within these limits, the job opportunities of working-class women increased spectacularly as a result of mechanization. They were held – along with children – to be particularly well fitted to the monotonous and repetitive tasks of so much early factory work.

It was not impossible for women to break out of these restrictions. Upper- and middle-class women could and did become writers, poets and artists. There were even some female entrepreneurs. Influential wives could operate under cover of a husband who acted as a front man; widows could take over an already flourishing concern. But usually the sexual prejudices were too strong and, when to those were added the social obstacles of class prejudice, women's escape was virtually impossible.

Very little progress was made in their position, despite the claims made on their behalf and the controversies stirred up by works like Mary Wollstonecraft Godwin's *A Vindication of the Rights of Women* (1792), William Thompson's *Appeal of One Half of the Human Race, Women, Against the Pretensions of their Other Half, Men, to Retain them in Political and Thence in Civil and Domestic Slavery* (1825), or John Stuart Mill's *The Subjection of Women* (1869).[15] The fact that as late as 1868 F. P. Cobbe could write an article in *Fraser's Magazine* entitled 'Criminals, Idiots, Women and Minors: is the Classification Sound?'[16] indicates the limits of that progress. For all the passionate debate women remained the victims of a double standard which operated almost wholly in favour of men. A delectable example of their position is revealed by a proposal in 1838 that an innocent wife, separated from her husband, might be allowed, if she were of irreproachable conduct, certain limited rights of access to her children. Brougham cunningly defeated the Bill in the Lords by suggesting that when women were the victims of so many unjust laws it was scarcely worthwhile to 'amend one small item of hardship'[17] – a debating technique almost on the

---

[15] See also William Alexander, *History of Women from Earliest Antiquity to the Present Time* (3rd ed., 1782); *Women Physiologically Considered* (1839); Mary Wollstonecraft Godwin, *Thoughts on the Education of Daughters* (1787); Thomas Gisborne, *An Inquiry into the Duties of the Female Sex* (1798); Priscilla Wakefield, *Reflections on the Present Condition of the Female Sex with Suggestions for its Improvement* (1798).

[16] *Fraser's Magazine*, 78 (1868), pp. 777–94.

[17] Joan Evans, *The Victorians*, p. 103.

level of the most famous second order argument of all, that one could
not abolish the death penalty because of the inevitable damage to the
rope trade.

It was not a minority group which suffered these various deprivations
and injustices. The female victims of prejudice were very numerous,
usually more numerous than men. For, although those who married
had to run the gauntlet of frequent pregnancies and a high infant
mortality rate,[18] more girls than boys survived the rigours of infancy.
By 1851, there were 365,159 more women than men. Indeed, by then
one of the major ingredients of the debate on women was the problem
of their surplus numbers,[19] and it is significant that one of the principal
concerns of those who wrote was the dangers of having 'a large single
female population seeking gainful employment and financial independence'. 'Why are Women Redundant?' was the title of an essay
by W. R. Greg; 'What Shall We Do With Our Old Maids?' was
another by F. P. Cobbe; and the ubiquitous Jessie Boucherett contributed an article on 'How to Provide for Superfluous Women' in
Joseph Butler's *Women's Work and Women's Culture*. The controversy
already flourishing in the *Edinburgh Review*,[20] *Blackwood's Magazine*,[21]
the *Westminster Review*,[22] and *Fraser's Magazine*[23] intensified. To a

---

[18] Even as late as 1900 one in six children died before the age of one year [154 deaths
per 1,000]. Now it is less than one in fifty.

[19] S. B. Kanner, 'The Women of England in a Century of Social Change, 1815–1914:
A Select Bibliography', *Suffer and Be Still: Women in the Victorian Age*, ed. M. Vicinus,
(1973), p. 183. See also below, footnotes 20 to 24.

[20] *The Edinburgh Review*: S. Smith, 'Advice to Young Ladies on the Improvement of
the Mind', 15 (1810), 299–315; E. G. E. Bulwer-Lytton, 'Spirit of Society', 52 (1831),
374–87; T. H. Lister, 'Rights and Conditions of Women', 73 (1841), 189–209;
M. Oliphant, 'Mill's Subjection of Women', 130 (1869), 572–602.

[21] *Blackwood's Magazine*: J. Neal, 'Men and Women', 16 (1824), 387–94; J. G. Phillimore,
'Women's Rights and Duties', 54 (1843), 373–97; M. Oliphant, 'The Condition
of Woman', 92 (1862), 183–201; M. Todd, 'Some Thoughts on the Woman
Question', 156 (1894), 689–92.

[22] *The Westminster Review*: H. Martineau, 'Criticism of Women', 32 (1838–39), 454–75;
M. Mylne, 'Woman and Her Social Position', 35 (1841), 24–52; T. H. Rearden,
'Mission of Woman', 52 (1849–50), 352–67; 'Capabilities and Disabilities of Women',
67 (1857), 42–59; 'Capacities of Women', 84 (1865), 352–80; 'J. S. Mill's "Subjection
of Women" ', 93 (1870), 63–89; 'Emancipation of Women', 128 (1887), 165–73; and
'Changing Status of Women', 818–28; E. Ethelmer, 'Feminism', 149 (1898), 50–62;
N. Arling, 'The Role of the New Woman', 150 (1898), 576–87; 'Privilege versus
Justice to Women', 152 (1899), 128–41; W. K. Hill, 'Equality with Man', 160 (1903),
647–64; F. S. Franklin, 'Women and their Emancipation', 161 (1904), 407–19.

[23] *Fraser's Magazine*: 'The Female Character', 7 (1833), 591–601; 'Woman and the
Social System', 21 (1840), 698–702; H. T. Buckle, 'The Influence of Women on the

society in which the only proper occupation for a woman was to be a wife and a mother, the 'excess of females' revealed by the 1851 census posed an obvious conundrum. Emigration was a much favoured alternative to employment – much favoured, that is, by the male commentators, for the reverse disproportion existed in the colonies and British spinsters could hopefully be banished to their proper or natural fate as wives for the frustrated colonists. To avoid alarming the anti-feminists, women who worked in family businesses were often classed in the census returns as 'unoccupied women', and female innkeepers and beer-sellers put in the 'domestic class', but nevertheless in his 1885 review of the census data Charles Mackeson called 'the growth of female industry . . . the most striking figure of the census'.[24]

Their numbers made women a vital part of the labour force, and so *a fortiori* did the numbers of children. For children in this period were not a small minority group. One of the most striking characteristics of pre-industrial society was 'its overwhelming youthfulness'[25] – an inevitable result of a high death rate and very low expectation of life. The characteristic was not changed in the first century of industrialization. It may have become even more marked. If we accept – as most demographers now do – an important role for an increase in the birth rate in bringing about the population explosion of the Industrial Revolution period, the average age of the population may have fallen lower still, despite the fall in mortality and the consequent increase in the expectation of life. Gregory King estimated that 47.8 per cent of the population in 1695 were under 19, and what reliable evidence we have suggests that this remained true up to at least the middle of the nineteenth century. Estimates for 1821 for England and Wales put the proportion in the 0–19 age group at 49 per cent – the proportion now

---

Progress of Knowledge', 57 (1858), 395–407; F. P. Cobbe, 'Criminals, Idiots, Women and Minors: is the Classification Sound?', 78 (1868), 777–94; M. Oliphant, 'Grievances of Women', n.s. 21 (1880), 698–710.

[24] C. Mackeson, *The British Almanac and Companion* (1885). See also Edward Cheshire, *The Results of the Census of Great Britain in 1851* (1853); Henry Mayhew, *London Labour and the London Poor* (1861–62), 4 vols., for statistical data concerning female employment. H. Martineau, 'Female Industry', *Edinburgh Review*, 109 (1859), pp. 293–336. J. Boucherett, 'On the Obstacles to the Employment of Women', *English Woman's Journal*, 4 (1860), pp. 361–75; J. Boucherett, 'Statistics as to the Employment of Women', *English Woman's Journal*, 12 (1864), pp. 400–8.

[25] Ivy Pinchbeck and Margaret Hewitt, *Children in English Society* (1973), vol. II, p. 387.

would be approximately 30 per cent because of the sharp fall in family size and the spectacular increase in life expectancy.[26]

Since they were so numerous it was essential that the young make their contribution to the labour force of the family and of the economy. A high proportion of young children can lead to what modern growth analysts call 'high dependency ratios'; and, as soon as they were able, children had to reduce that dependency by working. It was a commonplace of sixteenth- and seventeenth-century morality that a child should be set to some useful occupation by the age of six in order to avoid 'the sins and pitfalls of sloth and idleness'.[27] Children had found occupation in bird scaring, in stone picking, in weeding, in shepherding flocks, in milking, and in the domestic outwork industries for long before the coming of the Industrial Revolution, and in this way they had made their modest contribution to the household economy. But the coming of the factory changed both the work load and the returns in several significant ways.

The first and best-known result was to make the work longer, more regular, more punctual and, as a result, more financially productive. The technical breakthroughs in the textile industries reduced, and in some cases removed, the differential in strength between the adult and the child. Where certain kinds of finicky manual skills were required, the child was actually a more efficient and productive worker than its parent.

In rapid-growth sectors where demand for labour was high, the advantages for the entrepreneur were obvious. Unembarrassed by any sense of moral revulsion at child labour (and historically such a reaction would have been very strange in terms of the attitude of earlier generations to child labour – that is, that it was inevitable, desirable and beneficial), the enterprising manufacturers responded quickly to these advantages. What parental objection there was centred on the fragmentation of the family labour unit and the undermining of the father's dominant role as provider, teacher, trainer and disciplinarian. The work of Smelser,[28] Anderson,[29] Laslett[30] and their

---

[26] Peter Laslett, *The World We Have Lost* (1965), p. 103.

[27] See Philippe Ariès, *Centuries of Childhood* (1962), translated from the French (*L'Enfan et la vie familiale sous l'ancien régime* (1960)) by Robert Baldick.

[28] Neil J. Smelser, *Social Change in the Industrial Revolution* (1959).

[29] M. Anderson, *Family Structure in Nineteenth Century Lancashire* (1971).

[30] P. Laslett (ed.), *Household and Family in Past Times* (1972).

critics[31] has done much to illumine such changing relationships, and it is not my intention here to enter the controversies about the various competing sociological models. My concern is with the economic consequences of female and child labour, not with the internal tensions in the family unit.

According to the traditional view, the consequences of child labour are unambiguously disastrous. Those raised as children themselves on the pitiful experiences recorded in *A Memoir of Robert Blincoe*, with its history of savage punishment, sadistic cruelty, regular fourteen hours a day for six days a week, plus frequent overtime, will not wish to quarrel with the pessimistic verdict. When the Factory Act of 1802 tried – and, as was openly admitted, failed – to limit the work of poor law apprentices like Blincoe to not more than twelve hours' work a day, the case seems to be firmly closed and the verdict unarguable.[32] The verdict of Sadler's Committee of 1832 gives for many the official stamp of condemnation, and the ample literary evidence of the nineteenth century seems to confirm the truth of Sadler's charges. A couple of examples should suffice. Samuel Kydd wrote in 1857:

In stench, in heated rooms, amid the constant whirling of a thousand wheels, little fingers and little feet were kept in ceaseless action, forced into unnatural activity by blows from the heavy hands and feet of the merciless over-looker, and the infliction of bodily pain by instruments of punishment invented by the sharpened ingenuity of insatiable selfishness.[33]

Lord Shaftesbury recollected in 1873:

Well I can recollect in the earlier periods of the factory movement, waiting at the factory gate to see the children come out, and a set of sad, dejected, cadaverous creatures they were. In Bradford especially, the proofs of long and cruel toil were most remarkable. . . . A friend of mine collected a vast number together for me; the sight was most piteous, the deformities incredible. They seemed to me, such were their crooked shapes, like a mass of crooked alphabets.[34]

[31] For example, see M. M. Edwards and R. Lloyd Jones, 'N. J. Smelser and the Cotton Factory Family', Ch. 12 in *Textile History and Economic History: Essays in Honour of Miss Julia de Lacy Mann* (ed. by N. B. Harte and K. C. Ponting) (1973), pp. 304–19.

[32] See M. W. Thomas, *The Early Factory Legislation* (1948), pp. 9–13. See also P.P. 1816 III, Select Committee on the State of Children employed in the Manufactory of the United Kingdom. P.P. Report of the Inspector of Factories 1851 (1836–41).

[33] Samuel Kydd, *The History of the Factory Movement*, quoted by R. Fletcher, *The Family and Marriage in Britain* (1966).

[34] See Pinchbeck and Hewitt, *Children in English Society* (1973), p. 403, as well as Fletcher, op. cit. p. 101.

Such quotations are as moving as they are vivid, and they have been much cited. Together with the views of moralistic writers of the nineteenth century like Peter Gaskell,[35] with his overriding concern for the chastity of the working poor, and the earlier lamentations of writers like David Davies[36] and Sir Frederick Eden,[37] such quotations still colour most writers' attitudes to the role of women and children in the Industrial Revolution.

Despite the important addition to our knowledge and the corrections made to our judgement as a result of the work of Ivy Pinchbeck,[38] Margaret Hewitt,[39] Frances Collier,[40] Wanda Neff[41] and others,[42] the old orthodoxy dies hard and there remains much to correct. As Martha Vicinus wrote last year, 'little secondary work has been done

[35] P. Gaskell, *The Manufacturing Population of England* (1833), pp. 28, 31.

[36] David Davies, *The Case of Labourers in Husbandry Stated and Considered* (1795).

[37] Sir F. M. Eden, *The State of the Poor* (1797).

[38] Ivy Pinchbeck, *Women Workers and the Industrial Revolution, 1750–1850* (1930). Ivy Pinchbeck and Margaret Hewitt, *Children in English Society*, 2 vols. (1969–73).

[39] M. Hewitt, 'The Effect of Married Women's Employment in the Cotton Textile Districts on the Organization and Structure of the Home in Lancashire, 1840–1880' (London Ph.D. thesis, 1953). M. Hewitt, *Wives and Mothers in Victorian Industry* (1958).

[40] Frances Collier, *The Family Economy of the Working Classes in the Cotton Industry, 1784–1833*, edited by R. S. Fitton, with an introductory memoir by T. S. Ashton (1964).

[41] Wanda Neff, *Victorian Working Women: An Historical and Literary Study of Women in British Industries and Professions, 1832–1850* (1929).

[42] See also Martha Vicinus (ed.), *Suffer and Be Still: Women in the Victorian Age* (1973); D. M. Stanton, *The English Woman in History* (1957); D. Crow, *The Victorian Woman* (1971); B. L. Hutchins, *Women in Modern Industry* (1915); F. W. Tickner, *Women in English Economic History* (1923); C. W. Cunnington, *Feminine Attitudes in the Nineteenth Century* (1935); Dorothy Marshall, *The English Domestic Servant in History* (1949); J. Jean Hecht, *The Domestic Servant Class in Eighteenth Century England* (1956); Marjorie Plant, *The Domestic Life of Scotland in the Eighteenth Century* (1952); Alice Clark, *Working Life of Women in the Seventeenth Century*; W. R. Greg, 'Juvenile and Female Labour', *Edinburgh Review*, vol. 79 (1844), 130–56; John Milne, *Industrial and Social Employment of Women in the Middle and Lower Ranks* (1857); Barbara Leigh Smith Bodichon, *Women and Work* (1856); Anna Jameson, *The Communion of Labour: A Lecture on the Social Employment of Women* (1856); G. E. and V. R. Fussell, *The English Country Woman: the Internal Aspect of Rural Life, 1500–1900* (1953); *Victorian Studies*: 'The Victorian Woman: A Special Issue', 14 (1970); Patricia Thompson, *The Victorian Heroine, A Changing Ideal* (1956). See also P. Laslett, N. J. Smelser, M. Anderson, op. cit. For the best bibliographies see S. Barbara Kanner, 'The Women of England in a Century of Social Change 1815–1914: A Select Bibliography', Ch. 10 in *Suffer and Be Still* (ed. Martha Vicinus), pp. 173–206; O. R. McGregor, 'The Social Position of Women in England, 1850–1914: A Bibliography', *British Journal of Sociology*, 6 (1955).

on the nineteenth-century British woman in the context of wider social change'.[43] Dr Kanner confirmed that in her bibliographical study when she wrote: 'There are few systematic, historically oriented studies that relate changes in English women's status to national socio-economic phenomena in terms of time, place and circumstances.'[44] The difficulty of doing justice to the economic benefits which flowed from the employment of women and children (and indeed to some consequential social benefits) is exacerbated by the emotional response of so many critics of that employment.

It has been pointed out that alongside the pessimistic *Memoir of Robert Blincoe* can stand the optimistic verdict of the *Memoir of Kitty Wilkinson*; it has been pointed out that the Report of the Commission which enquired into the conditions of the employment of children in 1833 gave its opinion that: 'It appears that, of all employments to which children are subjected, those carried on in the factories are amongst the least laborious and of all departments of indoor labour amongst the least unwholesome. Handloom weavers, frame work knitters, lace runners, and work people in other lines of domestic manufacture are in most cases worked at an earlier age for longer hours and for less wages than the body of children employed in factories.'[45] As Plumb wrote over twenty years ago, 'The worst conditions, long hours, . . . gross exploitation of female and child labour, were to be found in small scale and domestic industry';[46] and, as Pinchbeck and Hewitt confirmed last year, 'Here, as in so many other respects, the experience of factory industry, far from being unique, was in fact the experience of cottage and workshop industry writ large for all to see. More readily observed in the factory than in the obscurity of the cottage, the conditions and consequences of employment in the mills, especially of women and children, were increasingly made a matter for concern.'[47] But for all the qualifications, for all the truth of the point that child and female labour was nothing new, that the hours and conditions of work which now evoked such passionate sympathy were a prolongation of what had long existed unseen and unremarked, the protests continued, and there were ample reasons why they should.

[43] Martha Vicinus, op. cit. p. vii.
[44] Barbara Kanner, loc. cit. p. 173. The three outstanding exceptions listed by Kanner are the works by Ivy Pinchbeck, Margaret Hewitt and Neil J. Smelser.
[45] Quoted by Fletcher, op. cit. p. 86, Pinchbeck and Hewitt, p. 403.
[46] J. H. Plumb, *England in the Eighteenth Century* (1950), p. 88.
[47] Pinchbeck and Hewitt, op. cit. p. 406.

The nature of this response was coloured by the genuine humanitarian feelings of many critics of female and child labour. It was coloured even more by the reaction to the stories of immorality in the factories – the lack of chastity among the women and the moral dangers which faced the young. It was deeply influenced by the changing size of the problem and the fact that female and child labour in the factories was difficult to overlook. It was much affected by the revelations of the Blue Books and the reaction of the literary world to those revelations.

Wanda Neff has shown how closely related to the revelations of the Blue Books was the literary response of the nineteenth century. As she says, 'By 1850 fiction was in harness to moral obligation.'[48]

The Victorians had 'discovered the sanctity of childhood' and, for all the work of apologists, they could not deny that frightful abuses of women and children *were* being perpetrated, even if they were not new or particular to, or even characteristic of, the factories. An emotional response to a social evil was more likely to succeed than scholarly qualification, and understandably so; and the emotional response attracted the better writers. Wordsworth was more effective than Andrew Ure with his picture of factory children as happy little elves at play. Dickens was a better propagandist than Chadwick, and Engels a more memorable polemicist than Cooke-Taylor. History and social comment are usually more acceptable when they provide one with a villain – helpless victims are a further bonus. When the moral absolutes are obvious, when the verdict is given in unrelieved black and white, the response can be equally whole-hearted, and so it was in the early nineteenth century. Wordsworth was not dealing in ambiguities when he wrote:

> Men, maidens, youths,
> Mothers and little children, boys and girls,
> Enter, and each the wonted task resumes
> Within His temple, where is offered up
> To Gain, the master idol of the realm,
> Perpetual sacrifice.[49]

Many authors had a clear picture of what their audience wanted and made sure that they provided it. 'Mrs Trollope, with a careful finger

[48] Neff, op. cit. p. 16.
[49] William Wordsworth, *The Excursion*, Book VIII, 11, 180–5.

on the pulse of her public, responded by writing *Michael Armstrong* to circulate the abuse of factory children. Charlotte Brontë apologized for *Villette* because it took up no "philanthropic scheme".'[50] Whatever the truth of the matter, female and child labour was seen as a novel abuse which must be condemned.

Female characters who are wage earners are introduced into fiction in a major way for the first time; child workers proliferate. The enormous popularity of writers like Mrs Tonna shows that there was a ready market. 'She saved herself from the evils of fiction by composing a species of tales, not novels, because they were based upon the truth. She took the unwieldy Blue Books of Parliament reporting the suffering of factory women and children, selected the most harrowing facts, and made them the experiences of imaginary characters.'[51]

To reinforce the sense of present injustice, the past became a romantic idyll. In the pre-industrial world, labour was romantically interpreted as creative, satisfying and wholesome. The prelapsarian myth of the golden past which had been shattered by industry – a myth which flourished in the days of Ruskin and William Morris – had started to sprout earlier. The grinding toil of previous centuries was transmuted into hymns of creativity and job satisfaction as

> Maids at the wheel
> Sit blithe and happy.[52]

It is doubtful whether the pre-industrial woman who lived in an environment which was sufficiently inhospitable to keep her average expectation of life at birth well below thirty;[53] whose prospective husband enjoyed such meagre rewards for his labour that he had to delay his marriage age and hers to the late twenties or even later;[54] whose life was constantly threatened by disease; whose children had a high likelihood of death before the age of five; whose home was a

---

[50] Elizabeth Cleghorn Gaskell, *The Life of Charlotte Bronte*, p. 364, quoted by W. Neff, op. cit. p. 16.

[51] Neff, op. cit. p. 16. See also Ivanka Kovacevic and S. Barbara Kanner, 'Blue Book into Novel: The Forgotten Industrial Fiction of Charlotte Elizabeth Tonna', *Nineteenth Century Fiction*, 25 (1973), 152–73.

[52] William Wordsworth, *Nuns Fret Not*.

[53] E. A. Wrigley, 'Mortality in Pre-Industrial England', *Daedalus*, Journal of the American Academy of Arts and Science, Vol. 97, 2 (Spring, 1968).

[54] E. A. Wrigley, 'Family Limitation in Pre-Industrial England', *Economic History Review*, XIX (April 1966).

miserable rural hovel;[55] and whose own labour yielded such small returns that probate records find very modest possessions to record – it is doubtful whether such women, and they were in all probability the norm, would exhibit 'the reactions which would satisfy a modern enthusiast for the peasant arts'.[56]

Historians dealing with female and child labour, like Ivy Pinchbeck, Dorothy George, Alice Clark, Lilian Knowles and Wanda Neff, have tried to demolish the prelapsarian myth, but its hold is still strong. As Wanda Neff acidly pointed out, 'even spinning before the cottage doorway has its hardships', and Alice Clark has indicated how meagre were the financial rewards for such 'happy toil': 2s. 6d. was the average weekly earnings of the woman spinner, and it often required a fourteen-fifteen- or sixteen-hour day to produce it.[57]

Long hours of work for women were not new, but the machinery to make these hours of work as productive as the work of men *was* new – and so, therefore, was the motive to offer greater rewards than ever before to women workers, and to employ a greater number of them than ever before, and no longer as a supplement to the domestic labour, or as a help in milking and harvesting, but as separate, independent wage earners. To a lesser extent the same change took place for the child worker. It was this which attracted so much contemporary antipathy. 'Classing women and children together as helpless creatures needing the protection of strong men, they were indignant at the knowledge that women had to support themselves.'[58] Others were indignant that they *could* support themselves – and that they could extravagantly display that independence in ostentatious expenditure on clothes and fashion and all the other products of the booming consumer industries.

The need of the Victorians to rewrite the role of women and children in the past stemmed from their view of their proper role in the present. The Victorians' view of the family and the role of the ideal woman in it also helps to explain why they so misunderstood and misrepresented the economic importance of these two groups of workers.

[55] Stanley D. Chapman, ed., *A History of Working Class Housing: A Symposium* (1971).
[56] Dorothy George, quoted Fletcher, op. cit. p. 82, and Pinchbeck and Hewitt, op. cit. p. 398–9.
[57] Alice Clark, *Working Life of Women in the Seventeenth Century*, pp. 95, 113, 114.
[58] Neff, op. cit. p. 14.

The literary reaction reveals this very clearly. Wanda Neff accurately described the change when she wrote: 'To the Victorian belongs the discovery of the woman worker as the object of pity, and in the literature of the early nineteenth century one first finds her portrayed as the victim of long hours, unfavourable conditions and general injustice.'[59] All the evils were of long standing, but the novel feature of the women who worked in the Industrial Revolution was that they earned substantial wages. 'It was women in the aspect of wage-earners . . . who aroused suddenly indignant defenders.'[60] Women and children left the cottages where they had toiled in obscurity and flocked to the mills to become the dominant part of the work force. It was argued by mid-century that two million women had to be self-supporting. The importance of their contribution to the economy has been less well recorded and appreciated partly because so much of the reaction to it was frankly hostile. Women workers simply 'did not harmonize with the philosophy of the Victorians'[61] and their glorification of the home and the mother's position in it. The changing attitude to women has been well characterized by Martha Vicinus in her perceptive study of the changing criteria for the perfect woman.[62] 'Prior to and at the beginning of the nineteenth century the ideal had been the 'perfect wife'. The perfect wife was an active participant in the family, fulfilling a number of vital tasks . . . she was expected in the lower classes to contribute to the family income. In the middle classes she provided indirect economic support. . . . This model gave way to an ideal which had little connection with any functional and responsible role in society.'[63]

Firstly, the perfect Victorian lady did not work. Since circumstances made it impossible for the working-class woman to attain this ideal, the perfect woman was one 'who kept to her family, centering all her life on keeping the house clean, the children well disciplined and her daughters chaste'.[64] In this way the ideal woman like the ideal lady would be wholly dependent on her husband. 'The worker with her own earnings was, accordingly, an affront against nature and the protective instincts of man.'[65] In nineteenth-century literature the

---

[59] Ibid., p. 11.　　　　[60] Ibid., p. 13.　　　　[61] Ibid., p. 14.
[62] Martha Vicinus, 'The Perfect Victorian Lady', introduction to *Suffer and Be Still.*
[63] Ibid., p. ix. See also J. A. and Olive Banks, *Feminism and Family Planning in Victorian England,*and C. Willet Cunnington, op. cit., for definitions of the Victorian ideal.
[64] Ibid., p. xiv.　　　　[65] Neff, op. cit, p. 37.

family economy to which the working wife contributed was replaced (in the ideal version) by the single male wage earner and the family-based wife. For this reason alone many contemporaries were better psychologically attuned to see the social drawbacks to female labour rather than any economic benefits. A woman's clear duty was to be a wife and mother, and the anti-feminist *Saturday Review* quite explicitly stated that women should be offered 'no alternative lest they never marry'.[66]

Another reason for the reluctance to recognize any good in female employment was the Victorians' view that women should be sexless, innocent and chaste. The final step in the campaign to protect female chastity was, wrote Keith Thomas, 'the most remarkable of all, for it amounted to nothing less than the total desexualization of women'.[67] The *Westminster Review* referred gratefully to that 'kind decision of nature' which, assisted by the English educational system, had ensured that sexual desire in women was dormant 'till excited by actual intercourse';[68] others went further and said that, 'happily for society', the supposition that women possess sexual feeling could be put aside as 'a vile aspersion',[69] and Mrs Ellis advised married women in a memorable phrase in her book of etiquette, *The Daughters of England*, that their 'highest duty is so often to suffer and be still'.[70]

When such views were current the statements by Place in 1822 that there was 'no chastity among the absolute poor',[71] and by Peter Gaskell that 'sexual intercourse was almost universal prior to marriage',[72] or by Engels that 'three fourths of the factory hands between fourteen and twenty were unchaste',[73] excited frantic concern. It has been suggested that early nineteenth-century reaction to conditions of female and child labour owed as much to sexual envy as it did to outraged social conscience. Certainly prurience played a major role. Statistics were bandied about with frenzied lack of logic. One of Mrs Tonna's charac-

---

[66] Vicinus, op. cit. pp. xiii–xiv.

[67] Thomas, op. cit. p. 215.

[68] *The Westminster and Foreign Quarterly Review* (April–July 1856), p. 457. Quoted Thomas, op. cit. p. 215.

[69] Ibid.

[70] Mrs Ellis, *The Daughters of England* (1845), p. 73, quoted by Vicinus, op. cit. p. x. As Thomas confirms, 'Respectable Victorian wives were educated to regard the act of procreation as a necessary and rather repulsive duty', op. cit. p. 215.

[71] Quoted in M. C. Stopes, *Contraception*, 6th ed. (1946), p. 280.

[72] P. Gaskell, *The Manufacturing Population of England* (1833), pp. 28–31.

[73] F. Engels, *Condition of the Working Class in England in 1844*.

ters declares that 'but one girl in fifty kept her character after she went to the mills';[74] and factory girls were at one and the same time accused of sexual immorality (the level of which was measured by the high number of illegitimate children they were alleged to bear) and of the sin of contraception (the level of which was measured by the low number of illegitimate children they bore).[75]

There are thus ample explanations for a pessimistic verdict on the role of women and children in the early stages of industrialization, and for the failure of most contemporary commentators to note the benefits which could stem from it. There were, of course, those who recognized that those 'families whose aggregate income is larger'[76] enjoyed a higher standard of living, and correctly identified the source of the extra income as the wages of wives and children.

As early as 1810 it was stated in Parliament that: 'If anyone would take the trouble to compute the amount of all the earnings of children . . . he would be surprised, when he came to consider the weight which their support took off the country, and the addition which, by the fruits of their toil, and the habits to which they were formed, was made to its internal opulence.'[77] And the value of the contribution of female and juvenile wage earners was well recognized by the working class. But the nineteenth-century criteria for maternal and family excellence meant that more often than not these earnings were regarded as a threat to male authority, a temptation to female luxury and indulgence, and an incitement of female independence. 'That's the worst of factory work for girls. They can earn so much when work is plenty, that they can maintain themselves.'[78] The moral disapproval of the luxurious spending of the poor is coloured in much contemporary literature, and when Mrs Gaskell recorded a working-class indulgence in ham, eggs, butter and cream, she felt she had to offer some explanation of the extravagance of such working class wives: 'But they were fine spinners, in the receipt of good wages, and confined all day in an atmosphere ranging from seventy-five to eighty-five degrees. They had lost all natural, healthy appetite for simple food, and having no

---

[74] Mrs Tonna, *Works*, Vol. I, pp. 554–5, for the case of Phoebe Wright.

[75] Neff, op. cit. pp. 53–6.

[76] Sir James Kay-Shuttleworth, *Four Periods of Public Education* (1862), pp. 7–8.

[77] *Parliamentary History*, Vol. XXXII (printed by Hansard, 1810), cols. 710–11, quoted Pinchbeck and Hewitt, op. cit. p. 39.

[78] Elizabeth Gaskell, *Mary Barton*, Ch. 3.

higher tastes, found their greatest enjoyment in their luxurious meals.'[79]

Foreign visitors to England in the late eighteenth and early nineteenth century laid great stress on the apparent prosperity of the English working classes. They wrote that one could not distinguish maids from their mistress;[80] that in Britain knee breeches and perukes, bonnets and panniered dresses could be seen on the very labourers in the fields;[81] that 'individuals of the lower classes were better clothed, better fed and better lodged than elsewhere (in Europe).'[82] K. P. Moritz wrote in 1782 that: 'Fashion is so generally attended to among the English women that the poorest servant is careful to be in the fashion, particularly in their hats and bonnets which they all wear.'[83]

The indigenous response confirmed the new conspicuous consumption but did so with a note of complaint and disapproval. Sir Frederick Eden constantly complained of the mis-spending of the poor on unnecessary luxuries and inessential fripperies:[84] others complained that those becoming marks of distinction between the classes were being obliterated by the extravagance of the lower ranks;[85] that working girls wore inappropriate finery, even silk dresses.[86] By some curious alchemy (explicable mainly in terms of their idea of what was proper for the working classes and for women in general) the ability of working girls to afford fashionable clothes was transmuted into a further reason to attack the employment of women. It encouraged independence, it loosened their morals, it made them extravagant. The note of disapproval grew stronger in the nineteenth century: Disraeli described mill girls 'gaily dressed, . . . their hair scrupulously arranged; they wore coral necklaces and earrings of gold';[87] and in *Mary Barton*, Esther was described as being 'dressed in her Sunday gown, with a new

[79] Elizabeth Gaskell, *Libbie Marsh's Three Eras*, Era I.

[80] See Richard Kent, 'Home Demand as a Factor in 18th Century English Economic Growth: The Literary Evidence' (unpublished M.Litt. thesis), (Cambridge, 1969).

[81] P. Kalm, *An Account of his Visit to England . . . in 1748* (translated by J. Lucas, 1892), p. 52.

[82] P. J. Grosley, *A Tour to London* (translated by T. Nugent, 1772), 11, p. 75. J. H. Meister, *Letters written during a Residence in England* (1799), p. 8.

[83] K. P. Moritz, *Journeys of a German in England in 1782* (1965), translated by R. Nettel.

[84] F. M. Eden, *The State of the Poor* (1797), I, Book II, Ch. II.

[85] See R. Kent, op. cit. *passim*.

[86] W. Neff, op. cit. p. 52.

[87] *Sybil*, Book II, Ch. IX.

ribbon in her bonnet, and gloves on her hands, like the lady she was so fond of thinking herself'.[88]

What foreigners remarked on with surprise, and what Englishmen described with disapproval, was a sign of the growing prosperity that could be enjoyed by some sections of the working classes as a result of child and female labour and the boost it could give to the earnings of the family unit. The new patterns of consumption played an important part in boosting home demand and fuelling economic growth. But it went largely unnoticed because child and female labour was so universally disapproved of. As Wanda Neff wrote many years ago,

No writer of the period found anything but evil in the downfall of the old feudal system. [The working woman] was dangerously independent because she had her own money. Even a wife began to adopt grand airs unbefitting her position. Although her husband was entitled legally to her wages and could get drunk on them while she and her children went without food . . . she often found a way of asserting her right to the money she had earned. . . . In these strange new ways the critics of the factory saw fresh evidence to support them in their position that women ought to be kept out of the mills. That both wives and daughters had worked even harder when they assisted the hand loom weaver at home, without the satisfaction of an independent wage was never suggested. . . . The economically independent wife who was a benefit to society because she was free, not a slave, was a figure of the future.[89]

For these reasons and as a result of what they suffered, the economic role of women and children in the Industrial Revolution has, perhaps understandably, excited more compassion than understanding, more disapproval than praise. They are pitied as victims of the economic process rather than honoured for their contribution to it; their work is seen as a moral evil rather than as a continuation of centuries of unsung and usually unpaid labour; their wages are regarded as being inhumanly low rather than as a significant increase on what the women and children of previous generations received; their earnings are regarded as a threat to male wage levels rather than seen as a vital contribution to the family income; their employment is condemned as competition for their husbands rather than praised for its contribution to an economy undergoing a uniquely rapid transformation. Too often they were, and are, simply stigmatized as necessarily inadequate wives

[88] Elizabeth Gaskell, *Mary Barton*, Ch. I, quoted Neff, op. cit. p. 52.
[89] Neff, op. cit. p. 53.

and mothers, rather than appreciated for their role in production and, even more important, for their role in consumption.

This is not to suggest that the traditional view is necessarily incompatible with the new. The old orthodoxy is not so much wrong as hopelessly incomplete. Much of the condemnation is right and reasonable. Much of the suffering and familial inadequacy was true. The lot of many women and children was as grim as it had ever been in the days of pre-industrial poverty and rural squalor, for some even grimmer. The fate of these victims has justifiably attracted pity, but they, and those who triumphed in these conditions, deserve more than that. It has been the fate of the working class in general to enjoy 'the enormous condescension of posterity': it has been the fate of women and children to receive the patronizing charity of posterity rather than recognition for the importance of their economic contribution.

The horrors, the injustice and the prejudice certainly existed. One cannot, and one would not wish to, deny their authenticity. One cannot deny that in years of depression such as 1839 to 1841 the inadequacy of their rewards was sufficiently widespread as to be typical in many northern industrial districts. Even in the more characteristic good years they always worked excessively long hours. In an age of inequitable distribution of wealth, the rewards of women and children were even more inequitable than men's. But to dwell only on the black side, and not to recognize what those long hours of work could yield in terms of family income, would be to misrepresent the past. It would be like dwelling solely on the horrors of war and ignoring the beneficial consequences that those who died had fought for. The sense of moral outrage for the casualties caused by industrialization, like that felt for the victims of war, is understandable but it should not block out all other reactions. To dwell only on the negative aspects of the phenomenon of child and female labour is to indulge in little more than propaganda, and propaganda is no less propaganda when it is on the side of the angels. Indeed, the kind of social history which lovingly picks over the scars and injustices of the past is like the kind of military history which confines itself to descriptions of the horrors of the battlefield and the agonies of the operating theatre. It has its descriptive uses but it does little to explain the past, and it does less than justice to the motives and aspirations and endeavours of those who actually suffered and achieved as a result of them.

There is a kind of social history which will always dwell lovingly on cancer of the scrotum in climbing boy chimney sweeps, or exploit the quick reaction to stories of the rampant immorality of the mill-hands, of female workers stumbling home 'blear eyed with drink and beastliness'[90] after a night of wanton toil – their torn garments and rumpled skirts a symbol of their fallen state and punctured maiden-heads. Purple prose is easier on such topics than on the thickets of wage data, family take-home earnings, and all the complications of regional variations, chronological fluctuations and occupational differentials in working-class prosperity. One kind presents the past as a battleground in which the fall of man occurred somewhere around 1760 and exploitation and immorality flourished on a hitherto unguessed-at level; the other approach might offer some explanation of the remaining paradoxes of how rapid economic growth accompanied these developments, how home demand absorbed such a proportion of the mass-consumption goods of the early Industrial Revolution. Who bought the cottons, woollens, linens and silks of the burgeoning British textile industries? Who consumed the massive increases in beer production? Who bought the crockery which poured from the Staffordshire potteries? Who bought the buckles, the buttons, the pins and all the minor metal products on which Birmingham fortunes were built? Who bought the Sheffield cutlery, the books of the booming publishers, the women's journals, the children's toys, the products o the nurserymen? Which families purchased the products of the early consumer industries? For it was in these industries that the Industrial Revolution began. All of these are questions of major importance to our understanding of the nature of demand.

There was a consumer revolution in the eighteenth century. J. H. Plumb has recently ransacked the work of 'a host of admirable antiquaries' to show how diversified that revolution was, but so far the explanations of why it occurred are inadequate and unsatisfying.

It has popularly been explained as a middle-class phenomenon – as Plumb wrote recently, 'All the activities that I have so far described point to the growth of a middle class audience'[91] – but why that middle-class audience grew in size, or in wealth or in propensity to consume, has been less satisfactorily explained.

---

[90] Quoted in Neil McKendrick, 'The Victorian View of Midland Industry', *Midland History* (1971), pp. 1–16.

[91] J. H. Plumb, *The Commercialisation of Leisure in Eighteenth-Century England*, The Stenton Lecture for 1972 (Reading 1973), p. 19.

In my view, the earnings of women and children and the important contribution they made to the family income can play an important part in providing a more satisfactory explanation. It is undeniable – for reasons I have tried to explore and to explain – that this aspect of female and child labour has been neglected. As the most recent critical bibliographer of female employment in the nineteenth century wrote last year, 'not as carefully noted is the situation of skilled and comparatively well-paid working-class women who improved their socio-economic condition and social status'.[92] The contribution of children's earnings to the status and buying power of their families has received even less attention.

It has been persuasively argued by Professor Eversley that 'the foundation of the industrial revolution . . . is laid by the home sale of articles of everyday life to a section of the labour force which was neither very poor nor very rich, but wielded effective purchasing power in the face of many difficulties'.[93] Eversley's new domestic market for mass-produced consumer goods is provided by the growth of a 'middle class of consumers' – accounted for by the emergence of an extra 150,000 households with an income over £50 a year.[94] For Eversley has recognized that 'the family, the unit of consumers and producers, plays a basic role'[95] . . . 'in the emergence, and maintenance' of a large domestic market for mass-produced consumer goods'.[96] He, like Professor Plumb, stresses that it is a middle-income market – 'What the postulated growth of the home market implies is merely that this middling group should have increased in size, relatively as well as absolutely, and had a greater margin of expenditure above necessaries.'[97] He sees this 'nascent *bourgeoisie*' as consisting of 'the artisans, the tradesmen, the more substantial farmers, the engineers and clerks. They are the new middle income group, they are also the rising part of the population.'[98] In my view, the market for mass consumer goods reached lower than that; it reached as far as the skilled factory worker and the domestic servant class, and it took much of its new impetus to consume from the earnings of women and children. It was, in my view,

[92] S. B. Kanner, loc. cit. p. 191.
[93] D. E. C. Eversley, 'The Home Market and Economic Growth in England, 1750–80', *Land, Labour and Population in the Industrial Revolution: Essays Presented to J. D. Chambers*, ed. by E. L. Jones and G. E. Mingay (1967), pp. 206–59.
[94] Ibid., p. 257.   [95] Ibid., p. 256.
[96] Ibid., p. 210–11.   [97] Ibid., p. 213.
[98] Ibid., p. 254.

their earnings which lifted so many household incomes over the
£50-a-year mark. The emotional outrage felt for female and child
labour has obscured their contribution; the moral disapproval of the
way in which they spent their new earnings prevented many contemporaries recognizing its economic and social importance. When the
pessimistic verdict dominated the historiography of the Industrial
Revolution, it would have been hazardous even to suggest that the
labour of women and children in the factories could produce benefits
for their families as well as profits for the entrepreneurs. Their earnings
were mentioned only to stress how low they were; their contribution
to the family income was mentioned more often for 'making up the
deficit in the family budget'[99] between the father's earnings and the
cost of subsistence, rather than for contributing to a surplus which
could be spent on non-essential consumer goods. In many families
'making up the deficit' must have been their main importance. In
depression years it was important even to the most prosperous sections
of the working class.[100] But in the more characteristic boom years
there existed, especially in the most rapid growth areas, conditions of
labour shortage and, therefore, high employment and high wages
which allowed the emergence of high family incomes as a result of
female and child labour – incomes between £100 and even £300 a
year being recorded by large families.[101] And what began in these
growth centres spread by diffusion and linkage effects, by imitation
and competition, to other parts of the labour force – to domestic
servants and even to agricultural labourers' families.

It is more possible to float such a hypothesis because of the changing
attitude to the industrial revolution, because of the recognition that
some at least of the labour force made substantial gains as a result of the
economic transformation of Britain.

As a result of recent research it is intrinsically more acceptable to
argue in favour of the beneficial aspects of female and child labour. The
'dark Satanic mills' view of the Industrial Revolution has received some

[99] See John Burnett, *A History of the Cost of Living* (1969), p. 181; Ivy Pinchbeck and
Margaret Hewitt, 'Children as Wage Earners in Early Industrialisation', Ch. XIV of
Children in English Society, p. 390; and Frances Collier, *The Family Economy of the
Working Classes in the Cotton Industry, 1784–1833* (1964).
[100] See F. Collier, op. cit. pp. 60–61, for the spectacular change in family earning between
1810 and 1811.
[101] Collier, op. cit. p. 50.

important corrective adjustments.[102] Some long-standing myths have been seriously questioned or even sucessfully challenged. In diet, it has been shown that 'throughout the industrial revolution most town workers ate better than countrymen';[103] in housing, 'the most recurrent theme' of a recent symposium 'is the response of the artisan élite to new economic opportunities and higher earnings. Individually, or in a co-operative enterprise, the skilled beneficiaries of industrial change can be seen striving to reach superior standards of accommodation and domestic comfort';[104] in wages and work load, it can be shown that for the skilled, and those willing to accept the responsibility of administrative posts, the rewards could be great and the hours of work less epic than sometimes assumed;[105] in attitudes to labour, it has been shown that eighteenth-century economists had abandoned a belief in keeping

[102] Some of the most important articles in the debate on living standards are R. M. Hartwell, 'Interpretations of the Industrial Revolution in England: A Methodological Enquiry', *Journal of Economic History*, XIX (1959); 'The Rising Standard of Living, 1800–1850', *Economic History Review*, XIII, no. 3 (1961); 'The Standard of Living during the Industrial Revolution', *Economic History Review*, XVI, no. 1 (1963); A. J. Taylor, 'Progress and Poverty in Britain, 1780–1850: A Reappraisal', *History*, XLV, no. 153 (1960); J. E. Williams, 'The British Standard of Living, 1750–1850', *Economic History Review*, XIX, no. 3 (1966); R. S. Neale, 'The Standard of Living, 1780–1844: A regional and class study', *Economic History Review*, XIX, no. 3 (1966). For the pessimistic verdict see E. P. Thompson, *The Making of the British Working Classes* (1963), and E. J. Hobsbawm, 'The British Standard of Living, 1790–1850', *Economic History Review*, X, no. 1 (1957); 'En Angleterre: Révolution industrielle et vie matérielle des classes populaires', *Annales*, XVII, p. 6 (1962); 'The Standard of Living Debate: A Postscript', Ch. 7 of *Labouring Men* (1964); 'History and "the Dark Satanic Mills" ', Ch. 6 of *Labouring Men* (1964); 'The Standard of Living during the Industrial Revolution', *Economic History Review*, XVI, no. 1 (1963). For other important statements see T. S. Ashton, 'The Standard of Life of the Workers in England, 1790–1835', *Journal of Economic History*, IX (1949), *Changes in the Standard of Comforts in Eighteenth-Century England* (Raleigh Lecture for 1955); J. D. Chambers, 'The Vale of Trent, 1670–1800: A Regional Study of Economic Change', *Supplement to the Economic History Review* (1957); W. Woodruff, 'Capitalism and the Historians', *Journal of Economic History*, XVI, no. 1 (1956); S. Pollard, 'Investment, Consumption and the Industrial Revolution', *Economic History Review*, XI (1958).

[103] John Burnett, *Plenty and Want: A Social History of Diet in England from 1815 to the Present Day* (1966).

[104] S. D. Chapman, *The History of Working Class Housing* (1971). This symposium contains studies of Leeds, Birmingham, Nottingham and Manchester which examine the process in detail. It also shows how 'a better class of dwelling could provide the incentive for the migration of labour'. This evidence is contrasted with 'the almost uniformly low standard of [housing in] Liverpool', and the plight of the framework knitters in Nottingham.

[105] Neil McKendrick, 'Wages and Workload in the Industrial Revolution: A Study of Wedgwood's Wage Policy' (forthcoming).

wages at subsistence level and recognized the relationship between higher real incomes and increased home demand;[106] in income distribution, it is difficult to argue on present evidence that it became more inequitable in the Industrial Revolution than it had ever been;[107] in factory discipline, the benefits have been recognized as well as the drawbacks.[108]

Few historians would now wish to take the view of Arnold Toynbee that the Industrial Revolution was 'a period as disastrous and as terrible as any through which a nation ever passed',[109] or the view of the Hammonds that 'surely never since the days when populations were sold into slavery did a fate more sweeping overtake a people than the fate that covered the hills and valleys of Lancashire and the West Riding with the factory towns'.[110]

There is a growing body of evidence to show 'that lower-income segments shared in economic growth'[111] during the Industrial Revolution; and 'whatever happened in the short run to the living standards of some or all of the wage earners in the critical second quarter of the nineteenth century, in the long run there can be no doubt of the result: during the nineteenth century real income per head for a population which itself more than trebled is estimated to have quadrupled.'[112]

This is not to accept a blandly optimistic verdict. For, as Keynes said, in the long run we are all dead, and what interests the individual is the short run of his own experience. Since the expectation of life two hundred years ago was little more than half what it is today that could be a very short run indeed, and short enough to run into hardship, unemployment and sickening poverty.

[106] A. W. Coats, 'Changing Attitudes to Labour in the Mid-Eighteenth Century', *Economic History Review*, 2nd series, XI (1958), pp. 35ff.

[107] Lee Soltow, 'Long Run Income Inequality in Great Britain', *Economic History Review*, XXI (1968).

[108] Neil McKendrick, 'Josiah Wedgwood and Factory Discipline', *Historical Journal*, IV (1961); S. Pollard, 'Factory Discipline in the Industrial Revolution', *Economic History Review*, XVI (1963).

[109] A. Toynbee, *Lectures on the Industrial Revolution in England* (1884).

[110] J. L. and B. Hammond, *The Town Labourer, 1760–1832* (1918).

[111] Lee Soltow, op. cit. p. 17. See also Lee Soltow, 'The Share of Lower Income Groups in Income', *Review of Economics and Statistics* (Nov. 1965).

[112] H. J. Perkin, 'The Social Causes of the British Industrial Revolution', *Transactions of the Royal Historical Society* (1969), p. 123. See also Phyllis Deane, 'Contemporary Estimates of National Income in the Second Half of the Nineteenth Century', *Economic History Review*, 2nd series, IX (1957), p. 459.

Whatever the most prolonged and disappointing controversy over living standards in the Industrial Revolution has done – and rarely have advances in knowledge been so slowly and so polemically achieved – it has revealed the simplicities and inadequacies of both the optimistic and the pessimistic camps. The evidence is enough to show that the Industrial Revolution does not merit either the blanket denunciation and condemnation of Engels nor the bland self-congratulation of G. R. Porter, W. Cooke-Taylor or Sir Robert Giffen.[113] Verdicts drawn only from the bad years of 1811, 1816–19, 1826 and 1839–41 are no longer acceptable; no more acceptable than the uninterruptedly rosy glow which emanates from the generally prosperous years before 1795, or the mainly prosperous 1820s, or the boom years after 1842. Pessimistic verdicts, based solely on the Blue Books and government inquiries and reports, which by their nature were usually inspired only by crisis years and therefore inevitably reflect the worst conditions, are increasingly seen for what they are – verdicts dependent on, and generalizing from, the authentic accounts of the *worst* that could, and appallingly often did, occur in *some* years of the Industrial Revolution: equally, optimistic verdicts based solely on the archival evidence of successful liberal employers which portray full employment, fat wages and general content can be seen as the *best* which could occur, and, for the fortunate ones, did occur in *many* years of the Industrial Revolution, but which were by no means the norm.

Such corrective comments on the evidence which has been used, and the methods by which it has been used, go some way to rid the debate of some of its militancy. How necessary this is can be judged by the adjectives and epithets which have been bandied about in this controversy. Thus the optimists (J. H. Clapham, T. S. Ashton, etc.) are "committed" to an "a priori case for amelioration" and have "a desire to prove preconceived notions"; their sources and evidence are suspect for their "optimist bias", "irrelevant", "anachronistic", "feeble props", "too negligible", "highly untypical"; their analysis and conclusions are "brash" . . . "unqualified", "implausible", "improbable", "frivolous", "careless", "cursory", "ill-informed", "inconclusive", "unsupported", "illegitimate", "futile", "not now based on reliable

---

[113] Engels, op. cit.; Cooke-Taylor, op. cit.; G. R. Porter, *The Progress of the Nation* (1847); Sir Robert Giffen, *The Progress of the Working Classes in the last Half Century* (1883), and *The Recent Rate of Material Progress in England* (1887).

evidence", "carry no serious weight", "purely rhetorical", "striking perversions of fact".'[114] Fortunately, the last decade has seen less of such polemic, and both sides now recognize the chronological fluctuations, the regional variations, the differing experiences of different occupational groups in different sections of the same class, as essential ingredients in the debate over living standards.[115]

But more is needed than an exercise in courtesy. More necessary are further exercises in historical methodology. For the evidence relating to the social and economic consequences of the Industrial Revolution reveals a series of connected paradoxes. Side by side with evidence of industrial squalor and economic hardship sit the aggregate figures indicating unambiguous economic growth; alongside the terrible unemployment figures for Bolton and Leeds in 1841 sit the sharpest increases in gross national product this country had ever known; next to the decline of the handloom weavers' wage from 30s a week to 5s a week sits the sharpest rise in gross national income this country had ever known; alongside the accounts of appalling infant mortality among the offspring of Lancashire mill workers, or the expectation of life of a mere eighteen or nineteen years for certain restricted groups of urban labourers, sits the sharpest rise in the size of the population this country had ever known. One could multiply such examples of apparent contradiction. The paradox between the aggregate indices of public affluence and the harrowing accounts of private poverty and personal deprivation is not easy to dismiss.

Attempts to explain it away are legion. It used to be argued that the capital needs of advancing industry would inevitably have absorbed so much of the increasing cake of national wealth that there would be little, if any, extra to share out among those whose labour was producing it.[116] It is a familiar argument: factories, mines and machines must come before men and consumption goods. It is not only familiar, it is also true of many advancing economies in the twentieth century when the capital costs of an advanced technology make very demanding inroads on the first dividends they yield. It was not true – or at least, it

---

[114] R. M. Hartwell, 'The Standard of Living...', *Economic History Review*, 2nd series, XVI, No. 1 (August 1963), p. 136.

[115] One of the more promising approaches is the class or regional study such as R. S. Neale, 'The Standard of Living, 1780–1844: A regional and class study', *Economic History Review* (1966).

[116] S. Pollard, 'Investment, Consumption and the Industrial Revolution', *Economic History Review*, XI (1958).

was far less true – of eighteenth- and early nineteenth-century England.
The early stages of the Industrial Revolution in Britain were achieved
with a very modest rate of capital accumulation.[117] Where economists
have, in such take-off circumstances, confidently predicted a rapid
doubling of the rate of capital formation – and even identified such a
rapid increase as *the* defining characteristic of an industrial revolution[118]
– economic historians have been unable to discover evidence to support
the theory. What they have discovered is the surprisingly low per-
centage of fixed capital which the early industrialists did need, and the
host of apparently ramshackle financial devices by which they raised it.
By credit finance, by self-finance, by renting their factories or by
mortgaging them, by partnership or by short-term loan, by plough-
back and by profit inflation, these early British entrepreneurs managed
to raise their comparatively modest fixed-capital needs and meet their
greater needs for circulating capital, without making significant inroads
in the nation's stock of reproducible capital.[119] When public utilities
are included, then clearly the rate of capital formation and of capital
consumption must rise, and, of course, they did. But the amounts by
which they did so are measurable,[120] and when measured against a
gross national income which increased by a factor of ten between 1750
and 1850, and by a factor of thirty between 1750 and 1900, then they
cease to look important. In fact, capital formation and capital consumption did diminish the cake of capital wealth to be shared out but
not to a substantial or socially significant extent.

In much the same way it used to be argued that the increase in
population was so rapid that it would wipe out any per capita gains in
consumption. Once again this is not the case. The population increased
dramatically, but never as dramatically as did the wealth of the nation.
If the increased wealth is divided by the increased population there is
still a very large per capita increase to account for.[121]

It was also argued, and by some it still is, that the per capita gains
would have been wiped out, or at least severely diminished, by in-

---

[117] S. Pollard, 'Fixed Capital in the Industrial Revolution', *Journal of Economic History*
(1964).
[118] W. W. Rostow, *The Stages of Growth* (1960), p. 37; W. Arthur Lewis, *The Theory
of Economic Growth* (1955), p. 208.
[119] François Crouzet, 'La Formation du Capital en Grande-Bretagne pendant la révolution
industrielle', *Second International Conference of Economic History* (1965).
[120] J. E. Williams, 'The British Standard of Living', *Economic History Review* (1966).
[121] J. E. Williams, op. cit., *passim*.

flation. Prices can be a more important regulator of living standards than income, and if prices rise faster than per capita income, and during the Napoleonic Wars they did, then per capita consumption will fall. But the occasions on which they did can be identified, and so, within an acceptable margin of error, can the rate at which they rose and fell; and, when per capita income is corrected by such a price index, one is still left with a very significant increase.

How fairly that increase in national wealth was shared out, and how much per capita consumption actually rose for the different sections of society, are still hotly debated problems.[122] The inequality of income distribution is too demanding a problem to attract the hordes who will always flock to the easy pickings of the vivid literary evidence of social and economic injustices. The richly quotable will always be preferred to the obscurely quantifiable. But the fact remains that if the controversy over living standards is to progress, answers about how income was distributed are absolutely essential, and the intellectual and academic rewards will go to those who provide them, not to those who work once more through the factory commissioners' reports and print the more appealingly horrifying verdicts.

What work has been done so far on the inequality of income distribution is inconclusive. Not surprisingly it shows that the wealth of England during the Industrial Revolution was, by present-day standards, very unjustly distributed, but it also shows, of course, that the much smaller sum of the nation's wealth in the pre-industrial phase was also very unjustly distributed or arguably even more so.

Agricultural societies of the British type are not normally characterized by great prosperity for the mass of the population.

A minority, enjoying the economic surplus produced from land or office, trade or taxes, may well be able to live in extreme luxury. There may well be magnificent cultural monuments and very wealthy religious institutions. But, with low productivity – low output per head – in a traditionally conducted agriculture, in any economy which has agriculture as the mainspring of its national income and the main source of employment the economic system does not produce much above subsistence needs.[123]

[122] Lee Soltow, 'Long Run Changes in British Income Inequality', *Economic History Review*, XXI (1968).

[123] Peter Mathias, preface to R. M. Hartwell, *The Causes of the Industrial Revolution in England* (1967), p. viii.

Before industrialization, 'life on the margins of subsistence' was the 'inescapable fate of the masses'. Poverty was the chief characteristic of the lives of most. In such conditions the working population can enjoy a golden age only when plague or famine happily decimates the population and reduces the competition for work and food as it did in late fourteenth-century England.

With its exploitation of the novel potentialities for growth, the Industrial Revolution offered new possibilities for prosperity for an ever widening proportion of the population. This brings us to a further paradox: the co-existence of a spectacular increase in production and no great gains in earning and buying power of the mass of the population.

But economic logic, as well as the fruits of much recent research, demands the recognition of an increasing home demand for mass consumer goods. The old explanation of the paradox, created by the spectacular increases in production accompanied by 'the immiseration of the workers', that exports swallowed the manufactured output of the Industrial Revolution, no longer commands general support.[124] Production expanded much more rapidly than foreign trade, and the export statistics, as at present interpreted, suggest that 'throughout the Industrial Revolution by far the greater part – about four-fifths – of production was consumed at home',[125] and that the leading entrepreneurs of the early stages of growth flourished as a result of home demand. The success of Strutt, Arkwright, Hargreaves, Crompton and Cartwright in textiles; of Pilkington in glass; of Whitbread, Truman and Barclay in brewing; of Wedgwood in pottery; of Bramah in locks; of Boulton and Fothergill in buckles – to mention but a sample of the most famous – shows, in Eversley's opinion, 'quite clearly . . . the predominance of the home market'.[126]

This is not the place to deal with the discussion surrounding the role of exports, or with the problem of re-exports, or the enclave theory. I have argued elsewhere that the current orthodoxy overrates the role of home demand, and is too dependent on Elizabeth Schumpeter's

---

[124] See D. E. C. Eversley, op. cit., *passim*.

[125] H. J. Perkin, op. cit. p. 143, n. 1. See E. B. Schumpeter, *English Overseas Trade Statistics, 1697–1808* (1960); W. Schlote, *British Overseas Trade from 1700 to the 1930s* (trans. W. H. Chaloner and W. O. Henderson) (1952), p. 51, table 11; A. H. Imlah, *Economic Elements of the Pax Britannica* (1958), pp. 40–1.

[126] Eversley, op. cit. p. 233.

interpretation of the customs and excise figures. Too little allowance is made for smuggling, or for the effects of inflation on prices and, most important of all, for the vast increase in the value of many items of manufactures.[127] The corrections, which I envisage, can be dramatic (manufacturers like Wedgwood and the Staffordshire potters can be shown to be exporting over 80 per cent of their goods by the middle of the 1780s – some five times more than the Schumpeter statistics suggest),[128] but, even with such corrections, home demand was probably of dominating importance between 1750 and 1775 and, even when it diminished in importance in relation to booming exports it continued to play a vital role in allowing the emergence of newer firms which cut their teeth on the home market, and by providing established firms with a solid base for their sales.

Economists like Berrill have argued that home demand is insufficiently elastic to provide a sharp enough upturn to trigger off rapid economic growth.[129] Indeed Berrill defies one to provide an example of such an increase. Theoretically it is easier to accept a sudden increase in demand coming from a new market overseas than from a home market suddenly galvanized into unprecedented spending. But most historians now feel that the statistics point so unequivocally to the predominance of home demand that exports were in danger of being dismissed 'as a mere reverberation of home demand',[130] and a number of persuasive arguments to explain the home market's eagerness to consume have appeared. A. H. John has argued that the good harvests in the second quarter of the century resulted in both a high demand for labour and therefore high money wages, and a fall in the price of food and therefore a rise in real wages – the consequence of which was that large sections of the working population could retain a margin between income and expenditure, a margin which could be spent on consumer

[127] See Neil McKendrick, 'Home versus Foreign Demand: The "Myth" of the Wedgwood Exports', *Economic History Review* (forthcoming).

[128] E. B. Schumpeter, op. cit. pp. 25–6.

[129] V. Berrill, 'Industrial Trade and the Rate of Economic Growth', *Economic History Review*, XII (1959–60): 'growth limited to meeting the "balanced" demand of the home market will be slow'. See also C. Kindleberger, 'Foreign Trade and Economic Growth', *Economic History Review*, XIV (1961–62).

[130] See M. W. Flinn, *The Origins of the Industrial Revolution* (1966), especially Ch. IV, 'The Commercial Origins'. See also Ralph Davis, 'English Foreign Trade 1660–1700', *Economic History Review* (1954), and 'English Foreign Trade, 1700–1774', *Economic History Review* (1962).

goods before 1750.[131] In the crucial period after 1750 there have been explanations turning on the role of London as a centre of conspicuous consumption encouraging consumer spending;[132] on the ability of entrepreneurs to exploit latent demand and create new wants by the brilliance of their marketing techniques;[133] on the effect of social emulation, class competition and emulative spending;[134] or on the growing class of consumers willing and able to buy not just the necessities but the decencies of life.[135]

What has been less satisfactorily explained is where the income for this consumer expenditure came from. To reach for the historians' *deus ex machina*, the rising middle class, is not a sufficient answer. Why did the middle classes spend more? Where did the increase in income come from? Was it sufficient to explain the economic effects? Was it middle-class expenditure which contemporaries commented on? Not all of these questions have been satisfactorily answered.[136]

One reason for this is that too much attention has been focused on wage *rates*. It is understandable that historians seeking long-run wage data should make use of the more easily available details of men's wage rates. Eighteenth-century wages were usually expressed in terms of a day rate for a ten-hour day, and to estimate weekly wages it is usual to assume that a man worked ten hours a day for six days a week. If a man was working for 2s a day, then he will be assumed to have earned 12s

[131] A. H. John, 'Agricultural Productivity and Economic Growth in England, 1700–1760', *Journal of Economic History*, XXV (1965). See also M. W. Flinn, 'Agricultural Productivity and Economic Growth: A Comment', *Journal of Economic History*, XXVI (1966), plus A. H. John's reply, ibid.; E. L. Jones, *Agricultural and Economic Growth in England, 1650–1815*, pp. 189–93; J. D. Chambers, *The Agricultural Revolution 1750–1880* (1966), and W. E. Minchinton, ed., *Essays in Agrarian History* (1968).

[132] E. A. Wrigley, 'A Simple Model of London's Importance in changing English Society and Economy', *Past and Present*, no. 37 (1967), pp. 44–70.

[133] Neil McKendrick, 'Josiah Wedgwood: An Eighteenth Century Entrepreneur in Salesmanship and Marketing', *Economic History Review* (1960); and 'Josiah Wedgwood and Thomas Bentley: An Inventor-Entrepreneur Partnership in the Industrial Revolution', *Transactions of the Royal Historical Society*, Vol. 14 (1964).

[134] H. J. Perkin, 'The Social Causes of the British Industrial Revolution', *Transactions of the Royal Historical Society* (1969).

[135] D. E. C. Eversley, 'The Home Market and Home Demand, 1750–1780', Ch. 9 in *Land, Labour and Population in the Industrial Revolution*, ed. by E. L. Jones and G. E. Mingay (1967).

[136] Elizabeth Gilboy asked many of them in her famous article 'Demand as a Factor in the Industrial Revolution' in *Facts and Factors in Economic History* in 1932, and Professors H. J. Perkin, op. cit., and D. E. C. Eversley, op. cit., have gone furthest in answering them.

a week. But if the demand for labour was low, if the leisure preference was high, if employment was intermittent and underemployment frequent, and many of these conditions were characteristic of the pre-industrial period, then such assumptions can exaggerate a man's likely earnings. In many areas it was common to work for four days in order to drink for three, Saturday, Sunday and good St Monday being devoted to pleasure;[137] Defoe complained that 'there is nothing more frequent for an Englishman to work till his pockets [be] full of money and then go and be drunk till 'tis all gone';[138] and the records of many Labourers Books show that hours worked often averaged closer to forty than sixty outside factories.[139] These considerations, plus seasonal unemployment, could all reduce a man's earnings below the assumed level.

Notoriously the discipline of the factories insisted on the new industrial virtues of punctuality, regular work and long hours. The factories, too, usually increased the demand for labour and the regularity of work. The resultant longer hours and more regular work brought larger take-home earnings – the hours of work of a man like John Engelfield who worked for Josiah Wedgwood show that over a substantial period of time he averaged seventy-five hours a week and therefore earned 25 per cent more than the sixty-hours-a-week norm – in the week he worked an epic ninety-eight hours he received ten days' pay for his week's work. A further inducement to work longer hours was noted by contemporaries; that is, that higher wages led to longer hours. Adam Smith commented in *The Wealth of Nations* that 'Workmen . . . when they are liberally paid by the piece, are very apt to overwork themselves.' Arthur Young put it more vividly when he said that 'two shillings and sixpence a day will undoubtedly tempt some to work who would not touch a tool for a shilling'.[140]

This process alone could boost a man's wage packet but, even for the very skilled workers of the Industrial Revolution, it was unlikely to produce the kind of inflated income needed to explain the boost in

---

[137] Elizabeth Gilboy, op. cit., and also *Wages in Eighteenth Century England*; E. M. Phelps Brown and S. V. Hopkins, 'Seven Centuries of the price of consumables, compared with builder's wage rates', *Economica*, XXIII (1956).

[138] Quoted Neil McKendrick, 'Factory Discipline', *Historical Journal* (1964), p. 55.

[139] Wedgwood MSS., 'Labourers Book', quoted Neil McKendrick, 'Wages and Workload in the Industrial Revolution: A Study of Wedgwood's Wage Policy' (forthcoming).

[140] Adam Smith, *An Inquiry into the Nature and Causes of the Wealth of Nations* (1776). Arthur Young, *A Six Months Tour Through the North of England* (1770), 4 vols.

home demand. But if the process was spread over the whole family, and if for many families this was the first time that the wife and children had received an independent wage, then the boost to the family income could be dramatic.

It was much noted at the time that women and children more willingly accepted the discipline of the factories, and submitted more easily to the long hours. What has been less often noted was the effect these long hours must have had on family earnings. When all the family laboured for long hours – on either piece rates or day rates – the family-unit earnings could provide the margin of income over expenditure that explanations of booming home demand require.

The hypothesis that I wish to propose is that when the wage rates of men, women and children were roughly of the ratio of 3 to 2 to 1, or, in those industries which rewarded women and children less well, 4 to 2 to 1; then one wife and one child, in those industries which paid the wife two-thirds and the child one-third of male rates,[141] or one wife and two children in those industries where the wife received a half and the children a quarter of the male rate, could double a working man's take-home earnings. Larger families could earn substantially more than double a single male wage, and as the older children moved on to higher wages and the family reached its peak earning capacity such families could earn up to four times the normal male rate.

The assumption that the arrival of a family prevented wives working and thus often put a stop to a wife's earning power is not borne out by the evidence. Many wives, despite frequent pregnancies, continued to work and to contribute to the family economy. There was admittedly a chorus of complaints about factory women being absentee mothers and the deplorable effect their absence had on their children, but, in fact, Dr Michael Anderson's recent work on family structure in nineteenth-century Lancashire shows that the absentee parent's place was frequently taken by the children's grandparents. 'The urban-industrial revolution . . . seems, contrary surely to all expectations ten years ago, to have been associated with a considerable increase in co-residence of parents and married children.'[142] Anderson's research

---

[141] This was the ratio which operated in Wedgwood's Etruria.

[142] M. Anderson, 'Household Structure and the Industrial Revolution; mid-nineteenth century Preston in comparative perspective', Ch. 7 in P. Laslett, *Household and Family in Past Time* (1972), p. 223. See also J. Foster, *Capitalism and Class Consciousness in early 19th century Oldham* (1967).

also shows that 'it was only those in more affluent states who took in those who could not support themselves',[143] and the reason for their affluence, it can reasonably be suggested, was the earning power of the wife because, as Anderson admits, the crucial reason for taking in a grandparent was that such 'a relative could also substantially *increase the family income* . . . by caring for the children and home while the mother worked in the factory. In this way a mother could have the child and home looked after . . . and the income she brought in kept the relative and gave a considerable surplus to the family budget.'[144] 'Households with children under ten where the wife worked were three times as likely to have a co-residing grandmother.[145] Married couples could even afford to take in unrelated old people rent free and all found to provide such a service.'

These pay differentials have been much criticized as exploitation of women and children, and so they were, but it is worth remembering that in April 1971 the average earnings of full-time female manual workers in Britain were only 55.6 per cent of the average weekly earnings of full-time men – a sex differential distinctly worse than those operated by Josiah Wedgwood two hundred years ago, and approximately the same as the average differentials recorded in many eighteenth-century factories.[146]

What is more to the point is that the earnings of women and children reveal a sharp increase on the earnings of those who had laboured in agriculture and in the domestic industries. There they were often a substitute for the father's labour when he was otherwise engaged, or a supplement to it which produced a very modest increment to the family earning.[147]

What is even more to the point was the increase in job opportunities for women and children. Since the differentials applied to particular skills, particularly skilful women could substantially out-earn their less

---

[143] Anderson, op. cit. p. 231.   [144] Anderson, op. cit. p. 230.
[145] Anderson, op. cit. p. 231.
[146] Admittedly the average female earnings of 1971 were the result of a 40-hour week, and the male earnings the result of a 46-hour week. See Audrey Wise, *Women and the Struggle for Workers' Control* (1974), p. 4. See also *Discrimination Against Women* (Labour Party Green Paper, November 1972), and *Women in Media Statistics* (23 January 1973).
[147] Agricultural workers who were married with children were often paid more in recognition of their families' work, but these increments increased as a result of higher wages paid to the factories.

skilful husbands. Mrs Wilcox, a skilled flower painter in Wedgwood's London workrooms, earned 3s 6d a day – exactly two-thirds the top rate for skilled male painters who received 5s 3d a day; her husband, also a painter but less skilled, and employed on simpler, more repetitive tasks, earned 2s 6d a day. When they both worked the standard sixty-hour week, their joint income rose to 36s a week instead of Wilcox's 15s a week, the norm for many men of modest skills in the 1770s.[148] At 6s a day between them they could afford to indulge themselves, and it is surprising how little they did so in terms of leisure: despite Mrs Wilcox's losing several work days at regular monthly intervals, they were still credited with an average of over ten days' work a week between them. Their joint average take-home pay – double the husband's standard wage – would give them an annual income of £75, which would provide an ample surplus for spending on consumption goods. Obviously, highly paid women workers, such as Mrs Wilcox, were exceptional. For most men to double their own weekly earnings they needed not only a working wife but one or more working children.

Such men were rapidly ceasing to be exceptional. Far more households than the extra 150,000 that Eversley requires to explain the leap in demand between 1750 and 1780 were enjoying the money wages of multiple earners by then. The small earnings of women and children had made their modest contribution to the family budget for centuries, but with the Industrial Revolution their earnings became central to the domestic economy. They made a significantly larger contribution and they made it to a significantly larger number of families.

For not only were women and children earning high wages, but far more women and children were working. Both are notoriously a characteristic of the British Industrial Revolution – and there is a massive literature on the increase in employment possibilities for them and the increase in the numbers actually employed.[149]

---

[148] Wedgwood MSS., Benjamin Mather to Josiah Wedgwood, 1774–75.

[149] See, for example, William Shaw, *An Affectionate Pleading for England's Oppressed Female Workers* (1850); Barbara Bodichon, *Women and Work* (1956); Clara Balfour, *Working Women in the Last Half Century* (1856). See S. Barbara Kanner, op. cit. pp. 190–5, for the full details of the pamphlet and journal literature, such as W. R. Greg, 'Juvenile and Female Labour', *Edinburgh Review*, 79 (1844), pp. 130–56. See also, for the statistics of textile industries, Huang Fu-san, 'The Role of Women Workers in the British Textile Industry, 1780–1850' (unpublished M.Litt. thesis, Cambridge University, 1972).

What I am mainly concerned to suggest, however, is a connection between the contribution of wives and children to the family income and the rise in consumer spending. I intend to argue that the surplus over subsistence produced by such earnings would be particularly likely to be spent on the consumer industries which flourished in the early Industrial Revolution, and to suggest that such spending had a disproportionate effect on boosting home demand because of the consequential effect it had on class competition, social emulation and emulative spending.

In terms of the proved take-home earnings of such women and children one can provide examples which show only that such a hypothesis is a possible explanation. The evidence is not available in sufficient quantity to *prove* that this was the explanation for the boom in home demand.

The relationship between family earnings and family budgets is a notoriously complicated one, requiring corrective weighting for price changes, payment in kind, the changing dependency ratios of children in the family as their ages changed and their earning power increased. The fluctuation in earnings from year to year, from one occupation to another, from one region to another, from town to country, are equally notorious and too complex to be dealt with here. But it is possible to demonstrate in simple terms the impact of the earnings of female and child labour on the family income levels.

In the Staffordshire Potteries, in which women workers were unknown before the 1760s, their earnings and those of their children could lift the average weekly income from the usual limits of between 12s and 21s, depending on a single male worker's skill, to examples of family income of 42s, 47s 6d, 55s and 60s.[150] Such earnings yield a far more dramatic increase in the surplus of income over expenditure than any of the increases in male wages that have been produced by those seeking to explain the source of the increase in home demand.[151] On the Patrick Colquhoun contemporary scale of family earnings, that would put an ordinary, not specially skilled potter and his wife and children on the level, in terms of income, with 'lesser clergymen,

---

[150] See Neil McKendrick, 'Wages and Workload in the Industrial Revolution: A Study of Wedgwood's Wage Policy' (forthcoming)

[151] See the increases quoted by Elizabeth Gilboy in 'Demand as a Factor in the Industrial Revolution', *Facts and Factors in Economic History* (1932), reprinted in R. M. Hartwell, *Causes of the Industrial Revolution* (1967).

farmers, shopkeepers, innkeepers, and dissenting clergymen' – well into the ranks of the lower middle class. Indeed the much trumpeted rise of the middle class came, in purchasing terms, from these recruits from below.[152]

The incomes of 119 families employed by Thomas Ashton, spinner and power-loom manufacturer of Hyde, set out by Dr Kay, no friend of the factory system, in the *First Annual Report of the Poor Law Commissioners for England and Wales*, 1835,[153] give even more dramatic evidence of the effect of wives' and children's labour on the family income. The proportion of adult males to women and children was about one to four: 'many males aged over twenty-one earned more than 20s a week, . . . and the next highest wage was 13s a week paid to 295 women weavers aged twenty-one and over', yet 'seventy-five out of the 119 families received over 40s a week'. Families of six earned up to £4 10s a week, families of eight earned up to £6 5s. In this same factory there were, admittedly, fathers bringing up a family of six on £1 6s 8d per week, and another raising a family of eight on £1 10s a week, but the low-income families were those in which the wife did not work and in which a high proportion of the children were still too young to contribute to the family income.[154] Dr Kay, Dr Ure and Peter Gaskell all sang the praises of Ashton's employees' standard of living and he cannot be taken as typical; but even the low wages offered by the Gregs (too low to attract town labour and attractive only 'to families eking out a miserable existence with the assistance of poor relief') were enough to double the wages of a father when four of his children worked with him – even though the doubling took his 12s a week to only 24s a week.[155] The wages of these children were clearly contributing to subsistence, more than explaining an increase in consumer demand. For Dr Kay had worked out (and this was corroborated by the evidence of the wife of a Manchester fine spinner before the Factory Commissions of 1833) that the family budget for food, rent, heat, soap and candles was 18s 1d a week. Even a highly paid man, like the fine spinner earning 25s a week, would generate a surplus of only 6s 11d a week for clothes, sickness, schooling and miscellaneous

[152] Patrick Colquhoun, *A Treatise on Indigence* (1806); and *A Treatise on The Wealth, Power and Resources of the British Empire* (1815).

[153] Pp. 203–4. See F. Collier, op. cit. p. 50–1.

[154] F. Collier, op. cit. p. 50.

[155] Collier, op. cit. p. 43.

items.[156] But married to a woman spinner, who earned approximately 53 per cent of the male wage, and with five children earning between 3s and 8s a week, that same fine spinner's family could earn over 60s a week. In boom years like 1810 their income could rise even higher, and even in a slump year like 1811 their joint earnings would be well above subsistence.[157]

When it is recognized that by 1790 over 55 per cent of the workers in the cotton industry were women, and that even higher proportions were non-adults, the potential importance of their earnings can easily be seen. Without accurate census breakdowns, the exact number of working women and children in the country during the early stages of the Industrial Revolution will never be known, but the mistake should not be made of limiting the importance of female and child labour to the factories. In the high-wage areas – like the industrial North, the industrial Midlands, London and the like – the growth of mining and manufacturing industry forced up agricultural wages in the vicinity and forced up the rewards of even domestic servants.

The prospective loss of a good ladies' maid to the mill led to an increase in wages and, although domestic servants continued to receive much of their payments in kind (in terms of lodgings, food, light, heat and even clothes), the increase in their money wages had an important impact on their ability to spend on consumer goods. As the group closest to the spending habits and life style of the upper and middle classes, they were a very important channel of communications for transmitting new fashions to the rest of society and spreading a desire for new commodities, and the increase in their spending power was therefore of disproportionate importance.[158] Domestic service was probably still the largest single employment for women by the turn of the century, and early in the nineteenth century a reliable observer like T. Somerville, a Scottish minister, was complaining that 'the wages of servants since the period of my becoming a householder have advanced at least four fold'.[159]

Agricultural workers were an even larger part of the workforce of the country, and there traditionally the wives and the children earned

[156] Factory Inquiry, Royal Commission 1st Report, Section D1, pp. 39–40, 1833 (450), xx. J. P. Kay, op. cit. pp. 8–9; F. Collier, op. cit. p. 52.
[157] See Collier, op. cit., Tables B/III and B/IV, pp. 60–1.
[158] See J. J. Hecht, op. cit.
[159] T. Somerville, *My Own Life and Times, 1741–1814* (1861), p. 340.

little. Rev. David Davies recorded the modest earnings of a labourer
and his wife in 1795 in Berkshire, where wages were still unaffected by
industrial competition: the man earned 7s a week for 35 weeks of the
year, and 10s a week (piece work) for 17 weeks, producing £20 15s
a year. His wife was credited with earning 6d a week, £1 6s a year.
If, on the contrary, he lived in an area where his wife and children could
take advantage of the new demand for their labour, then 'the wages of
a man and his children might double the man's earnings'.[160] Arthur
Young complains in 1771[161] that luxury is now universal and instances
the family budget of a family of four (two children aged ten and fifteen)
in which everyone works. The total income would be £37 15s and
total expenses would run from £22 7s to £24 17s. Such a family is
below Eversley's demarcation line between the market for necessities
and the market for decencies, but Young complains that very few
such families actually live on £22 per annum, because even the
poor must conform to fashion and eat the best white bread in
imitation of their social superiors. Social emulation clearly reached
well down the social scale, even if at this level its expression was
severely limited.

Much additional work on family incomes and family budgets will
need to be done before we can do more than indicate the potentialities
of this explanation of rising home demand. Much more work on wills
will have to be done to check whether the possessions of consumer
goods in such families markedly increased as a result of the process I
have described. A systematic analysis of the surviving inventories of
wills proved in the courts should yield some interesting confirmations
or denials, but most of the evidence that has emerged seems to suggest
that even the poorest, worth less than £10 like Richard Wainwright,
a nailer, 'had the little decencies of life';[162] that 'ordinary industrial
workers did own specimens of the products of neighbouring and even
distant manufactories'; that they owned pewter, glass and china, cast
and wrought-iron goods, brass and copper; that 'increasingly there
are textiles in the shape of blankets, linens, pillows . . . rugs, curtains
and cloths'. Moreover, increasingly these goods had been bought
in their own lifetime and, as Professor Eversley comments, 'this is
crucial. Mere inheritance, the passing on of wearing apparel and

---

[160] John Burnett, *A History of the Cost of Living*, p. 166.
[161] A. Young, 'A Farmer's Letters to the People of England' (1771).
[162] J. S. Roper, *Sedgley Probate Inventories* (1965), p. i. Wainwright inventory, No. 130.

daily linen, of utensils and furniture, could mean, at the margin, little demand.'[163]

The details of the earnings and possessions of the working classes have admittedly still to be evidenced sufficiently to prove the connection between the financial contribution of women and children and the recognition of the Parliamentary Papers of 1852 of 'this remarkable fact that incomes have increased more under the smaller classes of income than the larger'.[164]

Where the evidence is undeniably more thickly and easily available is in the literary comment of contemporaries on the phenomenon of the new spending habits of the working classes. Not only do they comment, they also offer their explanations as to the causes, and their fear of the consequences.

As to the motives and the consequences, most have no doubt at all. As the British Magazine wrote in 1763, 'The present rage of imitating the manners of high life hath spread itself so far among the gentlefolks of lower life, that in a few years we shall probably have no common folk at all.'[165] The process of social emulation was confirmed by Fielding in even more decided language: 'while the Nobleman will emulate the Grandeur of a Prince and the Gentleman will aspire to the proper state of a Nobleman; the Tradesman steps from behind his Counter into the vacant place of the Gentleman. Nor doth the confusion end there: It reaches the very Dregs of the People, who aspire still to a degree beyond that which belongs to them.'[166]

Not only was the emulative process fully recognized and described, but also the effect it had on the consumption of manufactures. According to Josiah Tucker,[167] English manufactures

are more adapted for the demands of Peasants and Mechanics, in order to appear in warm circumstances, for Farmers, Freeholders, Tradesmen and Manufacturers in Middling Life; and for Wholesale Dealers, Merchants and for all persons of Landed Estates to appear in genteel life; than for the Magnificence of Palaces or the Cabinets of Princes. Thus it is . . . that the

---

[163] Eversley, op. cit. p. 238.
[164] Parliamentary Papers, 1852, IX, p. 593. Quoted Soltow, op. cit. p. 29.
[165] British Magazine, IV (1763), p. 417, quoted H. J. Perkin, op. cit. p. 140.
[166] Henry Fielding, An Enquiry into the Causes of the late Increase of Robbers (1750), see Fielding's Works, II, p. 783.
[167] Josiah Tucker: A Selection from his Economic and Political Writings, ed. R. L. Schuyler (1931).

English of those several denominations have better Conveniences in their Houses, and affect to have more in Quantity of clean, neat Furniture, and a greater variety, such as Carpets, Screens, Window Curtains, Chamber Bells, polished Brass Locks, Fenders etc. (Things Hardly known abroad among Persons of such Rank) than are to be found in any other Country of Europe.[168]

To confirm how far down the social scale the new possessions had spread, he added: 'were an inventory to be taken of Household Goods and Furniture of a Peasant, or Mechanic, in France, and of a Peasant, or Mechanic in England, the latter would be found on average to Exceed the former in Value by at least three to one'.[169]

The effects of social emulation operating in a closely stratified society, in which vertical social mobility was both possible and much coveted, are richly evidenced.

Malthus specifically identified social ambition – 'the hope to rise or fear to fall in society' – as the cause of 'that animated activity in bettering our own condition which now forms the master-spring of public prosperity'.[170] Others deplored the results. 'It is the curse of this nation that the labourer and the mechanic will ape the lord',[171] wrote Hanway; 'the different ranks of people are too much confounded: the lower orders press so hard on the heels of the higher, if some remedy is not used the Lord will be in danger of becoming the valet of his Gentleman'.[172] Dibdin complained that 'the Tradesman vies with my Lord'.[173] Tucker made the same point when he wrote that 'the different stations of Life so run into and mix with each other, that it is hard to say, where the one ends, and the other begins'.[174]

The most obvious way this blurring of the class lines revealed itself was in dress. Writer after writer notes the 'absence of those outward distinctions which formerly characterized different classes'. Somerville, writing in the early nineteenth century, reflects on the changes which had taken place in his lifetime. 'At that time various modes of dress indicated at first sight the rank, the profession, and the age of every individual. Now even the servants are hardly distinguishable in their

[168] Tucker allowed the possible exception of Holland.   [169] Tucker, ibid.
[170] T. R. Malthus, *Essay on the Principle of Population* (1798).
[171] J. Hanway, 'Essay on Tea', printed in *A Journal of Eight Days' Journey* (1756), p. 224.
[172] Ibid., pp. 282–3.
[173] Dibdin, op. cit. I, 34–5.
[174] *Josiah Tucker: A Selection from his Economic and Political Writings*, p. 264.

equipment from their masters and mistresses.'[175] Davis, in his *Friendly Advice to Industrious and Frugal Persons*, drew attention to the same phenomenon: 'a fondness for Dress may be said to be the folly of the age, and it is to be lamented that it has nearly destroyed those becoming marks whereby the several classes of society were formerly distinguished.'[176]

This phenomenon was very widely commented on by both English and foreign observers, the major difference being that the foreigners usually recorded their amazed admiration for the prosperity of the English working classes while the indigenous commentators more characteristically denounced their extravagance and ostentation. Lichtenberg writes of England in the 1770s that the luxury and extravagance of the lower and middling classes 'has risen to such a pitch as never before seen in the world';[177] the German Moritz in 1782 notes that 'the distinction in dress amongst the various classes is not . . . great', and 'even the poor . . . wear silk stockings';[178] Karamzin in 1790 finds 'the Lord and the artisan are almost indistinguishable';[179] and von Archenholz confirms the picture, when he writes of the same decade, that 'the accumulation of riches, luxury and pleasures are enjoyed by all classes', adding that 'England surpasses all the other nations of Europe in the luxury of dress and apparel, and the luxury is increasing daily'.[180] England was found convicted of 'a certain inveterate national habit of luxury'. Grosley, St Fond, de Saussure and Count Pecchio add their confirmation.

English observers described the same process. Arthur Young in 1771 described a situation of 'UNIVERSAL' luxury; Dibdin in 1801 referred to the prevailing 'opulence' of all classes; and Wendeborne, Torrington, Postlethwayt and others saw the dominance of fashion and the pursuit of luxury as powerful explanations of the growth of the economy. As Richard Kent has written of the literary evidence, 'In the 1750s and 1760s the accounts of increasing luxury among the labourers – both urban and rural – were becoming much more frequent. These continued throughout the next thirty years and by the end of the century

---

[175] T. Somerville, *My Own Life and Times, 1741–1814* (1861), pp. 376–7.
[176] Davis, *Friendly Advice to Industrious and Frugal Persons* (1817), p. 23.
[177] *Lichtenberg's Visits to England* (1938), translated by M. L. Mare and W. H. Quarrell.
[178] K. P. Moritz, *Journeys of a German in England in 1782* (1965), translated by R. Nettel.
[179] N. M. Karamzin, *Letters of a Russian Traveller, 1789–90* (1957), translated by F. Jonas.
[180] J. W. von Archenholz, *A Picture of England* (1791), pp. 75–83.

what had previously been looked on as being a luxury for the worker was thought of in terms of being a decency or even a necessity.'[181]

This change was blamed by most English on the downward spread of fashion, and on the imitation by the poor of their social superiors in matters of dress, diet and possessions. A typical example was Hanway's denunciation of the social revolution which has changed tea drinking from being a luxury of the rich to a necessity of the poor: 'What a wild infatuation! it took its rise from Example; by Example it is supported; and Example only can abolish the use of it . . . with what countenance can my Lady's woman, or gentlewoman's chambermaid pretend to drink a liquor which her mistress no longer uses.'[182] As early as the 1750s Fielding complains that 'attorneys' clerks, apprentices, milliners, mantua makers and an infinite number of lower people' aspire to the pleasures of the fashionable: by the end of the century they were, according to contemporaries, already enjoying them. Wendeborne writes: 'Dress is carried to the very utmost, and the changes it undergoes are more frequent than those of the moon . . . this rage for finery and fashion spreads from the highest to the lowest; and in public places . . . it is very difficult to guess at [people's] rank in society or at the heaviness of their purse.'[183]

Women in particular were abused for their dependence on fashion and for their extravagant expenditure on clothes, a criticism which increasingly applied to all classes. Indeed the expenditure of the lower ranks spurred the middle and upper ranks to ever further efforts to stay ahead. The fact that the lead was given by upper ranks of society should not blind us to the fact that social emulation can work both ways – one of the reasons for the increased expenditure of the middle ranks was their desire to continue to outdistance the more competitive lower orders. As a result, fashionable competition in clothes reached manic proportions: in 1753 purple was the in-colour – 'all colours were neglected for that of purple: in purple we glowed from the hat to the shoe'; in 1757 the fashion was for white linen with a pink pattern; in the 1770s the changes were rung even more rapidly – in 1776 the fashionable colour was 'couleur de Noisette', in 1777 dove grey, in 1779 'the fashionable dress was laycock satin trimmed with

[181] Richard Kent, op. cit.

[182] J. Hanway, 'Essay on Tea', printed in *A Journal of Eight Days' Journey* (1756), pp. 215–6.

[183] F. A. Wendeborne, *A View of England towards the End of the Eighteenth Century*, p. 314.

fur'; by 1781 'stripes in silk or very fine cambric-muslin' were in; by 1785 steel embroidery on dresses was all the rage; by 1790 'the fashionable colours were lilac and yellow and brown and pale green'.[184]

Entrepreneurs exploited the situation with such skill that 'the fashions alter in these days so much, that a man can hardly wear a coat two months before it is out of fashion'.[185] Both men and women were made to conform.

The increasing expenditure of the rich and the prosperous is frankly explained by contemporaries as a reaction to the competition from below. In fact the eighteenth century not only provides us with the first evidence of the ability of the more prosperous sections of the working classes to enjoy some consumer behaviour patterns for long the province of their social superiors, it also provides the novel spectacle of the rich fighting back. Some of the increased consumption of the period was undoubtedly the result of the determination of the middle class women, spending in order to stay ahead of the pursuing pack and indulging in conspicuous consumption in order to do so. As von Archenholz wrote, 'in other countries the vulgar imitate the higher ranks, [in England] on the contrary, the great are solicitous to distinguish themselves from the mob'.[186] Fielding was full of admiration for the way the fashionable leaders used their arts 'to deceive and dodge their imitators . . . when they are hunted out in any favourite mode'.[187]

Many commercial pressures played their part. As Dr Johnson wrote, 'he that had resolved to buy no more finds his constancy subdued . . . he is attracted by rarity . . . seduced by example and influenced by competition'.[188] But no entrepreneur however skilful, and no advertisement however tempting, and no example however seductive, can persuade the public to buy unless it has some surplus to spend. Before 1750 that surplus doubtless stemmed from the run of good harvests, and the demand for labour and rising male wage rates would help to continue the process, but the entrepreneurial success stories of the late eighteenth century demanded more dramatic increases than these, and, before the appearance of large-scale exports, the increased family unit earnings, swollen by the wages of wives and children, played a major

[184] C. Willett Cunnington and Phillis Cunnington, *Handbook of English Costume in the 18th Century* (1957), pp. 320–4.
[185] Wendeborne, *A View of England*, pp. 160–1.
[186] Quoted Kent, op. cit.
[187] Fielding, *Works*, II, p. 239–40.
[188] *Idler*, no. 56.

part in providing them. As a contemporary put it, the new employment opportunities for children meant that 'all fears of a burdensome family are removed'.[189] It is true, as Hanway pointed out, that the bachelor could enjoy a considerable margin of income over expenditure but, when the marriage rate was rising and the age of marriage falling, there would be fewer bachelors in circulation. And the increased earning potential of wives and children was a frequently quoted explanation for those earlier and more frequent marriages.[190] A working wife earning two-thirds of a male wage was a very attractive financial proposition. Such childless couples could probably generate the greatest increase in consumption but, in a pre-contraceptive society, family limitation seems to have been closely geared to economic opportunity, and the promising conditions of the eighteenth century offered no serious financial obstacle to a family. Indeed they were held by many contemporaries to be positive inducement to breed, and the incentive most often identified was the increased earning power of children. Prudential checks could have increased prosperity, and doubtless for a small minority did so. But when most married couples wanted children, and had only unreliable and inconvenient methods of avoiding them, the earning power of their children was a further encouragement not to delay either marriage age or parenthood. The main point is that most couples did raise families, and the crucial difference between the industrial period and the pre-industrial was the earning potential of both wives and children. And, of course, the family household generated demand for manufactured goods, as well as generating the income to pay for them. Working mothers could no longer make their own clothes and the clothes of their children; they could make less of their own food. Once again the hostility to working wives meant that much middle-class comment directed itself mainly to the loss of household skills. It was a much publicized fact that many of the women in the textile mills in the early nineteenth century had never learned to make their children's clothes. More pertinent to their impact on demand for manufactured textiles was the fact that they did not need to make what they could now afford to buy.[191] As one contemporary commented, everything a working woman wore was manufactured

[189] J. Howlett, *An Examination of Dr Price's Essay on the Population of England and Wales*, p. 15.

[190] See E. A. Wrigley, op. cit.

[191] Neff, op. cit. pp. 48–53.

except her face; instead of being taught to mend, they were taught to spend.

It is significant, too, that, apart from the brewing industry, the consumer industries of the early Industrial Revolution were those in which women take the decision to consume: the cotton, woollen, linen and silk industries, the pottery industry, the cutlery industry, the Birmingham small trades. All were industries which produced for a mass market. For all there is evidence of demand from a large new market: 'even the most ordinary people in the streets sported the Birmingham-made fashion' – the buckle, the brooches, the ornamental buttons, the seals, the snuff box and the chain.[192]

Without the addition of female wages and the earnings of children, it is difficult to explain where a sufficiently large surplus of income over expenditure would have come from, and without a substantial rise in family income it is difficult to see where the increased home demand would come from.

It is not enough to rely on social emulation and the pursuit of fashion. We need some mechanism which will explain the extension of such pursuits to a wider audience. The tyranny of fashion was not new to the eighteenth century. William Harrison was referring to the 'phantastical folly of our nation (even from the courtier to the carter)' in wanting to pursue new fashions as early as 1577.[193] As Joan Thirsk wrote last year, 'since in every age fashions beguile all ages and classes in varying degrees, ordinary folks lower down the social scale were susceptible too, and strained their resources to ape their betters. As the proclamation of 1562 bewailed "such as be of the meaner sort, and be least able with their livings to maintain the same" felt they must follow the fashion'.[194] Miss Thirsk has demonstrated that sixteenth-century literature is 'full of baleful comment upon the dictates of fashion, which first seized the rich in thrall and then their servants'. 'No other nations take such pride in apparel as England', wrote Philip Stubbs in 1595. Moreover, 'no people in the world are so curious in new fangles as they of England be'. 'I have known divers [serving men]', wrote William Vaughan in 1600, 'who would bestow all the money they had in the

---

[192] Eversley, op. cit. p. 231.

[193] Joan Thirsk, 'The Fantastical Folly of Fashion: The English Stocking Knitting Industry, 1500–1700', *Textile History and Economic History* (1973), p. 50.

[194] Ibid.; see also W. Hooper, 'Tudor Sumptuary Laws', *English Historical Review*, XXX (1915), p. 439.

world on sumptuous garments.'[195] The novel feature of the eighteenth century was not its desire to pursue fashion, but its ability to do so.

It is important, then, that too much is not made of social emulation *alone*. By itself it can be of little economic importance. Over forty years ago Elizabeth Gilboy produced the perfect text for Professor Perkin's more recent argument that 'at bottom the key to the Industrial Revolution was the infinitely elastic home demand for mass consumer goods. And the key to that demand was social emulation, "keeping up with the Joneses", the compulsive urge for imitating the spending habits of one's betters, which sprang from an open aristocracy in which each member from top to bottom of society trod closely on the heels of the next above.'[196] To illustrate that phenomenon, Miss Gilboy quoted Forster, who wrote in 1767:

In England the several ranks of men slide into each other almost imperceptibly, and a spirit of equality runs through every part of their constitution. Hence arises a strong emulation in all the several stations and conditions to vie with each other; and the perpetual restless ambition in each of the inferior ranks to raise themselves to the level of those immediately above them. In such a state as this fashion must have uncontrolled sway. And a fashionable luxury must spread through it like a contagion.[197]

Forster's description neatly encapsulates all the features stressed by modern social historians of demand – the closely stratified nature of English society, the striving for vertical social mobility, the emulative spending bred of social emulation, the compulsive power of fashion begotten by social competition. What he does not explain, and what Professor Perkin does not satisfactorily explain, is why the potential for economic growth, contained in these long-standing social characteristics, was released to such effect in the eighteenth century.

Professor Perkin recognizes the problem, for he writes: 'There remains of course, the problem of timing. If the old society was ripe for an industrial revolution at least since the Civil War . . . why did it take a hundred years or more to reach the harvest?' His solution or 'short answer' is that 'every kind of growth takes time'.[198] Rather more specifically, and rather more satisfyingly, he offers a further explanation

---

[195] Thirsk, op. cit. pp. 50–1.
[196] Perkin, op. cit. p. 140.
[197] N. Forster, *An Enquiry into the Present High Prices of Provisions* (1767), p. 41.
[198] Perkin, op. cit. p. 141, 'The growth of so dynamically stable a society as Britain's could go on for generations without breaking out of its pre-industrial husk.'

based on the fact that in 'the last quarter of the eighteenth century British population hit the critical rate of growth squarely in the middle: slow enough to maintain, or even slightly improve, real wages and yet to encourage labour-saving innovation, fast enough to keep down labour costs and yet to expand aggregate demand for food and mass consumer goods'.[199]

In my view, if there was to be any qualitative increase in home demand, if there was to be the change in the demand schedules of the kind required by Miss Gilboy, then what was needed was more than 'a maintenance or slight improvement in real wages'. What was needed was a considerable body of family households with a substantially increased income – 'high enough to sustain the prolonged demand which we postulate as the core of industrialization'.[200] Eversley's required number of extra households generating an income of between £50 and £400 a year is most easily explained by recourse to the additional income provided by the independent wages of wives and families. Very few individual male workers earned enough to make substantial inroads into Eversley's required income limits.

Child and female labour made, of course, one very well-known contribution to rapid economic growth. It provided the entrepreneur with cheap labour. The rapid increase in the employment of women and children meant that, despite the rise in male wages, labour unit costs fell, but at the same time, because they had not usually earned serious money wages before, the earnings of women and children swelled the family unit income and so boosted demand.

The double effect of falling labour costs and rising demand produced a Utopian situation for many manufacturers, from which they were not slow to profit. It is a phenomenon which revives the possibility of profit inflation as an explanation of the speed with which many manufacturers ploughed back their profits.[201]

My present concern here is, however, centred on their contribution to demand. When a man's wages went up in the eighteenth century the first beneficial effects might be expected to occur in the brewing industry, and in the commercialization of sport and leisure which

[199] Ibid., pp. 142–3.
[200] Eversley, op. cit. p. 216.
[201] See Earl J. Hamilton, 'Profit Inflation and the Early Industrial Revolution, 1751–1800', *Quarterly Journal of Economics* (1942), and David Felix, 'Profit Inflation and Economic Growth', *Quarterly Journal of Economics* (1956).

Professor Plumb has recently described – gambling, boxing, horse-racing and the like. When a woman's wages went up the first commercial effects would be expected in the clothing industries and those industries which provided consumer goods for the home. Her increased earning released her desire to compete with her social superiors – a desire pent up for centuries or at least restricted to a very occasional excess. It is a common enough reaction. As a medical historian wrote recently, 'When a food that has been rare and long desired finally arrives within reach of the masses, consumption rises sharply, as if a long repressed appetite had exploded.'

Contemporaries were right to recognize a sudden jump in fashionable excess, because the competition was no longer between the upper and middle classes, but between them and the prospering working classes too. The extension was explicitly recognized by eighteenth-century observers. Early in the century the *Spectator* provided occasional examples of servants mimicking their masters, but the major competition was between the rich and the titled. By the middle of the century even the lower middle class aspired to compete. By the end of the century labourers and mechanics and their wives actually *can* compete. Kent has observed that expansion of the market, revealed by the literary evidence, occurs first among the domestic servant class, then among the industrial workers, and finally among the agricultural workers. Because of their dependence on payment in kind and on tips, or vails as they were then called, it is difficult to judge the changes that took place in the earning power of this servant class, but it seems likely that their wages went up as a result of the competitive effects of the higher paid factory workers, and that they are singled out first for their extravagant expenditure and emulative spending simply because they were a more accessible and more readily observed class than the factory workers for the articulate middle- and upper-class observers who wrote these records we rely on, and because, being so close to fashionable behaviour in their daily lives, they quickly reacted to it. The low food prices and the demand for labour in the second quarter of the eighteenth century had provided opportunities for a wide section of the working class to make modest gains before 1750. The increasing demand for labour after that date produced increased money wages for many groups of male labour but rarely sufficient to afford any major change in consumption patterns without the supplementary effects of female and child labour.

It is not necessary to suggest that the high income families I have described were typical. Clearly they were not. We are dealing here with an élite section of the labour force. For many families the earnings of their wives and children helped mainly to make up the deficit between their outgoing and their income, although even here it made a major contribution to comfort. But there were families in which it generated a handsome surplus which could be spent on the products of the mass consumer industries.

The spending of this aristocracy of labour sparked off further spending from those above in retaliation, and from those below in imitation. That so many of the products they bought have been identified as for the middle-class market was often because these working-class families now enjoyed an earning potential well within that range. The working class themselves certainly recognized the importance of the earnings of their wives and children, and it is interesting to note that Pinchbeck and Hewitt identify the high wage areas as those in which the abolition of the employment of children was most strenuously resisted. 'Later in the nineteenth century when women and children were employed in the same process as men and were used to undercut the men's wage rates, and sometimes even deprived them of a livelihood altogether, working-class organizations were to oppose the employment of children in factories as strenuously as they might. But in 1833 witnesses before the commissioners argued very differently.'[202] Once again it is important that the emotional Victorian backlash, and the very real humanitarian feelings of the mid-nineteenth-century reformers, do not blind us to the earlier benefits. Whether helping to provide the necessities of life, whether financing the decencies of life, and occasionally making accessible to this class for the first time some of the luxuries of life, the wages of women and children made a very significant contribution.

And how else are we to explain the boom in production and consumption which occurred in the second half of the eighteenth century? So many consumer industries flourished that required an extension of the mass consumer market, so many new trades appeared with a close association with the demands of women and children.

Many manufacturers frankly declared that it was the female market they were aiming at. The textile manufacturers understandably directed

[202] Pinchbeck and Hewitt, *Children in English Society*, II, p. 408.

their advertisements of the new fashions at women. A manufacturer like Foster used the Countess of Bective to give snob appeal to his products so that other women would, as Dr Johnson put it, 'catch from example the contagion of desire'.[203] Wedgwood used the Duchess of Devonshire for the same purpose because, as he wrote to Bentley, 'Few ladies dare venture at anything out of the common style till authorized by their betters – by the ladies of superior spirit who set the ton.'[204] Wedgwood's intention was always to 'amuse and divert, and please, and astonish, nay and even to ravish the Ladies',[205] because, as he wrote to Bentley, 'it will be in our interests to do so'. The lists of his customers show that he was right: in London they reveal a high proportion of titled and fashionable women; in the provinces they show an even higher proportion of women who aspired to own the products of the Queen's potter who had so brilliantly captured the market of the rich and the aristocratic. His customers' letters are richly stocked with evidence of the upwardly mobile ranks of society aping their social superiors at the centre of fashion. The woman in Newcastle upon Tyne who insisted on a dinner service in the 'Arabesque pattern' before her local shopkeeper had even heard of it, wanted it because it was 'much used in London at present', and she steadfastly 'declined taking any till she had seen that pattern'.[206]

It is not, I think, too fanciful to see the emergence of this increasing demand for such consumer goods as a direct result of the increasing financial independence of women in control of their own earnings. So many of the 'new wants' identified by contemporary comment were commodities bought and desired by women.

It *would* be too fanciful to see the sudden appearance in the 1760s of a host of new products successfully aimed at children as a direct result of children's earnings. We have evidence of industrial apprentices buying books with their wages, but the spectacular success of men like John Newbery and John Spilsbury clearly indicated 'a large growing class of people . . . with money to spend'.[207] Some, at least, of the money to

---

203 Dr Johnson, *Idler and Adventurer*, II, p. 463.

204 Wedgwood MSS., Josiah Wedgwood to Thomas Bentley, 21 June 1777. See Neil McKendrick, *Economic History Review* (1960).

205 Wedgwood MSS., Josiah Wedgwood to Thomas Bentley, 1 June 1767.

206 Wedgwood MSS., Joseph Harris of Newcastle upon Tyne to Josiah Wedgwood, 1780.

207 J. H. Plumb, *The Commercialisation of Leisure in Eighteenth-Century England*, The Stenton Lecture for 1972 (1973), p. 9.

spend came almost certainly from the pockets of the newly prosperous, socially aspiring working-class mothers who had achieved control not only of part of her husband's earnings, but of her own and her children's too. It seems too much of a coincidence that women's journals should begin and flourish in the 1760s,[208] that children's books should enjoy dramatic sales in the 1760s, that jigsaw puzzles should be invented and successfully launched in the 1760s, that new children's games were invented and launched in the 1760s. Clearly those who prospered in these areas had considerable entrepreneurial skills: John Jeffreys exploited what Linda Hannas has called 'this new children's market' by cunningly adapting an old gambling game and making it acceptable to both children and parents by adding a touch of instruction – he took a map of Europe and made it into a race game in which travellers were moved along a track through all the countries by the throw of a dice. *The Play of Geography*, as it was called, was sufficiently successful to have survived to this day. Spilsbury, too, made his puzzles instructive – the earliest ones were maps or the history of English kings;[209] and Newbery's *A Pretty Little Pocket Book*, which enjoyed such prodigious success, was designed to teach the alphabet. The appeal to the socially ambitious and socially emulative is clear. They were cunningly marketed in other ways too. Newbery gave some books away free – so long as you bought the binding. His *Pocket Book*, priced 6*d*, was neatly bound and gilt. It was illustrated and, as a further gimmick, for an extra 2*d* you got a pincushion for a girl and a ball for a boy.[210]

None of these more trivial signs of the extension of demand could have come into existence without the appearance of a growing market willing and able to spend, eager for instruction for their children, and financially capable of being exploited by the entrepreneurs. The demand can be explained in terms of middle-class prosperity but, unless that prosperity was a novelty, it was curious that it should suddenly reveal itself in the late eighteenth century. If these middle-class incomes were being enjoyed by a class which had previously been used to much lower incomes, their propensity to spend and consume in the current atmosphere of social emulation and competitive spending is much

[208] Alison Adburgham, *Women in Print* (1972).
[209] Linda Hannas, *The English Jigsaw Puzzle, 1760–1890* (1972).
[210] Plumb, *The Commercialisation of Leisure* (1973), p. 9; see also William Noblett, 'John Newbery, Publisher Extraordinary', *History Today*, XXII (April 1972), pp. 265–71.

easier to understand. After all, the reach of the market was not inconsiderable which could absorb 200,000 copies of Thomas Paine's
The Rights of Man within a year of publication; a reputed sale of over
one million copies of the *Last Dying Speech and Confession of William
Corder, the Murderer of Maria Martin* in 1828; and a weekly circulation
of 200,000 copies of Cobbett's *Political Register* in 1836.[211] The market
for a vast variety of inessential expenditure, which Plumb has recently
drawn attention to, was larger and more ramified than has often been
thought.[212]

There is still a great deal more evidence needed before we can move
with confidence in the problematic area of income, standards of living
and home demand. But enough has been established for us to recognize
that, although the pursuit of luxury can be seen as a reflection of the
structure of society and the relationship of the different social levels
within it, a sudden change in the social levels to which the pursuit of
luxury penetrated may require some further explanation. We may
agree with Marcel Mauss that 'it is not in production that society found
its impetus: luxury is the great stimulant'; with Jacques Rueff that 'production is the daughter of desire'; and with Gaston Bachelard that 'the
attainment of the superfluous causes greater spiritual excitement than the
attainment of necessities. For man is a creature of desire, not of need'.

But we must also realize that, as long as the pursuit of luxury was
limited to the few, it was more like an engine 'running in neutral than
an element of growth'.[213] Once this pursuit was made possible for an
ever-widening proportion of the population, then its potential was
released, and it became an engine for growth, a motive power for mass
production. Explaining the release of that power, in terms of the
release of a latent desire for new consumption patterns, would go a
long way towards explaining the coming of the Industrial Revolution.

No subject of enquiry has gained more from the increasing awareness of the social dimensions of economic growth than the studies of
home demand in the British Industrial Revolution. Comparative
studies have helped, too. We now know that in China in 1793 'the
form of clothing is rarely changed by fashion or whim. The dress which

211 R. K. Webb, *The British Working Class Reader, 1790–1848* (1950); R. D. Altick, *The
English Common Reader* (1963); Marjorie Plant, *The English Book Trade* (1965).
212 Plumb, *The Commercialisation of Leisure* (1973), *passim*.
213 Fernand Braudel, *Capitalism and Material Life, 1400 to 1800* (1973), translated from the
French (*Civilisation Matérielle et Capitalisme* (1967)) by Miriam Kochan, p. 124.

suits the status of the man or the season of the year when he wears it is always made in the same way. Even the women have scarcely any new fashions';[214] and we know that in the Ottoman Empire in 1741 'Fashions which tyrannize European women hardly disturb the fair sex in the east, hair styles, cut of clothing and type of fabric are almost always the same';[215] and such knowledge helps to explain why their response to a revolution in textile production would have differed from the response of eighteenth-century English society.

When economists increasingly concede that only a modest fraction of measurable growth in advancing countries can be traced to increasing inputs of capital, labour and resources, and when they have increasingly claimed that the major restraints upon the advance of economically backward nations are *non*-economic, then it is understandable that historians should have joined them in their famous 'hunt for the residuals' – a search for the other ingredients in a society beyond the major economic variables which explain a country's propensity to achieve economic growth.[216]

This search has led them increasingly to examine the ideas of sociologists, educational theorists, political scientists and psychologists. As a result, increasing emphasis has been placed on the motivational psychology of the entrepreneur, on the levels of technological education, and on the changing structure of society. The aspirations and values of a society are recognized to be as worthy of study as its raw materials, and the non-economic variables are now examined as assiduously as the major economic ones are.

The entrepreneur, for instance, has been examined, and indeed seen, as the mouthpiece or expression of the aspirations of his society, or more particularly of his class, or his religion, or even of his parents' frustrated ambitions. What Gerschenkron has ironically labelled 'exquisitely non-operative theories', which explain the British Industrial Revolution in terms of child-rearing patterns or the aspirational goals instilled by parents, have recently sprouted and flourished. To explain the entrepreneur's behaviour patterns there have been psychological theories of achievement motivation such as McClelland's,[217] or theories

[214] Ibid., p. 227.

[215] Mouradj d'Osson, *Tableau général de l'Empire ottoman* (1741), quoted Braudel, op. cit. p. 228.

[216] P. Mathias, *Cambridge Review* (30 January 1970), p. 90.

[217] D. C. McClelland, *The Achieving Society* (1961).

of status reorientation through economic achievement by disprivileged social groups such as Everett Hagen's,[218] or theories of profit satisfaction levels and psychic income such as Simon's[219] and Katona's.[220] The theory of games has been ransacked for insights.[221]

The schools, the universities, the religious minorities, the family and the firm are all being investigated for the values they instil. But, since demand moved to the top of the list of fashionable explanations of economic growth, it is society and its structure – its cultural differences, its attitude to work and leisure, whether it is contemplative or acquisitive, whether it is static or encourages social mobility – which has attracted the greatest attention. Economic historians are enriching their accounts of economic growth or refining their models, depending on their type, by increasingly taking note of the nature of the society they are studying. Professor Court's apparent truism that 'the first prerequisite for economic growth is a society of the kind required to produce it' has been fastened onto as the perceptive key to unlock the difficult problems of economic change.

Now much of this is right and reasonable. Such study is obviously very necessary. If Ancient Egypt was so preoccupied by death – its rites, ceremonies and artefacts – that death accounted for more wealth than any other sector of the economy but agriculture, then it obviously influenced that society's potential for economic growth. If eighteenth-century Portugal was a slave economy in which manual work was performed by slaves (and was therefore despised by the rest of society) and if, moreover, it was a society in which religion exercised such sway that, after all the holy days had been observed, there were only some 163 days left for work, then obviously it would influence their attitude to labour and employment, the pursuit of profit and, in consequence, their potential for growth. If, as in Mandarin China, the greatest social prestige was attached to the scholar-bureaucrat; or if, as in India, social mobility was prevented by the caste system; or if, as in some other eastern societies, the contemplative life was more highly valued than the active; or if, as in the classical world, the words for work and leisure

[218] E. E. Hagen, *On the Theory of Social Change* (1962).

[219] H. A. Simon, 'Theories of Decision-Taking in Economics and Behavioural Science', *Managerial Economics* (1968), ed. G. P. E. Clarkson, pp. 13–49.

[220] G. Katona, *Psychological Analysis of Economic Behaviour* (1951) and 'Rational Behaviour and economic behaviour', *Psychological Review*, 60 (1953), pp. 307–18.

[221] J. von Neumann and O. Morgenstern, *Theory of Games and Economic Behaviour* (1947).

were leisure and unleisure; or if, as in many societies, minority groups (ethnic, social, religious or merely immigrant) have been prevented by economic, legal or class barriers from enjoying the full spectrum of job opportunities, and, as a result, are channelled into particular directions by the restrictions – an effect which has had very striking consequences for the career choice of such minority groups as the Jews, the Parsees, the Huguenots, the Nonconformists and many immigrant groups – if any of these (and many other such distinctions could be listed) were important features of a society, then obviously it would be likely to influence that society's ability to expand economically. Such values help to explain why one society exploited its scientific inventions and another did not; they help to explain the different leisure preferences of different societies, the different social mobility, the different levels of class competition and social emulation, and the differing propensities to buy consumer goods of different societies.

But for all their importance – and this article is surely testimony to my belief in that – there is a danger of putting so much stress on the latent social causes of growth that one neglects the necessary economic catalyst which so often needed to release them. By this I do not mean merely the existence of a generally favourable economic climate in which to operate, but the more specific economic characteristics which linked social emulation with the production machine, and which turned class competition into realizable demand.

To argue, as Professor Perkin has done, that 'if there was one cause . . . that must bear more than any other the weight of responsibility for the British Industrial Revolution, it is social emulation, English snobbery, "keeping up with the Joneses" – a fitting verdict on the single greatest achievement of a nation of snobs',[222] is not to explain why that snobbery was suddenly so economically dynamic in the eighteenth century. Social emulation had existed for centuries, as had its offspring, the pursuit of luxury, and emulative spending could become a potent force in the economy only when its field of expression was widened by the appearance of significantly larger proportions of the population with surplus income to spend. A whole complex of forces was involved (involving capital, technology, demographic change and entrepreneurship), but the most important link in the

[222] Perkin, op. cit. p. 141.

chain between such social pressures and the working of the economy was the increased spending power of English working women and their families.

If the entrepreneur is rightly seen as the most important human link between the non-economic variables and the production end of the economy, then the female consumer should be seen as the most important human link between them and the demand side of the economy. The entrepreneur may have exploited demand, and released demand which was previously latent, he may even have created the need for 'new wants', but it was the increased propensity to consume and increased ability to do so of the female buyer which largely decided whether his efforts would succeed.

The consumer revolution was not, then, simply a reflection of social emulation, nor simply a reflection of the entrepreneur's ability to exploit it. It was a reflection of social emulation being released to operate with far greater force and over a far wider field by an increase in prosperity, much of which derived from female and child incomes. What ensured that the income would be spent on clothing the family and supplying the home was that, for the first time on any major scale, women had access to an independent income. The rise of the brewing industry may be a reflection of rising male wage rates; the rise of those industries in which women almost invariably took the consumption decisions – cotton, woollen, linen, silk, pottery, cutlery, glass and the Birmingham fashion industries – was a reflection of the increased proportion of family earning which women provided and over which they exercised increased control.

Social emulation provided an ideal environment for the purposeful economic deployment of this new prosperity; but it was the new source and new control of that prosperity which turned class competition into emulative spending, and thereby helped to turn a latent social force into a potent economic expression of growth. It was woman's increasingly important role in producing these family earnings which allowed her to release her frustrated desire to compete in the pursuit of fashion and conspicuous consumption; it was the fact that she took the consumption decisions which decided the direction of those earnings; it was her control of a larger portion of the family income – that earned by herself and her children – which decided where this extra prosperity was to be released into the economy; and the very fact of her increasing employment outside the home ensured that her demand for manufactured goods would increase because she could no longer make them herself.

There will be those who will say that to explain the consumer revolution and the growth of demand in terms of the wages gained from the demand for industrial labour, is to explain growth in terms of growth itself. But this is both a logical and historical fallacy. Our problem is not to explain why economic growth *began*. It is always beginning and petering out and beginning again. Our problem is to explain why growth was maintained, sustained and accelerated. That is what made the Industrial Revolution so important. That colonial demand or an agriculturally induced increase in home demand *initiated* eighteenth-century industrialization does not necessarily mean they are the most important elements to study. The first stage of a rocket's take-off can be the least difficult to explain, the second and third stages (the fact that the momentum can be accelerated and maintained) can be far more interesting and important. The response to the new demand for labour (the increasing employment of women and children) and the way in which their social aspirations made them spend their new earnings can be, at the very lowest, an interesting addition to the explanation of these second and third stages.

It was this new consumer demand – the mill girl who wanted to dress like a duchess, and who, according to a host of contemporary observers, could manage an increasingly close approximation to doing so – which helped to create the Industrial Revolution. It was consumer demand which attracted the attention of the textile entrepreneurs and made the fortunes of the manufacturers of mass consumer goods. And it was the despised labour of women and children which helped to finance that new consumer demand. The emotional response of the Victorians, and the compassion any historian must feel for the hours they worked and the conditions they endured, must not blind us to the importance of what they achieved.

The past paradise the Victorians created to describe the position of women and children in pre-industrial England has not survived inspection. The vivid picture they painted of an old England, which was 'the hell of horses, the purgatory of servants and the paradise of women, from the former having everything to do and the latter nothing' was created to serve as an instructive contrast with a present in which 'women had been led forth from their paradise into a life of labour and care'.[223] But the contrast was overdone and misleading. The propaganda has concealed important benefits for both the family and the economy. What they suffered in providing the labour for production must not obscure what compensation they were offered in terms of consumption. The abuses of child and female labour were real, and the accounts of them are often authentic, but the attempts of the Victorians (for a variety of motives) to blacken the *fact* of working women and children must not deceive us into underestimating their importance.

After hearing a paper I gave in 1972, to his postgraduate seminar at the City University of New York, on 'Demand in the Industrial Revolution' and after reading some of the subject's complex literature Professor Plumb[224] wrote: 'a clutch of historians is involved in the debate as to whether or not foreign demand was an important factor in triggering off the Industrial Revolution in Britain. To the outsider this may seem petty, but it is not, and the argument for and against is as complex, as fascinating and at times as beautiful as a game of chess by Fischer and Spassky. Also the question is very important, for the Industrial Revolution is one of the major changes in human history: to understand its causation is essential, on the other hand it is practically impossible to explain the intricacies of this problem [of demand] to anyone without professional training.' Gratefully accepting the tribute to the importance of the problem and its complexity, I also acknowledge the rebuke; and, since this piece is written in his honour, it is intended to be less technical, more comprehensible, and aimed at a wider public.[225]

---

[223] A review of Edward Cheshire, *The Results of the Census of Great Britain in 1851* (1853) in *The Edinburgh Review*, April 1959, no. CCXXII. See *Working Conditions in the Victorian Age*, by John Saville (1973).

[224] J. H. Plumb, 'The historian and the destiny of man', *The Daily Telegraph*, 19 October 1972, p. 18.

[225] For providing me with the larger perspective of the role of women in society and with a textbook example of how to extract that role from the literary evidence of the past, I am grateful to my wife: *see* Melveena McKendrick, *Woman and Society in the Spanish Drama of the Golden Age* (Cambridge University Press, 1974).

VIII

Legislation and Virtue:
An Essay on Working Class Self-Help and the
State in the Early Nineteenth Century*

BARRY SUPPLE

A good government will give all its aid in such a shape, as to
encourage and nurture any rudiments it may find of a spirit of
individual exertion. It will be assiduous in removing obstacles
and discouragements to voluntary enterprise, and in giving
whatever direction and guidance may be necessary: its pecuni-
ary means will be applied, when practicable, in aid of private
efforts rather than in supersession of them, and it will call into
play its machinery of rewards and honours to elicit such
efforts. Government aid, when given merely in default of
private enterprise, should be so given as to be as far as possible
a course of education for the people in the art of accomplishing
great objects by individual energy and voluntary co-operation.[1]

The recent revival of interest in the changing social and economic role
of the state in the early nineteenth century has stimulated new controversies about the roots and patterns of government intervention as
well as exploding (or, more accurately, re-exploding) the myth of a

* This chapter was completed before the publication of P. H. J. H. Gosden's *Self-Help:
Voluntary Associations in Nineteenth-Century Britain* (1973), which covers some of the
same ground. Unfortunately, time did not allow for any amendment of the text in
the light of Mr. Gosden's book. My thanks are due to the Centre for Insurance Studies
at the University of Sussex for a research grant, to Mr. William Smickersgill for his
invaluable research assistance, and to Professors Asa Briggs, John Harrison and Donald
Winch for their comments.

[1] John Stuart Mill, *Principles of Political Economy*, Book V, Ch. XI, section 16.

purely *laissez-faire* society.[2] But, even with respect to the latter point, the basis for an historical consensus hardly yet exists: first, because extensive institutional reform was perfectly compatible with a commitment to individualism and market forces, and was indeed a necessary prerequisite of a competitive society;[3] second, because, irrespective of the ultimate role of government, *laissez-faire* and individualistic doctrines were pervasive influences on contemporary debate and policy. The administrative state was not necessarily the antithesis of the *laissez-faire* state. Hence, even as the twin stereotypes of do-nothing *laissez-faire* and of government policies as direct reflections of pure doctrines recede, it becomes the more necessary to disentangle the respective influences on these policies of actual problems and of doctrine. For individualism was a powerful element in nineteenth-century intellectual systems – and men did not construct such systems for their private amusement.

The role of the state and the practical influence of social and intellectual doctrines can best be studied in relation to a wide range of problems. And in this respect the present chapter, which is concerned with merely a single aspect of the problem of the poor in nineteenth-century Britain, can provide only limited insight into the larger questions. Nevertheless, no problem provided such a fruitful source of official discussion and government action as the existence of poverty

[2] For examples of the recent literature, see David Roberts, *Victorian Origins of the British Welfare State* (1960); O. O. G. M. MacDonagh, *A Pattern of Government Growth, 1800–1860: The Passenger Acts and their Enforcement* (1961); Henry Parris, *Government and the Railways in Nineteenth-Century Britain* (1965); William C. Lubenow, *The Politics of Government Growth: Early Victorian Attitudes towards State Intervention, 1833–1848* (1971); A. W. Coats (ed.), *The Classical Economists and Economic Policy* (1971); William O. Aydelotte, 'The Conservative and Radical Interpretations of Early Victorian Social Legislation', *Victorian Studies*, XI, 2 (1967); Valerie Cromwell, 'Interpretations of Nineteenth-Century Administration: An Analysis', *Victorian Studies*, IX, 3 (1966); Robert M. Gutchen, 'Local Government and Centralization in Nineteenth-Century England', *Historical Journal*, IV, 1 (1961); Jenifer Hart, 'Nineteenth-Century Social Reform: A Tory Interpretation of History', *Past and Present*, 31 (1965); L. J. Hume, 'Jeremy Bentham and the Nineteenth-Century Revolution in Government', *Historical Journal*, X, 4 (1967); O. O. G. M. MacDonagh, 'The Nineteenth-Century Revolution in Government: A reappraisal', *Historical Journal*, I, 1 (1958); Henry Parris, 'The Nineteenth-Century Revolution in Government: A Reappraisal Reappraised', *Historical Journal*, III, 1 (1960); David Roberts, 'Jeremy Bentham and the Victorian Administrative State', *Victorian Studies*, II, 3 (1959).

[3] R. L. Crouch, 'Laissez-Faire in Nineteenth-Century Britain: Myth or Reality?', *The Manchester School*, 35 (September 1967); Nathan Rosenberg, 'Some Institutional Aspects of the Wealth of Nations', *Journal of Political Economy*, 68 (December 1960).

and the position of the new urban and industrial working class in society. This preoccupation was reflected in much of classical economics and population theory, in the great Poor Law of 1834 and the continuing evolution of poor-law administration, in the growth of a concern with education, and in the abundant legislation to improve the urban environment and working conditions. The result has even been interpreted as an embryonic welfare state:

In 1833 the central bureaucracies of few governments in Europe did so little for its citizens as did England's. . . . Yet in 1854 the central bureaucracies of few countries in Europe did more for the well-being of its subjects than did England's, and none of the governments intervened so decisively to regulate the hours of labour in factories, systematize poor relief, and promote the public health. . . . England, the historic home of Anglo-Saxon local government and the economic doctrines of Adam Smith, had begun to construct a welfare state.[4]

Yet whatever the energy and humanity which characterized the efforts of reformers, few men believed that state intervention could directly solve the national problem of poverty. If the poor had an economic salvation it lay not in their being helped, but in helping themselves, or at least in being provided with the means (education and a rationalized system of laws and institutions) with which they could help themselves. Social policy might ameliorate the condition of individuals and specific groups; it might successfully tackle specific evils (child labour, for example, or excessively long working days) or communal problems (e.g. bad sanitation) in relation to which individuals could do little. But in the last resort the welfare of the poor *as a class* was assumed to lie in changes in the values and habits and priorities of individuals – changes which would reduce birth rates, increase savings, and lead, via a conscientious striving after improvement, to a better and more secure life. Put crudely, the working class were expected to adopt the cardinal middle-class socio-economic virtues: self-help, character, thrift and duty, to cite the titles of Samuel Smiles's four most successful books. And if the state had a role in this process it was to help to overcome the obstacles to a better educated and more prudential working class.

This chapter discusses the evolution in the early nineteenth century of two types of working-class institution, friendly societies (essentially clubs for mutual insurance against sickness, old age and death) and

[4] Roberts, *Victorian Origins of the British Welfare State*, pp. 315–16.

trustee savings banks. It considers such associations in terms of their relationships to the growth of working-class thrift, the official attitudes towards the improvement of the position of the poor, and the tangled history of interventionism in a *laissez-faire* framework. Limited as the examples are, the topic is an important one because it raises questions concerning the roots and direction of social policy during a period when inherited ideological aspirations could not be made consistent with the specific problem of the labouring poor or with the general need to adapt society's laws and institutions to the nascent realities of the new industrial state. Government intervention in this, as in many other areas, was therefore a response to twin pressures: on the one hand, to solve particular problems by legislation or the adaptation of institutional law; on the other, to encourage, or remove obstacles to, those varieties of individual self-improvement which were judged to be consistent with the general social good. Three points are worth emphasizing at the outset. First, the poor created their own institutions: the policies with which we shall be concerned were supplementary influences on, rather than indispensable preconditions of, their growth. Second, legislation designed to shape and stabilize working-class financial institutions was based on a particular perception of social structure: the development and differentiation of a class society established new pressures for change in policies and attitudes. Third, these pressures involved a tension between ideology and activity. And, in manipulating market forces to attain social objectives, contemporaries embodied that tension in the superficially curious phenomenon of a state-sponsored individualism. In this sense the topic under consideration is merely one example of the attempt to legislate for an improved framework within which individual choices might operate freely and effectively. The basis of working-class thrift is to be found in the history of the poor, but the framework of legislative encouragement within which it grew illustrated that convergence of the ideas of Bentham and Smiles which was characteristic of so much of early Victorian social policy.

1

THE GROWTH OF FRIENDLY SOCIETIES AND SAVINGS BANKS

The principal standpoint of this essay is the formulation of national policy towards working-class thrift. Necessarily, therefore, financial prudence is here seen as a virtue which the relatively rich wished to inculcate in the relatively poor, and attention is concentrated on the means they adopted towards this end. Nevertheless, it is worth re-emphasizing that thrift, and the associated growth of institutions which embodied it, had very deep roots in working-class behaviour and habits. In both ideological and institutional terms, thrift was an *intrinsic* part of working-class history – an outgrowth of working-class attitudes towards moral and social independence and stability, and not merely a habit thrust on them by other social groups. Indeed, there is no other explanation of the impressive growth in the nineteenth century of social arrangements (friendly societies, savings banks, building societies, educational associations, co-operative societies, trade unions) which provided underpinnings to individual existence in an indus-trializing society.

Of the various sorts of thrift-orientated institutions which nineteenth-century working men supported, friendly societies were both the most popular and the oldest.[5] In essence, although there was considerable variety in terms of their structure and purpose, and the social and convivial elements were often very important, friendly societies were established on a co-operative basis to provide their members with mutual insurance against some or all of illness, death and old age. In terms of structure and purposes they were products of an earlier age than that of coal and iron. Nevertheless, their growth was a function of the economic and social upheaval of industrialism. Although the annual flow of premium payments is not known, the amount invested by societies with the National Debt Commissioners rose significantly: from an annual average of £38,000 in the period 1827–30 to £118,000 in 1847–50.[6] Concomitantly, membership of friendly societies grew rapidly: in 1801 an informed estimate gave the number of societies and local clubs as over 7,000 and their membership as over 600,000; by mid-century it was estimated that almost half the adult male population of England and Wales belonged to a society (in 1851 the male popula-tion aged 15 or over was about 5.7 million); and in 1858 the Registrar

---

[5] For the growth and problems of friendly societies in the mid-nineteenth century, see P. H. J. H. Gosden, *The Friendly Societies in England, 1815–75* (1961). Also see Gosden, *Self-Help*, Ch. 2–5.

[6] *British Parliamentary Papers* (henceforth referred to as *B.P.P.*), 1890–1, XLVIII, 281. It should be emphasized that by no means all friendly societies invested their funds with the National Debt Commissioners, and that those societies which did invest in this way could also invest in other outlets.

of Friendly Societies estimated that there were 20,000 societies in England and Wales with funds of over £9 million. Between 1815 and 1872 the membership of friendly societies in England and Wales increased from just under one million to over four million. By the latter date, there were over 30,000 societies – many of them, of course, very small – with accumulated funds of almost £12 million.[7]

As this timing suggests, and as has been pointed out by their historian,[8] friendly societies were like co-operative and trade unions in the sense that they were the products of voluntary effort on the part of those seeking both greater material security and a lessening of the social isolation of the individual at a time of accelerating economic growth and change. Naturally, therefore, their principal expansion came not only in the period, but also in the areas, most affected by industrial growth. As early as 1815, when Lancashire alone accounted for about 15 per cent (147,000) of all members of English friendly societies, the concentration in the manufacturing counties of the midlands and, more particularly, the north had been marked. And in the course of the subsequent development of the friendly society movement, the influence of northern industrial areas was very striking.

There was very considerable variety in both the types and the membership of friendly societies. The more conventional 'local societies', many of them very small, were characterized by complete independence and self-government. Their membership probably remained steady at just under one million between 1815 and the early 1870s. By the latter date such local societies were overshadowed by the affiliated orders which had attained a membership of some 1,250,000. These orders were themselves deeply rooted in localism through their branches, which were the basic units of organization. They experienced a particularly rapid growth in the north in the late 1830s and the early 1840s. The two biggest – the Independent Order of Oddfellows, Manchester Unity, and the Ancient Order of Foresters – which accounted for 800,000 members between them, both originated in Lancashire; and the Royal Commission on Friendly and Benefit

---

[7] There is a wealth of information on friendly societies in the Fourth Report and Appendix of the Royal Commission on Friendly and Benefit Building Societies, B.P.P., 1874, XXIII. Also see Gosden, *Friendly Societies*, pp. 1–7, 13–16; [W. R. Greg], 'Investments for the Working Classes', *Edinburgh Review*, XCV (1852), 407; B.P.P., 1857–8, I, 251.

[8] Gosden, *Friendly Societies*, pp. 6–7.

Building Societies emphasized that affiliated societies in general 'have
... their headquarters, or at least their chief centres of influence, among
the manufacturing or mining population of the midland and northern
counties, and of Wales'.[9] As with local societies, the premiums of the
affiliated societies varied from place to place. In 1845, for example, the
different lodges of the Manchester Unity paid conventional benefits of
about 8s weekly in sickness, and £10 death benefit in return for
premiums of 4d, 5d or 6d weekly.[10]

In addition to local and affiliated bodies offering a range of friendly
society benefits, the economic, although not the social, function of
societies was fulfilled by a relatively small number of what the Royal
Commission called 'ordinary large (or general) societies', which
provided life and sickness insurance, often on a national basis and with
no personal or social connection between members. Operating from
London with more or less conventional governing bodies of directors
and managers, societies like the Hearts of Oak (founded 1841) and the
much smaller Royal Standard, United Patriots, Royal Oak, London
Friendly, etc., catered for the better-off members of the working class
(membership of the Hearts of Oak was limited to those earning £1 2s
or more weekly)[11] and even to members of the lower middle classes.
Altogether, however, there were less than ten of such societies in 1874,
with a membership of about 60,000.[12]

Finally, it is important to bear in mind the existence of 'burial
societies',[13] which were founded primarily, and often exclusively, to
provide a life insurance benefit to cover funeral expenses in an age
when the poor dreaded a pauper funeral, whether for themselves or for
their children. (The insurance of children figured particularly strongly
in burial societies.) Such societies normally used a house-to-house
canvass to secure subscription – and were therefore also described as
'collecting societies'. Although many of them were insecure and open
to mismanagement, some of the local societies, particularly in the north,
were singled out by the Royal Commission in 1874 as examples of the
potentialities of local effort to provide a cheap service on a large scale.
Thus one of 'really gigantic dimensions', the Blackburn Philanthropic
Burial Society, founded by workmen at a cotton mill in 1839, had over

---

[9] B.P.P., 1874, XXIII (i), 49.   [10] Gosden, *Friendly Societies*, p. 105.
[11] B.P.P., 1874, XXIII (i), 46.   [12] B.P.P., 1874, XXIII (i), 45.
[13] See Gosden, *Friendly Societies*, pp. 52–61, following the Royal Commission's Fourth
Report, for a description of the other, less important, types of society.

130,000 members, mostly factory workers, by 1872 (it paid a death
benefit of £5 – or £4 if the member was under 10 years old – for a
premium of 1*d* per week). The total membership of local burial
societies in England and Wales stood at some 650,000 in 1872.[14] But
they, too, were overshadowed by a parallel type of national organization – the 'general' burial or collecting societies, which operated from
a central headquarters and were, in effect, life assurance offices catering
for the poor, operating under the Friendly Societies Act and employing
a complex apparatus of salaried officials and well-remunerated can-
vassers. Their main growth was to come in the 1850s and 1860s: by
1872 their membership in England and Wales was about one million
(1.4 million in the United Kingdom).[15] Like the proprietary industrial
life assurance companies which developed in the 1840s and 1850s,[16] the
general collecting societies were better indications of an attitude to
death than to savings. But they, together with all the other types of
friendly societies, provide an indication – no matter how rough and no
matter how distorted by the mixture of motives which explain their
growth – of a rising tide of financial prudence among the relatively
poor of Victorian Britain.

Compared with friendly societies, the trustee savings banks, – non-
profit making institutions, managed by trustees, and paying a moderate
rate of interest on relatively small-scale deposits – were more dependent
on private philanthropy and official encouragement for their foundation
and continued existence. Nevertheless, even considering this fact, once
the circumstances were favourable, their growth was an important
indication of the rise of the small-scale saver in nineteenth-century
Britain. The initial period of rapid expansion came after the Napoleonic
Wars, and particularly after legislation in 1817 had provided official
security for and a high return on their funds:[17] by December 1818 there

[14] *B.P.P.*, 1874, XXIII (i), 93, 100–1.
[15] *B.P.P.*, 1874, XXIII (i), 91–105. The group was dominated by the Royal Liver
Friendly Society (founded 1850: with some 550,000 members by 1872) and the
Liverpool Victoria Legal (1843: 200,000 members by 1872). Such societies had no
shareholders, but were managed by salaried officials.
[16] In addition to societies registered under friendly society legislation, the business of
industrial life assurance – the provision of small insurances for the poor, based upon
the payment of small weekly or fortnightly premiums collected at the policyholder's
house – attracted proprietary companies. Industrial life assurance (supremely exemplified by the Prudential Assurance Company) was the product of the 1840s and 1850s,
a period of rising living standards for the working class.
[17] Below, pp. 239–40.

were some 465 banks in the United Kingdom, of which all but six had been established in the previous four years, and deposits shot up in the 1820s to about £15 million.[18] In the 1830s and subsequently, the pace of expansion slackened, as legislation reduced the yield on deposits, as the average deposit decreased, and as the savings bank movement had to tap a wider field of depositors. Even so, between 1829 and 1850 the number of banks rose from 476 to 573, while the number of individual depositors (i.e., excluding charitable institutions and friendly societies) grew from some 400,000 to over one million and their total savings doubled, from £13.4 million to £27.2 million.[19]

Although they were largely promoted in order to encourage prudence among the poor, the growth of trustee savings banks cannot be taken as a precise index of working-class thrift. As far as the occupational structure of depositors can be determined, the banks tended to attract funds from domestic servants, from relatively well-off members of the working class (tradesmen, clerks, mechanics), or even from members of the middle class or their children.[20] Although the surviving data are hard to interpret, it is fairly obvious that only a relatively small proportion of depositors was derived from those socio-economic categories – the labouring classes in industry and trade – originally contemplated by the supporters of the trustee savings bank movement.

The view that friendly societies, savings banks and similar institutions were the outcome and embodiment of working-class effort and behaviour obviously has to be modified in the light of the complicated social history of ostensibly working-class institutions. Some, like friendly societies, were supported by workers, both independent and dependent, of middling as well as low incomes. Others, like the savings banks, which had been established with philanthropic motives to help the poor, were in fact used by the not-so-poor. And yet others, like the building societies, while originally initiated by working and lower middle class groups, had to a large extent been transmuted, by the third quarter of the century, into outlets for middle-class savings. At another

---

[18] Albert Fishlow, 'The Trustee Savings Banks, 1817–1861', *Journal of Economic History*, XXI, I (March 1961), 31, 39.

[19] *B.P.P.*, 1890–1, XLVIII, pp. 266–7. By 1860 there were 638 banks, 1.5 million depositors, and £38.5 million of deposits.

[20] See Fishlow, 'Trustee Savings Banks', *Journal of Economic History* (1961), 34, 36. Only 14 per cent of deposits were accounted for by the category of labourers, farm servants, journeymen and their wives.

level, some institutions were created by the efforts of middle-class philanthropy; and most successful burial societies and all industrial life offices, while attracting increasing numbers of the working class as they grew rapidly in the 1850s and 1860s, were based upon a spirit of active and successful commercial enterprise. In spite of this variety, however, each type of institution had ramified connections with the lower strata of Britain's developing class structure in the nineteenth century. Together, they represent a network which included, even when it also went beyond, the institutionalization of the genuine working-class impulse to thrift.

That network was obviously related to the course of British industrial growth. At one level, for example, the development of financial institutions can be seen as a defensive response to the greater personal insecurity and mobility of an industrializing society. For, irrespective of its effects on incomes, rapid economic change dislocated inherited institutional arrangements and relationships – whether in the family or between members of a hitherto quasi-traditional society. The anxieties and dissatisfactions which resulted from the disruption of the family, and of other established agencies of welfare and stability, helped produce new or newly important institutional arrangements. From this viewpoint, for example, the threat apparently posed to traditional modes of welfare policy by the Poor Law Amendment Act of 1834 (whatever its real consequences) led to a spurt in both the number and membership of friendly societies.[21] More generally, it can be argued that friendly and building societies, savings banks and insurance companies were responses to the disruption of 'the social environment of the family economy' by the pattern of economic growth. The result was the creation of 'new social units differentiated as buffers for the family's tenuous market position'.[22]

On the other hand, the purely 'defensive' aspects of the rise of thrift institutions should not be exaggerated. For not only was it the case that the facilities of many of these institutions were extensively used by those whose living standards had already been considerably improved by the process of industrialization, but the development of habits of thrift and the search for security were – among the working as among

---

[21] Gosden, *Friendly Societies*, Ch. VIII.
[22] The quotations are from Neil J. Smelser, *Social Change in the Industrial Revolution: An Application of Theory to the British Cotton Industry, 1770–1840* (1959), pp. 342, 377.

the middle classes – more often than not the consequence of increasing personal wealth. Active participation in friendly societies, savings banks, building societies and the like could be afforded only when the basic necessities of life had been provided for. And to this extent the growth of such institutions – like the growth of the ordinary life insurance offices patronized by the middle and upper classes – was in large part the outcome not only of the search for stability, but of changes in living standards which left more and more groups with at least a modest surplus of wealth above their minimum daily needs.

In these various respects the influence of industrialism was obviously very powerful. The dominant role of northern industrial areas in general, and Lancashire in particular, has already been mentioned. At the same time, the decades of the 1830s and, more especially, the 1840s, in which the process of industrialization was significantly accelerated and extended, and which saw the beginning of the end of a prolonged period of abject working-class poverty, comprised a critical era in the institutional history of working-class thrift. Moreover, a notable feature of much of this growth was the extent to which it exemplified an enormously powerful pressure for co-operative self-help, volun-taristic self-government and social and fraternal cohesion. This was illustrated in the extremely democratic methods of government chosen by many societies, in their independence of spirit as well as organization, in the essentially local character of various sorts of societies, and in the desire for conviviality and group identification which was apparently such a strong motive for many members.

Nevertheless, powerful as the tendency to self-improvement was, it offered a sharp contrast, in terms of economic reserves and social effects, to the much broader tendency among the middle classes. And it was this continuing contrast which moved many of those who wrote about or tried to legislate for the problems of the poor, to concentrate so much of their attention on working-class thrift.

2

THE ENCOURAGEMENT OF VIRTUE

The debate about working-class thrift naturally derived from the debate about the 'condition of England question' in the early nineteenth century. There were, of course, many commentators who felt that nothing short of a radical change in the social and economic system would provide the basis for a significant improvement in the lot of the poor. And others, perhaps unduly influenced by the gloomy side of classical economics, could hardly envisage *any* development which might have this desirable effect. But among the relatively rich there was probably a majority view that the solution of the problem of poverty would be found in the long run if the poor learned or were taught new habits of prudence in relation to the size of their families, their pattern of expenditure and savings, and their attitudes to work. The ethos which so powerfully encouraged the virtues of financial independence and prudence among the Victorian middle class was logically generalized by its adherents to embrace all those in humbler stations of life. 'It is wonderful what a power the working-people of this country might become', urged *Chambers's Edinburgh Journal* in 1844, 'were they to take, to the extent of their ability, the same advantage as the middle classes of the ordinary recognized means of advancing themselves in the social scale. A right ambition and self-respect is one of their greatest wants.'[23] And at the end of the next decade, when thrift institutions were already well developed among the poor, that most assiduous advocate of private virtue as social policy, Samuel Smiles, preached the same gospel: 'The whole body of the working classes might (with few exceptions) be as frugal, virtuous, well-informed, and well-conditioned as many individuals of the same class have already made themselves.'[24] And a constant refrain of such exhortations was that moral and social independence would inevitably follow financial independence. By frugality the poor, like the rich, would not only safeguard their living standards but would thereby enhance their self-respect by avoiding charity and personal dependence.

The view that working-class living standards could be raised by the unaided power of economic virtue had a very long history. With industrialization, however, there was an attempt to translate that view directly into social policy. The prospects of the poor did, indeed, improve in the third quarter of the nineteenth century. But the apparent rise in average real wages should not obscure the reality of the situation, which was that, at that or any other time in the nineteenth century, very large numbers of the poor were too poor to accumulate a significant amount of savings or insurance. As the statistician George Porter put it:

[23] *Chambers's Edinburgh Journal*, I (new series), 12 (23 March 1844), 124.
[24] Samuel Smiles, *Self-Help* (1859 ed.), Ch. X, 'Money: Its Uses and Abuses'.

Want of providence on the part of those who live by the labour of their hands, and whose employments so often depend upon circumstances beyond their control, is a theme which is constantly brought forward by many whose lot in life has been cast beyond the reach of want. It is, indeed, greatly to be wished, for their own sakes, that the habit were general among the labouring class of saving some part of their wages when fully employed, against less prosperous times; but it is difficult for those who are placed in circumstances of ease to estimate the amount of virtue that is implied in this self-denial. . . . Those persons . . . whose passage through life has been unvisited by the cares and anxieties that attend upon the children of labour, are very inadequate judges of the trials on the one hand, and of the means of surmounting them on the other, which are offered to those who must always form the most numerous class in every community.[25]

In spite of occasional reminders along these lines, however, the broad stream of exhortation to the poor remained unstemmed. Moreover, thrift – whether in the form of regular saving or mutual insurance against sickness, unemployment and old age – was not only a matter of private, individual advantage. The nineteenth-century attitude to savings was merely one aspect of an already conventional ethos which identified the moral and the material, the welfare of the individual and the good of society. And the advocates of working-class thrift were well aware of its more generalized social benefits. An obvious one, which was the complement of the individual's material independence, was the lessening of the cost of public poor relief if individuals could be persuaded to make greater provision for an uncertain future. This particularly applied to friendly societies, which received a good deal of attention as alternative institutions to the Poor Law, and as devices for economizing on public welfare payments through private insurance schemes. In fact, the late eighteenth century saw some determined (although unsuccessful) attempts to link friendly societies and poor law administration by legislating for parochial subsidies to, and even management of, local societies;[26] while the course of subsequent legislation showed quite clearly that the presumed 'beneficial influence exercised upon Poor Law expenditure by Friendly Societies' was a powerful motive for encouraging them.[27]

[25] G. R. Porter, *Progress of the Nation* (1851), Ch. XIV, pp. 454–5.
[26] *B.P.P.*, 1874, XXXIII (i), 192–3; H. Oliver Horne, *A History of Savings Banks* (1947), pp. 6–8.
[27] *B.P.P.*, 1874, XXXIII (i), 189. It was estimated that friendly societies saved the ratepayers some £2 million annually in the early 1870s.

A more subtle, and in the last resort more important, reason for the widespread encouragement of working-class thrift was that, in an age of rapid industrialization and social change, it was seen as one way of 'socializing' groups whose potential alienation from, and dissidence towards, the new industrial state might pose grave social and political problems. The working-class saver and insurer, it was assumed – and presumably rightly assumed – would have a greater attachment to social stability by virtue of his financial stake in its continuance. To Bentham in 1800 the offer of government securities 'to the least opulent and most numerous class of individuals' would have the incidental advantage of 'creating on the part of the lower orders, in respect of the proposed new species of property, a fresh and more palpable interest in the support of that government, on the tranquillity of which the existence of such their property will depend'.[28] In 1806 Patrick Colquhoun advocated a national scheme for savings and insurance partly for the same reasons. And two generations later, in 1852, after a sustained experience of the social consequences of industrialization, class differentiation and social unrest, the encouragement of working-class thrift was considered 'a matter of deep interest to the state; for the man who has invested a portion of his earnings in securities, to the permanence and safety of which the peace and good order of society are essential – will be a tranquil and conservative citizen. . . . To have saved money and invested it securely, is to have become a capitalist [and] . . . for the poor man, to have overleaped a great gulf; to have opened a path for himself into a new world.'[29] Moreover, it was not only the advocates of thrift who connected it with conservatism. In 1833 Thomas Attwood attacked savings banks in the Commons as 'a sort of screw in the hands of the Government to fix down the working classes to its system'. And in 1839 the socialist John Francis Bray protested that, through the savings banks, 'the government . . . holds . . . so many golden chains to bind men to it and to the existing order of things'.[30]

---

[28] 'Circulating Annuities', in John Bowring (ed.), *The Works of Jeremy Bentham* (Edinburgh, 1843), III, p. 143. Also see pp. 145–6.

[29] Colquhoun: quoted in Horne, *Savings Banks*, p. 32; 1852: [W. R. Greg], 'Investments for the Working Classes', *Edinburgh Review*, XCV (April 1852), 407–8. Also see [S. Smiles], 'Workmen's Earnings and Savings', *Quarterly Reviews*, CVIII (1860), 106–7.

[30] *Hansard*, XVII, Col. 200 (16 April 1833); John Francis Bray, *Labour's Wrongs and Labour's Remedy* (1839), p. 152.

The exhortation to thrift was, of course, part of the broader stream of the literature of success – which itself gathered real pace only in the 1850s – urging the lowly to pursue the virtues of hard work and frugality, self-help and temperance.[31] It was the more positive counterpart of the popular and comforting view that 'habitual improvidence – though of course there are many admirable exceptions – is the real cause of the social degradation of the artisan. . . . Misery . . . is the offspring of individual improvidence and vice; and it is to be cured, not so much by conferring greater rights, as by implanting better habits.'[32]

Smiles was not voicing a unanimous view. There were others, notably such early socialist writers as Robert Owen, William Thompson, John Francis Bray and Thomas Hodgskin, who argued equally strongly that material improvement was more a function of social and economic, than of individual, reform, and that public action, more than private regeneration, was a prerequisite of the elimination of misery and poverty. But the 'great majority of the leading advocates of mere political changes', in Bray's critical words, looked at the world simply as it was, and did not 'conceive the possibility of human society being constituted otherwise than as they find it'. Their aim was 'the partial amelioration of the condition of the working class as a *working class*'.[33] For such men the individual and social role of private financial prudence was given a significant emphasis. And it is this which provided the context for the attempts of successive governments, within the constraints of their political ideology, to encourage the poor to look after their own financial destinies.

3

LEGISLATION AND THE GROWTH OF WORKING-CLASS
FINANCIAL INSTITUTIONS

The principal characteristic of friendly-society legislation in the period under consideration was that it offered legal status and financial benefits

---

[31] For this literature see J. F. C. Harrison, 'The Victorian Gospel of Success', *Victorian Studies*, I (1957–8), 155–64. The baneful financial effects of drink, and the relationship between intemperance and improvidence, were constant themes in the literature of thrift. See, for example, [Smiles], 'Workmen's Earnings', *Quarterly Review* (1860), 101–3.

[32] [Smiles], 'Workmen's Earnings', *Quarterly Review* (1860), 84.

[33] Bray, *Labour's Wrongs* (1839), p. 98.

to societies willing to register and to submit themselves to a modicum of official oversight.[34] The main statutes were enacted in 1793, 1819, 1829, 1846, 1850 and 1855. The first was largely confined to the legal recognition and protection of societies. That of 1819 attempted to introduce some regulation by local officials and offered a very favourable interest rate on friendly-society investments. In 1829 the main *locus* of official supervision was shifted to the central government, the rate of return on new investments was reduced and a regular return of actuarial data was called for. The Act of 1846 reinforced the centralizing tendency and attempted (unsuccessfully) to intensify the Government's actuarial supervision of friendly societies. Finally, in 1850 and 1855 the financial benefits which had been offered to registered friendly societies were further reduced, societies were encouraged to register without having to submit their actuarial workings to official oversight, and the branches of affiliated orders were encouraged to seek legal protection.

The relationship between the state and friendly societies was largely determined by the fact that they were the most vulnerable as well as the most versatile of the various institutional embodiments of working-class financial prudence. Indeed, the two characteristics were closely related. For in offering insurance not only against death but against sickness and old age, and in doing this on the basis of localized and limited membership and frequently insufficient statistical data, many friendly societies were actuarially unsound and therefore financially at risk. In the long run, the question of their financial stability and the statistical rationale of their operations was the principal basis for the debate about the government regulation of friendly societies. Yet there was a prior set of considerations, relating to their legal status, which was important to societies, and which afforded the state its principal opportunity for exercising some influence on their development.

Friendly societies were organized on a mutual basis. But, as with other sorts of commercial institutions, unless they could secure legal recognition of their corporate status, they were deemed to be partnerships, and were therefore subject to the various disabilities of unincorporated associations: they could not sue or be sued in courts of law; they had no legal means of enforcing internal rules or 'agreements'

---

[34] The course of legislation up to 1870 was summarized by Augustus K. Stephenson (the Registrar of Friendly Societies) before the Royal Commission on Friendly Societies and Benefit Building Societies: *B.P.P.*, 1872, XXVI (Parts I and II, Q.2). Also see Appendix I to Fourth Report: *B.P.P.*, 1874, XXIII (i).

as to ways to settle disputes; they might lose their assets if they were held by an officer who went bankrupt or died (and whose other creditors had priority); and it might be impossible for them to recover assets embezzled by their officers, since until 1868 the law did not allow partners to sue each other for the recovery of funds. (The situation was not as serious in Scotland, where commercial law was much more favourable to partnerships.)

These particular disadvantages were tackled in 1793 by the first statute to give friendly societies legal recognition. In this case, however, and in the case of most of the subsequent legislation with which we are concerned, the privileges were offered only to societies agreeing to enrol or register, and to make themselves liable to varying degrees of government supervision. Thus, in 1793, societies wishing to take advantage of the Act, which offered exemption from the various legal disabilities already mentioned, had to deposit their rules with local justices of the peace, who were empowered to annul those repugnant to the Act, and ensure that the clerk of the peace enrolled confirmed rules. Enrolled societies were granted exemption from stamp duty on bonds.

The Act of 1793 provided the legal context for the rapid expansion of friendly societies which took place during the Napoleonic Wars. But it is a measure of both the imperfection of procedures and the spirit of independence and insularity which characterized the movement that, both then and later (when the privileges offered were even greater), a large number of societies refused or failed to enrol, and thus denied themselves the advantages of official recognition.

Yet even with respect to those associations which *were* enrolled, the 1793 Act was not particularly successful in ensuring the soundness and stability of the rapidly growing numbers of friendly societies. This was acknowledged in the 1819 Act, which indicated that many societies established under previous legislation had been characterized by mismanagement and fraud. The new statute therefore extended the scope of regulation as well as offering important new privileges to enrolled societies. Instead of automatically enrolling all societies which submitted their rules, justices of the peace had to assess how far a society's actual rules were consonant with its professed object; the tables of mortality and sickness data used for actuarial calculation had to secure the approval of at least two actuaries or 'persons skilled in calculation'; and the law now covered the appointment of trustees to each society and stipulated the circumstances and terms by which societies could be dissolved. At the same time, however, societies agreeing to subject themselves to these restrictions by enrolment were granted a significant extension of their privileges: they were allowed to invest funds in savings banks (confirming a clause of the Savings Bank Act of 1817) or directly with the Commissioners for the Reduction of the National Debt at the attractive rate of 3d a day per £100 (i.e., £4 11s 3d per cent per annum).

The 1819 Act (although it, too, failed to achieve its main objectives) exemplified the principal threads which ran through friendly-society legislation in the early nineteenth century. First, it embodied the warm approval which those in authority extended towards non-reforming, non-radical institutions of mutual self-help among the working class. Second, friendly societies were given not only the legal recognition but also financial advantages (security of investment and a high rate of interest) which were designed to act as a positive incentive to the growth of working-class prudence. These privileges, however, were also used as an enticement to persuade friendly societies to place themselves under some form of control: for legislation was passed in a voluntary spirit, and societies were not obliged to submit themselves to regulation. Third, the unquestioned aim of legislation was to improve the stability of working-class financial institutions, although there was considerable doubt as to how far the Government should or could go in its supervision of the actual affairs of friendly societies. Finally, whatever the degree of supervision, it was necessary to decide the respective roles of local and central government.

By the mid-1820s the failure of legislation to place friendly societies on a secure and financially sound basis had again become obvious. Many societies were too small and/or poorly managed to be secure; there was a lack of effective actuarial supervision; and there were insufficient or unreliable data from which useful and safe tables of benefits and contributions for sickness and superannuation could be deduced. In investigating the position and prospects of friendly societies in 1825 and 1827, two Commons Select Committees paid particular attention to their actuarial weaknesses and the paucity of statistical information.[35] And it is significant that, in reviewing the reports of these two committees, Edwin Chadwick (in his first pub-

---

[35] B.P.P., 1825, IV, 323–44; B.P.P., 1826–7, III, 871–80.

lished essay), while criticizing the subsidy implied in the guarantee of over 4.5 per cent interest, argued that the Government alone was in a position, and therefore had an obligation, to collect, calculate and disseminate data about sickness and mortality for the purpose of mutual insurance.[36]

Broadly speaking, although characterized by a good deal of uncertainty as to the best means of ensuring financial stability, the official discussion of friendly-society problems in the 1820s concentrated on the apparent need to enhance the role of central government and to improve the flow of statistics concerning the contingencies against which societies insured. These two principles were embodied in the Act of 1829, which replaced all previous friendly-society legislation. Yet this legislation, even though it marked an important shift of responsibility from local to central government, also began a significant dilution of attempted government control. Thus, friendly-society rules were to be inspected in the first instance by a state official: the barrister appointed by the National Debt Office in 1828 to certify savings banks. He, however, had no effective regulatory powers, but was expected merely to certify that the rules conformed to the law. Upon receipt of the barrister's certificate by the local justices, the rules were to be automatically confirmed by them and enrolled by the clerk of the peace. (The previous requirement that the justices should reassure themselves that the proposed society was useful or beneficial disappeared.) These more or less formal procedures were associated with a relaxation of actuarial control: the sanction of two actuaries or other skilled persons was no longer needed for the relevant tables. The statute also maintained most of the privileges of friendly societies, which reflected their special status as vehicles for the encouragement of thrift. For example, they were to continue to receive a favourable interest rate on their investments with the National Debt Commissioners, although this was reduced to £3 16s 0½d per cent except for societies established and investing with the National Debt Commissioners before 28 July 1828, which could continue to earn £4 11s 3d per cent. Further exemption from stamp duty was confirmed; and an exemption from the burdens and costs of probate was granted to estates (policies) under £50, which could now be distributed without letters of administration. In return for these privileges, societies were given extra

[36] [Edwin Chadwick], 'Life Assurances', *Westminster Review*, IX (April 1828), 384–5.

responsibilities: they had to provide members with annual returns of receipts and expenditures, and to make a quinquennial return of sickness and mortality, which could then be collected to improve national statistics 'on the duration of sickness and the probabilities of human life'.

The tenor of this legislation and an Act of 1834 demonstrated an important change in official attitudes towards, and legal provision for, friendly societies: self-help was to be put on a 'purer' basis, individuals were acknowledged as the best judges of their own welfare, and the state's principal duty was seen as the rationalization and improvement of the framework within which individuals would be encouraged and educated to make their own choices. In its own sphere the 1834 Poor Law was evidence of a similar retreat from direct paternalism in social policy. And, as with the Poor Law, the avoidance of paternalism in relation to friendly societies also entailed the lessening of a reliance on local authorities, and the appeal to a new tradition: the use of central government agencies (departments of state, special commissions, registrars, inspectors) to oversee social affairs. On the other hand, quite apart from the continued activity of advocates of state intervention, it would be misleading to view the early years of Victoria's reign as a period in which, as far as friendly societies were concerned, actions and attitudes tended inexorably towards an ideal of *laissez-faire*, if only because distinctive privileges were still made available to working-class institutions, while the task of improving their legal bases involved fairly continuous intervention in the 'private' sector. In fact there were three general areas of involvement and discussion which stand out in this period: the working-out of the role of the central government in the registration procedures which survived 1834; the participation of the state in the vital matter of improving actuarial statistics; and the exploration of the consequences and implications of the various corporate and financial privileges which had heretofore been extended to friendly societies.

The piecemeal evolution which characterized the central government's role with respect to various financial institutions created a multi-purpose public office for which the supervision of friendly societies was only one task, albeit one of the most important. It will be remembered that the 1829 Act obliged new friendly societies in England and Wales to submit their rules to a certifying barrister (an office originally designated for savings banks), attached to the Office of the Commissioners for the Reduction of the National Debt (Scotland and Ireland had their own certifying barristers). At different times this official was given a similar role with respect to trade unions, loan societies, building societies, co-operative societies and literary and scientific societies. And in 1846, by the terms of an important new Act, his status and role were both strengthened. His office was formally designated as that of Registrar of Friendly Societies at an annual salary of £1,000, and he was given power over incapable trustees and authority to settle disputes or require the production of documents. As if to symbolize the new emphasis on the centralizing tendency, friendly-society rules which had been filed by local clerks of the peace since 1793 were to be transferred and retained by the Registrar. (This had been anticipated in the case of savings banks in 1844, when it was enacted that their rules, when certified, should be retained by the National Debt Commissioners, rather than by clerks of the peace.) At the same time actuarial certification was reintroduced in a somewhat more demanding way than in the period 1819–29, by the requirement that friendly societies could not be registered until an actuary had certified the sickness, mortality and interest-rate data on which the tables had been based. This last provision, which had the effect of greatly reducing the number of registrations,[37] was abandoned in 1850. Yet the centrality and variety of the Registrar's role, which was made more complicated by legislation in 1850, should not be confused with the possession of a large degree of effective power. Throughout the period, admittedly, the individual concerned – John Tidd Pratt, who held the office between 1828 and 1870 – was an excellent publicist with a well-earned reputation. And the multiplicity of his tasks earned him the pleasant Victorian sobriquet of 'minister of self-help to the whole of the industrious classes'.[38] But his actual authority was severely circumscribed by the laws within which he operated. For example, he was 'in no way responsible for the accuracy or sufficiency of any tables'[39] which he registered, and he could not refuse to register a society on the grounds that a proposed table of premiums was inadequate. The Royal Commission of the early 1870s went to some pains to point out that he and his office lacked any effective power of control or punishment: 'The law may be trifled with or violated by every class of society.'[40] More than this, he was very much on his own:

[37] Below, p. 236
[39] B.P.P., 1852, V, Q. 1315.
[38] B.P.P., 1874, XXIII (i), 244.
[40] B.P.P., 1874, XXXIII (i), 204.

in 1852, it emerged that he was the only person, other than the handful
of clerks who worked for him, who knew and understood the workings
of the office of Registrar – a fact which led him to propose, without
success, the establishment of a five-man Board, which would not only
oversee registration and ensure that rules were correct, but would help
friendly societies by proffering information and advice.[41]

The role envisaged for the Registrar was obviously not a positive
and active administrative one. In the last resort, the function of his
office was to afford a modicum of reassurance that friendly societies
conformed to some simple legal requirements,[42] and to act as a
repository of useful information, not all of which was used because of
the shortage of staff.

All this was consistent not merely with the general situation in
government departments at the time, but also with one widely accepted
mid-century view of the role of the state in matters affecting individual
choice concerning the allocation of resources: the Registrar represented
merely the legal recognition and encouragement of private activity,
its protection against the vagaries of law, and the possibility of gathering
and providing information to improve the way in which men might
govern their own affairs.

Yet even at this level, as its opponents were quick to point out,
relatively innocuous government action, merely because it had the
overtones of official sanction, might have unexpected and undesirable
consequences. This happened in the case of the sickness and mortality
statistics which were collected as a result of friendly-society legislation.
In the early 1850s the Government published tables compiled by John
Finlaison, Actuary to the National Debt Office, from the returns of
1846–50. However, Finlaison's definition of sickness was stringent and
narrow, and therefore unsatisfactory for the broad day-to-day needs of
most societies. Nevertheless the Registrar urged the use of the official

---

[41] *B.P.P.*, 1852, V, QQ. 1310–14.

[42] Even this task could not always be filled adequately; the Royal Commission of the
early 1870s found that it was only too easy for the Registrar's office to lose contact
with many of the thousands of societies, or to be unable to secure information (e.g.
as to funds or membership) from a large minority. Quite apart from the estimated
one third of all societies which, quite legally, abstained from registering or depositing
their rules, almost half of those which registered failed to make a yearly return, and
of those which did so, over 14 per cent omitted to return the number of their members.
See *B.P.P.*, 1872, XXVI (Parts II and III), QQ. 3–6; *B.P.P.*, 1874, XXXIII (i), 203,
296–7.

tables, thus giving an imprimatur to a technical device which had only a strictly limited applicability. The result was what opponents of state intervention feared: it persuaded people that a procedure was safe which should, in fact, have received much more careful scrutiny. As the Royal Commission subsequently pointed out, 'There is no doubt that the plan on which these tables were formed has proved unfortunate and that many societies and even actuaries have made use of the Tables without discovering that they were inapplicable to societies which do not limit the benefit to sickness as defined by Mr. Finlaison.'[43] More generally, the existence of the Registrar's certificate often deluded men into believing that the state in some way guaranteed the soundness of the relevant tables, for the certification of such statistics seemed to imply government responsibility.[44] (Similar problems arose after 1844 with the official registration of joint-stock companies, which was frequently confused with their official approval or sanction.)

Legislation has also had other unanticipated consequences. Thus, as we have seen, the legal privileges and convenience afforded by registration under the Friendly Society Acts encouraged the formation of 'burial societies' – large-scale, centralized societies which were in effect industrial life assurance companies, established for the financial benefit of their salaried officials and well-paid agents.[45] The Registrar of Friendly Societies, Tidd Pratt, who was accused of carrying on a 'memorable crusade against his special *bêtes noires*, the Burial Societies',[46] was particularly scathing about this system of 'commercial speculation', masquerading as friendly societies.[47] This was largely a development of the second half of the century, when the financial benefits were negligible. Before 1850, however, another class of societies had appeared which took advantage of the state's efforts to encourage and protect the working-class movement in order to secure exceptional privileges for an essentially middle-class activity.

By the early 1830s, in an effort to encourage working-class thrift and

---

[43] Quoted by Gosden, *Friendly Societies*, p. 104.

[44] *B.P.P.*, 1849, XIV, 69, Q. 771–2.

[45] *B.P.P.*, 1874, XXIII (i), 106–28. In the early 1870s successful collectors would earn as much as £400 annually, and 'books' of established policy holders became valuable properties, changing hands for hundreds of pounds.

[46] F. G. P. Neison, *Legislation on Friendly Societies* (1870), p. 13.

[47] See memorandum to W. E. Gladstone, 1864: Gladstone Paper, B.M., Add. MSS, 44402, fo. 147; and Tidd Pratt's *Report* for 1867: *B.P.P.*, 1867–8, XL, 504.

to entice friendly societies to register, the state offered not only the legal advantages of incorporation but also important financial advantages. First, societies received annual interest on deposits ($£4$ 11s 3d per cent from 1817, $£3$ 16s 0½d for societies founded after 28 July 1828)[48] which compared well, particularly considering the security, with rates on ordinary mortgages and Consols (the latter stood at between 3 and 3.5 per cent in the 1830s and 1840s). Second, friendly societies were exempted from the payment of stamp duties, which at that time, in the case of life insurance policies, varied on a sliding scale from $£1$ for policies of less than $£500$ to $£5$ for policies of $£5,000$ and upwards. Third, with respect to death benefits, the 1829 law gave friendly-society policies exemption from probate duty for small policies and the 1834 Act, in allowing members of a society to nominate beneficiaries other than their wives or other relations, in fact exempted them from probate and legacy duty.

These various privileges were obviously designed to encourage habits of thrift and financial prudence among the poor. Yet they were legally available to any group of people, whatever their economic or social status, who enrolled themselves under the Acts. They could, therefore, be used to cater to the needs of middle-class policyholders. The Clergy Mutual Society, for example, was established in 1829 for the benefit of Church of England clergymen and enrolled as a friendly society. Initially, although it benefited from the exemption from stamp duties and the guaranteed yield of $£3$ 16s 0½d on its investments, its activities were restricted by limitations on the scope of its investment and by being able to make policies payable only to wives and relations.[49] In 1834, however, the Friendly Societies Act made it possible to make sums assured by friendly-society policies payable not only to wives, children or relatives but also to their nominees – a provision which made such life policies very much more useful to policyholders and in the case of the Clergy Mutual 'immediately led to an extension of our society amongst the clergy in general, and the number of our insurances increased in consequence'.[50] The Clergy Mutual was not alone: in 1832 a group of Bradford Quakers had formed the Friends' Provident Institution, and in 1835 (in response to the stimulus of the new legislation) two of its members were instrumental in establishing

[48] In 1850 the official rate for societies registered after 1843 was reduced to $£3$ 0s. 10d.
[49] B.P.P., 1852, V, Q. 468.
[50] B.P.P., 1852, V, Q. 467.

the National Provident Institution with an eye to a broader membership base.[51]

The distinctive characteristic of these and other societies was not that they operated a life business (in this respect they were no different from many other friendly societies). Rather, it was that, operating as friendly societies with the associated privileges, they issued really substantial life policies: the Clergy Mutual's policies went as high as £5,000 sum assured (its average in 1852 was £950, a very high figure). As the Chancellor of the Exchequer argued in 1850, friendly societies 'had been instituted for the benefit of the lower classes; but, as often happens in such cases, persons of a higher class availed themselves of those benefits'.[52] The societies actually involved had in fact 'outgrown the particular class of objects which were in the contemplation of Parliament when those statutes were passed, and have become in fact Life Assurance Offices'.[53] As a result of the general expansion of life assurance within the framework of friendly-society legislation, the consequent loss of revenue to the Exchequer, and the determined opposition of ordinary life assurance companies (complaining about unfair competition), Parliament moved to close the loopholes. In 1840 friendly-society life policies above £200 were denied financial privileges, and from 1850 new societies were limited in their death, annuity and sickness benefits. On the other hand, however, the existing societies were not affected by the limitation on the scale of their operations, and they still enjoyed significant privileges in the types of transferable policies they could issue, which were in effect exempted from probate and legacy duty and could be used for a wide variety of private and commercial uses. Finally, in 1853, after a detailed investigation by a Select Committee, those societies issuing policies in excess of £200 were restricted from investing *any* of their funds with the National Debt Commissioners, and in 1854 they were at last discharged from the operation of the Friendly Societies Acts.[54]

By mid-century, the attention paid to the unanticipated consequences

---

[51] Stanley Hazell, *A Record of the First Hundred Years of the National Provident Institution, 1835–1935* (1935), pp. 1–2.

[52] *Hansard*, CXIII, col. 928 (7 August 1850).

[53] *B.P.P.*, 1852, V, 300.

[54] For the operation of the five societies involved, see the Report and Evidence of the Select Committee: *B.P.P.*, 1852, V. In 1852 the five societies had total sums assured of almost £9 million (covering some 16,000 policy holders) at a time when total sums assured by ordinary life assurance companies were about £150 million.

of friendly-society legislation did not obscure – indeed, it merely emphasized – the fact that the basic objectives of that legislation had not been adequately achieved. Thus, a Select Committee of the House of Lords in 1848 gloomily noted that there had been thirteen statutes since 1793, but that 'notwithstanding the attention paid by Parliament to the subject, their efforts have failed to produce the desired effects. . . . From a deficiency in the means adopted to facilitate or enforce compliance with their provisions, these Acts have neither secured the stability of the societies enrolled under them, nor prevented the rapid growth of independent and illegal associations.'[55] By the late 1840s it was apparent that there were various ways in which the incentives had failed even to persuade societies to register.

First, a very large number of individual societies did not register after 1846 because they used tables of contributions and benefits which no actuary could certify – the tables being either inherently bad or the society being reluctant to base tables upon age structure, strongly preferring a single premium for all members.[56] Second, it was argued that 'the members of many of them have an unfounded but general fear lest the management of their own affairs, or of their money, would be taken out of their hands by the state if they enrolled'.[57] Third, there were many small local societies founded and dominated by publicans for their own profit and whose members were relatively uninterested in financial stability. Finally, the social character of many societies led them to use secret signs at meetings, which thereby brought them within the terms of the Corresponding Societies Acts and made them illegal. Nor was it only small and insecure societies which grew up outside the protection and 'interference' of friendly-society legislation. Great affiliated societies like the Oddfellows had developed 'without assistance from the state and unprotected by the law'. This was because their branch structure was contrary to the provisions of the Corre-

[55] B.P.P., 1847–8, XVI, 491.

[56] The various reasons for non-enrolment are given in B.P.P., 1849, XIV, 5. Charles Ansell, of the Atlas Assurance Company, also submitted data to show that in the two years before certification was required there had been 2,101 applications for enrolment of which 1,683 were actually enrolled; whereas in the two subsequent years the figures were 1,780 and 423 (ibid., 72, 103). In 1853 Tidd Pratt, the Registrar, argued that over half of the ordinary societies admitted members aged 18–45 at one premium and 'do not understand' the idea of the premium varying according to age 'and they will not do it': B.P.P., 1852–3, XXI, Q. 522.

[57] B.P.P., 1849, XIV, 5.

sponding Societies Act, because their idiosyncratic constitutions were not covered by the provisions of friendly-society legislation, and because of the general problem of dealing with friendly societies with numerous branches. In 1846, however, registered friendly societies were exempted from both the Corresponding Societies Act and the Seditious Meetings Act. And in 1848, partly as a result of the discovery that the Manchester Unity could not legally recover £4,000 embezzled by its Secretary, the affiliated orders pressed for a change in the law. This was secured in 1850, when the registration of societies with branches was facilitated. But the Lords Committee which had considered the case argued that legalization was desirable, not merely in order to try to improve financial security, but 'to increase the attachment of so numerous a body of the industrious classes to social order'.[58]

In addition to the large number of unenrolled societies, it was also fairly clear by the late 1840s that the stability of those which had registered and thereby obtained legal protection and financial privileges was in no way guaranteed by the obligations imposed on them as a consequence of registration. Annual reports were available only to members, the tables were unreliable, and the rules were defective. It was also anticipated that 'the quinquennial valuations, when they shall be sent in, will be found likewise so defective that they will be of little or no use, either as an index of solvency, or as a source of statistical information'.[59]

The Friendly Societies Act of 1850 marked a decisive stage in the relationship of such societies to the state – although little was done to enlarge or improve their regulation or statistics. Annual returns were to be brought into the public domain by being sent to the Registrar. But the main purpose of the Statute was to diminish the financial privileges of registration and to encourage a larger number of working-class societies to come forward: the rate of interest payable by the National Debt Commissioners on new investment was reduced to £3 0s 10d; the benefits of the Act were limited to societies issuing life

[58] Select Committee of House of Lords, *B.P.P.*, 1847–8, XVI, 492, 494. The Committee urged that the law should be relaxed so as to include affiliated orders. It cited the extent (260,000 members, £340,000 annual income) of the Oddfellows as evidence of its being 'a powerful instrument of good or evil in proportion as its objects are useful or dangerous': 'Without a sense of protection from the law, or a feeling of obligation to the state, such associations may lose their attachment to existing institutions, and become discontented from the impression that their interests are neglected.'

[59] Report of Commons Select Committee: *B.P.P.*, 1849, XIV, 4.

policies of £100 or less, or annuities of £30 or less, or weekly sickness
benefits of £1 or less. Further, a distinction was drawn between
'certified' societies, the rules and tables of which had to be certified
(the guaranteed interest rate and the right to issue annuities were confined to such societies), and 'registered' societies, which received no
special treatment but were granted enrolment and, therefore, a legal
existence and a protection against embezzlement and fraud. Finally,
and perhaps most significantly, branches were expressly recognized,
thus allowing affiliated societies to secure the protection of the law.

The 1850 Act seems to have been fairly successful: from its passage
until May 1852 some 1,900 societies, including branches of affiliated
orders, were registered – although only twenty-nine were 'certified'
and had their tables approved by an actuary. The Registrar reported
that the new situation was significantly for the benefit of the societies
and that they were more eager to seek information and advice.[59a]
Finally, in the consolidating Act of 1855, which settled the position of
friendly societies until the 1870s, the somewhat meaningless distinction
between certified and registered societies was abolished; actuarial
certification was abandoned, except for registered societies issuing
annuities; the fee for registration was dispensed with; and all societies
were allowed to invest with the National Debt Commissioners.

Some aspects of the early nineteenth-century development of friendly
societies were also exemplified in the contemporaneous history of the
trustee savings banks: for in that instance, too, the incentives offered
to one sort of institution encouraged developments which had not been
contemplated at the outset, while the Government found itself being
expected to undertake responsibilities which implied an administrative
role that it was unwilling to accept. On the other hand, the savings-
bank movement was more obviously the outcome of state encouragement and the relationship between private activity and government
action was therefore always more intimate.

Of the various examples of working-class thrift institutions, savings
banks owed the most not merely to the privileges derived from legislation, but to the efforts of philanthropists drawn from the middle and

---

[59a]B.P.P., 1852, V, 350.
[60] The standard history of savings banks is H. Oliver Horne, *A History of Savings Banks*
(1947). In the case of friendly societies, the so-called 'county societies' sponsored by
local landowners and tradesmen, clergymen, etc. were not very important. The
officers or leaders of the large affiliated orders, however, tended to be drawn from the

upper ranks of society.[60] These efforts were to a large extent associated with the beginnings of savings banks designed for working-class depositors in the late 1790s. They were necessary at that time because the working-class saver, even if he or she was sufficiently sophisticated to envisage using savings as investment, could find few outlets for very small sums of money. And it was to redress this balance that clergymen and other professional men, industrialists, landowners, tradesmen, and the like, sponsored and managed (and sometimes quite literally worked in) savings banks. In Scotland, where the savings-bank movement originated, it was possible to secure adequate interest on savings-bank deposits in ordinary commercial banks. In England, however, the trustees of the earliest banks were obliged either to act as personal guarantors, accepting funds as individuals and paying a return on them, or to invest the bank's funds in government securities. But the former practice obviously acted as a limit on the growth of savings banks, and the latter exposed the bank to the risk of unpredictable fluctuations in capital value.[61] These financial limitations were perhaps the main reason for the relatively slow start of the savings-bank movement outside Scotland: by 1817 England had only about eighty banks.

It was principally the financial problems of savings banks which led to legislation on their behalf but, as with friendly societies a generation earlier, the need to give a legal existence and protection to their operations also prompted the state to intervene. Indeed, the Savings Bank Act of 1817 (there was also one for Ireland) was sponsored by George Rose, who had been responsible for the Friendly Societies Act of 1793, and in part was literally copied from the earlier legislation. It was designed to encourage working-class thrift at a time when problems of poverty and instability were being emphasized by the economic situation after the end of the Napoleonic Wars: trustee savings banks could be established with the rights of suing and being sued through their officers, of referring disputes to binding arbitration, and of securing summary legal remedies. Their rules had to be deposited with

---

ranks of 'self-made men and members of the "middle class" . . . (who had) freedom to organize their own time.' The management of local societies continued to be dominated by working-class members. See Gosden, *Friendly Societies*, pp. 52–3, 88–93.

[61] A third alternative – to transfer the risk by making the depositors the proprietors of the purchased government stock – was adopted by so-called provident institutions, which were corporate ways of enabling small savers to invest in government securities. See Horne, *Savings Banks*, pp. 60–3.

the clerks of the peace (in 1818 it was enacted that the rules had to be approved by justices of the peace). The principal privilege was, however, financial: savings-bank funds had to be deposited in the Bank of England to the credit of the Commissioners for the Reduction of the National Debt, who invested the money in government securities. These deposits, the security of which was absolutely guaranteed, were to earn a rate of interest of 3d a day, i.e. £4 11s 3d annually, per £100. No trustee, treasurer or manager was to derive any benefit from his office; and deposit accounts were limited to £100 in the first year and £50 in later years, except for friendly societies, which could deposit unlimited amounts. Minor privileges in relation to stamp duties and the distribution of small testamentary estates were also awarded. But there is no doubt that the guaranteed rate of interest was the most important aspect of the new legislation: not only did it provide a basis for the payment of a reasonably attractive interest rate to small savers (usually about 4 per cent after deduction for management expenses) but, given the fact that in November 1817 the effective yield on 3 per cent Consols was only £3 15s per cent, it represented a substantial government subsidy to the savings banks.

With this solution of the main financial problem of savings banks, there was an immediate and rapid increase in their number: 150 were formed within twelve months of the 1817 Act and by December 1818 there were some 465 savings banks in the United Kingdom, of which all but six had been established in the previous four years.[62] Thenceforth, the growth in the number of banks slowed down; but in their first decade the growth rate of deposits was very substantial: they increased by virtually 25 per cent *annually* between 1818 and 1828; and between 1817–21 and 1827–31 the average balance of trustees with the National Debt Commissioners grew from £2.6 million to £14.8 million.[63]

It is a significant comment on official attitudes to working-class thrift in these early years that the question of the preferential interest rate for savings banks was treated almost entirely in terms of the need to help those who might not otherwise save. Admittedly, some M.P.s – notably Joseph Hume, whose consistent campaign for economy and

[62] Horne, *Savings Banks*, pp. 76–81. Scottish savings banks were outside the terms of the Act. Ireland had an Act of its own.
[63] Fishlow, 'The Trustee Savings Banks, 1817–1861', *Journal of Economic History* (1961), 31, 39.

laissez-faire efficiency led him to advocate the reduction of the interest rate to market levels – were opposed to the subsidy on principle. But successive Chancellors of the Exchequer defended it on social grounds. In 1818, for example, Vansittart rejected the idea of a decrease:

To a certain extent this plan might be inconvenient to the public and might take from the public purse from one to one and a half per cent but he was certain that the House would not think the amount of from six to ten thousand a year too much in aid of a plan which tended so much to the industry and morality of the people in general. He confidently hoped that the benefit to be derived would not be threefold or even tenfold but would extend to a hundredfold.[64]

On the other hand, there was constant anxiety about the social background of depositors. The legislation could not, after all, stipulate that only the poor or the working class could make use of savings banks. And it soon became clear that much of the growth of the banks was based upon fairly large deposits (in England in 1830, for example, a third of total deposits was accounted for by accounts in excess of £100, and two-thirds by accounts in excess of £50). The deduction that the 'wrong' people (i.e. people who did not need to be encouraged to save) might be benefiting from the privileges extended to savings banks is confirmed by the apparent dominance among the depositors of domestic servants, small tradesmen and occupationally unidentified women and children. The labouring poor, the putative beneficiaries of legislation, were not able to take very much advantage of savings banks.[65] As a result, in 1824 and 1828 there were drastic reductions in the limits of initial and annual deposits, in the hope that the attractiveness of investment to the relatively well off would thereby be reduced.

But the real attraction to investors obviously lay in the favourable interest rate. Moreover, the insouciance with which Chancellors of the Exchequer contemplated the deficit on the Savings Bank Fund in early years could hardly survive its growth. By the mid-1820s, for example, annual interest payments averaged over £400,000, and in the period 1818–28 the average loss exceeded £67,000.[66] In 1828, therefore, the interest paid by the National Debt Commissioners was reduced to £3 16s 0½d (with a maximum payable to depositors of £3 8s 5¼d).

[64] Quoted in Horne, *Savings Banks*, pp. 98–9.
[65] Fishlow, 'Trustee Savings Banks', *Journal of Economic History* (1961), 33–9.
[66] Fishlow, 'Trustee Savings Banks', *Journal of Economic History* (1961), 39; Horne, *Savings Banks*, p. 100.

The changes of 1828 reduced the attractiveness of savings banks to large investors. But even though the relative importance of small savers grew in subsequent years (the average account fell from £33 in 1830 to £25 in 1852),[67] there seems to have been little change in the social composition of the depositors and a marked slowing down in the growth of total deposits.

From these viewpoints there was some disillusion with the trustee savings bank movement as an instrument of social change in the 1840s, and early in that decade, when the National Debt Commissioners were paying what was still a favourable rate of interest on almost £30 million of deposits, there were new moves for reform. In 1844 the Chancellor argued that the high interest rate 'afforded a constant inducement to persons who were not the specific objects intended to be benefited by them to invest money in them', and therefore recommended a further reduction (to £20) of the limit on annual deposits, and a drastic cut in the rate of interest.[68] Although an effective campaign by the banks confined the changes to an adjustment of interest rates to £3 5s payable to banks and £3 0s 10d to their depositors, it was clear that the state, much as it wished to encourage working-class thrift, was not prepared to attempt to do so by the continuation of a generous subsidy to savings banks: between 1817 and November 1852 the National Debt Commissioners had paid £2.4 million more to savings banks than had been earned on the stock purchased with the deposits.[69]

Throughout most of the period under consideration the relationship between the state and the savings banks had been viewed primarily as a financial one. However, the savings banks, like friendly societies, in becoming the object of legislation, had become involved in the web of government relationships. Thus, in 1818 their rules had become subject to confirmation by the justices of the peace. Ten years later, in 1828, an amending Act for savings banks stipulated that their formation

[67] B.P.P., 1890–1, XLVIII, 266–7.

[68] Hansard, LXXIV, cols. 576–7 (2 May 1844).

[69] British Museum, Add. MSS. 44574, fo. 22 (Memorandum on Savings Banks, 2 April 1853). In the long run the state lost money on the arrangements. However, in the three years after the reduction of interest of 1844, when the price of stock was also exceptionally low, the National Debt Commissioners had received some £102,000 excess interest above that paid to savings banks. Yet even then, there occurred a marked withdrawal of funds from banks by individual depositors, presumably in order to invest their money directly and more profitably in government securities (B.P.P., 1850, XXXIII, 619; Add. MSS. 44305, fos. 218–19, 19 July 1854).

needed the approval of the National Debt Commissioners, as well as local justices, and that their rules, before being deposited with local clerks of the peace, had to be certified by a barrister appointed by the National Debt Commissioners. The Certifying Barrister was also to act as umpire in cases of arbitration. The 1828 legislation was a turning point in the history of both savings banks and friendly societies (it was used as a model for the relevant parts of the 1829 Friendly Societies Act): responsibility was passing from local to central government, as a national official took over functions for which magistrates were ill-equipped.

In 1844 local registration was entirely abolished (as it was to be in 1846 for friendly societies): rules were to be submitted directly to the Barrister, who was also given power to settle all disputes between depositors and trustees or managers. The nature of savings banks offered fewer problems to the state than that of friendly societies. Yet the similarities were significant. For example, the fact that the banks were the object of legislation, that trustees were obliged to deposit funds (albeit at a good yield) with a government agency, and that savings bank rules had to be scrutinized by the Barrister to the National Debt Office, all gave the impression to the unsophisticated that the stability and security of these institutions were also in some sense guaranteed by the state. As long as the banks *were* stable there was no need to question the government's role, or to seek for any greater security than the personal sureties of officers and the responsibilities of trustees. The effect of the small number of frauds was counteracted by trustees repaying depositors in full. In 1844, however, in response to the anxiety of trustees, the Savings Bank Act stipulated that trustees were liable to make good any deficiencies only if they had expressed their willingness to do so in writing, and as a result most absolved themselves from such legal responsibility by not signing such a declaration.

In the event, the security of savings banks deteriorated markedly. In 1848 two frauds in Irish banks – at Tralee and Killarney – involved depositors in losses of £36,000 and £20,000 respectively; while in 1849 frauds amounting to over £70,000, of which less than half were recovered for depositors, were exposed at Rochdale. Other frauds, in some but not all instances followed by full payments by trustees, steadily eroded the reputation of the banks in the late 1840s and early 1850s. And this must have been a factor in the relative stagnation of the movement: withdrawals exceeded deposits in 1847–50.

As a result of this relatively new situation, the Government began to take much more notice of the question of financial security and of its own responsibility. As one *laissez-faire* critic of the system, Joseph Hume, ironically pointed out, 'the public had a right to complain of the Government in this matter, because it was always understood that the Government were pledged to the depositors, and thus the public were deluded'.[70] Yet the fact remained that the state had only two very limited means of 'control' over savings banks: legalization when first established, and the administration of invested funds combined with the power of securing financial returns. In 1850 the Chancellor of the Exchequer, Sir Charles Wood, introduced a Bill which would have had the effect not only of reducing deposit limits and interest rates and reimposing trustees' liability, but of introducing a government system of audit, pass-book inspection and the official appointment of bank treasurers. In 1853–54 Gladstone, when Chancellor of the Exchequer, had similar ambitions. If the Government was to guarantee deposits, he argued, then it would have to control the receipt and payment of money: 'there must be complete superintendence and control by the National Debt Office.' 'The poor depositors have a claim of right upon the Government for protection. . . . If I place money in my Banker's hands he is personally liable to me – why should not the poor man have the same security?'[71] Gladstone also introduced a Bill for official control and guarantee. But in each case these proposals were defeated by a well-drilled campaign by influential savings-bank trustees who objected not merely to lower yields and deposit limits, but to the introduction of a class of officials appointed by the Government.[72] Yet the argument about the role of the state was, in fact, a case of a clash of traditions rather than ideologies: the trustees objected to new paid officials (other than auditors of whom they approved) not so much on *laissez-faire* principles as because of the presumed advantages of the existing system of amateur and philanthropic management and the difficulty of working a system 'involving . . . a divided management and a divided responsibility'.[73]

The limitations as well as strengths of the existing system of trustee savings banks were reasonably clear by the early 1850s. They had, of

---

[70] *Hansard*, CX, col. 905 (29 April 1850).
[71] Add. MSS. 44305, fos. 49–50 (27 April 1853).
[72] Horne, *Savings Banks*, pp. 129–34, 148–9.
[73] Quoted in Horne, *Savings Banks*, p. 132.

course, enjoyed a fair measure of success and, whether or not they catered for precisely those sections of the working class originally envisaged, they had apparently encouraged a good deal of small-scale savings by relatively poor people. They reflected, too, much of the charitable and improving impulse of the middle and upper class, proud of their hoped-for ability to inculcate 'provident and economical habits among the industrious classes' and to contribute 'to the elevation of moral character and the enhancement of social and domestic happiness'.[74] Yet expansion was increasingly exposing their imperfections: the development and growing complexity of banking institutions not only made it difficult for amateur trustees to grasp their workings, but offered growing temptations to underpaid officials. In many banks standards of administration and book-keeping were inadequate. An institutional framework, based upon a combination of government subsidy and private philanthropy, had found it extremely difficult to adapt to the basic business needs of important financial intermediaries. Ultimately, in 1861, and with little hesitation on ideological principle, the state carried the situation to its logical conclusion and created its own alternative, the Post Office Savings Bank.

4

CONCLUSION: WORKING-CLASS THRIFT AND THE
NINETEENTH-CENTURY 'REVOLUTION' IN GOVERNMENT

The early 1850s mark a watershed in the history of working-class thrift. On the one hand, they begin a period of rising prosperity and tranquillity: thenceforth the years of mid-Victorian prosperity were associated with the accelerated development of old and new types of financial institution. On the other hand, they brought to a close the initial phase of the state's attempt to deal with poverty by positively encouraging individual prudence. Legislation had in fact achieved a good deal in terms of incentives to working-class savings. But in the stock-taking of the middle years of the century it was apparent that the more 'forward' aspects of social policy had been effectively tempered by a reluctance to interfere too decisively and by an awareness of the dangers of offering financial privileges on an indiscriminate basis. This was, indeed, one of various respects in which it is possible to

[74] Quoted by Horne, Savings Banks, pp. 136–7, from a resolution passed at a mass meeting of members of the Glasgow Savings Bank, 1852.

see more general themes reflected in a fairly specialized aspect of social history.

First, it must be emphasized that the style of the state's preoccupation with working-class thrift in the early nineteenth century was a logical consequence of the perception of poverty as an evil which could be mitigated by an alteration in the opportunities and habits, rather than the basic economic circumstances, of the poor. In the event, therefore, not only did official attitudes preclude any fundamental change in social and economic systems, but social policy with respect to working-class financial institutions – which was designed to encourage and protect a particular mode of behaviour – was less interventionist than those policies which aimed at the eradication of 'positive' and observable evils, such as poor sanitation or conditions aboard emigrant ships. At the same time, however, although policy was formulated in the context of an individualistic ideology, the urgency and character of the need to encourage the development of self-help among the poor led to a far more broad-based and active intervention with market forces and private arrangements than was the case with such middle-class institutions as ordinary life assurance companies.

In fact little of the discussion and none of the legislation concerning thrift institution envisaged a detailed managerial or supervisory function for government officials. Quite apart from the technical and administrative problems involved,[75] such proposals ran counter to strongly held opinions about the need to preserve scope for private and local initiative. This was particularly related to the nature of the institutions with which the Government was dealing, and the widely accepted view that a more direct government role would also involve some financial responsibility: 'by interfering in details', reported the Select Committee on Friendly Societies in 1849, 'Parliament would incur the risk of shaking the principle of independence and self-management upon which all voluntary associations depend'.[76] Similar sentiments were expressed with regard to savings banks.[77] Even an

---

[75] In 1849, in his evidence to the Select Committee on Friendly Societies, Charles Ansell argued that it was doubtful if a law obliging societies to make regular actuarial valuations and returns could be enforced since 'it seems practically impossible that any Government can enter into the details of working 10,000 or 12,000 societies . . . except through an amount of supervision which no government could give, or would be willing to pay for' (B.P.P., 1849, XIV, QQ. 782–3).

[76] B.P.P., 1849, XIV, 6. Also see B.P.P., 1847–8, XVI, 612; B.P.P., 1852, V, 402–9.

[77] Hansard, CX, col. 900 (29 April 1850).

institution's relationship with the state was placed on a voluntary basis. Friendly societies were perfectly entitled to remain free of government attention, and many did. Savings institutions could also shun official attention, although this was a much less realistic posture, since they would thereby cut themselves off from a critically important legal and investment privilege.

These attitudes were consistent with the prevailing view of the dangers of excessive interference with voluntary associations. As the 1825 Select Committee put it, even though the restrictions of the law were 'calculated for the benefit and security of individuals', nevertheless it is for the individuals themselves to determine whether 'to adopt the provisions of the Statute, which offers them at the same time regulation and privilege; or to remain perfectly unfettered by anything but their own will'.[78] This voluntaryism was also exemplified in the details of 'regulation' which really assumed that the state's main hope of influencing the stability and security of friendly societies lay in its powers of persuasion. And this, too, was consistent with broader themes in the nineteenth-century 'revolution in government'. In Professor Roberts's words, 'Persuasion not coercion was the ideal of the Victorian administrator' – a verdict for which there is evidence in the fields of the education, mining and factory inspectorates, the Poor Law, the Railway Board and the commissioner of lunacy.[79] In the case of friendly societies, too, coercion tended to be ruled out; and there was probably general, although not universal, agreement with the spirit behind the proposal that the role of any public board or department should be that of 'a friendly counsellor'.[80]

On the other hand, however, it is possible to make too much of the apparent passivity of the state. The incentives which were offered to associations to submit to some sort of state supervision were very powerful in the case of friendly societies and irresistible in the case of savings banks. And these incentives – a legal personality, protection against embezzlement, exemption from stamp and probate duties, security for investments, a subsidized interest rate – were designed as the bases of stable and successful institutions as well as inducements to place themselves within the framework of the law.

The rationale of such help to the working classes was of course

[78] B.P.P., 1825, IV, 324–5.
[79] Victorian Origins of the Welfare State, pp. 287–8.
[80] B.P.P., 1849, XIV, Q. 774.

obvious; given their education and outlook on the one hand, and the nature of such savings as they could accumulate on the other, it was necessary to eradicate some of the institutional and legal obstacles to the small saver, and to offer larger incentives than were needed for the wealthy. Early nineteenth-century governments therefore intervened extensively in the operations of the market by manipulating the incentives to private activity. Although there was little detailed administrative interference, the pattern of intervention by public authorities was similar to that in other fields: there was a marked tendency to move from local to central supervision; intervention led to a better acquaintance with the complexities of legislative supervision (as well as creating some of its own) so that the process of state action tended to be cumulative; and an important part of the central government's role was the collection and publication of statistical data, which could provide the essential basis of private action as well as public policy. More generally, the need to ensure that useful information was widely disseminated was itself a powerful reason for shifting new responsibilities from local to central authorities. Like the Registrar of Births, Deaths and Marriages (1836) and of Joint-Stock Companies (1844), the Registrar of Friendly Societies was armed with powers primarily of communication rather than of control. As John Stuart Mill argued, 'Power may be localized, but knowledge, to be most useful, must be centralized; there must be somewhere a focus at which all its scattered rays are collected.'[81]

In the case of friendly societies, as with other aspects of economic and social policy, the question of centralization was by no means clear-cut. Nor did it receive a clear-cut solution. As, in general, the anti-government feelings of the eighteenth century took the form of localism which was a powerful element in the legislative battles of the period 1830–70,[82] so with friendly societies the pull of local interests and suspicions served to mitigate the centralizing tendency as well as to give it a distinctive, and relatively innocuous, character.

At the same time, however, the need for action made it imperative to reduce some of the responsibilities of local authorities, even if the central government had to be even more sensitive to the charge of

[81] Quoted from *Considerations on Representative Government* in Lubenow, *The Politics of Government Growth*, p. 181.
[82] Valerie Cromwell, 'Interpretations of Nineteenth-Century Administration: An Analysis, *Victorian Studies*, IX, 3 (March 1966), 250.

interference. Initially, as we have seen, friendly societies and savings banks were treated within the tradition of local registration (with clerks of the peace) and supervision (by justices of the peace). From the late 1820s, however, the acceptance and approval of rules were transferred to an official of the central government, and from the mid-1840s these rules had to be permanently filed with the Registrar of Friendly Societies. There is little doubt that the shift to central government, which was common to many areas of social policy, was based on the inability of magistrates to handle complex and often highly technical matters, and on the greater effectiveness of a single, central authority in the formulation of a national policy, the systematic application of rules and the collection of statistics.[83] As far as friendly societies and savings banks were concerned the tide of centralization began to run before the great symbolic act of centralization (the new Poor Law of 1834). In the 1820s, however, the issue was clearly a very sensitive one. In 1825, for example, the Select Committee on Friendly Societies rejected a proposal for a 'Central Board' in order not to 'excite alarm or jealousy'. And two years later another Select Committee recommended that societies should not have to establish direct contacts with London, but rather should deal with local authorities, who would in turn contact London – all with the purpose of 'avoiding jealousy of what may be deemed interference on the part of the Government'.[84]

Local suspicion of the motives and policies of central government continued throughout the period. It was, as we have seen, one of the most important reasons for the lack of co-operation of friendly societies with the government's voluntary scheme of registration. More generally, however, it combined with broader ideological principles to diminish the authority which was being focused in central government. As a result, in the case of thrift institutions, the victory of the principle of central supervision was a victory more for administrative convenience than for centralized power.

Having acknowledged this, however, it must also be acknowledged that the distinction between the government's accepting registration or proffering advice and information only on request, and its assuming an important degree of responsibility, was not always clear. In the first

---

[83] For the controversy about centralization in the early Victorian state, see Roberts, *Victorian Origins of the British Welfare State*, Ch. 3; Lubenow, *The Politics of Government Growth*, pp. 16–19, 30–106, 113–14.

[84] *B.P.P.*, 1825, IV, 339; *B.P.P.*, 1826–7, III, 880.

case some degree of responsibility was thrust on it merely by virtue of
the certification and registration of friendly societies and the nature of
the investment of savings-bank funds. For these generated a misplaced
confidence on the part of many of their members. As a result the Select
Committee on Friendly Societies in 1849 recommended that every
Registrar's certificate should 'have words inserted at the foot of it to
correct any opinion that the Government guarantees the stability of
the Society' and the Registrar of Friendly Societies was obliged to
agree that it was 'a popular delusion, which is constantly leading people
into error' to assume that his certificate was a certificate of accuracy,
whereas it was merely a certificate that a society's rules were in
accordance with the law.[85]

Second, the fact that the state intervened at all on a selective basis
had complex and unanticipated results in terms of the institutional
development. In particular, the privileges which it extended to the
poor could not be confined to them. In the 1850s and 1860s they were
to lead to the dramatic growth of new forms of associations (general
burial societies) which, although catering to the working classes, did so
in pursuit of private profit and in ways which were not always in the
best interests of their 'members'. In the 1830s and 1840s the advantages
of registration as a friendly society led a handful of middle-class life
offices to bring themselves within the legislation; and the guaranteed,
relatively high interest rates offered to savings bank depositors attracted
relatively well-off investors, many of whom resorted to fraud as well as
legitimately taking the attractive interest rates. 'Thus, skilfully,' wrote
a Benthamite in 1828, 'do our legislators attempt to cultivate good
habits among one portion of the community, and succeed in promoting
bad habits among another!'[86] In the last resort, the legislation designed
to encourage prudence among the very poor missed its aim. Instead,
it provided one more set of incentives to self-help and improvement
among the wealthier strata of the working class and among the lower
middle class. Social policy did not yet have a sufficiently discriminating
armoury to fight the battle against poverty on this sort of front. And in
tackling the consequential problems, and the financial embarrassment of

---

[85] *B.P.P.*, 1852, V, QQ. 1333–5.
[86] [Edwin Chadwick], 'Life Assurances', *Westminster Review*, IX (April 1828), 408.
Similarly, the building societies of early Victorian Britain soon came to be dominated
by the middle and lower middle classes – the working classes tending to have too
low and insecure an income to maintain their membership.

the high interest rate paid, the state was led to restrict the privileges of thrift institutions. The rate of interest was progressively reduced until the element of security of investment far outweighed in importance the attractiveness of the return; severe limits were placed on the amounts which individuals could invest in savings banks; and the privileges of friendly societies were denied where policies above a certain value were issued.

By the early 1850s the result was a streamlining of the pattern of incentives to working-class thrift: the more positive inducements were almost eliminated and the state's contribution to prudence among the labouring poor was confined largely to the provision of a rationalized framework of law, registration and communication. In the 1850s and 1860s, therefore, the state relied on a fairly 'neutral' policy with regard to the prudence of the poor. The inducements which it offered were directed mainly to ensuring that there were no exceptional handicaps to working-class thrift. Government did not ignore the problem; but it was confident that its role could be confined to ensuring that reasonable opportunities were made available. Its approach was similar to Mill's version of

intervention which is not authoritative: when a government, instead of issuing a command and enforcing it by penalties, adopts the course so seldom resorted to by governments ... of giving advice and promulgating information; or when, leaving individuals free to use their own means of pursuing any object of general interest, the government, not meddling with them, but not trusting the object solely to their care, establishes side by side with their arrangements, an agency of its own for a like purpose.[87]

Characteristic of such a non-authoritative departure from *laissez-faire* were two mid-Victorian experiments in state-sponsored thrift: the founding of the Post Office Savings Bank in 1861 and the official offer of life assurance in 1864.[88]

These moves were, of course, responses to deficiencies in the private arrangements for savings and insurance. At the same time, however,

---

[87] John Stuart Mill, *Principles of Political Economy*, Book I, Ch. XI, section 1.
[88] The Savings Bank was quite successful: by 1875 deposits exceeded £25 million, compared with £43 million in trustee savings banks. The insurance scheme was less successful (its minimum limit of £20 for the sum assured exceeded normal working-class needs). The state had, of course, sold annuities for decades, but these did not appeal to the working classes. I hope to deal with the later history of government policy and working-class thrift in a separate monograph.

they were seen by Gladstone, who introduced both, as measures to fulfil responsibilities already imperfectly assumed by the state. The Post Office Savings Bank was a commitment to the government guarantee of private savings which depositors had wrongly imagined to exist in the case of trustee savings banks. The insurance scheme was presented on the basis of a vitriolic attack on many burial societies sustained by friendly-society legislation. Gladstone argued that the state was doubly obliged to intervene since it subsidized and encouraged them: 'we stimulate, we force the production of Friendly Societies . . . and when we have done that it is too late to say that it is something novel to . . . see whether it is possible, by any means, to mitigate the evils they have produced.'[89]

Yet neither move amounted to a minatory or positively inter-ventionist policy. And in these years other and more general forces were also apparently working to abate the strength and extent of government intervention in a wide range of affairs. In the field of social policy as a whole, weak governments combined with the resolution of some of the worst problems of the 1830s and 1840s to usher in a period of relative 'administrative acquiescence' which contrasted with an earlier period of bold and prolific action.[90]

From this viewpoint the period up to the early 1850s was one of positive government action and experiment with regard to thrift insti-tutions. Such action reflected not merely the enlistment of the state in the attempt to influence working-class patterns of thrift, but also the inescapable need to accommodate the legal framework of institutions and social relations to new patterns of economic and social behaviour. From one point of view, therefore, friendly societies could be seen as an independent development which produced a new body of law. As a continental visitor to England put it a generation later, 'It is not legislation that dictated to the Friendly Societies their line of march, but the efforts of those societies for reform led to facts which required legal regulation. . . . Legislation has not created these institutions, but, on the contrary, their growth has necessitated legislation.'[91] More generally, industrial growth, through its effects on the distribution of wealth, consumption and savings inevitably influenced the outlook of

---

[89] *Hansard*, CLXXIII, Col. 1556 (7 March 1864).
[90] W. L. Burn, *The Age of Equipoise* (1964), pp. 153, 217–18; Cromwell, 'Interpretations of Nineteenth Century Administration', *Victorian Studies* (1966), 253–4.
[91] J. M. Baernreither, *English Associations of Working Men* (1889), p. 166.

legislators. In the words of the Select Committee on the Savings of the Middle and Working Classes in 1850, 'The great changes in the social position of multitudes, from the growth of large towns and crowded districts, renders it more necessary that corresponding changes in the law should take place both to improve their condition and content-ment, and to give additional facilities to investments of the capital which their industry and enterprise is constantly creating and augmenting.'[92]

In spite of all this, however, the main purpose of state action had been to offer a fairly substantial incentive to working-class thrift. In this respect the system which was created hardly amounted to a radical transformation of the circumstances or moral education of the poor. In fact, the problem of poverty – in so far as it had been approached through the encouragement of the poor to help themselves – had been seen in a middle-class context. This decisively shaped the nature of the intervention of the state. The subsidizing of working-class thrift was viewed as a temporary measure and was soon nullified, although while it lasted it was probably fairly important. The Government was well aware that it had to reduce a number of obstacles to prudence, and did so by offering legal privileges to working-class institutions, and by providing an absolutely safe outlet for their funds. But the ultimate trend of legislation was still conditioned by voluntaryism and the assumption that freedom of action and the improvement of com-munication and publicity would be far more productive than direct government action and regulation. And it is significant that the Select Committee on the Savings of the Middle and Working Classes which met in 1850 devoted most of its attention to the obstacles to limited liability investment – a question which, in retrospect, hardly seems relevant to the workaday problems of the mass of the labouring poor.

The economic and social situation of the very poor in industrial society would have to be rediscovered in future generations. Mean-while, both the compassion and the apprehension of the governing classes had led the state into extensive and cumulative experiments designed to transform individual and social behaviour. The outcome was a compromise between the *laissez-faire* state and the administrative state. That it failed to achieve some of its most important objectives was not due to a want of trying. It derived in large part from the nature

[92] *B.P.P.*, 1850, XIX.

and dimensions of contemporary poverty. At the same time, however, the relatively small effect of state intervention was also a function of the perception of the problem of the poor. As long as it was assumed that the psychology and habits of the working classes were the causes rather than the effects of their poverty, there were intractable obstacles in the way of successful government action. When even a John Stuart Mill saw the poor as having a 'deficiency in the power of reasoning and calculation, which makes them insensible to their own direct personal interests', and talked of the importance of 'converting these neglected creatures into rational beings'[93] there was little hope that more conventional men would be able to transcend his own determined belief in education in the broadest sense. It is in this light – as part of an imperfect and inadequate, but nevertheless commendably humanitarian, attempt at re-education – that early nineteenth-century social policy with respect to working-class thrift must be seen. Mill, as much as Smiles, was speaking for his generation when he urged on behalf of the poor that 'any one who could instil into these people the commonest worldly wisdom – who could render them capable of even selfish prudential calculations – would improve their conduct in every relation of life'.[94] Strictly interpreted, this might have been true. But as a prescription for poverty it missed the main point.

[93] John Stuart Mill, 'The Claims of Labour', *Edinburgh Review*, April 1845, reprinted in J. M. Robson (ed.), *Essays on Economics and Society*: vol. IV of *The Collected Works of John Stuart Mill* (1967), 377–8.
[94] Ibid., 377.

IX

'The Village Community' and the Uses of History in Late Nineteenth-Century England*

J. W. BURROW

Sir Henry Maine published his *Village Communities in the East and West* in 1871. Building on the work of German students of the early European village community, particularly Georg von Maurer and Erwin Nasse,[1] Maine drew comparisons with his own knowledge, acquired as a former Legal Member of the Viceroy's Council from 1862 to 1869, of Indian village communities, in an attempt to establish a common pattern of early agricultural and tenurial arrangements among all the peoples of 'Aryan' stock. The original form of land-ownership and cultivation, Maine argued, had been the co-proprietor-ship of self-governing village communes. The book, like Maine's other works, was received with considerable scholarly interest and acclaim, but Maine, whose political attitudes can be loosely described as a hard-headed Peelite élitism varied by a taste for Burkean rhetoric, was

* A first draft of this article was given as a paper to the Nineteenth Century Group of the University of Sussex and to the Historical Society of University College, London; the final version owes a good deal to the comments offered on those occasions, for which I am grateful. I also wish to thank Rodney Barker, Quentin Skinner and John Thompson for their criticisms and suggestions, and to acknowledge my initial and pervasive debt to J. H. Plumb, *The Death of the Past* (London, 1969).

[1] G. L. von Maurer, *Einleitung zur Geschichte der Mark, Hof und Stadtverfassung* (Munich, 1854); *Geschichte der Markenverfassung in Deutschland* (Erlangen, 1856). The common land of the village is the *mark*, and hence the village community is the *Markgenossen-schaft*. Also, E. Nasse, *On the Agricultural Community of the Middle Ages* (English translation, London, 1871). For Maine's sources, see his *Village Communities in the East and West* (3rd ed., London, 1876, Appendix ii).

incensed to find himself hailed in the press as a 'prophet of agrarian radicalism'.[2] The mistake was not altogether unnatural, for references to early agricultural communes inexorably attached themselves, in the absence of explicit disclaimers, to that long tradition of nostalgic agrarian radicalism whose course Christopher Hill has traced in *The Norman Yoke*,[3] and which was being given a fresh if relatively short-lived impetus in the 1870s by the agitation for land reform. John Stuart Mill, for example, though more cautious than the *Examiner* or the *Daily News* about Maine's own inclinations, used his review of *Village Communities* to preach a sermon on the mutability of concepts of property and the desirability of the redistribution of land.[4]

In doing so, he was, of course, touching on an issue of pressing contemporary interest.[5] Not only had land nationalization been for some time a political panacea – Herbert Spencer, for example, had advocated it in *Social Statics* in 1851 – but some of the most hotly debated issues of the early 1870s could give to even the most strictly historical inquiries into different systems of land tenure the character of test cases of their justice or their viability. There was, for example, the familiar problem of security of tenure for the Irish peasantry, brought to a head by the Irish Land Bill of 1870. On the other side there was the Cobdenite call for free trade in land and the liquidation of 'feudalism'. Nasse's short but seminal work, for example, on medieval English agricultural arrangements was translated in 1870 under the auspices of the Cobden Club and prefaced by a passage from a speech by Cobden himself. Nasse may not have been entirely happy at being so closely identified with political polemics, because the Cobden passage was omitted from the 1872 edition with a brief explanation that this had been done lest it should seem to detract from the work's scholarly objectivity. It was hard, however, to treat the village community merely as a matter of purely antiquarian interest in the last decades of the nineteenth century.

The *Examiner*'s mistake about Maine was therefore understandable,

[2] G. A. Feaver, *From Status to Contract: A Biography of Sir Henry Maine 1822–1888* (London, 1970), p. 120.

[3] Christopher Hill, 'The Norman Yoke', *Puritanism and Revolution* (London, 1958).

[4] J. S. Mill, 'Mr. Maine on Village Communities', *Fortnightly Review*, IX, 1871, reprinted in Mill's *Dissertations and Discussions*, IV, noted in Feaver, loc. cit.

[5] See also, for example, Mill's admiring review of T. E. Cliffe Leslie's *Land Systems and Industrial Economy of Ireland, England and Continental Countries*, in *Fortnightly Review*, VII, 1870.

and it provides a useful starting point for a review of the uses of early English history in the late nineteenth century, focused in particular on the concept of the village community. It has, moreover, an epilogue, in the letter which F. W. Maitland wrote to Paul Vinogradoff in February 1889, commenting on the manuscript of the latter's *Villeinage in England* (1892).[6] In his introduction Vinogradoff gives a review, impressive in its learning and European scope, of the idea of early European, and particularly Teutonic, land law as rooted in the practices of ancient free agricultural communes. Vinogradoff saw the historical treatment of this concept as having been conditioned, throughout the nineteenth century, by ideological considerations. As a Russian liberal, he himself necessarily approached it, though he was far from being a Slavophil or Populist, with, as he says himself, a strong sense of contemporary relevance.

Questions entirely surrendered to antiquarian research in the West of Europe are still topics of contemporary interest with us – such questions as 'How far legalisation can and should act upon the social development of the agrarian world'. 'Are economic agencies to settle for themselves who has to till land and who shall own it?' 'Or can we learn from Western history what is to be particularly avoided and what is to be aimed at?' I do not think that anybody is likely to maintain at the present day, that, for instance, a study of the formation and dissolution of the village community in the West would be meaningless for politicians and thinkers who have to concern themselves with the actual life of the village community in the East.[7]

In his historiographical survey Vinogradoff implies that the 'village community school' from the time of Jacob Grimm to von Maurer, Nasse and Maine, is associated with a liberal cult of the concept of a primeval Teutonic freedom, tinged with social democracy. This becomes most clearly apparent when he comes to discuss the recent reaction against these ideas. Vinogradoff was persuaded that 'the reaction against Maurer's teaching has gone so far and come from such different quarters, that one has to look for its explanation beyond the range of historical research'. The answer he finds in political reaction:

The brilliant achievements of historical monarchy in Germany, the ridiculous misery to which France has been reduced by conceited and impotent poli-

---

[6] C. H. S. Fifoot (ed.), *The Letters of Frederick William Maitland* (C.U.P., 1965), pp. 59–60.

[7] Sir Paul Vinogradoff, *Villeinage in England* (O.U.P. repr., 1968), p. vi.

ticians, the excesses of terrorist nihilism in Russia, the growing sense of a coming struggle on questions of radical reform – all these facts have worked together to generate a feeling which is far from propitious to liberal doctrines.[8]

Petit-Dutaillis, making the same kind of observation, saw the consequences for historiography of liberal disillusionment only as a cooler and more objective temper in historical writing, a recession from the liberal enthusiasms of Stubbs and Freeman.[9] Vinogradoff, addressing himself to its consequences for the study of the village community, saw something more specific: 'For the representatives of the New School, this "original Teutonic freedom" has entirely lost its significance, and they regard the process of social development as starting with the domination of the few and the serfdom of the many' – and he goes on explicitly to mention Frederic Seebohm.[10]

Maitland immediately sensed something wrong with this argument or at least with Vinogradoff's presentation of it. In a letter which is worth quoting at length he warned that:

it will seem strange to English readers, this attempt to connect the development of historical study with the course of politics, and it leads you into what will be thought paradoxes – e.g., it so happens that our leading village communists, Stubbs and Maine, are men of the most conservative type, while Seebohm, who is to mark conservative reaction, is a thorough liberal. I am not speaking of votes at the polling booth but of radical and essential habits of mind. I think that you hardly allow enough for a queer twist of the English mind which would make me guess that the English believer in 'free village communities' would very probably be a conservative. On the other hand, with us the man who has the most splendid hopes for the masses is very likely to see in the past nothing but the domination of the classes.[11]

Professor Fifoot, the editor of Maitland's letters, has been unable to trace Vinogradoff's reply, but clearly Maitland was left feeling that he might have offended his correspondent, and he made a gracious, if qualified, retraction, obviously with the intention of turning away wrath:

[8] Ibid., p. 31. The same kind of ideological interpretation of the historiography of the village community is to be found still more emphatically stated in Alfons Dopsch, *The Economic and Social Foundations of European History* (New York, 1969), Ch. 1.
[9] Charles Petit-Dutaillis, *Studies and Notes Supplementary to Stubbs' Constitutional History* (Manchester, 1908), p. xiii. Cf. A. V. Dicey, *Law and Public Opinion in England during the Nineteenth Century* (2nd ed., London, 1914), pp. 440–3.
[10] Vinogradoff, op. cit. p. 32.
[11] Fifoot, op. cit. pp. 59–60.

All you say about Stubbs and Seebohm and Maine is, I dare say, very true if you regard them as European, not merely English phenomena, and attribute to them a widespread significance – and doubtless it is very well that English-men should see this. Still, looking at England only and our insular ways of thinking, I see Stubbs and Maine as two pillars of conservatism, while as to Seebohm, I think that his book [*The English Village Community*] is as utterly devoid of practical importance as, shall I say, Madox's *History of the Exchequer*. But you are cosmopolitan and I doubt not that you are right. You are putting things in a new light, that is all. If 'the darkness comprehended it not', that is the darkness's fault.[12]

This correspondence has not escaped the notice of scholars, but Maitland's concluding words have been quoted as though they constituted a complete, and justified, retraction.[13] In fact, however, it seems quite clear that Maitland's courtesy should not be taken absolutely at face value – he was clearly not really satisfied – and also that his initial objection was, so far as it went, entirely correct. Of course, seeming strange to English readers is not necessarily an incapacitating disability for an historical argument, and Maitland was right subsequently to disavow it as an objection. It is also apparent that part of the dispute arises from using, as Maitland rightly senses, a vocabulary of too broad a mesh. Maitland's brief struggle with 'conservative not Tory' reminds us of our debt to Sir Herbert Butterfield for licence to use the word 'Whig' in an historiographical context, also with a fine disregard for the polling booth. And, of course, much of what Vinogradoff says rings true. There was a liberal-patriotic inspiration in the myth of primeval Teutonic freedom, embodied in the concept of the free village community. Von Maurer did have liberal and democratic sympathies, while in other continental works his historical theories were given a much more explicitly socialistic and polemical turn, by Marx and Engels, Lavelaye, Letourneau, Kropotkin and others.[14] In

---

[12] Ibid.

[13] E.g. J. W. Thompson, *A History of Historical Writing* (New York, 2 vols., 1942), ii, p. 389 and n. 16, W. S. Holdsworth, 'Sir Paul Vinogradoff', *Slavonic Review*, iv, no. 12, 1926, p. 532. Feaver, however, describes Maitland's comment as shrewd, op. cit. p. 297.

[14] Karl Marx, *Pre-Capitalist Economic Formations* (trans. J. Cohen, London, 1964). F. Engels, *The Origin of the Family, Private Property and the State* (4th ed., Moscow, 1954). Emile de Lavelaye, *Primitive Property* (trans. G. R. L. Marriott, London, 1878). Charles Letourneau, *Property, Its Origin and Development* (London, 1892). P. Kropotkin, *Mutual Aid* (London, 1906). Henry George made glancing use of Lavelaye, Maine and Nasse as warrant for saying that 'Historically, as ethically, private property in land is robbery', *Progress and Poverty* (London, 1906 ed.), pp. 262–3.

England, too, J. M. Kemble, who had been a pupil of Jacob Grimm and was responsible, in his *The Saxons in England* (1849), for the classic picture of the Teutonic *mark*-community on English soil, was a radical who had relearned the Whig habit of grounding libertarian doctrines on ancient rights. While as for Freeman, the cap fits so well that he wears it constantly.

Yet the suggested correlations do break down, as Maitland says they do. Stubbs was a Tory, Seebohm a liberal and Maine at the very least a strong conservative, while Vinogradoff's defence, to which Maitland refers, that 'I am speaking of general currents of thought and not of the position of the man at the polling booth. An author may be personally a liberal and still his work may connect itself with a stream of opinion which is not in favour of liberalism'[15], gives away more than Vinogradoff perhaps realized. Any attempt to explain the tendencies of historical works by general political attitudes is clearly vitiated if the political attitudes in question are to be discerned only in the historical work and are *prima facie* contradicted by the more explicitly political evidence.

Yet again, on the other side, Maitland is surely not altogether right either. If he was right, for example, in holding that Seebohm's book was of no political relevance, then it was a truth that Seebohm himself would certainly have disputed, as his preface to *The English Village Community* makes amply clear.[16] In fact both Vinogradoff and Maitland seem to be partly right, though it is not perhaps immediately easy to see why this should have been so. Clearly the situation in England was not simply one in which romantic liberal apologists for primeval free village communes were confronted by disillusioned realists or political authoritarians who denied the existence or significance of such communes and insisted instead upon the importance of individual property rights or seigniorial control. Nevertheless, Vinogradoff was clearly right about men like Kemble or Freeman, and there is something a little bluff about Maitland's English historian's disposition to regard historiography as historians writing about what was what in the best ways they know how. The situation was certainly more complicated than Vinogradoff allowed for, but it was also more politically charged than Maitland implied.

In order to unravel these threads, we need first to consider some of

[15] Vinogradoff, op. cit, p. 30.
[16] F. Seebohm, *The English Village Community* (3rd ed., London, 1884).

the different ways in which late Victorian historiography could assume a political relevance, especially in relation to the village community. For Maine and for the surviving apostles of Anglo-Saxon freedom, the last bearers of the Norman Yoke, the *mark*-community was a sensitive political issue, but they were arguing from history not only to different conclusions but in quite different ways. Moreover, the village community concept, by its very vagueness, could be many things to many men; to take only the most basic distinction, it could lend itself to quite different kinds of political persuasiveness depending on whether one emphasized its economic or its political aspect; in historiography there was a liberal ancient village community and a socialist one. Christopher Hill has observed that 'Only when Saxon freedom had ceased to be a rallying cry for the discontented masses did it begin to be enthusiastically taught in the lecture rooms of Oxford'.[17] This may well be so, but we would be misled if we drew the inference that no more need be said about the political implications of the late nineteenth century middle-class professional study of early English history than that it was more or less complacent, eirenic, Whig and tinged with chauvinism and Teutonic racialism – though that is certainly some of the things it was.

Only, however, when some basic distinctions have been made are we able to see in reasonably orderly fashion the various ideological uses of the concept of the ancient Teutonic village community, and some of the more general ideas reflected in the historical treatment of early English history in the 1870s, '80s and '90s. The most fundamental distinction is the one made by Macaulay, between history as 'a collection of experiments from which general maxims of civil wisdom may be drawn', and history 'as a repository of title deeds on which the rights of governments and nations [and, one could add, of classes] depend'.[18] The latter might, indeed, seem by the late nineteenth century so archaic a way of thinking of history as to be scarcely worth attention. Maitland, commenting on this very passage of Macaulay, with its conclusion that 'our antiquaries conducted their researches in the spirit of partisans', remarked cheerfully: 'Well, that reproach has passed away.'[19]

This is, of course, what one would expect. The doctrine of full

---

[17] Hill, op. cit. p. 115. For Victorian attitudes to the Saxons, see also Asa Briggs, *Saxons, Normans and Victorians* (Historical Association, Hastings and Bexhill Branch, 1966).

[18] Lord Macaulay, *The History of England from the Accession of James the Second* (Popular ed., London, 1889, 2 vols.), i, 13.

[19] 'Why the History of English Law is not Written', F. W. Maitland, *Collected Papers*, ed. H. A. L. Fisher (C.U.P., 1911, 3 vols.), i, 492.

parliamentary sovereignty, and the practical supremacy of the House of Commons, makes politically inspired antiquarianism, it seems, irrelevant, and makes consequences the only measure of right and wrong.[20] We are left with 'maxims of civil wisdom', and certainly attempts were not lacking in the later nineteenth century to make history, objectively and even comparatively treated, provide inductive support for such maxims. Yet it would, of course, be absurd to suppose that late Victorians were utilitarians *pur sang* in their attitudes to history simply because of an acceptance of the predominance of the House of Commons and the sovereignty of Parliament. Constitutional arguments as such might no longer assume quite their classic seventeenth-century forms, but, even apart from the abiding importance of case law and prescriptive rights, the question still remained: what kind of a society was it for which Parliament legislated? Unless one adopted the heroic expedient of resolving the society into its constituent individual members – something which could have plausibility only as a theoretical exercise of the kind Bentham and James Mill sometimes conducted, and which was growing increasingly unrealistic, as men like Maitland and Dicey realized – some richer descriptive texture was needed, something which could take systematic account of the rights, claims, sympathies and the various forms assumed by men's sense of their social identities, which social life was felt to contain. For some it might be provided principally by rights which the courts would recognize, by vague notions of class, or Utopian Owenite ideas of co-operation; for others, by a systematic sociology, Comtist or Spencerian perhaps. But for others again, it continued to be provided by some version of the national history, providential, catastrophic or simply unique.

It is in the light of this that we have to see some of the arguments over the historic existence of ancient free village communities. Although Saxons and Normans may have increasingly lost their place in radical polemics as the century wore on, there was still sufficient indignation on behalf of a dispossessed peasantry to keep the argument from usurped ancient rights flickering, if indeed it can ever be altogether exorcized from agrarian economic history; and surviving common rights were still in the process of being extinguished. Even Mill, utilitarian as he was, can be seen, in the review of Maine mentioned

---

[20] E.g. Henry Sidgwick, *The Development of European Polity* (London, 1903), p. 44.

above, delicately skirting the claims of ancient right. Modern property relations rest on 'usurpation' and the nation, in putting the process into reverse, would have 'an unquestionable moral right',[21] while the common rights which survive are older than manorial rights 'and can claim more of the sacredness which the friends of existing land institutions consider to attach to prescription'.[22]

In the case of the academic 'Germanists', Stubbs, Freeman and John Richard Green (who apart from Maine were the chief and least critical proponents of the ancient mark-community in academic historiography), though there was a marked idealization, in the two latter at least, of this supposed germ cell of Teutonic liberties, there was of course no such aching and outraged sense of dispossession as that which had sometimes guided the more radical denunciations of the Norman Yoke or of the extinction of common rights in the land. They therefore had less need of a theory of ancient rights as rights, that is as moral or even quasi-legal claims. Nevertheless, in a more general way the notion of history as a charter of rights was by no means alien to them. Indeed, in a society whose title deeds often run far back, the historian can have a modest practical role as an expert. It must have been gratifying to Freeman to be thanked by the Duke of Norfolk for his expert help in a lawsuit,[23] while Stubbs played a significant part in the Royal Commission on Ecclesiastical Courts which reported in 1883, on account of his knowledge of ecclesiastical history.[24] Stubbs, in his inaugural lecture, made the concept of rights the basis of his famous distinction between the study of ancient history, which the political theorist can treat as his playground, and the more awful responsibilities borne by a modern historian such as himself; the classical historian, he implies, can be intellectually more irresponsible because his results 'exercise no direct influence on the interests of real life', whereas the modern (i.e. post-classical) historian 'must not, as in Ancient History, amuse himself with principles, however valuable or however generally applicable, because he has to deal with rights'.[25] Thirteen years later, in 1880, he

---

[21] Mill, op. cit. pp. 544, 550.   [22] Ibid., p. 547.

[23] W. R. W. Stephens, *The Life and Letters of Edward Freeman* (London, 1895, 2 vols.), ii, 200–1, n. 1.

[24] See W. H. Hutton (ed.), *Letters of William Stubbs, Bishop of Oxford, 1825–1901* (London, 1904), pp. 208–15: Freeman was also a member but played little part. Stephens, op. cit. ii, 270–1.

[25] W. Stubbs, *Seventeen Lectures on the Study of Medieval and Modern History* (O.U.P., 1887), pp. 16, 19.

was reiterating that 'the rights and wrongs of the political life of modern
Europe are rooted in the medieval history of Europe, and we can trace
sufficient connection between the extreme past and the present to give
interest to the earliest investigation'.[26] To see what this could mean in
practice, however, we have to turn to Freeman, writing, for example,
that 'if it is worth our while to show that Queen Victoria is in every
sense the true successor of Cerdic and Aelfred and Edward I, it is no
less worth while to show that Louis Napoleon Bonaparte is in no
conceivable sense the successor of Clovis and of Charles the Great',[27]
or again, defending the German annexation of Alsace (always 'Elsass'
to Freeman): 'I have ventured to speak of historic right, because it is
on that which the whole thing turns.'[28]

   But of course, in a national state with constitutional means of
expressing the national will, ancient rights could not be quite so over-
bearing. It was, after all, half a century since even so good a Whig as
Hallam had refused to allow the right to a free government to be tried
by a jury of antiquaries,[29] and Stubbs acknowledged that 'the past has
no power, no moral right, to dispose of the present by a deed in
mortmain'.[30] And when Freeman made his own bow to ancient rights,
he made it clear that it was a retrospective one: 'the holders of liberal
principles in modern politics need never shrink from tracing our
political history to its earliest beginnings. As far at least as our race is
concerned, freedom is everywhere older than bondage. . . . Our
ancient history is the possession of the liberal.'[31] One major function of
this declaration for Freeman is to reassure himself that his democratic
and republican sympathies are unimpeachably English, Teutonic and

---

[26] 'On the Characteristic Differences between Medieval and Modern History', ibid.,
p. 238. Stubbs's distinction between medieval and modern history – that the former
is less politically controversial and the latter concerned with 'forces' rather than rights
(ibid., p. 275), may seem to tell against the argument offered here; it does, however,
reinforce the connection between the ideas of 'rights' and 'origins'.

[27] 'The Franks and the Gauls', National Review (1860), reprinted in E. A. Freeman,
Historical Essays, first series (5th ed., London, 1896), p. 165. Freeman's point was not
a Legitimist one, but appears to have been directed against French claims to Nice
and Savoy.

[28] Stephens, op. cit. ii, 3–4. Freeman was prepared to disregard the wishes of the
inhabitants.

[29] Henry Hallam, View of the State of Europe During the Middle Ages (London, 1819,
3 vols.), iii, p. 235.

[30] Stubbs, Seventeen Lectures, p. 25.

[31] E. A. Freeman, The Growth of the English Constitution from the Earliest Times (3rd ed.,
London, 1870), p. x.

historically rooted with no taint of abstract cosmopolitan arguments from metaphysical rights of man.[32] But Freeman is not, of course, simply opposing one static notion of original rights by another; he is instituting a preamble to an account, in the classic Whig mould, of the success of piecemeal reform guided by precedent, glossed by his own endorsement of late nineteenth-century democracy; he even incorporates the Burkean image of house repairs and improvements, as Stubbs does also.[33] The concept of ancient freedom here becomes chiefly important as a healthy starting point for future growth, distanced from immediate political claims by the more mature Whig notion of history not so much as a deed box but as the demonstration of the rewards of historical continuity and political pragmatism. The office of the supposed continuity of English history is not so much to guarantee any particular institution as to promote and underwrite a particular temper and habit of mind; it is, as one would expect, the Whiggism of Burke rather than of Coke.

To both Freeman and Stubbs, though far more vehemently for the former, the chief enemies of this historically tutored pragmatism were lawyers, though Stubbs also found time to rebuke philosophers and publicists.[34] The pages of both are studded with outcries against the abstract, over-tidy, unhistorical systematizations purveyed by lawyers,[35] and Freeman's attacks were sufficiently violent to irritate Dicey into a rejoinder and a refutation of what he called 'historical constitutionalism'.[36] For Freeman, moreover, lawyers' 'distortions' and 'subtleties' have a special function, that of chief scapegoat whenever

---

[32] This is not intended to imply that Freeman simply used history to justify political preconceptions. His whole political consciousness was entangled with history, and it seems to have been the study of Saxon history which eroded his early Toryism and high churchmanship; Stephens, op. cit. i, 88, 103. The interaction of history and politics is a two-way process; sometimes, as Lecky said, 'We are Cavaliers or Roundheads before we are Conservatives or Liberals'; W. E. H. Lecky, *The Political Value of History* (London, 1892), p. 19.

[33] E.g. The passage beginning 'The wisdom of our forefathers was ever shownnot in a dull and senseless clinging to things. . . .', Freeman; *Growth of the Constitution*, p. 20. Cf. Stubbs, *Lectures on Early English History* (London, 1906), p. 332.

[34] *Seventeen Lectures*, pp. 124, 135. *Early English History*, p. 194.

[35] The examples are too numerous for quotation. See Stephens, ii, 262, 270. Freeman, *Growth of the Constitution*, pp. x–xi, 127–9, 145–7. *Comparative Politics, Six Lectures Before the Royal Institution* (2nd ed., London, 1896), pp. 92, 279. Stubbs, *Early English History*, pp. 37–8; and Hutton, op. cit. pp. 88, 305.

[36] A. V. Dicey, *Introduction to the Study of the Law of the Constitution* (7th ed., London, 1908), Ch. i. Cf. *Law and Public Opinion*, p. 459, n. 1.

English history particularly glaringly fails to exhibit the degree of continuity which Freeman feels becomes it.[37] Freeman does not perhaps, as Dicey saw, sufficiently recognize that if a country's lawyers systematically interpret things in a certain way, then there is a sense in which they are so. Freeman here hovers on the brink of a really crude distinction, between an ideal or 'real' England and an actual historical one, in a way which has perhaps been more common in French or German than in English thought, and which can indeed give ancient rights a bolder role than is common in the later refinements of the Whig tradition. If so, it is Freeman's democratic radicalism which leads him along this metaphysical path; lawyers are largely to blame for the 'interruptions' of feudalism and the near absolutism of the Tudors and Stuarts.

Yet, though Freeman ostensibly associates lawyers primarily with authoritarian and anti-democratic habits of mind,[38] one senses in his and Stubbs's references to abstract theorizing another malign figure, the revolutionary ideologue. The sin, after all, is from this point of view the same: an a-historical neglect of the fine organic complexity of social and constitutional arrangements. The constant pejorative references to French authoritarianism and instability in this connection[39] cut in both directions, and sometimes the two are explicitly aligned, as when Freeman contrasts 'bit-by-bit reform' with 'magnificent theories and . . . massacres in the cause of humanity'.[40]

There is, however, a nuance which divides Stubbs's and Freeman's historically based political pragmatism. For the former it is a temper, judicious, practical reason; for the latter unashamedly a 'spirit'. Stubbs emphasizes not only the superiority which English institutions derive from their deep roots, but also that one learns political judgement from the practice of history as a craft, from negotiating the stubbly contours of concrete historical situations;[41] Freeman, rather, that one learns it from the *contemplation* of history, and specifically of English or Teutonic history moreover. 'We must recognize the spirit which dictated the Petition of Right as the same which gathered all England around the

---

[37] E.g. *Growth of the Constitution*, pp. 21, 126, 129.

[38] Ibid., p. 128.

[39] E.g. Stephens, i, 171–2. Stubbs, *Early English History*, p. 2.

[40] Freeman, *Historical Essays*, 1st series, p. 45. Cf. *Growth of the Constitution*, p. 66. Compare the scathing remarks on the 'natural rights of man' by the strongly liberal Green; see Leslie Stephen (ed.), *Letters of John Richard Green* (London, 1902), p. 370

[41] *Seventeen Lectures*, pp. 19–20, 84, 275. *Early English History*, pp. 37–8.

banners of returning Godwin.'[42] But in Freeman there is a further ambiguity. One is perhaps at a loss to know here whether we are being presented with a metaphysics or an induction. That is, Freeman seems to present English history as a demonstration of the success of an historically sensitive pragmatism, yet he also seems to speak of the latter as an emanation of something active *in* history. Here, in fact, we have to recognize that in this view of history there is no abrupt hiatus between what we have so far been taking as distinct categories of historically based political claims. Arguments from ancient rights modulate almost insensibly into arguments from historical continuity; thus to know the title deeds is already a step to the appropriate civil wisdom. The argument from continuity has, in turn, a dual function. Historical continuity is both the inductive guarantee that respect for precedent builds more lastingly than abstract theories, and also the content of the myth by which that respect is sanctioned and inspired. At its most emphatic, the myth presents the national history and identity as the continuous self-renewal and development of a spirit. And if this description seems to lean inappropriately on an alien metaphysics, how else can one interpret such a remark of Freeman's as that 'New and foreign elements have from time to time thrust themselves into our law, but the same spirit which could develop and improve whatever was old and native has commonly found means sooner or later to cast forth again whatever was new and foreign'?[43]

'Spirit' or 'character'? Again, as we turn from the intellectual to the emotional significance of historic continuity, we find the same differences of tone between Stubbs and Freeman, Stubbs employing the language of character-formation, Freeman that of epic. Stubbs laments that nations like France, which lose continuity, lose 'character and independence'.[44] In Freeman, Hallam's 'generous pride that entwines the consciousness of hereditary freedom with the memory of our ancestors'[45] is rampant. He has all Macaulay's love of a roll call, and intones the names of Saxon kings as though they were the companions

[42] Quoted Stephens, i, 125.
[43] *Growth of the Constitution*, p. 19. Cf., e.g., Coleridge's notion of the progressive self-realization of an Idea of the Constitution, in his essay *On the Constitution of Church and State*. Freeman himself, of course, took no interest in metaphysics as such.
[44] *Early English History*, p. 2.
[45] Hallam, loc. cit.

of Agamemnon;[46] it is partly this trait which gives the ancient *mark-community* a significance for him which it could not have for the sober Tory Stubbs. It gives the notion of origins a meaning for him, that is, which political pragmatism in no way requires. The village community had in fact a double significance; for Freeman the mythologist and Freeman the Gladstonian liberal.

Because he was the latter, Freeman's version of English history is only in a very loose sense one of unbroken continuity. Its pattern is really much more that very popular nineteenth-century triadic one of rude idyll, overlaid by decadence, and ultimately restored, or about to be, at a higher level. At a time when both democracy and socialism found an increasing number of advocates, but when both still had more ancient than modern precedents, it was a plausible sequence. Mill toyed with it in the essay quoted above.[47] Gladstone referred to it;[48] Lewis Henry Morgan looked forward, in a passage quoted by Engels, to a 'revival, in a higher form, of the liberty, equality and fraternity of the ancient *gentes*'.[49] Freeman presented a liberal democratic version of it, based largely on the notion of the democratic, self-governing, ancient village community. Modern democracy is the revival and perfection of ancient Teutonic democracy on a wider scale, and he can thus reconcile the Whig's consciousness of a genealogy of freedom with a belief that one has earned one's noble forbears' approval and done nothing to smirch the family name by subscribing it to a lodger franchise.[50]

Freeman made no contribution to the scholarly study of the village community,[51] but he contributed notably to the myth. Not only did he present the chief, though not the only, liberal-democratic version

---

[46] This was partly a conscious attempt to match the Hellenic and Teutonic heroic ages by use of the comparative method. *Comparative Politics*, pp. 33–7, 169ff. It was still a matter of concern to claim an equal status for modern compared with ancient history.

[47] Mill, op. cit. p. 544.

[48] 'restoring the good old constitution which had its root in Saxon times', quoted Hill, op. cit. p. 112.

[49] Quoted Engels, op. cit. p. 292.

[50] 'We have advanced by falling back on a more ancient state of things . . .', etc.; *Growth of the Constitution*, p. 21, cf. ix–x, 143. Freeman was careful to emphasize that ancient democracy 'does not forbid the existence of magistrates clothed with high authority and held in high reverence, nor does it forbid respect for ancient birth or even an attachment to an hereditary line of rulers',; ibid. p. 11. Apart from the necessary development of representation, the symmetry was complete.

[51] Freeman's sources are given most fully in *Comparative Politics*, pp. 272–3.

of it, but he gave it colour and imaginative depth. Just as evolutionary anthropologists gave substance to abstract notions of 'stages' of development by modern ethnographical details, so Freeman assumed that the direct democracy of the Swiss *Landesgemeinden* was a living survival of the ancient democracy of the *mark*-communities, the nuclei from which all subsequent constitutional development had sprung, 'the true kernel of all our political life'. 'Year by year, on certain spots among the dales and mountain sides of Switzerland' one can look 'face to face on freedom in its purest and most ancient form'.[52] In its idealized evocation of the world of Tacitus's *Germania*, Freeman's description is comparable, by way of contrast, with the even lusher and more famous set-piece in which Frazer crystallized his notion of primeval savagery in the opening of *The Golden Bough*.

Freeman is able to take the attitude he does to the *mark*-community – at once idealistic and complacent – partly because he has none of the critical attitude to what he sees as the tendencies of the modern world which normally accompanies an atavism such as his, but also partly because of a limitation in his conception of the village community itself. For him it was essentially a political unit – a face-to-face democratic society. It is not for him the archetype of a *Gemeinschaft*, or primarily a producer's co-operative.[53] Hence nothing essential is lost when the democracy of the village community is 'revived' in representative, parliamentary form, and any hankerings for the intimacies of kinship and locality are satisfied for him by his pan-Teutonic or pan-Aryan racialism. Stubbs treated the economic aspect of the *mark*-community more fully, but also rather equivocally, and he accepted the view of Maine, to which he refers, that co-ownership was a drag on progress.[54] Stubbs too, of course, was heavily committed to the

---

[52] *Growth of the Constitution*, p. 1. To have seen the annual assembly 'I reckon among the highest privileges of my life', ibid., p. 2. Freeman makes frequent reference to the *Landesgemeinden*, which represent, of course, groups of villages rather than individual village communities.

[53] Contrast the detailed attention given to the economic aspects of the *Landesgemeinde* by a continental 'socialist of the chair' like Lavelaye (Lavelaye, op. cit. p. 71ff.). Freeman discusses common property in land briefly in *The History of the Norman Conquest of England* (O.U.P., 1876, 5 vols.), i, 83–4, v. 463.

[54] *The Constitutional History of England* (3rd ed., O.U.P., 1883), p. 35, n. 2. Stubbs's treatment of the question of communal ownership is rather obscure, partly because of the obscurity of the subject, of which he himself complained (ibid., p. 37), and partly because, as Maitland pointed out, he made some revisions in successive editions but never thoroughly or systematically.

view of liberty as rooted in Germanic soil, and begins his *Constitutional History* with Tacitus, but he identified it with allodial tenure and such institutions as frank-pledge, which he saw as 'a more likely basis of freedom than the . . . community of land . . . and the clannish spirit that one finds in the Highland Scot and Irishman, or in the Pole or Hungarian'.[55]

How liberal individualism could be introduced into the Tacitean picture of the village community can be seen in two other writers, J. R. Green and Sir George Gomme. In Green the individualist gloss is brief but obvious. Quoting the famous passage from Tacitus in which he refers to the separate houses of the Germans: 'They live apart, each by himself. . . .' Green's paraphrase continues 'each dweller within the settlement was jealous of his own isolation and independence. . . .'[56] But the passage in Tacitus explaining the open spaces round the houses suggests fire precautions or poor building techniques[57] rather than 'jealous independence'. Like Freeman, Green speaks of the *mark-community* with an appropriate awe: 'It is with a reverence such as is stirred by the sight of the head-waters of some mighty river that one looks back to these tiny moots . . .'.[58] But again it is as a political, not an economic entity. Of this Green merely says rather unsympathetically that the 'toil necessitated by the system of common culture was severe'.[59]

Gomme's treatment of the theme of 'jealous independence' is considerably more elaborate. Initially we seem to begin with a rather simplified but classic account based on the usual sources. In early times 'individual ownership in land is not recognized', and 'the individual is the child of the community'.[60] Then, however, in a fashion that seems to owe a good deal to Fustel de Coulanges's *La Cité Antique*, the disentangling of individual from communal property begins, in association with the development of a religion of the sacred hearth which

---

[55] *Early English History*, p. 204. Stubbs emphasized that in Saxon England 'it is as an owner of land, or as a fully qualified "lawful man", not as a member of the mark community that the freeman has rights and duties', *Constitutional History*, p. 91.

[56] J. R. Green, *A Short History of the English People* (New ed., London, 1902), p. 3. Cf. Stubbs, 'every man's house is his castle', *Early English History*, p. 5. Also *Constitutional History*, p. 21.

[57] 'sive adversus casus ignis remedium sive inscita aedificandi', Tacitus, *Germania*, 16.

[58] *Short History*, p. 4. Cf. J. R. Green, *The Making of England* (4th ed., London, 1904, 2 vols.), i, 218–9.

[59] *Making of England*, i, 211.

[60] Sir George Laurence Gomme, *The Village Community* (London, 1890), pp. 14–15.

replaces the vague nature worship found in pure savagery.[61] In the classic, all too simple theory of the *mark*-community, as found, for example, in Kemble,[62] and based ultimately on Tacitus, there were three ingredients: the common land or *mark* itself, the arable strips which were subject to annual redistribution, and the individual homesteads. According to Gomme, it was the religion of the sacred hearth which, by making the homestead and its surroundings sacred and taboo, constituted the origin at once of private property, individualism and progress. It is what differentiated the 'Aryan' from the lesser breeds, sunk in animism and quite literally without the law, and hence doomed to stagnation.[63] Both Gomme and Stubbs agree, that is, that there was an original co-ownership,[64] but they, and particularly Gomme, tend to place the origin of liberty and progress at the point where it breaks down, though for Gomme this point is much earlier, the emergence of an 'Aryan' hearth religion.

At this point, with the suggestion, on Gomme's part at least, that we have not merely detected origins, but found the clue to the difference between the progressive and the unprogressive peoples – what Maine called 'one of the great secrets which inquiry has yet to penetrate',[65] we move emphatically from the concepts of ancient rights or unbroken tradition to that of history as a comparative, inductive discipline, whose most valuable lesson will be the causes, or at least the conditions, of human progress. And it is in this context that Maine's own treatment of the village community must be placed. Maine was misunderstood because, as a proponent of the fact of an original co-proprietorship, he was suspected of being concerned with rights, when in fact he was trying to write a comparative kind of history from which sociological inferences could be drawn.

Not that Maine had not paid his own tribute to the concept of original rights, but it was a backhanded one. Maine was concerned at various points in his writings[66] to refute the notion, which he associated primarily with Rousseau, and seems to have seen as dangerously democratic, of an original state of nature and individual natural rights.

[61] Ibid., p. 131.

[62] J. M. Kemble, *The Saxons in England* (London, 1849, 2 vols.), i, Ch. ii.

[63] Gomme, op. cit. p. 150.

[64] Stubbs saw individual property rights emerging smoothly and naturally as a consequence of 'the practice of careful husbandry', *Constitutional History*, p. 56.

[65] Sir Henry Maine, *Ancient Law* (O.U.P., World's Classics, 1954), p. 19.

[66] Ibid., pp. 2–3, 77. Cf. Maine, *Popular Government* (2nd ed., 1886), pp. 157–9.

He always treated this as a (spuriously) *historical* claim, and set himself to refute it historically, by showing that 'Ancient law knows nothing of individuals'.[67] It does not seem to have occurred to him that if men could endow the spuriously primeval with moral authority, they might suppose him to be doing the same with what he claimed to be the genuine article. For, of course, it was not in the least Maine's intention to present his ancient village communities as constituting either models or title-deeds. He was an individualist and an élitist, equally hostile to democracy and to socialism, which he regarded as related.

Maine's sources for the village community were the same as Freeman's, and indeed Freeman drew on his work, except that Maine supplemented the historical sources by his own knowledge of Indian village communities. And no doubt this makes a difference. For not only was Freeman democratic in his sympathies, but it is also no doubt one thing to look in on one day of the year, on a fine Alpine spring morning, upon Swiss patriarchs exercising an immemorial franchise; quite another to deal, as a busy and irritable Anglo-Indian official, with the resistance to change and the tenurial complexities of Indian village agriculture. Not that some Anglo-Indians, like Sir John Malcolm or Sir Thomas Munro, did not manage to view Indian peasant life with affection and even idealization, but Maine was not among them.[68] Yet essentially Maine's political attitudes were set before he embarked for India in 1862;[69] his knowledge of Indian land tenures chiefly provided him with additional empirical arguments. Maine was a leading late Victorian critic of democracy, and his concept of the village community and the sociological truths it embodied was pivotal in that critique.

Placed in the context of Maine's works as a whole, the village community occupied a central role in his polemics, and it faced both ways. On the one hand it helped him to refute the philosophic radicals whose influence had been dominant in his youth, and whose clear-cut concepts of sovereignty and private property could be shown to have only a limited relevance in the face of such legal and tenurial complexities as those exhibited by the village community.[70] Government, which had

---

[67] *Ancient Law*, p. 214.
[68] For the study of the Indian village community see L. Dumont, 'The Village Community from Munro to Maine', *Contributions to Indian Sociology* (Paris, The Hague), ix, 1966.
[69] See Feaver, op. cit. Also J. W. Burrow, *Evolution and Society* (C.U.P., 1966), Ch. iv.
[70] Maine, *Lectures on the Early History of Institutions* (London, 1875), Lecture xii. Cf. *Popular Government*, p. 86.

stood in danger of being revealed as essentially simple, could be re-established as complex and difficult, its task to be fully understood only by men of historical knowledge and administrative expertise. Maine had an abiding distaste for demagogues, newspapers and public opinion.

But he did not, of course, in any way *endorse* such arrangements as co-proprietorship. If he opposed Bentham and John Austin because he was an élitist, and in some sense a traditionalist, the face he turned to the socialists and democrats of the 1870s and '80s was that of a *laissez-faire* individualist.[71] The village community, having by its mere existence done its duty in refuting the a-priorism of Rousseau and the philosophic radicals, could now be wheeled about and help to refute the doctrines of late nineteenth-century democrats and socialists, as a sociological example; that is, by helping to show that democratic and socialistic communities were inherently repressive and stagnant. 'Nobody is at liberty to attack several property and to say at the same time that he values civilization.'[72] Individualism is not the birthright of mankind, it is a precious historical achievement, confined to the progressive nations, whose progress is the work of creative minorities and free competition. 'The movement of the progressive societies has hitherto been a movement from status to contract.'[73] Its precondition is the break-up of the stagnant village community and the development of private property. So far Maine's account agrees with Gomme's, but he places the vital steps in different places: first, in the codification of Roman Law; and second, in the beginnings of feudalism and the emergence of the *seigneur*.[74] Towards the end of his life, in *Popular Government* (1885), Maine, like Freeman, saw signs of European society returning to its origins but, whereas for Freeman this meant only democracy, for Maine it meant not only democracy, which he detested in any case, but socialism and the stifling of human progress.

Apart from Maine, the most distinguished English writer on the village community who seems to have regarded his work partly as a basis for inductive political generalization was Frederic Seebohm, and it is no surprise to find that he attended Maine's lectures and warmly acknowledged his influence.[75] In terms of historiography, of course,

[71] *Popular Government.*
[72] *The Effects of Observation of India on Modern European Thought* (C.U.P., 1875), p. 30.
[73] *Ancient Law*, p. 141.   [74] *Early History of Institutions*, pp. 120, 126.
[75] Seebohm, *The English Village Community*, p. xi.

they were far apart: Maine was one of the founding fathers, in England, of the concept of the early medieval village community, while Seebohm traced the communal features of medieval agriculture to the Roman *villa* and dissolved the village community in the manor – to Maine's considerable irritation.[76] But at a deeper level they concurred in their manner of using history, and even in the specific inferences they drew from it: the connection between private property, freedom of contract and human progress. Seebohm, a Liberal Unionist of a more straight-forward kind, did not share Maine's violent hatred of democracy, or his traditionalist sympathies; but a version of *laissez-faire* individualism was common to them both. Seebohm, indeed, offers one more historical variation on the themes of private property, individualism and pro-gress. Where for Gomme the Aryan hearth-religion had been crucial; for Stubbs, Teutonic allodialism; and for Maine, Roman Law in the ancient world and the emergence of the landlord out of the Dark-Age village community in the modern; for Seebohm it was in the first place the Roman *villa* whose legacy, the manor, differentiated the heartlands of medieval Europe from the purely tribal societies of the Celtic fringe, which he also studied.[77] More important, though he devoted less detailed attention to it, was the break-up of feudal society in the later Middle Ages with the emergence of a free landless peasantry.

Seebohm wrote in his preface to *The English Village Community* that he had approached his studies 'not as an antiquary, but as a student of Economic History, and even with a directly political interest. To learn the meaning of the old order of things, with its "community" and "equality", as a key to a right understanding of the new order of things, with its contrasting independence and inequality.'[78] To look forward to a return to a past communalism was, for Seebohm, to put progress into reverse, and he hoped that 'the knowledge of what the community of the English village and the Celtic tribe really were under the old order may at least dispel any lingering wish or hope that they may return'.[79] The 'freedom of the individual and growth of individual enterprise and property which mark the new order . . . has triumphed by breaking up both the communism of serfdom and the communism of the free tribe', both of which had represented 'a forced equality'.[80]

[76] Feaver, op. cit. p. 296.
[77] F. Seebohm, *The Tribal System in Wales* (London, 1895).
[78] *The English Village Community*, p. vii.
[79] Ibid., p. 441.   [80] Ibid., p. 439.

A spontaneous communalism of free men, such as the more idealistic 'village communist' scholars envisaged, seems to have been unacceptable to Seebohm because, as Vinogradoff said, 'It seemed to him that free men are naturally inclined towards individual acquisition, disposition and alienation of property'.[81]

Seebohm's revelation of the political relevance of his work was no afterthought. Throughout the latter part of the 1860s, in a series of articles in the *Fortnightly Review*, he had spelt out the political implications, as he saw them, of medieval economic history. In 1870, the year of the Irish Land Bill, and in contradiction to Mill's article in the same volume, he was concerned to show by historical precedent that 'what justice obliges us to do for Ireland, can be done upon principles recognized in England, and in such a way as to strengthen, instead of in the least degree to undermine, the rights of property in England'.[82] In the debate over land reform he came out firmly in favour of free trade in land, and equally strongly against land nationalization, peasant proprietorship, or the remaining 'feudal' restrictions on the sale of land.[83] And in 'The Black Death and its Place in English History' he traced the initial steps in the severance of the English peasantry from the land – so often deplored and condemned as usurpation on the part of the landlord – not, initially at least, to coercion but to free choice. 'The freedom of the peasantry was not a one-sided bargain. Serfs having claimed the right to do what they liked with their labour, landlords soon learned to do what they liked with their land.'[84] Again, a backhanded tribute to the persistence of the argument from ancient rights.

Maitland, who denied incorrectly – at least so far as intentions went – a political character to Seebohm's work, might well have seen an irony in his own conception of the village community being given a political significance by 'those who, ignoring the contents of English ballot boxes [a reminiscence of Vinogradoff], assign to historiographers their respective places in the thought of the nineteenth century'.[85] Maitland is counted, in relation to the village community, as a moderate Germanist. Fundamentally, that is, and with considerable qualifications,

[81] Sir Paul Vinogradoff, *Collected Papers* (O.U.P., 1928, 2 vols.), i, 274.

[82] 'Feudal Tenures in England', *Fortnightly Review*, vii, (new series), 1870, p. 89.

[83] 'The Black Death and its Place in English History', Part ii, *Fortnightly Review*, ii, 1865. 'The severance of the English People from the Land', ibid., vii, (n.s.), 1870. 'The Westminster Review on the Land Question in England', ibid., ix, n.s.), 1871.

[84] Ibid., ii, 1865, p. 276.

[85] F. W. Maitland, *Collected Papers* (henceforth cited as *C.P.*), iii, 508.

he was prepared to remain in the tradition of Kemble, von Maurer and Stubbs, rather than crossing over to the Romanist camp of Seebohm and Fustel de Coulanges. Yet he was, by the standard of the whole-hearted village communalists, a cautious and unenthusiastic ally. He disapproved of Maine[86] and Gomme,[87] and the 'obscurity' and 'indefiniteness' of the subject, which bothered Stubbs, bothered Maitland still more: 'How little is gained by our easy talk about village communities.'[88] Furthermore, it is clear that, even apart from his scholarly reservations, ancient communal arrangements could have had no claim on him in the form of rights. One of his earliest essays was an amusing but weighty attack in the *Westminster Review* on atavism in jurisprudence, and from this he never wavered: 'no practical convenience, however small, is to be sacrificed on the altar of historic continuity'.[89]

Yet there is, of course, another side to Maitland, and the historian revered partly for the political chastity of his historical writing, compared with Freeman's or even Stubbs's, was revered also – though generally not by the same people – as the man who almost casually gave a new direction to English political thought. There is, in other words, not only the Maitland of *The History of English Law*, which Petit-Dutaillis rightly considered the paradigm of a new historical objectivity,[90] but the Maitland of the famous preface to his translation of Gierke, of 'Trust and Corporation' and 'Moral Personality and Legal Personality', who became for a time a political inspiration to socialist pluralists like Cole and Laski.[91] The question we have to consider is the relation between the two.

The apparent starting point of Maitland's political ideas is not very dissimilar from Maine's: a critical examination of the theory of natural rights, and a certain suspicion – in Maitland's case the milder term is appropriate – of a sovereign democratic parliament. In his unsuccessful

[86] Fifoot, *Letters*, p. 222.
[87] 'The Survival of Ancient Communities', *C.P.*, ii, 313ff. Cf. Fifoot, p. 104.
[88] 'Tenures in Roussillon and Namur', *C.P.*, ii, 252.
[89] 'The Law of Real Property' (*Westminster Review*, 1879), *C.P.*, i, 195. Cf. 'A Survey of the Century' (1901), *C.P.*, iii, 434ff.; and 'The German Legal Code' (1906), ibid., 476ff.
[90] Petit-Dutaillis, op. cit. p. xiii.
[91] There is no need to labour this well-known connection. See, e.g., G. D. H. Cole, *Social Theory* (London, 1920), pp. 11, 209. Harold Laski, 'The Early History of the Corporation in England', *Harvard Law Review*, xxx, 1917, p. 588; and *The Problem of Sovereignty* (O.U.P., 1917), Preface.

Trinity Fellowship dissertation, published privately in 1875, Maitland argued that the concept of natural rights offered no protection to minorities in a democracy.[92] He considered Coleridge's notion of a representation of interests rather than individuals, but settled instead for a qualified acceptance of J. S. Mill's arguments for non-interference;[93] Mill was obviously a substantial influence on the essay. Yet Maitland's reasons for rejecting Coleridge's idea are interesting in the light of his later championship of voluntary associations and corporate rights: not that the representation of interests is unrealistic, though it may be dangerous, but rather that Coleridge's restriction of those interests to two, the landed and the commercial, is unjustified.[94] Maitland does not at this early point, however, extend the notion of the rights of various 'interests', in pluralist fashion, to the multifarious groups and corporations which embody them. Yet this is precisely what he was to do twenty-five years later, in his preface to the translated section of Gierke's *Das Deutsche Genossenschaftsrecht*. Where the Maitland of 1875 had only questions, the Maitland of 1900 has begun to get answers.[95] It is German *Genossenschaftstheorie* which has taught him to see in the organized social group 'no fiction, no symbol, no collective name for individuals, but a living organism and a real person . . .'.[96]

Nevertheless, in Maitland's pluralism it is not hard to see, through the metaphysical refinements of *Genossenschaftstheorie*, the essentially Burkean English political style, displaying, of course, its customary affinities with kindred but more philosophically wrought German ideas. There is the usual protest against the inadequacies in social and political thought of the metaphor of contract,[97] and the rejection of a too

[92] 'An Historical Sketch of Liberty and Equality as Ideals of English Political Philosophy from the time of Hobbes to the time of Coleridge', *C.P.*, i, 84–6.

[93] Ibid., pp. 93–5, 109.

[94] Ibid., pp. 138–40.

[95] The coincidence which links Henry Sidgwick with both Maitland's essays is probably little more than that. The fellowship dissertation was certainly written under Sidgwick's influence (see H. A. L. Fisher, *F. W. Maitland: A Biographical Sketch* (C.U.P., 1910), pp. 7–10); and it was Sidgwick who, a quarter of a century later, suggested that Maitland should translate Gierke (Fifoot, p. 189). But Sidgwick's own published references to Gierke are scanty (*Henry Sidgwick: A Memoir*, by A. S. and E. M. S. (London, 1906), p. 437; *European Polity*, p. 33). In *The Elements of Politics* (London, 1891), he treated voluntary associations coolly, stressing their dangers and possible 'moral coercion' of their members; op. cit. Ch. xxviii.

[96] Otto Gierke, *Political Theories of the Middle Age*, translated with an Introduction by Frederick William Maitland (C.U.P., 1900), p. xxvi.

[97] Maitland, in Gierke, op. cit. pp. xxiii, xliii.

abstract individualism. There is the unabashed confrontation of theory
with the contents of common sense: 'For the morality of common
sense the group is person, is right-and-duty bearing person.'[98] There is
the antithesis of theory and history: 'our popular English *Staatslehre* if,
instead of analysing the contents of a speculative jurist's mind, it
seriously grasped the facts of English history, would show some
inclination to become a *Korporationslehre* also'.[99] And this marches
alongside the traditional parallel contrast between 'organic' and
'mechanical', which Maitland quotes on Gierke's behalf,[100] though it
was not really Maitland's natural language; 'organic' was itself too
'mechanical' a term to be really congenial to him, or to reside easily in
that 'rich, flexible, delicate vocabulary' which he recommended to
historians and exemplified so beautifully.[101] But the thought is there in
part – the contrast of flowing, changing human life constrained by
theories insensitive to its needs: 'the dead hand fell with a resounding
slap upon the living body.'[102]

But the last comment, on the inadequacy of the law of Trusts in the
Free Church of Scotland case to supply the place of a true *Korporations-
begriff*, also points to a quality of detachment in Maitland. Just as
Maitland saw no virtue in archaism, so he could tease his countrymen
with their lack of intellectual system, and see its drawbacks. The famous
essay on 'Trust and Corporation' is in part a celebration of English
pragmatism, but it is subtly qualified in a way Freeman would never
have allowed himself, just as Maitland's tone, Cambridge-conversa-
tional rather than Oxonian-prophetic, is different too. The difference
of generation is no doubt a factor; Maitland shared the admiration of
many of his contemporaries for German efficiency, while Freeman's
attitude, though warm, had contained more patronage and senti-
mentality. Yet Maitland could also use France, just like Burke or
Freeman, as a foil to pin down a moral; France, where 'we may see the
pulverizing, macadamizing tendency in all its glory, working from
century to century reducing to impotence and then to nullity, all that
interferes between Man and State'.[103]

[98] 'Moral Personality and Legal Personality', *C.P.*, iii, 314.
[99] Gierke, op. cit. p. xi.   [100] Ibid., xxviii.
[101] 'The Body Politic', *C.P.*, iii, 288.
[102] 'Moral Personality and Legal Personality', *C.P.*, iii, 319.
[103] Ibid., p. 311. 'Pulverizing' and 'macadamizing' were obviously words with a Gallic
    connotation for Maitland; he also uses them, rather oddly, of Fustel de Coulanges,
    C.P., ii, 252.

There is a more fundamental difference, however, between Maitland and the classic apologetics of Whig historiography in that, besides paying no reverence to ancient title deeds, Maitland accords no special legitimating role to tradition and unbroken lineage. Joint-stock companies qualify for group personality as readily as ancient corporations – indeed they are actually crucial because more difficult to construe 'as a piece of the State's mechanism'.[104] The test is sociological and jurisprudential, not traditionalist. It is typical that in the case of the Church of England's historic claims, Maitland, the great pluralist, always hostile to the Church establishment,[105] took for once the side of the central authority.[106]

Yet it could be argued that Maitland was over-tolerant, that his readiness to endorse group personalities in general was a drawback from the point of view of a general, sociologically based theory of associations and the corporate rights their existence created. One might retort that Maitland was not attempting anything so comprehensive, yet his demand for a *Korporationslehre* to supplement a mere *Staatslehre* closely parallels the nineteenth-century attempts – Tocqueville's, for example – to provide a sociological analysis to fill out the abstractions of political philosophy. Hence one might argue that Maitland's pluralism remains somewhat drily legal; that is, it is presented not so much as a prolegomenon to a sociology of groups, though it points that way, nor as a general theory of the moral and political claims constituted by the existence of such groups, but as a warning to the law not to make an ass of itself by treating things as if they were not what they manifestly are. There is more to Maitland's arguments than that, but it is true that he does not distinguish between *types* of collectivities except in such specifically legal terms as the distinctions between co-ownership and corporate ownership, partnership (*Gesellschaft*) and corporation; *Gemeinschaft*, 'organic' and 'mechanical' solidarity, the categories so important to continental sociologists like

---

[104] Gierke, op. cit. pp. xxi, xxiv.
[105] E.g. H. E. Bell, *Maitland: A Critical Examination and Assessment* (London, 1965), p. 78.
[106] *Roman Canon Law in the Church of England* (1898). It is interesting in this connection to note the different strategies adopted respectively in defending the rights of the Church by Stubbs and J. N. Figgis. The former, in the Royal Commission on Ecclesiastical Courts, hovered rather uneasily between 'historical claims' (the argument from ancient rights) and the metaphor, half-heartedly borrowed from rationalist political philosophy, of a 'quasi-contract' (letter to Lord Chief Justice Coleridge, 28 Dec. 1881, Hutton, op. cit. pp. 214–15). Figgis, instructed by Gierke and Maitland, was able to present in *Churches and the Modern State* (London, 1913) an argument full-bloodedly based on the concept of the real personality of groups.

Tönnies and Durkheim, find no place in Maitland. The nearest he gets to a sociological exploration is in remarks like: 'morally there is most personality where legally there is none. A man thinks of his club as a living being, honourable as well as honest, while the joint stock company is only a sort of machine into which he puts money.'[107] The hero of 'Trust and Corporation' is in a sense 'the spirit of association' (Maitland's phrase) but it is a modest English hero – clubbability, almost – and there is a lack of continental solemnity about Maitland's examples from the Turf and Pall Mall which recalls more recent English moral philosophers' attention to such questions as the ethics of returning library books. Remaining, for all its suggestiveness, essentially jurisprudential (as he obviously intended it to be), Maitland's endorsement of corporate rights broke with traditionalism without becoming fully sociological.

But one thing his refusal to take sides as between types of collectivities indisputably did was to detach, for those who wished it, the Burkean, organicist political style from any exclusive attachment not merely to traditional but to local and territorial units. For, of course, there was always an element of pluralism, the patriotism of Burke's little platoons, in the traditionalist position but, despite the loyalties attracted by colleges, universities and churches, and even the commercial institutions of the City, it was of necessity a sentiment attached primarily to notions of *place*. Freeman, Stubbs and Green[108] were all imbued with a sense of the importance of local institutions, recognizing local self-government as an important element in English freedom and stability, and deploring the redrawing of the administrative map of France.[109] Green was, as Freeman said, in everything 'municipal' in his

---

[107] 'Trust and Corporation', *C.P.*, iii, 383. But contrast Maitland's treatment of joint-stock companies considered as corporate persons with, e.g., Lavelaye's references to them as 'Means of associating capital not men' (Lavelaye, op. cit. p. 63) or, for that matter, with Gierke's notion of association as a remedy for the squeezing out of small artisans and landowners by *laissez-faire* capitalism. R. Emerson, *State and Sovereignty in Modern Germany* (Yale, 1928), p. 136.

[108] Freeman, like Seebohm, was a justice of the peace. Stubbs had held a parson's freehold (Navestock). Gomme was an L.C.C. official who wrote on the principles of local government. The migratory professional historian was not yet the dominant type; Maine came nearest to it among the figures discussed here.

[109] For Freeman: Stephens, op. cit. i, 187, 277–9, 309. Also James Bryce, *Studies in Contemporary Biography* (London, 1904), p. 272. Freeman wrote extensively on town histories and edited the 'Historic Towns' series for Longman. He was also interested in federal questions. Also Stubbs, *Early English History*, pp. 2, 17, 311, 333.

sympathies,[110] a trait which led him to sympathize even with the Paris Commune.[111] Part of the veneration with which Freeman and Green approached the ancient *mark*-community was due precisely to the vague notion that it was in some way the nucleus of that local self-government from which in turn the strength of the national constitution significantly derived.[112]

Maitland, in the same spirit but less romantically, agreed that local authorities are best left to make fools of themselves,[113] and of course he wrote conspicuously on borough origins. But essentially he adapted the veneration which among English constitutional historians had attached to small, spontaneously created self-governing social units, to the more fluid conditions of a commercial and industrial society. His advocacy of *Korporationstheorie* was in part an attempt to enrich the texture of men's understanding of society, beyond the point at which it can plausibly be represented by an omnipotent sovereign and individual citizens, and to promote a recognition of the corporate character of much human activity, from which can be derived a new theory, no longer rural, archaic or traditional, of corporate rights. The ground of argument has shifted from the rights supposedly possessed by ancient rural communities to the rights created by the fact and consciousness of human corporate association as such, and hence to a distinctively different style of political philosophizing. Maitland's position contained elements of all the arguments we have been considering; it was concerned with rights, but not necessarily ancient rights; it shared some of the Burkean ingredients of the arguments from tradition, but it gave no special place to tradition; it was sociological, but not merely a matter of learning from examples the means to given ends.

This might seem to leave no role to historiography but the establishment of truth and the satisfaction of a laudable curiosity, but this is not

[110] Stephens, i, 303. Cf. Green, *Short History*, pp. 92–3.
[111] L. Stephen, *Letters of John Richard Green*, pp. 288, 298.
[112] Freeman, *Growth of the Constitution*, p. 10; *Comparative Politics*, pp. 30, 75, 272. Green, *Making of England*, i, 214; *Short History*, pp. 4–5. But Stubbs accepted Gneist's argument that the *mark* was not the basis of Anglo-Saxon local government (*Const. Hist.*, p. 89, n. 1) and Freeman, in private, acknowledged an uncharacteristic bafflement (Stephens, ii, 354). The association of municipal sympathies and study of the *mark* was a long-standing one. J. J. Möser (1701–85), the pioneer of village community studies (Dopsch, op. cit. pp. 5–6), wrote a history of his native Osnabrück and propounded '*Lokalvernunft*'. G. Parry, 'Enlightened Government and its critics in Eighteenth Century Germany', *Historical Journal*, 6, no. 2, 1963, p. 189.
[113] 'The Shallows and Silences of Real Life', *C.P.*, i, 473–5.

quite so. Maitland's own view of the early village community neatly complemented and reinforced his view of the modern world. Not, of course, that the former was tailored in any way to fit the latter, but simply that he saw both in terms of essentially the same concepts – those of *Korporationslehre*. This was no intrusion of an alien theory. Von Maurer had influenced Gierke, and Maitland himself acknowledged that any account of the development of *Genossenschaftstheorie* in Germany would need to refer to 'the persistence in Germany of agrarian communities with world-old histories, to the intricate problems which their dissolution presented, and to the ancient complaint that Roman Law had no equitable solution'.[114] The concept of the *mark*-community set up many ripples.[115]

Maitland applied to the historiography of the village community the basic distinction expounded in the preface to Gierke, the distinction between co-ownership and corporate ownership, and found it lacking in the attributes of corporateness. A body of co-proprietors, such as Maitland considered the village community to have been, is merely a partnership, *societas*, or *Gesellschaft*; 'the *universitas* is a person; the *societas* is only another name, a collective name, for the *socii*'.[116] It is well known that in *Township and Borough* Maitland argued, in a way that must have been and was obviously intended to be, highly paradoxical to anyone for whom Maine's concept of the group as the unit of ancient law was received wisdom, that for the Cambridge burgess of the early Middle Ages, far from corporate ownership being something he understood in his bones, while individual ownership was a concept he had to grasp, it was the other way about.[177] Individualism, or some version of it expressed in a confused notion of a partnership, was primitive; corporateness, the recognition of associations of men as constituting legal persons who were neither individuals nor any aggregate of them was modern, and Maitland, agreeing with Gierke, speaks of 'a moral and economic achievement accomplished in the medieval boroughs, the differentiation of "its" from "ours".'[118]

As for the concept of the ancient village community, it was deplor-

---

114 Gierke, op. cit., p. xxv.
115 Max Weber served part of his sociological apprenticeship on the same contemporary problem. Reinhardt Bendix, *Max Weber: An Intellectual Portrait* (London, 1960), pp. 38ff.
116 Gierke, op. cit., p. xxii.
117 *Township and Borough* (C.U.P., 1898).
118 Ibid., p. 12.

ably vague, and instrinsically, as a theory of group ownership, implausible:

It apparently attributes ownership of land to communities. It contrasts communities with individuals. In doing so it seems to hint, and yet be afraid of saying, that land was owned by corporations before it was owned by men. The hesitation we can understand. No one who has paid any attention to the history of law is likely to maintain with a grave face that the owner-ship of land was attributed to fictitious persons before it was attributed to men. But if we abandon ownership by corporations and place in its stead co-ownership, then we seem to be making an unfortunate use of words if we say that land belonged to communities before it belonged to individuals. Co-ownership is ownership by individuals.[119]

The full extent of Maitland's argument, familiar in any case to all students of medieval history, cannot be summarized here. But his assertion of a 'core of individualism'[120] in the village community justified Vinogradoff's reference to Maitland's own 'antiquarian individualism',[121] which was also the complement of his perception of modern life as increasingly characterized by a plurality of overlapping social groups, with what he wishes to call, in many cases, real personali-ties and real wills. Conversely, the notion of society as composed of individual citizens, whose collective life is embodied essentially in a sovereign state, its relation to its citizens expressed in the metaphor of a contract of individuals, he finds increasingly implausible, just as at the beginning of his career he had found it inadequate as a basis for rights. It is implausible because of the immense growth of groups endowed with legal personality. 'Nowadays it is difficult to get the corporation out of our heads. If we look at the doings of our law courts, we may feel inclined to revise a famous judgement and to say that while the individual is the unit of ancient, the corporation is the unit of modern law'.[122] But the reversal of Maine's *laissez-faire* individualist version of progress – from status to contract – is complete only because it has an historical component: the analysis of the early village community into its individual co-proprietors.

---

[119] *Domesday Book and Beyond* (C.U.P., 1907), p. 341. Cf. Frederick Pollock and F. W Maitland, *The History of English Law Before the Time of Edward I* (2nd ed., C.U.P., 1911, 2 vols.), i, 610, 616–7, 620–34; ii, 240–8. Also *C.P.*, ii, 86–8, 313, 359–63.

[120] *Domesday Book and Beyond*, p. 353–4.

[121] Vinogradoff, *Collected Papers*, i, 259.

[122] *Township and Borough*, p. 13.

For Freeman and Green the 'village community' had been both in some sense individualistic as well as communal, and also a prefiguration of the modern world. For Maine and Seebohm it had been essentially communistic and irretrievably archaic. For Maitland, prompted by *Korporationslehre* to see it as lacking true corporateness, just as he was prompted in the same way to recognize the modern world as increasingly peopled by a multiplicity of corporate personalities, the village community was both archaic *and* individualistic: indeed, by a slight exaggeration which Maitland, who was as indulgent to paradox as he was stern to falsehood, might have pardoned, it was archaic *because* individualistic, because its members had not learnt 'to distinguish between *res civitas* and *res omnium civium* – a grand intellectual achievement comparable to the discovery of the differential calculus'.[123]

These various examples should have been enough to show that the historiography of the early Middle Ages did not cease to be a locus of ideological interest when the Norman Yoke no longer chafed, nor is the content and manner of that interest exhausted by the notion of Whiggish complacency, a mimic flourishing in Oxford lecture rooms of obsolete class weapons. Rather, it is Freeman who has the last word: 'Past history and modern politics are always influencing one another, but the forms which their mutual influence takes are infinitely varied.'[124]

Note: Since this article was completed a substantial contribution to the literature on the subject has been made by Dr Clive Dewey's interesting article 'Images of the Village Community: A Study in Anglo-Indian Ideology', *Modern Asian Studies*, 6, 3, 1972.

[123] 'Archaic Communities', *C.P.*, ii, 337.
[124] 'The Franks and the Gauls', *Historical Essays*, 1st series, p. 164.

X

'The Voice of the Hooligan':
Kipling and the Commonwealth Experience*

ERIC STOKES

History as a retrospective, recording activity traces the long defeat of
the past by the present. Clio's devotees, we know, awaken only in the
twilight at the hoot of Minerva's owl and meditate on the splendours
and miseries of a day that is done. So there can be no surprise that its
professional priesthood of recording scribes has never been more
numerous or more active at the very moment when the Commonwealth – that ghost of the British Empire sitting crowned on the ruins
thereof – itself appears to be passing into the historical night, and when
the Old World is being called back into existence to redress the balance
of the New. Perhaps for the professional historian that should be
enough; his subject flourishes, and he should not be squeamish that it
flourishes in the expiring shadow of that which once was great. Acton
wrote on one occasion that history should be as chaste and all but
purposeless as mathematics, and it might well seem to be no proper
part of the historian's task to question the source of his curiosity about
the past but to bend all his energies in the endeavour to satisfy it. And
indeed most of our working activity is spent unreflectively in this way.
Yet I would like to use an occasion such as this to look a little more
closely into the impulse which at present drives historical inquiry into
what, from our local standpoint, still appear as the outer regions of the

---

* An Inaugural Lecture delivered in Cambridge by the Smuts Professor of the History
of the British Commonwealth in 1971. References to Kipling's works are to the Sussex
Edition. Dates for the first publication of short stories are taken from Louis Cornell,
Kipling In India (1966), Appendix 1; or, for work published after his residence in India,
J. M. Stewart, *Rudyard Kipling: A Bibliographical Catalogue* (Toronto, 1959).

earth. For it is one thing to erect academies of learning and fill them with scholiasts, and another to ensure that what they disseminate bears an efficient and fruitful relationship to our general intellectual culture.

Historical curiosity, it is clear, is neither random nor yet is it logically determined. The object upon which it fastens is delivered by some *donnée* in our experience rather than by a chain of ratiocination. For my own generation the Commonwealth experience came early and unasked. Tossed casually by war halfway across the globe and brigaded willy-nilly with men of diverse Commonwealth nations and races – as fortuitously as the young are tossed into colleges and campuses today – we passed through a crucible that for some of us set the pattern of our lives. The sum and substance of that experience was the conviction, or illusion if you will, that part of the total meaning of things was to be discovered in this encounter with the world beyond the European continent. So stated, such a notion seems too trite to record, but it is a feature of any strongly entrenched national culture like that of the British, a feature embracing all shades of political persuasion, that while it pays nodding deference to the importance of other societies it moves in practice within the extraordinarily narrow circle of its own immediate experience. Now it seems to me that the sub-rational impulse that lies behind much of the intellectual drive into overseas history is a paradoxical attempt to register the authenticity of a totally separate world of experience, and at the same time to appropriate that experience into this narrow domestic circle; to enjoy, as it were, a dual emotional citizenship, like men, as Maine said, bound to make their watches keep true time in two longitudes at once.

How far a person may genuinely enter into an alien culture is, of course, a matter of personality, but also of time and place. My group of war-bred historians, whose primal experience was the sudden companionships of war followed by the colonial withdrawal, were thrown into an examination of the nature of British colonialism, a study which already had a lengthy pedigree and which the labours of Keith Hancock and my distinguished predecessor in this Chair, Nicholas Mansergh, had done much to revivify in their *Survey of British Commonwealth Affairs* and other writings. Already, however, there was a significant difference; our overwhelming emphasis was on the brown and black rather than the white Commonwealth. (On any objective reading the comparative neglect in this country of the white overseas world, including the United States until the colour question became dominant, must appear totally irrational.) Nevertheless, it can plausibly be urged that the first post-war studies were singularly unsuccessful in breaking out of the constraining circle of domestic experience; that we grappled intellectually with the world beyond Europe in terms of our own common-sense experience, directing our attention to that which was modern, Anglophone, utilitarian and comprehensible within the terms of Western analogues.

Yet I do not believe that subsequent work that came with the hot upsurge of the new nationalisms in Asia, Africa and Latin America, and more avowedly sought to throw off the ethnocentric and metropolitan standpoints, have eluded – or can hope to elude – the fundamental dilemma that besets the enterprise. The circumscribing arc of the English-language culture still confines the generality of our studies to the Anglophone areas of the earth; the historian most hotly engaged in throwing off the dependency of the colonial bond and asserting the intellectual autonomy of an alien society is also a missionary seeking to communicate to the larger English-speaking world and must work within its academic conventions. And in historical terms he cannot escape the fact that the importance of his chosen subject on the modern world stage was mediated through the colonial bond or the colonial confrontation, and that this still supplies the orientating, integrating element by which the deliberate shattering of the former colonial world into discrete, autonomous intellectual entities can be redressed in the interests of overall intellectual coherence. So it is that so much of the work which set out to smash the intellectual constructs of imperialism has gone to swell the incomparable academic swag-bag that we may still designate as Commonwealth history. And the fact that Commonwealth history should rest on natural convenience rather than artificial political presupposition seems to me its most solid safeguard. The Commonwealth remains our entrée into the Third World.

But why this obsession with the Third World? Here I think we touch on the sub-rational impulse I spoke of. Overseas history has always represented some sort of imaginative attempt to break through the confines of urban industrial civilization to societies which still appear to rest on their own centre outside its grip. In the past the veld, the prairie and the outback have appeared such an outlet, but the rapid urbanization of settler societies has deprived them of much of that emotive attraction. We have indeed become caught up in a much more powerful Romantic movement in the last decade or so, a movement to return to the only fields and woods yet unpolluted by industrialism, to the last natural men before the Fall, to the Third World peasantry rightly struggling to be free. But there's the rub. The impulse to strike off from the wretched of the earth the fetters of poverty and all that makes oppression bitter destroys the receptivity and passivity of our intellectual tourism and sets us to invade and conquer alien societies with the appropriate intellectual armoury of modern technology – that of the social sciences. The historian is lost without the concept of change which supplies the *differentia* of his subject, and that concept, however subtly refined and qualified, is never freed from the crude simplicity of the dichotomy between tradition and modernity and that whole imported thought-world which inheres in the one contemporary term 'development'. The problem is compounded for the overseas historian by the deep-seated difficulties under which his discipline as a whole is labouring. That the ever-intensifying degree of detail and statistical precision which has been required of historical, like other scientific, statements has resulted in the fragmentation of history into a staccato series of arcane studies, is familiar enough. But for overseas history technical specialization has thrown up a double barrier, enormously enhancing the difficulty of assimilating alien experience into our general intellectual culture, and more seriously muffling the flash of apperception that momentarily makes us one with an alien world. Not that technical history does not yield a keen delight to its practitioner. To call the tune for the dance of the bloodless categories is often an exhilarating, certainly a useful, but not, I suggest, a permanently satisfying activity. Like A. E. Housman, we may derive professional pleasure from editing Manilius but we need the unfinished manuscript of *The Shropshire Lad* in the desk-drawer. To communicate beyond our fellow craftsmen we are drawn inevitably to the objects of more common concern, and cannot dodge the central paradox that besets our subject. So we find that the more *engagé* becomes our society to the overseas world, the more rampant are the walls it erects of intellectual concept and political presupposition, fencing it off from the land where its spirit seeks the healing of its divided self.

There is no magic remedy for our condition other than what awareness can give. For this reason I make no apology for turning aside from the beaten paths of professional history to look at a remarkable literary sensibility, the most *engagé* in our literature to the overseas world, that of a man who also wrestled to scale the walls that his own mind and emotions erected against it. Rudyard Kipling pre-dated the modern multi-racial Commonwealth, and was, of course, largely antipathetic to it; but his was the one recording sensibility which took in, as far as one man could, the extraordinarily diverse and untidy experience of the British overseas, and tried to distil its inner significance.

Once the outward *persona* has been stripped away, Kipling's temperament and interests still look remarkably modern. But the *persona* is not readily detached. Since Robert Buchanan in 1899 led the assault on Kipling as 'the Voice of the Hooligan' and branded him as being 'on the side of all that is ignorant, selfish, base, and brutal in the instincts of humanity', the weight of educated opinion has been cast massively against him. When T. S. Eliot, one of Kipling's few eminent admirers, edited a selection of his verse in 1941, he felt it necessary in his introduction to defend him against the charge of racialism and Fascism – a defence that immediately prompted George Orwell to retort that Eliot was on a false trail:

... there is a definite strain of sadism in him, over and above the brutality which a writer of that type was to have. Kipling *is* a jingo imperialist, he *is* morally insensitive, and aesthetically disgusting. It is better to start by admitting that, and then try to find out why it is that he survives while the refined people who sniggered at him seem to wear so badly.[1]

Eliot was without doubt excessively charitable towards Kipling's racial and political stance, but much nearer than Orwell to guessing the secret of his 'permanent hold'. For Orwell Kipling simply had the gift of memorable phrase for thoughts which were both commonplace and permanent in human nature; a judgement which made little advance beyond that of Oscar Wilde, who commented in 1891 that on turning the pages of Kipling one felt 'as if one were seated under a palm-tree reading life by superb flashes of vulgarity'.[2]

Now Eliot recognized that over and above the gift of words there was 'a queer gift of second sight, transmitting messages from elsewhere, a gift so disconcerting when we are made aware of it that henceforth we are never sure when it is *not* present'. But like Bonamy Dobrée and

---

[1] George Orwell, 'Rudyard Kipling', in *Critical Essays* (1946), cited A. Rutherford (ed.), *Kipling's Mind and Art* (1964), pp. 70–1. T. S. Eliot (ed.), *A Choice of Kipling's Verse* (1941), p. 29 *passim*.
[2] Cited R. L. Green (ed.), *Kipling – The Critical Heritage* (1971), p. 104.

others of Kipling's small handful of literary admirers, Eliot squirmed
at his imperialism and, following the lead of Edward Shanks, chose to
regard it as a transient phase before the riper middle years which saw
'the development of the imperial imagination into the historical
imagination'. Adverse critics, like Edmund Wilson and Lionel Trilling,
whose youthful reading had been influenced by the *Jungle Books* and
Kim, saw Kipling's imperialism as a stage in his early deterioration, the
defeat of the artist by the politician and propagandist. Wilson believed
that this deterioration took firm hold at the end of the 1890s when
Kipling and his family were driven from America by local ostracism
(after a row with his American brother-in-law became public). His
elder daughter's death on Long Island in 1899 sealed the break in
inconsolable bitterness, and he drove furious roots into the Sussex soil.
In this way, according to Wilson, the open-minded, cosmopolitan and
racially tolerant New England immigrant reacted defiantly to become
the bigoted and sadistic British-race patriot of the Boer War period,
to whom almost all foreigners, white or coloured, were 'lesser breeds
without the Law'.[3] Dobrée had already anticipated this notion of
Kipling's deterioration, but placed it still earlier. Kipling's best work,
he believed, was done by 1893, the year from which 'he began to
proselytize and shout too loud into the deaf ears of Demos'. And as an
example of Kipling's unspoilt early genius he pointed to the *Letters of
Marque*, composed in 1888–89, 'with their profound tolerance of
India'.[4]

But the case will not hold water. The open inconsistencies in
Kipling's racial and national attitudes cannot be resolved by neat
periodization in this way, for they remained permanent. He reacted
defiantly and savagely whenever any group appeared to present a threat
to his world. His work exhibited no development, only the elaboration
of separate and discordant elements that co-existed uneasily from the
beginning of his writing career.[5] Indeed a major part of Kipling's
fascination resides in the violence with which his nature experienced
attraction and repulsion towards the same objects. His mind may have

[3] Edmund Wilson, 'The Kipling that Nobody Read', in *The Wound and the Bow* (1952),
cited Rutherford, op. cit., esp. p. 32ff. Lionel Trilling, *The Liberal Imagination*, cited
Rutherford, p. 85 *et. seq.*

[4] Bonamy Dobrée in *The Monthly Criterion*, December 1927, cited Green, op. cit. pp.
349–50. An expanded version of the essay appeared in *The Lamp and the Lute* (1964),
cited E. L. Gilbert (ed.), *Kipling and the Critics* (1966), p. 37 *et seq.*

[5] Cf. W. W. Robson, 'Kipling's Later Stories' in Rutherford, op. cit., p. 258.

compartmentalized this contradictory response; it never compromised it. This inconsistency of view is familiar enough in the opinions he advanced on the Irish, the Americans, the Jews and the British 'establishment'. But even in the early *Letters of Marque*, praised by Dobrée for their tolerance, a worm was eating at the heart of the rose. A cursory inspection could easily mistake it for the canker of racialism. I am not referring to the stinging contempt which Kipling poured on the educated Bengali gentlemen who spouted advanced political theory in the Legislative Council at Calcutta while the stench of the uncleansed city wafted through the doors.[6] That was no more than the stock response he had learned in the Punjab Club towards the first political stirrings of educated India. In Rajputana of the princes, where he fell under the spell of an India remote from modernity, he experienced a much deeper revulsion. In the ruined citadel of Chitor, where centuries before the beautiful Rajput queen, Padmini, had cast herself on the funeral pyre rather than fall into the hands of the Muslim invaders, he ventured down the steps into the dark shrine of the Gaumukh:

Almost under the little trickle of water was the loathsome Emblem of Creation [presumably a phallic *lingam* stone associated with the worship of Siva], and there were flowers around it. Trees sprouted in the sides of the tank and hid its surroundings. It seemed as though the descent had led the Englishman, *firstly*, two thousand years away from his own century, and *secondly* into a trap. . . . The Englishman endured as long as he could – about two minutes. Then it came upon him that he must go quickly out of this place of years and blood – must get back into the afternoon sunshine. . . . He desired no archaeological information, he wished to take no notes, and above all, he did not care to look behind him, where stood the reminder that he was no better than the beasts that perish. But he had to cross the smooth, worn rocks, and he felt their sliminess through his bootsoles. It was as though he were treading on the soft, oiled skin of a Hindu. As soon as the steps gave refuge he floundered up them, and so came out of the Gaumukh, bedewed with that perspiration, which follows alike on honest toil or – childish fear.[7]

'. . . as though he were treading on the soft oiled skin of a Hindu' – the deep psychological revulsion is expressed appropriately as an intimate physical sensation, testifying to the power of the recoil that takes hold

[6] *From Sea to Sea, Works*, Vol. XXII.
[7] Idem, pp. 96–7. Kipling used the experience for his account of Tarvin's descent into the Cow's Mouth in *The Naulahka, Works*, Vol. XIX, p. 157ff.

of the explorer of alien experience when he strays unwittingly beyond the frontiers of empathy.

One might assume that this recoil had only to be politicized to produce 'the prophet of British imperialism in its expansionist phase',[8] as Kipling appeared to the world from 1893. But this would be seriously to misunderstand his genius whose mainspring was ambiguity. The vicious political strain like the racial animus or the addiction to brutality were not later developments but were present from the beginning and remained to the end, just as were his more attractive qualities – his humour, his compassion, his ability to throw himself into the mentality of others. No doubt these discrepant elements ranged themselves on one or other of the 'two separate sides' of his head, of which he declared himself so proud and by which he explained his constant inconsistencies. One might assign the peremptory political edge of his writing to Kipling the reporter rather than Kipling the artist, had not Louis Cornell properly noted that the two cannot be kept separate, his reporting possessing much of the character of fiction, and his fiction the character of reporting.[9]

Kipling's powers reached their highest expression when the two separate sides of his head *both* contributed to produce his many-layered sensibility, his rational intelligence yearning for hard definition and the erection of secure, defensive outworks of conviction and prejudice and his artistic consciousness, in contrast, roaming freely without arrest across every dimension. His finest work depicts the sharply defined, rationally controlled world of modern professionalism held over against the fluid, mysterious and dark underworld beyond the range of waking consciousness. He experienced the contrast most vividly in India:

> A stone's throw out on either hand
> From that well-ordered road we tread,
> And all the world is wild and strange:

Or describing the moonlit route from the European civil lines to the old walled town of Lahore: 'Straight as a bar of polished steel ran the road to the City of Dreadful Night'.[10]

---

[8] The phrase is Orwell's, cited Rutherford, op. cit. p. 72.

[9] Louis Cornell, *Kipling in India.*

[10] The verse quotation is from 'In the House of Suddhoo' (30 April 1886), collected in *Plain Tales from the Hills, Works,* Vol. I. The other quotation is from 'The City of Dreadful Night' (10 September 1885), collected in *Life's Handicap, Works,* Vol. IV.

It has long been recognized, at least since Edmund Wilson's important essay, that the polarities between which Kipling's creative sensibility oscillated were powerfully charged by his psychological history. The nervous breakdown and fear of blindness he suffered as a foster child in the 'House of Desolation' at Southsea, and the partial breakdowns he suffered from overwork when alone in Lahore and later in 1890 in London, left him a prey to 'the sensation of nameless terror, he described in his early tale 'The Strange Ride of Morrowbie Jukes'. Through all his writing life, as he said, 'the darkness stayed at his shoulder blade'.[11] Hence his psychological need to grasp the certitude of outward reality with 'violent precision';[12] hence the importance of work, the tribal group, and the ordered authority structure. In these he was safe. As Lionel Trilling wrote: 'You feel that the walls of wrath and the ramparts of empire are being erected against the mind's threat to itself.'[13]

Undoubtedly his cult of the life of action and his *Schadenfreude* in the cleansing power of pain as escape mechanisms from the fear of mental emptiness and terror were powerful ingredients in the formation of his imperialist attitude. Yet Kipling – to adapt a phrase of Johnson's – was perpetually a moralist but an imperialist only by chance. And here is probably the secret of his 'permanent hold'. For although he believed, like Sartre in his latest mood, that the highest function of the artist as the journalist was 'to serve his day' and immerse himself in the short-sighted concerns of common men, he saw empire only as 'the day's need', the particular, transient moral task by which a much more general condition of modern man was to be alleviated, and of which he himself was a victim. Indeed, although his life was a constant attempt to escape the fact, he was cast in the mould of the modern intellectual who is condemned to live vicariously in the experience of others. There was little he needed to learn of the *anomie* of urban man, which his contemporaries Durkheim and Freud were investigating in their different ways.[14] He himself had trodden the road of rootlessness,

[11] Cited J. M. S. Tompkins, *The Art of Rudyard Kipling* (1959), p. 215.
[12] The term 'violent precision' is Desmond MacCarthy's in *The Sunday Times*, 19 January 1936, cited Green, op. cit. p. 7.   [13] Cited Rutherford, op. cit. p. 91.
[14] Cf. Noel Annan, 'Kipling's Place in the History of Ideas', *Victorian Studies*, Vol. 3 (1959–60), cited Rutherford, p. 97 *et seq.* For the connection between Kipling's psychology and his imperialism, Alan Sandison's writings offer the most recent and most sensitive interpretation. Cf. 'Kipling: The Artist and the Empire' in Rutherford, p. 146 *et seq.* Also Sandison, *The Wheel of Empire* (1967).

scepticism, and lack of self-identity, and of the yearning to overcome them through violent action and passionate attachment to a cause. When in his early story, 'On the City Wall' (December 1888, *Soldiers Three*), he drew the character of Wali Dad, the uprooted Western-educated Muslim intellectual, whose scepticism was momentarily dissolved in the violence of riot and in a total, irrational surrender to communal passion, Kipling was nearer to depicting his own underlying condition than he knew. There was, of course, an important difference. If there was in Kipling an undue addiction to violence, it was countered by an equally strong fear of the psychological insecurity resulting from complete surrender to emotion, so that his final position was that of the authoritarian personality and its satisfaction in the ordered, controlled violence of military force. Brooding silently over the City of Dreadful Night with all its symbolism of the exciting, elemental chaos of the subconscious, the reassuring mass of Fort Amara stands at a distance, representing the rational intelligence and the overwhelming coercive force of organized society. The garrison comprises individuals who instinctively are drawn to the unrestrained exercise of violence, like 'the Garrison Artillery, who to the last cherished a wild hope that they might be allowed to bombard the City at a hundred yards' range'.[15] But the rational social will as expressed in military discipline throttles down the indulgence of passion to the exercise of minimum force. The riot of a hundred thousand Muslims and Hindus is put down by five hundred Tommies, bayonets unfixed simply stamping with their rifle butts on the rioters' bare feet.

Louis Cornell has argued that 'On the City Wall' is an important parable of empire, and if one believes that Kipling constructed his stories within a series of widening frames of meaning, like a set of Chinese boxes, this may well be so. Lalun, the courtesan, is India, full of mystery, charm and deep intuitive wisdom, who offers her favours or aid (but never her inner freedom) equally to the old traditionalist rebel, Khem Singh, as to the modern-educated Wali Dad.[16] The British stand at a still further remove, suggesting that, within three months of finally quitting India, Kipling had concluded that the two worlds symbolized by British power and Indian life had to be mediated at a distance.

[15] 'On the City Wall', *Soldiers Three*, *Works*, Vol. II.
[16] Cornell, *Kipling in India*, p. 153.

Such a conclusion was not simply determined by the circle of European ethnocentricism within which, Kipling knew, lay in the end his psychological safety. Indeed, as a young man, he was the first to argue that the conventions of English bourgeois society were far too tightly drawn, stamped as he found them by the primitive methodist constriction of experience, and breeding a hypocritical morality that killed comprehension and compassion. A powerful vein of cynical realism, nurtured by his unhappy childhood and blighted first love, came to the aid of his journalist's passion to see things as they were, 'to move at will', as he said 'in the fourth dimension'. So he frequented the barracks at Mian Mir, poked into the farthest recesses of the old city of Lahore, with its opium dens and brothels, and sought in his tales to enter into the skin of men not like-minded with himself. Hence many of the early tales are of quite different and self-contained worlds of experience, many being idyllic vignettes of Indian life, while others attempt to explore the relationship between these worlds. Critics have frequently pointed out that all Kipling's tales in which the characters attempt to breach the racial or cultural barrier come to comic or tragic grief, like Lispeth (29 November 1886, collected in *Plain Tales from the Hills*) or Georgie Porgie (3 March 1888, *Life's Handicap*) or, more movingly in 'Without Benefit of Clergy' (7 June 1890, *Life's Handicap*). And many of his more hostile critics have concluded that he was simply exploiting the motif to titillate his public's palate without disowning the racial code. But the exploration was genuine enough.

Somerset Maugham thought Kipling remained a schoolboy who never grew up; and, as a solipsist shut in his own private world, it is true that for much of the time he communicated at the only level at which he had experienced a degree of intimacy with his fellows – in the camaraderie of the schoolroom, the mess and the club.[17] But this persistent streak of puerility did not mean that his convictions were naïve. He was hurt early, and responded with a youthful cynicism which, for all its light raillery of tone, was delivered like the flick of a whip across the complacent countenance of his countrymen. From the Hill of Illusion on which they dwelt he pointed to the dry, shrivelled

[17] On Kipling's solipsism, cf. letter to W. E. Henley, 1890, cited C. E. Carrington, *Rudyard Kipling* (1955), p. 156: 'Since we be only islands shouting misunderstandings to each other across seas of speech or writing . . .', a phrase he repeated in almost identical terms in *The Light That Failed*, Vol. XVIII, p. 69.

plains of Naked Reality below. In 'The Dream of Duncan Parrenness' (25 December 1884, *Life's Handicap*) – the six-page tale that cost him three months' labour – he set down his bitter truths in the guise of an eighteenth-century pastiche. Parrenness, 'writer in the Company's service and afraid of no man', typifies the English pioneers who founded the Raj, driven by the illusion of fortune not only to dare every physical peril but, like Faust, to surrender even the moral security of faith and conscience itself. Their reward during their brief dissolute lives was but 'a little piece of dry bread' and the tearing aside of the veil of illusion which hid from ordinary men the empty horror of ultimate reality. In a companion-piece, among the very first tales at which he worked, he pursued this notion of India as a setting in which men could see too far into the truth of things. In 'The Strange Ride of Morrowbie Jukes' (25 December 1885, *Wee Willie Winkie*) he constructed a nightmare situation in which an unimaginative Englishman finds himself imprisoned with a strange community of Indians who had come alive after being deemed dead and had been banished to a desert place where they dwelt in fetid burrows in the sand. It is the image of an India depicted in all its most repellent aspects and of a Hobbesian condition of society in which all distinctions founded on colour, caste, wealth and authority have entirely vanished. In other words, Kipling carefully removes all the physical and, more important, the psychological props – especially those of authority and social distance – which enabled the ordinary Englishman to come to terms with India. In a coldly precise narrative style learned from Swift and Poe he depicted the loathsome condition of this community of latter-day Yahoos: '... a most sickening stench pervaded the entire amphitheatre – a stench fouler than any which my wanderings in Indian villages have introduced me to.' The Englishman is forced to spend the night in one of their burrows, nearly as narrow as a coffin and whose 'sides had been worn smooth and greasy by the contact of innumerable naked bodies, added to which it smelt abominably'. However, these physical conditions are nothing to the loss of all moral norms and the collapse of the mind into 'a sensation of nameless terror', a sensation as overwhelming as the nausea of sea-sickness, but 'the agony was of the spirit and infinitely more terrible'. It is not a pretty tale nor was it meant to be. One is forcibly reminded of Conrad's *Heart of Darkness*, where Kurtz, at the end of a similar nightmare in the Congolese jungle, completely cut off from the security of Western society, encounters the black emptiness within himself and goes to his death screaming: 'The horror, the horror.'[18]

A young man who had seen thus far into the nature of racial and social prejudice and the psychological role of moral convention was unlikely to lapse into any simple blimpish attitude. But his conclusion that boundary maintenance, as expressed in inherited prejudice and behaviour patterns, was an essential defence of the structure of personality confirmed his notion that society in India, as elsewhere, was a series of walled compartments out of which the individual strayed at his peril. All this could, and did, issue in a highly conservative political philosophy; but it was far from being a defence of the *status quo*. Kipling was as concerned as any modern existentialist that men should liberate themselves from their alienated existence, find their true being, and do their own thing. And he recognized that, for a man to discover his true identity, it was necessary to embark on a voyage of discovery beyond the limits of the known and the familiar.

It was paradoxically when he had quitted India and purportedly entered upon his most rabidly imperialist phase that he fully addressed himself to this question. As his teeth clenched on bitter political dogma he let his imagination escape to the rear where the frontiers had still not yet been closed – to the world of childhood imagination and an idealized memory of India. Mowgli in the *Jungle Books*, and *Kim*, completed at the height of the Boer War, were essays in the quest for self-discovery and identity, a quest successfully accomplished, Kipling suggests, because his heroes plunge into an alien medium only for a limited apprenticeship and from the secure base of their personal or artistic integrity.

We would observe that they scarce risk a fall since the medium is no longer hostile or cruelly indifferent. The Jungle symbolizes an ideal traditional India or, at a higher remove, Nature as the archetype of a model society. Mowgli represents something of Kipling's own ex-

[18] Cf. also Conrad's *An Outpost of Progress*, cited A. Fleishman, *Conrad's Politics* (Johns Hopkins Press, Baltimore, 1967), p. 93: 'They were two perfectly insignificant and incapable individuals, whose existence is only rendered possible through the high organization of civilized crowds. Few men realize that their life, the very essence of their character, their capabilities and their audacities, are only the expression of their belief in the safety of their surroundings. The courage, the composure, the confidence; the emotions and principles; every great and insignificant thought belongs not to the individual but to the crowd: to the crowd that believes blindly in the irresistible force of its institutions and of its morals, in the power of its police and its opinions.'

perience – suckled in the bosom of Nature or India in all her innocent simplicity and colour, then exiled to the world of man, recalled for a period of service, and then finally exiled for ever. Here is the essential encounter and rejection between the two worlds. 'We be of one blood, ye and I' is the claim of blood brotherhood he makes, only to recognize the final truth; 'Man goes to man at the last.' The service Mowgli returns for his upbringing symbolizes the idealized function of the Raj; it is the transient gift of technological superiority and organizing power to defend the Jungle people from internal predatory leaders (Shere Khan, the tiger) and external foes (Red Dogs or Russians). But, if this is his functional role, it is what Mowgli learns from the Jungle that is the more significant. The Law of the Jungle is a Platonic notion of natural law by which each individual finds his place in the scheme of things, and by so doing discovers his true self, lives on his own centre, and attains freedom. Such a functionalist conception of society rests on the principle of differentiation and the impossibility of one species or individual identifying itself with or becoming another. But it is contact across the walls of separation that supplies and sustains the life-giving knowledge and spark. And Kipling's real concern in these stories was not to teach children but to sustain his own artistic inspiration. India became for him a world of memory and imagination, and, as he hoped, some sort of permanent reservoir of spiritual power which he could draw upon in time of need. Hence Baloo's blessing on Mowgli: '. . . take thy own trail; make thy lair with thine own blood and pack and people; but when there is need of foot or tooth or eye, or a word carried swiftly by night, remember, Master of the Jungle, the Jungle is thine at call.'

Embedded in the *Second Jungle Book* is a more sophisticated parable of the reconciliation of the worlds of rationality, modernity and political power, with nature, spirituality and the timeless meaning of things. 'The Miracle of Purun Bhagat' (October 1894) is a wholly Indian tale, presumably because Kipling wished to avoid the misunderstanding that he saw the contrast between the two worlds simply in racial or national terms. Purun Das, Brahmin diwan of an Indian princely state, is a paragon of all the virtues, imbibing English education and all the latest notions of moral and material improvement but never losing anything of his true Indian personality. At the height of success and power he obeys the Vedic teaching and leaves all to become a penniless *sanyasi* or holy man. In the high Himalayan foothills he takes up his solitary abode, befriended by the animals and silently worshipped and fed by the nearby villagers. Here he meditates on final reality: 'He knew for a certainty that there was nothing great and nothing little in this world: and day and night he strove to think out his way into the heart of things, back to the place whence his soul had come.' Roused one night of torrential rain by the animals, he wrenches his mind back into the world for his final service of warning the villagers against the impending landslip, and expires in the effort. It is a vignette which paves the way for the much more ambitious attempt which Kipling embodied in *Kim* to suggest the nature of Oriental spirituality and its importance in keeping alive the dimension of the Other for modern urban man.

The relation between Kim and the Buddhist Lama is evidently meant to signify the relation between the white man's civilization and traditional India, the one practical, resourceful, limited in perception; the other aged, dependent, but steeped in the fundamental truths about the ultimate nature of life. The Lama leans on Kim for physical support . . . 'till the young branch bowed and near broke'. But, as Kim tells him, 'Thou leanest on me in the body Holy One, but I lean on thee for some other things.' The Lama attains his vision by finding the River of the Arrow, although to the world he appears a stupid old man who throws himself into a stream and has to be rescued. Kim comes to the knowledge of himself – which is his own quest – by discovering his role in society. That it is the Way of Action in no way disturbs the Lama, who believes that for aiding him in his Search Kim is 'assured as I am when he quits this body of Freedom from the Wheel of Things. . . . Let him be a teacher; let him be a scribe – what matter? He will have attained Freedom at the end. The rest is illusion.' And as the story ends the Lama lifts his voice to express what Kipling believed, beyond his own artistic concerns, might be the function of India, or the world of imagination and spirituality it represented, in cleansing the soul of urban man. Like Purun Bhagat or Plato's visionary in the Cave, the Lama turns back to save the world of action. "Son of my Soul, I have wrenched my Soul back from the Threshold of Freedom to free thee from all sin – as I am free and sinless. Just is the Wheel! Certain is our deliverance. Come!" He crossed his hands on his lap and smiled, as a man may who has won Salvation for himself and his beloved.'

This was a short-lived moment of vision and proved Kipling's farewell to India rather than a fresh fount of inspiration for his future work. Indeed this overcontrived masterpiece already suffered from his most serious defect as a writer, the foreclosure of sensibility that shut out all conflict, so that the mind could bathe in idealized images, and every element and character observe a perfect fit. For the sake of inner certainty and security he came near to abandoning the split level at which his genius worked at its best and to bring everything into a single flat surface. *Kim* is just saved by the creative tension between the story and its symbolism, but The Wheel of Things has no hint of the horror glimpsed by Duncan Parrenness and Morrowbie Jukes or of the primal revulsion he himself experienced in the Gaumukh.[19] Kipling had almost conflated the two worlds which he knew must stand apart, and had surrendered reality to sentiment.

In the next few years after 1901 he roamed desperately in search of fresh inspiration, to South Africa and then to Canada, but he struck no root that ran deep. While he fought his ferocious political vendetta with the Liberal Government after 1905, he let his imagination sink into Sussex and the English past, and the fruits – *Puck of Pook's Hill* (1906) and *Rewards and Fairies* (1910) – have something of the virtues and defects of *Kim*. But it was the sight of Old Cairo in 1913 that brought back the memory of his first and most fecund source of inspiration, the East: '. . . the Shadow on the dial had turned back twenty degrees for me, and I found myself saying, as perhaps the dead say when they have recovered their wits, "This is my real world again".'[20]

Collingwood saw in Kipling 'the artist as magician', and, if we believe with Yeats that the ultimate object of magic is to obtain control

[19] Cf. 'The Prayer of Miriam Cohen', *Rudyard Kipling's Verse – Definitive Edition* (1946), p. 614:

> 'From the wheel and the drift of Things
> Deliver us, Good Lord,
> And we will face the wrath of Kings,
> The faggot and the sword!
>
> Hold us secure behind the gates
> Of saving flesh and bone,
> Lest we should dream what Dream awaits
> The Soul escaped alone.
>
> A veil 'twixt us and Thee, Good Lord,
> A veil 'twixt us and Thee –
> Lest we should hear too clear, too clear,
> And unto madness see!'

[20] *Letters of Travel, 1892–1913* (1920), Vol. XXIV, p. 278.

of the sources of life, the literary magician's touch is not without relevance to the historian of that encounter between two worlds which we term the Commonwealth experience.[21] The historian's paradoxical double engagement is constantly threatened with the foreclosure of sensibility that Kipling knew. Either the alien experience, which is also in a sense the past, lapses into a sentimental image, or more usually with us it is brutally subjugated by our intellectual imperialism. Yet, rightly understood, it remains the historian's highest function to liberate rather than to colonize the past. Even though he knows the past stands defeated, he must hasten to fix its traces by the last gleams of the dying day, which is carrying with it into oblivion the pre-industrial world itself, its magic, and its gods.

Great Kings, the beginning of the end is born already. The fire-carriages shout the names of new Gods that are *not* the old under new names. Drink now and eat greatly! Bathe your faces in the smoke of the altars before they grow cold! Take dues and listen to the cymbals and the drums, Heavenly Ones, while yet there are flowers and songs. As men count time the end is far off; but as we, who know, reckon, it is to-day.'[22]

---

[21] R. G. Collingwood, *The Principles of Art* (1938), p. 70, cited Green, op. cit. p. 2. Yeats on magic is quoted by Lionel Trilling, *Beyond Culture* (Peregrine Books, 1967), p. 193.
[22] 'The Bridge Builders' (November 1893), in *The Day's Work* (1898), Vol. VI, pp. 41–2.

J. H. Plumb: A Select Bibliography

SEPARATE WORKS

Fifty Years of 'Equity Shoemaking': A History of the Leicester Co-operative Boot and Shoe Manufacturing Society Ltd, Leicester, 1936. 94pp.

England in the Eighteenth Century, Penguin Books. First published 1950. Reprinted 1951, 1953, 1955, 1957, 1959, 1960, 1961. Reprinted with revised bibliography 1963, 1964, 1965, 1966, 1968, 1969, 1971, 1973. 224pp.

West African Explorers (with C. Howard), Oxford University Press (The World's Classics). First published 1951. ix+598pp.

G. M. Trevelyan, Longman, 1951. Revised edition 1971. 35pp.

A Handlist of the Cholmondeley-Houghton MSS: Sir Robert Walpole's Archive (with G. A. Chinnery), Cambridge, 1953.

Chatham, Collins (Brief lives). First published 1953. Published in *Makers of History* 1965. American edition (St Martin's Press), 1953. 159pp.

British Prime Ministers, by various hands, 1953. Includes essays on Sir Robert Walpole and the Earl of Chatham.

Studies in Social History (with others), Longman, 1955. xv+287pp.

Sir Robert Walpole: Volume I, The Making of a Statesman, The Cresset Press. First published 1956. Reprinted 1957. Republished by Allen Lane 1972. American edition (Houghton Mifflin), 1956. xv+407pp.

The First Four Georges, B. T. Batsford. First published 1956. Reprinted 1957 and 1961. Published in Fontana paperback 1966, 1967, 1968, 1969, 1970, 1971, 1972 and 1974. 188pp. American edition (John Wiley), 1967. New edition, enlarged, revised and illustrated (Hamlyn), 1974. American edition (Little Brown), 1974.

Sir Robert Walpole: Volume II, The King's Minister, The Cresset Press. First published 1960. Reprinted 1963. Republished by Allen Lane 1972. American edition (Houghton Mifflin), 1961. xii+363pp.

The Renaissance, Horizon Books. English edition (Collins), 1961. First published 1961. Penguin paperback 1964. American paperback: *The Italian Renaissance*, Harper Torchbooks, 1965. 431pp.

Men and Places, The Cresset Press. First published 1963. ix+294pp. Published in the United States as *Men and Centuries*, 1963. Penguin paperback 1966.

Crisis in the Humanities (with others), 1964. 172pp.

The Growth of Political Stability in England 1675–1725 (The Ford Lectures), Macmillan. First published 1967. American edition (Houghton Mifflin), *The Origins of Political Stability*, 1967. Peregrine edition (Penguin) 1969. Penguin University Books, 1974. xviii+206pp.

Churchill Revised (Churchill the Historian). First published 1969, in the United States by Dial Press.

Churchill: Four Faces and the Man (with others), Allen Lane, 1969. Penguin, 1974.

The Death of the Past (The Saposnekow Memorial Lectures at the City College, New York), Macmillan. First published 1969. Reprinted 1973. American edition (Houghton Mifflin), 1969. Paperback in the United States (The Century Edition, Houghton Mifflin), 1970. Penguin, 1972.

Man versus Society in Eighteenth Century Britain (by various hands), Cambridge University Press, 1969. American edition 1969. Paperback in the United States 1972. Includes 'Political Man', W. W. Norton.

Some Aspects of Eighteenth Century England (with Vinton A. Dearing), University of California Press, 1971. Includes 'Reason and Unreason in the Eighteenth Century: The English Experience', 26pp.

In the Light of History (collected essays), ALPP. First published 1972. American publisher, Houghton Mifflin, 1972. Paperback, Dell, 1974. ix+273pp.

The Development of a Revolutionary Mentality (by various hands), Library of Congress, Washington, 1972. Includes 'The Fascination of Republican Virtue amongst the Known and the Unknown'.

The Triumph of Culture: Eighteenth Century Perspectives, edited by Paul Fritz and David Williams. Includes 'The Public, Literature and the Arts in the 18th Century'. Toronto, 1972.

Great Britain: Foreign Policy and the Span of Empire, 1689–1971: A Documentary History (with Joel H. Wiener), 4 vols., 1972. Published in the United States by Chelsea House. liii+3423pp.

Parliamentary Lists of the Early Eighteenth Century: Their Compilation and Use (edited by Aubrey Newman), Leicester University Press, 1973. Preface and comment by J. H. Plumb.

The Commercialisation of Leisure in Eighteenth-Century England (The Stenton Lecture), The University of Reading, 1973.

WORKS EDITED AND INTRODUCED

Graham Clark and Stuart Piggott, *Pre-Historical Societies*, 1965. Hutchinson. Published in the United States by Alfred Knopf, 1965. Introduction by J. H. Plumb, pp. 15–26.

C. R. Boxer, *The Dutch Seaborne Empire, 1600–1800*, 1965. Introduction by J. H. Plumb, pp. xiii–xxvi.

J. H. Parry, *The Spanish Seaborne Empire*, Hutchinson, 1966. Alfred Knopf, 1960. Introduction by J. H. Plumb, pp. 13–25.

John R. Alden, *Pioneer America*, 1966. Introduction by J. H. Plumb, pp. xv–xxix.

Anthony Andrewes, *The Greeks*, 1967. Introduction by J. H. Plumb, pp. xi–xxiii.

C. R. Boxer, *The Portuguese Seaborne Empire: 1415–1825*, 1969. Introduction by J. H. Plumb, pp. xiii–xxvi.

Donald Dudley, *The Romans*, 1970. Introduction by J. H. Plumb, pp. xi–xxiv.

Raymond Dawson, *Imperial China*, 1972. Introduction by J. H. Plumb, pp. 5–18.

Jacquetta Hawkes, *The First Great Civilisations*, 1973. Introduction by J. H. Plumb, pp. xiii–xxvi.

Daniel Defoe, *A Journal of the Plague Year*, Signet Classics, 1960. Foreword by J. H. Plumb, pp. v–x.

Henry Fielding, *Jonathan Wild*, Signet Classics, 1961. Foreword by J. H. Plumb, pp. xi–xvii.

Oliver Goldsmith, *The Vicar of Wakefield*, Signet Classics, 1961. Afterword by J. H. Plumb, pp. 183–190.

John Cleland, *Memoirs of Fanny Hill*, 1965. Introduced by J. H. Plumb, pp. vii–xiv.

EDITOR, FONTANA HISTORY OF EUROPE

J. R. Hale, *Renaissance Europe, 1480–1520*, 1971.

G. R. Elton, *Reformation Europe, 1517–1559*, 1963.

J. H. Elliott, *Europe Divided, 1559–1598*, 1968.

John Stoye, *Europe Unfolding, 1648–1688*, 1969.

David Ogg, *Europe of the Ancien Régime, 1715–1783*, 1965.

George Rudé, *Revolutionary Europe, 1783–1815*, 1964.

Jacques Droz, *Europe Between Revolutions 1815–1848*, 1967.

Elizabeth Wiskemann, *Europe of the Dictators, 1919–1945*, 1966.

ARTICLES

(A selection of some of the more important and more
characteristic articles)

'The Elections to the Convention Parliament of 1689', *Cambridge Historical Journal*, vol. V, no. 3, 1937, pp. 235–254.

'Sir Robert Walpole and Norfolk Husbandry', *Economic History Review*, Second Series, V, no. 1, 1952, pp. 86–89.

'Political History of Leicestershire, 1530–1885', *A History of Leicestershire*, vol. II (The Victoria History of the Counties of England), 1954, pp. 102–134.

'Thomas Babington Macaulay', *University of Toronto Quarterly*, October 1956, pp. 17–31.

'R. Walcott, *English Politics in the Early Eighteenth Century.*' A review in *English Historical Review*, LXXII, 1957, pp. 126–129.

'The Organization of the Cabinet in the Reign of Queen Anne', *Transactions of the Royal Historical Society*, 5th Series, vol. 7, 1957, pp. 137–158.

'Nature of Politics', *New York Review of Books*, 11 February 1965.

'Horace Walpole's Correspondence', *New York Review of Books*, 30 September 1965.

'Slavery, Race and the Poor', *New York Review of Books*, 13 March 1969.

'The Growth of the Electorate in England from 1600 to 1715', *Past and Present*, no. 45, November 1969, pp. 90–116.

'Oliver Cromwell', *Encyclopedia of World Biography*, 1969, pp. 211–221.

'Captain Swing', *New York Review of Books*, 19 June 1969.

'Sir Lewis Namier', *New Statesman*, 1 August 1969.

'The World the Slaveholders Made', *New York Review of Books*, 25 February 1970.

'The Public and Private Pepys', *Saturday Review*, October 1970.

'From Peking to Rome', *New York Review of Books*, 25 February 1971.

'The Function of History', *Encounter*, June 1971.

'Hogarth', *New York Review of Books*, 16 February 1971.

'Political Pornography', *Horizon*, Winter 1972.

'The World of Saint Simon', *Horizon*, Spring 1972.

'In Search of Benjamin Franklin', *New York Review of Books*, 2 March 1973.

'Bigness in Scholarship', *Horizon*, Winter 1973.

'Lordly Pleasures', *Horizon*, Winter 1973.

'Nixon and Disraeli', *New York Times Magazine*, 11 February 1973.

'Is History Sick?', *Encounter*, February 1973.

'Capitalism and Material Life', *New Statesman*, 30 May 1973.

'The Surprise of History', *Horizon*, Summer 1974.

'History and Tradition', *Great Ideas for Today*, Encyclopaedia Britannica, Chicago 1974.

'The French Connection, 1776–1782', *American Heritage*, August 1974.

'La Nouvelle Révolution', *Comprendre: Revue de Politique de la Culture* no. 39–40, 1974, pp. 2–12.

Index